OUT OF THE RUINS OF EUROPE

WALTER LAQUEUR

PROPERTY OF
AURORA PUBLIC LIBRARY
AURORA COLORADO

NO LONGER PROPERTY OF

THE LIBRARY PRESS
New York
1971

Copyright © 1971 by Walter Laqueur

3 1277 00248 8911

"Homecoming," "Remembering Stalin," "Nazism and the Nazis," "Russians and Germans," "Thoughts at the Wall," "The Tucholsky Complaint" and "The Jewish Question Today" reprinted with permission of *Encounter*, copyright © 1963, 1963, 1964, 1965, 1962, 1969, 1971 by Encounter Ltd.; "From a Russian Notebook" reprinted by permission of the *New Republic* and *Encounter*, copyright © 1960 Harrison-Blaine of New Jersey, Inc. and 1959–62 by Encounter Ltd.; "Prague Revisited" reprinted by permission of *Midstream* (April 1966); "Reflections on Youth Movements," "Bonn is Not Weimar" and "New York and Jerusalem" reprinted with permission of *Commentary*, copyright © 1969, 1967, 1971 by the American Jewish Committee; "The Archaeology of Youth" and "The Illusions of the Zionist Left" reprinted by permission of the *Times Literary Supplement;* "Literature and the Historian" from the *Journal of Contemporary History* reprinted with permission of George Weidenfeld & Nicolson Ltd.; "Russia Through Western Eyes" (Survey No. 50) and "In Search of Russia" (*Survey* January 1964) reprinted by permission of *Survey;* "The Third World" (*Dissent* September/October 1967) reprinted with permission of *Dissent;* Review of "An Introduction to Contemporary History" (Chapter 10) from the *New York Times Book Review,* May 2, 1965, "A Look Back at the Weimar Republic—The Cry Was, 'Down With Das System'" (Chapter 11) from the *New York Times Magazine,* August 16, 1970 and "Weimar Culture" from the *New York Times Book Review,* November 24, 1968, copyright © 1965, 1970, 1968 by the New York Times Company, reprinted by permission; "The End of the Monolith: World Communism in 1962" (*Foreign Affairs* April 1962) reprinted by permission of *Foreign Affairs,* copyright © 1962 by the Council on Foreign Relations, Inc., New York; "Russian Roulette", "Roots of Nazism", "Plotting Against Hitler", "Propaganda and Terror" and "Middletown, Germany" reprinted with permission from the *New York Review of Books,* copyright © 1965, 1965, 1964, 1965, 1965, by The New York Review.

901.946
Laq
cp. 1

INTERNATIONAL STANDARD BOOK NUMBER: 0-912050-01-2

LIBRARY OF CONGRESS CATALOG CARD NUMBER: 71-141855

Printed in the United States of America

AUTHOR'S NOTE

"1938" and "Utopia Plus Twenty" have not appeared before in English. The other essays were originally published in *Commentary* (chapters 5, 19, 28), *Dissent* (chapter 9), *Encounter* (chapters 1, 15, 17, 18, 20, 26, 29), *New Republic* and *Encounter* (chapter 13), *Foreign Affairs* (chapter 14), *Journal of Contemporary History* (chapter 7), *Midstream* (chapter 4), *New York Times* (chapters 10, 11, 21), *New York Review of Books* (chapters 16, 22, 23, 24, 25), *Survey* (chapters 8, 12) and *Times Literary Supplement* (chapters 6, 27). I am grateful for the permission to reprint these articles. In several instances the original, more detailed versions have been used for this collection; in other instances minor cuts have been made.

W.L.

CONTENTS

PREFACE

A FRIEND of mine sedulously refuses, as a matter of principle, to discuss any event that happened before 1945, unless indeed it took place a very long time ago; he did not have what is now commonly referred to as "a good war." When I once showed him a special library devoted entirely to the period he abhors, he suggested that since mankind does not learn from its past it might be wiser to destroy those books rather than preserve them. His behavior could probably be explained in terms of self preservation: after all a fairly common and, in some ways, inevitable phenomenon—"and we forget because we must and not because we will . . ." Lucien Febvre once wrote that an instinct tells us that forgetting is necessary for societies that want to live; and the same is no doubt true, perhaps more compellingly, for individuals. But not everyone reacts in this way. For others the preoccupation with history, especially its more recent aspects, may represent a need in terms of mental hygiene; re-living the past may well have an effect not altogether dissimilar to psychoanalysis. It was once the belief among historians that study of the recent past was more exhilarating and edifying than a concern with distant times. "What a fool I was," Droysen wrote in 1841, "to waste my time with the nonsense of ancient history rather than feasting on the colorful and dramatic recent past . . ." Dramatic, yes—but is there much scope for edification and enjoyment in the study of the 1930's and '40's?

My own interest in 20th-century history was not awakened by classical musings among the ruins of the Capitol or by strolling in a London lane. I hope I will be forgiven the flippant allusions. But I can well remember certain days in the valley of Esdraelon in the summer of 1942: I was on guard duty, lying in the shade of a Palestinian tree to which a horse and a watchdog were tied. The grain was just about to be harvested, the birds chirping, and miles away there was the sound of a passing train. It was a most peaceful scene, and it occurred to me that I was very fortunate to be simply alive at a time when so many of my friends and European contemporaries had already perished. But I also reached the conclusion that, having been the plaything of historical forces over which there was seemingly no control, I might one day soon at least try to comprehend the events which had led up to that sudden and altogether inexplicable catastrophe.

This recognition did not come at once, nor in retrospect does it seem surprising. People who have been uprooted are often compelled to search for explanations for their private and collective misfortunes, and those not religiously inclined are likely to turn to history. In my own case there was, perhaps, also some hereditary predisposition. I have been able to trace the origin of my family (unfortunately, without any degree of certainty) to an Alsatian village near Colmar in what many regard as the heartland of Europe. Shortly before, or after, the French Revolution the family moved to Eastern Germany. The family tree includes artisans and, later on physicians and historians who, as far as I can gather, did satisfactory and occasionally outstanding work in their respective fields. It is more than likely that but for the stormy events of the 1930's I would have studied history in my home town, and received a convenient and traditionally solid grounding in both the techniques and the philosophical implications of the discipline. As it happened I had to acquire them by hard toil in later years, and some of them to my regret I have not mastered to this day. Perhaps—it could be that I am flattering myself—I would now be enjoying a certain renown as the author of a weighty study of the Carolingian age.

For many years I used to lament this, but now I am not sure that the years between were all wasted and the lack of a *Doktor Phil.* degree no longer haunts me. My working life so far has consisted, broadly speaking, of three separate periods (as can, I think, be seen from the essays in the present volume). If the captain of the Hampshire Grenadiers was not useless to the Roman empire (as Gibbon confessed in his *Autobiography*), then the agricultural laborer, the building worker, the book-seller and the journalist may have been of some assistance to the student of contemporary history. It is possible—there are, alas, innumerable books to prove it—to write whole volumes on the working class and on the proletarian way of life without ever having shared it; yet a little first-hand knowledge helps. It is quite easy to generalize about politics, past and present; but, again, it is useful to have observed its workings in the melée. It remains, of course, true that we cannot *"learn men"* from books or, at any rate, not all about them. I often marvel at the technical competence of our contemporary professors of history, but in some important respects they differ from their predecessors of the last century who had greater experience, more vivid and intimate, of the real world. Of Acton it was said that "he knew everyone"; Thiers and Guizot, Tocqueville and Lamartine, Masaryk and Milyukov were cabinet ministers or presidents; Bryce, Bancroft, and Motley were diplomats; Macaulay, Gibbon, Burke, Mommsen, Treitschke, Sybel, Lecky and Croce were Members of Parliament; Jaurès was the leader of the French Socialist party; Namier, political secretary of the Jewish Agency; Pieter Geyl was deeply involved in Dutch politics. The list could be extended: all celebrated historians who were involved in the affairs of their age. They were prejudiced no doubt, and lacked detachment. But the experience they gained sharpened their understanding of bygone times. It is more difficult to understand politics, past or present, if one has spent all one's life in scholarly pursuits, or to interpret decision-making if the only decisions one has had to make concerned the competition of the curriculum or faculty appointments. To be sure, as has often been pointed out, a psychiatrist need not be partially demented in order to study successfully the mentally ill, and one surely does not have to be a flesh addict to grasp the phenomenon of cannibalism. But, equally, it is almost impossible without some first-hand knowledge to make sense of subjects totally alien to oneself. The lack of comprehension often shown by the younger generation of historians and political scientists when dealing with such topics as Fascism or Stalinism, or even the immediate post-war period, may serve as an illustration.

There are many ways to acquire experience and each has something to recommend it. Journalism, with all its pitfalls, delusions, and its inherent danger or superficiality, has certain uses. A distinguished American historian once said in a presidential address to the American Historical Association that he would have gone into journalism had he been more gifted with his pen. He was taking, perhaps, an idealized view of the profession; but even now in its present depressing state of doldrums, journalism may not be the worst training ground.

But is contemporary history a "legitimate" subject? The idea that it could not, and should not, be written had many vigorous proponents between, roughly speaking, the last third of the nineteenth century and the Second World War.

The grounds of the arguments shift yet a basic critical attitude persists. The essential hostility derived from the fact that the source materials were usually not available, and that even if the necessary facts were accessible and could be verified, the human detachment required to deal with them in an objective and balanced way would be lacking. Gradually it has been realized that the main danger facing the modern historian, so far as sources are concerned, is not one of drought but of drowning, and that the archives (opened in most democratic countries after an interval of thirty or fifty years) contain relatively little material to change the over-all picture. As for historical detachment, the limitations of historiography are more obvious now than in the last century. Antiquarians can write *sine ira et studio;* historians cannot. Even the man who coined the phrase did not live up to his own prescriptions: Tacitus accused Domitian of having killed Agricola on what historians today would regard as the flimsiest of evidence. There is only one foolproof form of detachment—what Michelet called *"le désintéressement des morts."* Distance in time may help us to see events in wider perspectives and thus to add an important dimension to historical understanding, but it does not make for a consensus. If historians cannot agree on the French Revolution or the Wars of Religion, not to mention more distant happenings, there will be no consensus on events much nearer to us in time. That history is always rewritten in the light of contemporary events is not necessarily a disaster, provided of course that the historian is aware of the dangers of distortion and tries to minimize them rather than to write partisan history with an untroubled conscience. It is true that there is no history, that there are only historians, but only in the sense that there can be no consensus. Some historians are still more reliable than others.

Contemporary history needs no apology. It is more likely

that the contents of this volume do. They were written over a period of twelve years, they cover a fairly wide variety of subjects, and some of them are autobiographical. Marc Bloch once compared the historian to the man at the rear of the marching column—admittedly not an ideal position for observation. In these memoirs the man at the rear has strayed from the column without illusions as to the wider significance of these forays into personal history.

W.L.

London, April 1971

I
HOMECOMING

HOMECOMING

ON ONE RECENT DAY I found myself in a somewhat bewildered state on a bench in the *Park Poludnia* in the Polish city of Wroclaw. It was a fine morning, sunny but not too warm, some well-nourished swans were cruising effortlessly on the little lake, a cuckoo was calling, and great plots of pansies, a flower that is to the Poles these days what the shamrock is to the Irish, were in bloom. I had not lost my way; in fact I knew every little path in that splendid park. I could recall having sat on that very bench twenty-five years before, almost to the day, and listening to what may have been the grandparent of that cuckoo; but then it had been the *Südpark* in the German city of Breslau. The city I had known has disappeared like Herculaneum or Pompeii (or, as some may prefer, like Sodom and Gomorrah); many landmarks are still the same, the Oder still flows through the town and quite a few streets and buildings look exactly as they did a quarter of a century ago. But then I had parents, acquaintances, friends, in that city. Now I did not know a soul. The character of the city had really changed, there were new people around who talked a language that I could understand only with difficulty. I felt somewhat like the hero of H. G. Wells' *The Time Machine*. The combination of the *déjà vu* with the totally unexpected was confusing; it would almost have been easier to accept if the city had disappeared altogether.

Even now I find it difficult to write. I try to concentrate on the present, and yet my thoughts return to those days in May, 1938. I had just graduated from school, and my future was entirely in the hands of various committees, boards, and consulates. I had much free time and came to the *Südpark* almost every morning; I remember reading here Céline's *Voyage au Bout de la Nuit*. What fascinated me in this story of cynicism and despair I do not know; perhaps I had an inkling that another journey to the end of the night was about to begin? Or would it be wrong to attribute so prophetic an instinct to one who had not yet turned eighteen? I recall meeting an old teacher of mine one of those mornings in the *Südpark*. He was no Nazi and had been forced to retire before he had reached the age limit. He was deeply pessimistic about the future, and strongly advised me to clear out as soon as possible. He spoke about very difficult days ahead, about envying my ability to get away, and he ended by asking me to come back when the worst was over. He turned to go but suddenly seemed to remember something and said: "You will recall that I tried to explain to you, not always with success, the song of the Nibelungen. Do look up Hagen's story one of these days." That was the last I saw of Dr. U., walking away from me with his ebony walking-stick. There is no trace of him now, nor of any of his pupils (1921 proved to be a bad year to be born as far as the chances of survival were concerned in those parts of Europe). I have looked up the story of Hagen, but I am not sure what he meant. He may have referred to Hagen's words before he went to his last battle, that everything had happened just as he had forseen. (". . . *es ist auch so ergangen, wie ich mir hatte gedacht"*). But there is another incident in the story of the Nibelungen which has intrigued me for some time: when Hagen crosses the Danube together with King Gunther's armed escort on his way to Attila's court, a party of mermaids tells him that they are all going to perish—with the exception of the King's chaplain. To prove them wrong, Hagen pushes the priest into the torrent. But he is carried by the current to the safe shore, while Hagen and his comrades are killed in the battle they foolishly provoked.

The stranger coming to Breslau in the 1930s received a leaflet at the central railway station which told him all he needed to know: that the city was located in the alluvium of the Oder valley, 119.98 meters above sea level, that it was the biggest, the most beautiful, the most important city of East Germany, with a population of roughly 625,000. He was advised to look at the magnificent baroque buildings as well as the monumental modern structures such as the *Jahrhunderthalle*, with the largest cupola (and the biggest organ) in the world. He learned that there was "a very active social life," and, generally speaking, a very *gemütlich* atmosphere. If he was a philosopher he could join either the Kant or the Schopenhauer Society, as a Mason he would find Herman sur Bestäadigkeit" or "Settegast zur deutschen Treue" very hospitable lodges, and the Association of Christion Maidens would take care of young women without relations in the city. Anyway, he was bound to like *Breslauer Korn* (a local *schnaps*), and *Schlesisches Himmelreich*, a dish which, if memory serves me aright, consisted mainly of baked fruit.

The guide was well-meaning but somewhat misleading. In fact, Breslau did not differ greatly from other cities in Eastern Central Europe. The streets in the older parts of the town were rather narrow, the façades of the houses very much like one another—and not only the somber, dark-grey blocks of flats of the working-class quarters—and there were large factories and markets. In brief, it was a city of work, not of *savoir vivre*. There were no aristocracy or high society as in Berlin, no royal merchants as in Hamburg, no artists' quarter as in Munich. The university was a fairly recent establishment by Central European standards, and the city had not produced any important politician with the single exception of Ferdinand Lassalle—but of him the burghers preferred not to be reminded. There were some fine actors and musicians, but they went off to Berlin as soon as they had made their names. There had been some outstanding writers and poets, but that was after the Thirty Years War, a long time ago. People did not travel much in those days and many thought, therefore, that Breslau was simply wonderful.

Before 1914, people said, things had been different; my own recollections go back only to the late 20s. But my father came to Breslau from a little provincial town around the turn of the century and I remember him and his friends telling me about the "good old days": the colorful parades on the Emperor's birthday, the concerts with Bülow, Nikisch, and Mahler, the *Frühschoppen* breakfasts at Hansen, Kempinski or Brill (dinner *à la carte* for 75 Pfennig, and what a dinner!), the Sunday morning walks on the promenades along the former city walls and the town moat. They seldom mentioned the other side of the picture: poverty and drunkenness in the working-class quarters; the insipid taste manifested in painting, furniture, and interior decoration; the Byzantine manners and customs of Wilhelminian Germany, led by an aristocracy that had long ago outlived its social function, and an arrogant officer corps that deemed itself far superior to all other mortals. Yet, despite ugliness, poverty, and the lack of fresh air, it must have been a very confident age. Progress was in evidence, prosperity was widespread, technical advances were made almost each year; amenities that have become known in England only in recent days, such as central heating, were already in general use. There had been no war for forty years and everybody was very optimistic, including those sinister fellows, those radical revolutionaries, the Social Democrats. The first taxi-cabs appeared in front of the central railway station and gradually replaced the horse-drawn carriages; first-class coachmen had white lacquered top hats, their second-class colleagues wore black hats with silver lace—there must be no mistake about a man's station in life. Everybody was very patriotic, and in 1914 went off to fight for *Kaiser* and *Vaterland*.

When the war was over, the province of Posen and parts of Upper Silesia had to be ceded to Poland; Breslau lost much of its *Hinterland*. There was a feeling of stagnation, of narrowed horizons and limited prospects, though economic progress continued on a modest scale despite inflation and world economic crisis. Yet the former confidence had disappeared; Breslau, once an important junction, had become a terminus. I have some memories of the city as it was around 1930; the crowds of unemployed men in the streets discussing politics, the frequent elections, and the brawls almost every Sunday in which a few people usually got killed. My own interests at the time were directed more to soccer and athletics, in which, unfortunately, my home town never excelled; I remember the terrible thrashing the Everton team gave our city eleven. We had half a dozen daily newspapers, and I tried to see all of them, the beginnings of a disease which became chronic in later life: the *Schlesische Zeitung*, arch-reactionary and very proud to have published in 1813 the King's "appeal to his people" to rise against Napoleon; the democratic *Breslauer Zeitung*, which folded because there were so few liberals left apart from the Jews; and the Catholics, the Social Democrats, the Communists, and of course the Nazis, had their own papers as well. (Now the Polish journalists have a magnificent club near the town moat with first-rate abstract paintings on the walls, very good coffee, and modern furniture. But the two newspapers they produce are even poorer than were the local *Käseblättchen*.) In the elections of March 5th, 1933, the Nationalist Socialist German Workers' Party received 50.2 per cent of the votes in the Breslau district. What happened subsequently in the city did not differ greatly from events in other parts of Germany. I vividly remember the speeches, the demonstrations, the torchlight parades which hailed the dawn of the new era. The teachers in the *humanistisches Gymnasium* told us, with varying degrees of conviction, what bliss it was to be alive in that dawn.

I wanted to see the house in which we lived when I was a child, but had some difficulty in finding the street. The names of the streets had of course been changed; but that was not the main problem. I had expected to see a house, or its ruins, or perhaps a new building, but there was nothing, not even a trace that human beings had lived and died there. There was a forlorn signpost in the middle of nowhere marking the spot as "ULICA SKWIERZYNSKA—CROSSING ZELAZNA." The rubble had been removed years ago, weeds were sprouting and dandelions, a few shrubs and a solitary tree had taken root. Some children were playing in a nearby street in which a single house was standing; they did not hurry to let me pass; cars are rarely to be seen in these parts. Half a mile or so further on St. Carolus Church was standing; a nurse had once taken me there and explained in great detail the horrors of purgatory and hellfire. In a different direction, a few hundred yards away, there were signs of life in a big ugly redbrick building, apparently a school. For a few minutes I stared at the great sundial and the city coat-of-arms beneath it—of course, there were trees in front, we used to collect chestnuts there! The area would have seemed, to visitors who had not known it before, very peaceful and utterly empty. The effect it had on me was different; nothingness can make a stronger impact than destruction and ruin.

In this area, the southern part of the town, tens of thousands of people had once lived; yet the story of its destruction is very brief. During the first five years of the war Breslau was a long way from the front. It became, in fact, the air-raid shelter of the Reich at one stage, and its population grew to about a million. In January, 1945, with the approach of the Soviet armies, a fanatic *Gauleiter*, Hanke, had the defeatist burgomaster hanged in public, and organized a last-ditch defense. In this Hanke was, in a way, successful; it took the Russians about three months to advance a mile and a half. As a reward, Hitler, in his Testament, made him supreme leader of the S.S. in succession to the traitor Himmler—by that time the S.S. had, however, ceased to exist. *Gauleiter* Hanke literally vanished into thin air; he flew out of Breslau a few days before the city capitulated—it was the only major city not to surrender before the armistice. We do not know what became of that efficient *Gauleiter*. The price the city had to pay for having been turned into a fortress was appalling; the whole southern and western part was destroyed, and the center of the town was a shambles. When the surveyors came to assess the damage they said that 60 per cent of the city had been destroyed, which was a lower figure than that for Warsaw and some German cities. I do not know how destruction is measured beyond a certain point; in Breslau, at any rate, unlike Berlin, Kassel, or Nuremberg, it seemed fatal because it coincided with the expulsion of the population of the city. Fewer than 20,000 had stayed there when it became a fortress, the others had been evacuated during the winter. Then *Breslau* became *Wroclaw*. In the following year all but a few thousand of the remaining Germans were expelled. Slowly the immigration of Poles got under way. By 1947 the city again had 200,000 inhabitants; in 1949 it passed the 300,000 mark. The newcomers were people of very different social and cultural backgrounds: peasants from backward Carpathian mountain villages which had been ceded to Russia; intellectuals from Lvov (Lvov University was tranferred to Wroclaw); soldiers from German P.O.W. camps; reemigrants from Western Europe. Russian military administration handed the city over to the Poles, the big railway wagon factory resumed production, and the local theater staged *Pygmalion*—all while the rats were still feeding on corpses in the streets that had once been a battlefront. Wroclaw remained a rubble heap long after other cities had re-emerged from the ashes.

The leading bookshops were on the West and North Side of the central city square, opposite the statue of a Prussian king. The statue, needless to say, has been replaced by a new one—of Aleksander Fredo, the Polish Molière. The secondhand bookshop provides a welcome surprise; the employees are knowledgeable and helpful, the prices reasonable, and—unlike in Russia—one is permitted to approach the shelves. Many of the books are in German; I even spotted copies of the telephone directory for 1937 and 1942 and similar items of local interest. There are hundreds of books—side by side—claiming that Silesia and Breslau were "always German," and others that maintain that Wroclaw and Dolny Slask have been "Polish from time immemorial." The Germans take the year 1242 as their starting point; the German city of Breslau was founded after the Mongol assault had been repulsed. But no! say the Poles, we were there much earlier; excavations in the city and the suburbs have proved the existence of pre-Slavonic settlements during the early Stone Age. During the Iron Age the Lusatians lived there, and they were, for sure, the forefathers of the Slavs. The Germans violently disagree. During the excavations for the *Autobahn* south of the city they found two big subterranean caves containing tons of amber, which they say "could only have belonged to the Wandalers" (not to be confused with the Vandals). And who were the Wandalers but the forefathers of the Germans? Nobody seems to dispute that. The Poles, however, counter that around the year 1000 Wratislawa was a Polish city. At that time the Polish kings, the Piasts, called in German settlers to help colonize the country. True enough, the Germans reply, but "the Piasts became Germans by intermarriage, and anyway, who made the miserable village of 1000 A.D. what it subsequently became—one of the most important towns of medieval Europe, more important as a trading center than Frankfurt, or Berlin, of which hardly anybody had heard at the time. . . ." I have always found these disputations somewhat tedious; how can serious people invest so much time and energy in proving and disproving half-truths? But the struggle continues unabated, each side insisting on its version of the past. The Germans insist that a great historical injustice has been done them; the Poles conclude that the German *Drang nach Osten* was always aggressive and reactionary.

The Poles feel strongly about those Pan-German ideologists who claim that the conquest of territory and the assimilation of the Slavonic people were a "historic trend," one which indicated the "physical and intellectual vigor" of the German nation, and which had "spread civilization in a part of the world in which there existed the necessity to import all elements of culture from Germany." The quotations I have used are from Karl Marx. I know it is unfair. But the Poles, too, ought to be reminded of some of the facts of life. Like the Russians, they prefer not to rely on what Marx wrote about their country; their heroes are Boleslav Wrymouth, Ladislav the Short, Casimir the Restorer, and their like. These absurd exercises were provoked, it is only fair to add, by generations of German *Ostforscher* who proclaimed that the Slavs were and always would be an inferior race.

At school we were never told that there had been any Poles in Silesia; but there was an organization called *Bund Deutscher Osten* (headed by a Professor Oberländer from Königsberg) which distributed maps and leaflets on the German East with many quotations starting with Tacitus and Procopius and ending with Adolph Hitler. One of them I found again in my Wroclaw bookshop. It ended with the following words: "So let us all remember the old inscription on the Reval town hall,

> *He is right who fights.*
> *He who stops fighting*
> *has lost all rights. . . ."*

It made curious reading that morning in the Polish city of Wroclaw.

I cannot recall having met a Pole when I grew up in Breslau in the '20s and '30s. True enough, there were many people with names like Stefanski or Osnojewitch, but this was not uncommon in Germany; the forward line of the German soccer team used to read like an excerpt from a Warsaw telephone directory. Anyway, these bearers of Polish names were completely assimilated, they were 150 per cent German. There was a small Polish minority, but somehow one never met them, or more probably one did not recognize them; they had been to local schools and they spoke German without an accent. In Upper Silesia the situation was different; east of the Oder there had been a Polish majority, particularly in the villages, until 1914.

When the war ended there were some 40,000 people in Breslau who opted for Poland. Some were slave laborers who had worked in the city, others were Polish prisoners of war, but the majority consisted of local residents. Some had never made a secret of the fact that they belonged to a national minority. Others discovered their Polish patriotism only when faced with the threat of expulsion and loss of property; because they were Catholic, had a Slavonic family name and remembered a few words of Polish, they thought they would pass. (Many of them did pass, but the new authorities had to introduce Polish language courses for them.) The percentage of these *autochthoni*, small in Wroclaw, was substantial in Upper Silesia; the newcomers from Eastern and Central Poland regarded them as Germans, and often as ex-Nazis; there was tension and it continues to this day.

There is a great deal of anti-Polish literature on the shelves of those bookshops, starting with publications of the early years of the century. By their side are the Polish anti-German publications (from Roman Dmowski to the books and magazines of the Polish Western Institute in Poznan). I cannot help thinking that these historians could be more profitably employed. Breslau/Wroclaw has a past that is both German and Slav. But what happened to the city in 1945 has nothing to do with medieval history, nor even with events in the 19th century. Don't we all by now know the causes?

All traces of German rule in Breslau have been very carefully removed. This includes statues, inscriptions, memorial tablets, road signs, and so on. Sometimes the old inscriptions have been erased but nothing put in their place, and the result is confusing (particularly in certain public conveniences). The German language is not heard or seen, except in conversations with strangers who want to help, in the secondhand bookshop just mentioned, and in cemeteries. There was a small German-language newspaper in Wroclaw in the middle 1950's but it has since disappeared. There was one remaining sign—an inscription in Ulica Wlodkowica (Wallstrasse); it indicated that this had been the office of the Jewish community. (It still is, of an infinitely smaller Polish Jewish community which had nothing to do with the German Jewry who had lived in the city.) The inscription was cut into the stone and so could not have been removed without doing damage to the building. It is a bitter irony—and yet somehow it seems appropriate—that chance should have singled out the local Jews to bear witness to the German past. There were some 20,000 Jews in Breslau of whom half emigrated in time, the remainder being deported and killed. This comparatively small section of the population had a disproportionate influence on the cultural life of the city—and beyond. The assimilation of a large section of German Jewry was very far advanced (much more so than in Britain or the United States). The result of this German-Jewish symbiosis was a culture disapproved of by German nationalists. Nevertheless it had an impact the effects of which can be discerned to the present day.

Its influence extended far beyond Breslau: for writers and musicians born in the city who became prominent emigrated to Berlin. There were also many physicians, physicists, chemists, botanists, and biologists of world distinction whose origins were in Breslau or the surrounding countryside. Looking through a biographical dictionary of the world's leading scientists recently, I noticed how often the entries read *b. Breslau,* or, even more frequently, *b. Lissa* (or *b. Ostrowo*); small villages such as these on the former German-Polish boundaries produced more leading scientists between 1860 and 1910 than any Western capitals with the possible exception of London and Paris. With official careers virtually closed to them in pre-1914 Germany, many bright young German Jews were almost inevitably drawn into the then rapidly expanding sciences.

The fact that Breslau became a cultural center in the 19th century was to a great extent a Jewish achievement. True enough, the German-Jewish symbiosis was a hybrid, and therefore dubious, problematical: but it had outstanding achievements to its credit. Who could have foreseen that it would end as it did, with a few thousand elderly people assembled on the platforms of the central railway station one summer night in 1942? Fortunately, most of them did not know that from this journey there would be no return. My parents were among them.

As I write these lines in the late hours of the evening in my hotel room, the figure of the city's liberal rabbi comes back to my mind. He lived very near this place, on what is now Kosciuszko Square. Dr. V. was one of the most widely educated men I have known, and one of the kindest; he had written a most erudite book on the history of Rome and had one of the largest private libraries in town. Sometimes I saw him in the municipal library with an apologetic smile: "I am sure I have that book somewhere at home but I can't find it." When I went to see him last in 1938 he was a broken man. He had always been a German patriot, bitterly opposed to any Jewish nationalist aspirations; his whole world was now in ruins. These were the days of Hitler's great successes, and we talked about the uncertain future. He was a mild man, yet on that day there was something of the fire of an Old Testament prophet in him; he quoted Isaiah to me, the passage about the coming day of vengeance, and even Paul's *Epistle to the Romans* 12.19—I have mentioned that he was a *liberal* rabbi. . . . When I was already in the corridor he added as an afterthought: "Though the mills of God grind slowly. . . ."

Gottes Mühlen mahlen langsam, mahlen aber trefflich klein.
Ob aus Langmut er sich säumet, bringt mit Schärf er alles ein.
(Friedrich von Logau)

I often read with interest the sophisticated travelogues, in magazines like *Holiday,* on the charm of the quaint little streets on the *rive gauche,* the enchanting corners of the Ile St. Louis, and the appeal of the Champs Elysées on a sunny

Sunday afternoon. I wish my task were as easy. For all the world loves Paris, but who is interested in Breslau, let alone Wroclaw? A detailed description of the strange charm of the cemetery in Cosel, the exquisite beauty of the abattoir in Ulica Legnica and its surroundings, the splendor of the ruins at the Neumarkt, or the fascination of the desert south of Gartenstrasse would probably create the effect the Spaniards call *contraproducente*. I did see the sights, but the written word does not seem an adequate means of communication in this context; a film using the flashback technique would perhaps be more appropriate and more convincing.

The *Monopol* had been the best hotel since the turn of the century; it still is, though its name is somewhat provocative for a hotel in a communist country. After 1945 its reputation for bad service became legendary; one day even an otherwise unflappable British ambassador is said to have shown signs of annoyance. It is much better now; a local wit maintains that a few waiters were shot *pour encourager les autres*. It would be almost perfect if only Polish economic planning had made provision for the manufacture of sleepable beds.

To the right of the hotel there was, and is, a big open square, which has changed its name and function several times during the last hundred years. In the 19th century the local garrison held its exercises here. Subsequently agricultural machinery was sold, and still later Adolf Hitler used to address mass meetings from the ramp of the castle on the north side of the square. The castle was destroyed but the square is decorated with little red-and-white flags and it is full of people; a Polish military band plays marches; it is the 18th anniversary of the capitulation of Breslau. Beyond the square there were the enormous courtyards and warehouses built in the 18th century; Breslau was then a big center for trade with the East. The houses now look shabbier and more dilapidated, there is little trade, and children play where carriages and trucks once unloaded enormous bales of cotton and other large freight. It used to be a very orderly city, the tanners had their own little street, and so did the coppersmiths and also the prostitutes; Krullstrasse lies in ruins, is uninhabited and cordoned off—one cannot even enter it by car. This is the very center of the town—there are old churches—old inns, most of them in ruins now; whole streets have disappeared, but the house where we lived for some years in the '30's still stands. I had always thought of it as rather small, dark, and in no way distinguished. Now it looks much brighter and most imposing, because so many buildings in the neighborhood have disappeared. It has become something of a national monument, because it was designed by Langhans the younger, the architect who built the Brandenburg gate in Berlin. Someone looks down at me from our old flat; he must be the "specialist in nervous diseases," who, according to the doorplate downstairs, now lives there. Business appears to be slack; Wroclaw's new residents seem to be people with iron nerves.

It used to take me twenty minutes to reach school; it should have been half the time, I realize now, but there were so many distractions. Alas, I can't see any now. Half the buildings have come down, most of the shops have disappeared. There is hardly any traffic at all in the side-streets of most Polish cities, all the life is concentrated in the main thoroughfares. The school is there all right, a very ordinary grey building, smaller than it appeared to me in memory. It is still a school—the Wroclaw Economic High School. Overcoming some strange fear of authority (these things, it seems, last forever) I ventured into the building. The teachers' rest-room still gives comfort to tired lecturers, but the colored glass panel commemorating those fallen in World War I (*dulce et decorum est . . .*) has been removed. The little shops nearby which sold exercise books, toy guns, sweets, and buttermilk have disappeared; there are heaps of coal in the street, an execrable but widespread custom in Polish cities.

I only dimly remember the other things I saw on this day; there were some surprises but no major shocks, one got accustomed to the different character of the town. I went to see Wertheim's, once the big department store, and the city's most modern building, now the *Powszechny Dom Towarowy* (the leading state chain-store). When it was established in 1930 the small businessmen made a terrible fuss; they were going to lose their customers, they said, and they threatened to support the Nazis (which I suppose in the end they did). The outcry was not worth while; after 1933 the place was "Aryanised"; in 1945 they "Polonized" the store and very faithfully rebuilt it. The selection and the display compare favorably with Moscow; there are good inexpensive cigars and a lot of well-made (and highly priced) motorcycles. In the olden days prospective customers were invited to taste the products of new baking mixes and custard powders and what not. The new régimes in Eastern Europe do not believe in free samples; the customer must not be spoiled. I went to see the hospital near the big watertower in the south. A doctor had decided one day long ago that I would be better off without tonsils; he was right, I suppose, but the timing was all wrong. Some slight complication developed. I had to stay a few days longer than planned. It was September 25th, 1938; Chamberlain had just returned from Bad Godesberg to London; war seemed imminent. Never had I felt so helpless, it was like being in a mousetrap about to close. But I will tell this story later. I went to see the Cathedral which, dating back to the 13th century, was largely destroyed in the last war but has been re-built by the Poles. There were groups of sightseers; the new Silesians are certainly eager to know their new homeland and to grow roots. There is the university on the other side of the river; nothing much has changed there.

The new dean, recently elected, is himself a graduate of the university.

How curious that while trying to eradicate all traces of the German tradition, the Poles should in some ways be so eager to continue where the Germans left off. The original function and character of many shops, public buildings, institutions, has been preserved. The place where I got my first spectacles still sells them and the C & A shop opposite has merely given way to the Polish "state trust," selling coats and trousers.

An old aunt was bound to ask me what became of the *Jahrhunderthalle,* so I went to see it too. It was built in 1913, in commemoration of the war against Napoleon a hundred years earlier; at the time it was one of the world's seven wonders, a building of concrete and iron covering 10,000 square meters. Gerhard Hauptmann wrote a bad play for its opening; there was also an enormous orchestra and choir of a thousand. Now they call it Hala Ludowa; it houses a cinema, the biggest in Poland. Not far off the Oder steamers anchored on their run up river. On sunny afternoons the ships were full, the families went to a big open-air restaurant some miles away, where they spent a few hours by the river, fighting off the gnats, eating huge pieces of cake and drinking lemonade. There were small motorboats and canoes, and people in all sorts of bathing costumes. The little orchestra played *"Nun ade, du mein lieb Heimatland"* as the steamer left for the city once again. How peaceful it all seemed. One Sunday evening in 1932, on our way back, a swimmer clambered on to the ship and wiped his bottom with the Black-Red-Gold flag of the Weimar republic. There was a roar of laughter; few of the passengers thought much of the flag. The tranquillity was deceptive.

I was not eager to mention the fact that I was born in

Breslau, for whenever a Pole heard about it there was the inevitable question: "And how do you find the city now?" It was a question I would have preferred not to answer; it involved comparing two different peoples, cultures, ways of life, political régimes, and going on to pass value judgments. German Breslau was not only a bigger city than Polish Wroclaw, it was more orderly and prosperous, it had a culture of its own and a certain character. But is it fair to compare the toughs from Carpathian mountain villages who now lounge about the *Blücherplatz* with the local intelligentsia of 1910 (or 1930) assembled in the *Café Fahrig* after an evening at the opera? German Breslau was not only efficiency, *Gemültlichkeit*, and culture. The head of one of the West German refugee organizations said the other day that most of his compatriots who now visit Wroclaw are not really qualified to judge the present state of the city because they had not known the place in "the old days." Maybe so, but what past does he have in mind? 1910 or 1938—or perhaps April, 1945? Does he remember only the Fair on the Eve of St. John? Or also the infamous guillotine in the local *Gestapo* prison? The frenetic applause when Hitler came to watch the gymnasts in 1938? The deportation and murder of thousands of Jews? The rowdy student demonstrations (Middle Eastern style) against professors who did not display enough enthusiasm for the Nazi cause? "Temporary aberrations," some will say; German history does not begin with Hitler, nor does it end with him. True enough, but for such historic aberrations nations pay dearly.

There is a great and growing literature on the new Wroclaw and I had bought in Warsaw some of the more important publications: the urban survey of 1956, the development plan for the city published in 1961, and Irene Turnau's investigation into the social composition of the new population. They all help one to understand the present state of affairs—but only up to a point. The cultural and social differences between the planners and many of the local population are simply too great. They have helped to clean up the shambles and to get the factories working again. Their children or grandchildren may make Wroclaw a modern city which is more than a conglomeration of factories, shops, and schools. It must have been a dreadful place in the early '50's; even the most orthodox party members tell you that life was grim in those days. The reconstruction of the city had not yet got under way, but a local underworld had developed—drunks, prostitutes, and terrifying criminals. There was nowhere to go in the evening, the general mood was one of gloom and despondency. After October, 1956, conditions improved owing to the general changes that took place in Poland, but also owing to an able local leadership. Matwin, the party secretary and a liberal by East European standards, has done much to improve living conditions and is genuinely popular; so is Mayor Iwaszkiewicz, a former mathematics professor. The number of inhabitants, less than 200,000 in 1946, is now up to about 450,000; it is expected to reach the half million mark in a year or two, and, according to the overall plan, 700,000 in 1985. (It was 625,000 in 1939.) The central city squire with its baroque *Bürgerhäuser* has been most faithfully reconstructed, with its gables, portals, and richly decorated attics. The Gothic town hall has been repaired, and with its triangular gable towers, its turrents and sculptural ornaments, is still one of the noblest monuments of Gothic architecture in Europe. There are 30 bookshops, 27 pharmacies, 23 cinemas, 6 theaters (counting the opera), and 650 taxicabs (of which 90 per cent are privately owned). Some of the shops too, are still in private hands, and about 15 per cent of the smaller workshops. The cinemas show films from all over the world; the mark of *"Zorro"* on the town hall showed the progress of Western civilization. A lethargic elephant in the Zoological Garden may be one of the few survivors from the German era. Perhaps the SS omitted to kill him in the last days of the siege. Thirty-seven per cent of the population of Wroclaw are engaged in industry; employment in machine industry has gone up, in textile plants it has gone down. Public transport is mainly by a noisy and not very fast streetcar service and no radical change is envisaged for the future. I am not a city planner but I foresee certain difficulties. Few people want to live in the inner part of the city; the local intelligentsia lives in such suburbs as Biskupin, or Oporów. There are museums, milkbars, and a number of new, very big, and always overcrowded coffee-houses around Kosciuszko Square; old General Tauentzien, one of Frederick the Great's paladins, who is buried there, had to give way. There is an International Press and Book Club where the *Herald-Tribune* is sold, sometimes with only three days' delay (the British press seems in less demand); there are even a few filling stations though it takes some effort to find them. According to the city plan the destroyed quarters in the south of the city will be rebuilt in the next few years; I saw a few surveyors at work. There are many schools; Polish Silesia is demographically a very young country; there are more schoolchildren now in Wroclaw than there were in Breslau.

All this does not sound too bad. It is a real achievement, considering that the Poles started from very nearly nil in 1945. In Silesia the Poles do not merely want to make their own lives more tolerable, they want to show the Germans that they are capable of building a city as well as, if not better than, the Germans.

One recent autumn evening during an interval at a conference near Athens, the conversation turned to "the need for roots." We were eight around the table, and it emerged that none of us lived where we were born and that only one would be able to see again the parental home if he went back to his birthplace. (This was a girl who came from a small North Italian village that had been by-passed by the war.) The destruction of houses and the uprooting of many millions of people has been a commonplace on the continent of Europe in our time, and not only there. I envy those who survive and manage never to look back; from the point of view of mental hygiene I suppose it is the right thing to do. I was glad, nevertheless, that I had come back to my native city despite the unquiet memories. I was even more glad when the visit came to an end. Wroclaw is now very much a going concern; the recent protests in the West German *Bundestag* against a documentary film showing the new realities will do no good. I do not doubt that, as a new Polish guide to Wroclaw says, the new citizens have become attached to the town in the pioneering days among the ruins and the wreckage left by the war.

In a few decades the city may be among the finest in Poland; today much imagination and good will is still needed to envisage such a prospect. The importance that Breslau had in the 19th and early 20th centuries will hardly be regained, if only for the reason that the city was then part of the leading country in Central Europe; the language spoken in Breslau was the *lingua franca* of all Central, Eastern and Southeastern Europe. All this is gone and past help; it should be also past grief. It is also, as far as I am concerned, past personal interest. I will not deny that I was excited when the train that was bringing me to Wroclaw entered it suburbs, and for the benefit of my wife I gave a running commentary from the open window interrupted only by exclamations. But when we entered the train that was about to leave the city in the early hours of the morning, I took no "last look." I went into my empty compartment and almost immediately fell asleep. An utterly confused dream is all I can remember: *"Deutschland, Deutschland über Alles,"* played by an enormous brass orchestra, directed by a gentleman in very old-fashioned attire; it must have been my Breslau neighbor, Hoffmann von Fallersleben, who wrote the text. Yet the German anthem was soon drowned out by *"Jeszcze Polska nie zginela,"* played by a group of ladies and gentlemen looking even more anachronistic. The trumpets sounded a well-known march: "Poland has not yet perished! March, march Dombrowski!" Among the musicians one excelled, Jankiel the honest Jew, about whom I only know that he was the best performer with the dulcimer at *Pan Tadeusz'* marriage. Yet even this touching scene did not last long. The Poles disappeared as on a revolving stage, a calm, measured voice came in, announcing that this was a fine morning in London, and that a gentleman in Asmara had asked the B.B.C. General Overseas Service to play *"Abdul, the Bulbul Emir."* And so to this cheerful tune the East European confusion dissolved and gave way to British certainties. I reached out and turned the dial of the little radio. The train had just passed Opola (Oppeln). I had left my native city for the second and, I suppose, last time in my life.

1938—A MEMOIR

FROM time to time my work takes me to the Foreign Office Library on the South Bank of the Thames, not far from Waterloo Bridge. It is an old building; the library is on the third floor, down corridors lined with tall shelves, crowded with books, old newspapers, and documents. Admittance is not easily gained. A pleasant elderly lady accompanies the visitor to show him the way, even if he has been there hundreds of times. But there is a reason: after all, this library contains confidential material which must be protected from prying eyes until it is authorized for release decades after the events.

I am chiefly interested in the photocopies of German Foreign Ministry files which fill several rooms. Here, the atmosphere is congenial; there are learned discussions with young undergraduates working on themes such as "Danzig between Germany and Poland in 1928." At half past ten, there is coffee, and if the sun is shining and if—as is often the case—one's attention is not altogether riveted on the files, one's eyes may wander down to the scene below, towards the big barges on the Thames, the motor launches of the river police, and the little yellow Fleet Street vans waiting for the latest edition of the evening papers.

In these files, I often come across documents dating from 1938. This is hardly surprising: after all, 1938 was a fateful year. Yet at the beginning of that year, anything still seemed possible; there was no knowing how things would turn out. There is no doubt that in the history of Europe, 1938 was a year fraught with more drama and suspense than any other in the twentieth century: 1939 was the anticlimax.

All this is known from countless books, memoirs, and published documents. But the historian is interested not only in the *post hoc,* he wants to know not only "what actually happened," but also how things appeared at the time to the man in the street, whether he was aware of the historic significance of events and how—if at all—he reacted to them. To help me in my efforts in reconstructing the scene, I sometimes recall my own memories of 1938. They are probably quite untypical; they certainly contribute nothing towards an understanding of the intricate political events of that time. In subsequent years I have on occasion managed to get a glimpse into the inner world of high politics, or to be precise, the border region between politics, journalism, and academic life; I have shaken hands with foreign ministers, plied secretaries of state with questions and exchanged small talk at diplomatic cocktail parties. Whether one gains any real insights in this way is open to question, but at any rate there is the illusion that one is very close to the center of power and comprehends what it is all about.

In 1938, I was seventeen; I passed my exams for an *Abitur* diploma in February, and I left Germany in November. I read every newspaper I could lay my hands on—sports vied with politics, and I somehow managed an equal interest in Rudolf Harbig, the track star, and in Rudolf Hess; I listened to more radio broadcasts than was good for me. And yet I was barely aware of the connection between politics and everyday life. Politics seemed to be something rather theoretical, which might possibly have some meaning for a few people in Berlin, Paris and London and which, in itself, might well be a serious and important subject like, for instance, the study of philosophy. But I felt that the ordinary mortal could not possibly have any influence on politics and it was therefore best ignored. Life would go on somehow. At the age of seventeen—as I later discovered with a confused sense of guilt—one possesses an astonishing capacity for overlooking unpleasant facts. For me, 1938 was a year of waiting, a year of unsuccessful attempts to train for a career, a year of cycling tours in the mountains of the Taunus and Riesengebirge, a year in which I did a lot of swimming, fell in love with at least two girls, saw dozens of films and read countless books. I am asked sometimes—and indeed I ask myself—how this was possible: a Jew, in Germany, on the eve of the Second World War? However incredible it may seem in retrospect, the spring and the summer passed without any great excitement, although the autumn crisis left its mark. Came September, came November. Right into the late summer, I must have been so immersed in my own thoughts and problems that I only noticed the events around me out of the corner of my eye. The only excuse I can muster is that it was no different for many others who were older and more experienced than myself. The awakening was a slow process.

I visited Breslau recently, and drove out to the Stadium by way of the Scheitniger Park. In 1938 it was probably one of the most modern sports arenas in Germany. It was built in the early 1930s, designed by the father of a school friend. Everything seemed unchanged: the Silesian Arena where I had run the 100 meters in school sports, the grounds where we had played soccer every Thursday afternoon, the swimming pool where, as a small boy, it had taken me two hours to summon up courage to dive off the ten-meter board. Now the pool was noticeably neglected, the soccer

fields overgrown with grass, in the whole huge sports stadium there was not a body to be seen. But my mind's eye
saw a crowded stadium—thousands of spectators, athletes
in track suits, hot-dog and ice-cream vendors. The last occasion on which I had seen the Hermann-Göring Stadium
(as it was then called) was during the Gymnastics & Athletics Festival of July 1938: it was packed to overflowing
and I still remember the monster demonstrations and the
public appearance of Hitler, Himmler, and Goebbels.

The official propaganda machine had been preparing the
ground for some time beforehand. There was much talk
of the "precious blessing of physical fitness," of the big rally
in Silesia, the border land which had for centuries been
living proof of "the binding strength of German blood"
and of "the might of the German spirit," where Germans
would link up with their brethren regardless of frontiers.
There were many fringe events; at the Municipal Theatre
they were playing *Gregor und Heinrich,* but what Kolben-
heyer had to say about the conflict between Emperor and
Pope was of no particular interest to me. A cousin of mine,
a "half-Jew" serving in the *Wehrmacht,* was enthusiastic
about developments he had seen on the Gandau aerodrome:
the new *DO-17* (the "flying pencil"), gliders and parachu-
tists and aerobatics. He talked about Achgelis. Count Hag-
enberg, von Lochner and others. He was particularly impressed by the daring maneuvers performed by some of the
pilots. But Hans had a great and fatal capacity for enthusiasm. He perished at the beginning of May 1945, one day
before the siege of Breslau came to an end—a wanderer
between two worlds who did not know, perhaps could not
know, where he belonged.

I went to the Stadium on a Saturday. It was "the Day of
Community," *der Tag der Gemeinschaft.* There was a
full program, though things were a bit chaotic; there had

been a heavy thunderstorm in the morning. I well remember the 800-meter race. The favorite, Harbig, was the last to take his place on the starting line where the others were jogging about impatiently. A trainer gave some last-minute advice to one of the runners, two got into the starting position, the starter fired his pistol, and they were off. The pace was not fast, and one could scarcely expect a record time on a track sodden with rain. Harbig occupied a middle position. After the first lap, tension suddenly mounted, some of the spectators jumped up, others shouted, "Sit down." The crowd was shouting *Harbig* as he sprinted and began to overtake the whole field on the outside. He reached the winning-post with a 10-meter lead, but his time was rather slow. And then came the ceremonial to honor the winners. It started with a spectacular display by the SS and music by massed bands of the *Wehrmacht*. Himmler and his staff had timed their arrival to coincide with the SS gymnastics. A little man with a mouse-like face—was this the supreme leader of the fearful élite corps? Then came units of the *Wehrmacht* parading in historic uniforms—a company of the ancient regiment of the Elector of Brandenburg, and a landing corps of the old Imperial Navy. Finally there followed a sort of war game, a reconstruction of the Battle of Eckernförde. Flags and bunting fluttered, the bands played the Düppeler-Schanzen march, the blue coats smartly turned right and left, and the public was highly edified by it all.

After a brief moment, there was a burst of applause from the many Sudeten Germans present. On the speakers' platform appeared a man in a white shirt and white trousers—Konrad Henlein, the athletics master from Asch. It took several minutes for the cheering and shouts of *Heil* to subside; finally he removed his glasses and started his speech. He was not an able orator and seemed altogether ill at ease. He said he was immensely impressed by the enormous progress made by the New Germany, that he himself had come from sports and knew how great a contribution athletes had made to the unification of all Germans. "With awe and deep emotion, I stand before the mighty, living work of Adolf Hitler. That we Germans have found our way to this great inner unity, is due to one man only, Adolf Hitler." Thunderous applause.

Henlein left the platform. Now Dr. Goebbels spoke, and a few sentences were sufficient to make one realize how fully "our Doktor" was accepted by the public. "Certain cultural apostles abroad claim that we in Germany have forgotten how to laugh", the little man said. . . . Gales of laughter swept the stadium. Then, turning to more serious matters, he screamed into the microphone that the enslaved people of 1918 had become a new Great Power. "We are fully conscious of our strength! And we know what we want!" Tumultuous applause. He waved it aside impatiently, and silence returned. Was it not a miracle that the unknown conscript of the World War was today in charge of the destiny of the *Reich* and of the whole nation? Tomorrow the *Führer* was to come to Breslau whose citizens would be inspired to renewed faith and fresh hope by beholding his countenance. More than anyone else they needed this faith and hope "which you must preserve for the greatness of our nationhood and the honor of our blood." Once again, deafening applause. Press reports next morning were to describe the meeting as "a mighty demonstration of the unity of Germany on both sides of the frontier, which can no longer be sundered by any power in the world." I made my way home in a more thoughtful mood.

Hitler had arrived in Breslau, and on the following morning the huge festive procession wound its way through the streets of the city. I can no longer remember the Führer's speech on this occasion. In three ranks several kilometers

long, ten and twelve abreast, the participants in the Sports
Festival marched to the Castle Square, where a colossal
rostrum had been erected opposite the opera house. Beneath a large swastika made of oak leaves, Hitler stood with
his staff on a platform swathed in red draperies. Beside him
were Goebbels, Himmler, and a third man whose name was
not very well known at the time: Martin Bormann. I was
impressed by the feat of sheer physical endurance: with
outstretched hand, Hitler saluted column after column of
marchers: the march-past continued for several hours, the
Führer's face became more and more rigid; the effort clearly
showed, but he stuck it out. The marchers swarmed through
the beflagged streets of the town:

> Es fragen nicht nach Spiel und Tand
> Die Männer aus Westfalenland
> (They seek not fun and regalia
> The stalwarts of Westphalia)

Then came a troupe of Swabian girls in regional costume:
"Wir sind schwäbische Mädels—(We are Swabian girls) . . ."
they chanted, as if anyone could have mistaken them. They
were followed by the Austrian athletes, the first contingent
since the Anschluss. Twelve abreast they marched past the
Führer's platform:

> Wir sind der Ostmark Söhne
> Unser Land, das schöne.
> Unser der Kampf und der Sieg.
> (Sons of the Ostmark [the Nazi name for Austria]
> are we.
> Ours is that beautiful country,
> Ours the struggle and victory).

The procession went on and on, until at last came the turn
of the hosts, ecstatic faces, sparkling eyes, tumultuous cheering. From my vantage-point on the corner of Schweidnitz
road, I heard them singing an old tune:

> *. . . wo vor einer Tür mein Mägdlein steht.*
> *Da seufzt sie still, ja still, und flüstert leise*
> *Mein Schlesierland, mein Heimatland.*
> *(. . . where my maiden stands by a door.*
> *And she sighs and whispers*
> *My Silesia, my homeland.)*

The SS which was responsible for keeping the streets clear had great difficulty in holding back the crowds.

> *My Silesia, my homeland,*
> *We will meet again on the banks of the Oder.*

The bands were playing the Badenweiler march, the York march, the Hohenfriedberg march. And then came the Sudeten Germans, thousands of them, all clad in white. A group of young girls ran towards the platform, lifting their hands up to Hitler. For several minutes, the *Heils* and spoken choruses continued:

> *Wir wollen heim ins Reich.*
> *Ein Volk, ein Reich, ein Führer.*
> *Wir wollen heim ins Reich.*
> *(We want to come home to the Reich.*
> *One nation, one country, one leader.*
> *We want to come home to the Reich.)*

So now for the first time they beheld the man whose countenance would inspire them with renewed faith and fresh hope, as Goebbels had told them the day before. The enthusiasm was boundless: "As through a floodgate, the broad stream of happiness and joy flows between the Führer's platform and the marchers," reported the *Völkischer Beobachter* next day. "Here was an expression of the passionate love of all Germans for the man who is the embodiment of the youthful German people." The march suddenly came to a halt, and the whole procession was threatened with momentary confusion. Himmler left the platform and thanked the Sudeten German girls in Hitler's name, asking them to continue on their way, which they finally did. Further groups marched past and were welcomed enthusiastically, especially the *Volksdeutsche* (Germans living beyond the borders of Germany) in their white embroidered shirts, with long flowing ribbons, and carrying bouquets of flowers in their hands. And again and again the chanting.

Wir wollen heim ins Reich . . .

I did not watch the march to the stadium in the afternoon. That evening, Hitler flew back to Berlin. When, at a late hour that night, I went to visit a friend in town, I could still hardly make my way through the crowds. Everybody was in high spirits, great events were casting their shadow before them. The Sudeten German brothers would not have to suffer much longer under the "despotism of the licentious Czech soldiery."

During the same period that the *Volksdeutsche* were clamoring so loudly to come "home to the *Reich*," several hundred thousand German Jews had no dearer wish than to leave Germany as quickly as possible. They were pariahs in the Third *Reich* and were living—figuratively speaking— in a ghetto which was closing in on them all the time; many of them were no longer able to carry on with their daily work. In Breslau, for example, almost half the Jewish community had to be supported by Jewish charities. The measures by which the Jews were to be excluded from the life of Germany had by now been in force for over five years, but many thought that this process was still too slow. In February of that year, *Das Schwarze Korps,* the SS newspaper, had devoted an important editorial to the Jewish problem. In answer to the question "Where are the Jews to go?" it said: "We must point out that the Jews have not exactly been seized by a feverish desire to emigrate. The behavior of the Jews in Germany does not give the impression that they are sitting on ready-packed suitcases . . . With admirable agility, they have switched over from retail to wholesale trade, from manufactured goods to raw materials, they have cleverly developed the art of camouflage. . . ." Needless to say, there was not a shred of truth in this statement. I did not know of a single case where Jews had "switched over" to wholesale trading or raw materials. But the intention was unmistakable. The Jews were still too well off. What was to be done to hasten their departure? What indeed? The Jews were besieging consulates, administrative offices for Palestine, emigration advice bureaus and language schools and were preparing themselves hectically for departure.

When I think back to 1938, I still hear some snatches of songs which have imprinted themselves on my memory. To me, they symbolize a whole era in Germany: *Steige hoch du roter Adler* (Rise, thou red eagle) and *Geduld verratne Brüder* (Patience, betrayed brethren) and of course *Wir seh'n uns wieder am Oderstrand* (We'll meet again on the banks of the Oder). But when I recall the Jewish situation of that summer, certain phrases come to mind, among them this compulsive advertising jingle which I can recite by heart to this day—probably because I had to spend several hours waiting in an office where there was nothing else to read:

Willst den Wohnsitz du verändern
Sei's auch nach den fernsten Ländern,
Ob nach Indien oder China
Oder auch nach Palästina
Zieh getrost zum fernsten Ort,
Eckstein bürgt für den Transport.

(If you're on the move,
Let Ecksteins prove

The farthest spot
On earth is not
Too hard to do.
From Timbuctoo
To Samarkand
Or the Holy Land
Eckstein's take care
To get you there.)

Most of my acquaintances would have cheerfully moved to the farthest spot on earth with Eckstein's, but certain little difficulties stood in their way. These difficulties could be drily formulated in scientifically precise terms; the clamp-down on the international movement of capital and the crisis in world trade exerted an unfavorable influence on emigration overseas. Or, to express it more simply and brutally: there was no country in the world waiting for the German Jews (or any other immigrants for that matter). But the words which were on everyone's lips and which, in my memory, characterize the whole period, are *re-training, livelihood* ("create a livelihood" and "a secure livelihood"), *certificate of good conduct, Hachsharah* (preparation for Palestine), *health certificate, police clearance, harbor charges, Affidavit* (a necessary condition for obtaining a U.S. visa), *Chamada* (the same for Brazil), and so on. In addition there were the many new abbreviations, such as ICA, HIAS, HICEM, ALTREU, PALTREU which had suddenly acquired supreme importance. All this must seem rather odd, if not funny; however, it soon turned out that the certificates, affidavits, and *chamadas* were a matter of life or death. I know a number of people who are by no means of a nervous or sensitive disposition but who even today, over a quarter of a century later, are seized, with violent palpitations when entering a consulate—although they have, in the meantime, become unimpeachable citizens of the U.S.A., Israel, or Honduras . . .

While rummaging in some old papers recently, I came across a hectographed leaflet, yellowed with age, which had been handed to me at an emigration office. The imagination boggles at these extracts:

> *LUXEMBURG: frontiers closed to all immigrants and passengers in transit.*
> *MINISTRY OF JUSTICE, AMSTERDAM: in future any refugee will be regarded as an undesirable alien.*
> *Notice from the UNITED STATES CONSULATE IN BERLIN: in view of the extraordinarily high number of entry applications, the quota figures for the immediate future are exhausted.*
> *The following are required in the Fiji Islands: a Jewish pastry cook and a single watchmaker who must not be younger than 25 or older than 30.*
> PARAGUAY was looking for an accomplished, self-employed sweetmeat cook, BRITISH BECHUANALAND wanted a qualified tanner, CENTRAL AFRICA an unmarried Jewish butcher (specializing in the manufacture of savory sausages) and SAN SALVADOR required a single, Jewish engineer for the construction of electrical machinery. The greatest opportunities existed in MANCHUKUO where there were vacancies for a Jewish cabaret producer/choreographer who had to partner the prima ballerina, together with a troupe of 6-8 ballet dancers able to dance solos. In addition, they wanted a Jewish ladies' orchestra and a pianist able to play the accordian.
> There was a peremptory notice from MEXICO to the effect that a visa issued by a Mexican consulate did not guarantee official permission to disembark in Mexico.
> The Canadian delegate to the Evian Conference on Refugees stated that CANADA could not make any binding promises.
> The British delegate, Lord Winterton, declared that BRITAIN was faced with heavy unemployment.

Such were the openings for German Jews in the summer of 1938. They could emigrate to the Fiji Islands if they happened to be pastry cooks aged between 25 and 30, or to Manchukuo—if they belonged to the female sex, played an instrument, and were prepared to entertain the Japanese armed forces.

The scenes in these offices are the most harrowing that I can remember. At the same time as the Athletics Festival was being held at Breslau, an international conference had been convened at Evian on Lake Geneva for the coordination of aid and emigration facilities for refugees. All the delegates expressed their deepest sympathy with the prospective emigrants (who, since the spring of 1938, also included the Jews of Austria). Most Jewish communities held a day of fasting and prayers in the synagogues. But the prayers remained unanswered, for no country in the world was prepared to accept refugees without any means of support; and National Socialist Germany made it impossible, even for those Jews who had any property left, to take their possessions with them. However, one land would have been prepared to welcome them: Palestine, the "Jewish National Home." But in 1936 there had been violent disturbances, and the British had severely limited immigration in order not to jeopardize their relations with the Arabs.

Occasionally, a ray of hope broke through the clouds. Magic worlds like "Shanghai", or "Bolivia" appeared on the horizon, or rumors were heard about the Berlin representative of a Central American republic who was selling passports for money and kind words—but above all, for lots of money. The only drawback was the dismal fact that these passports were apparently valid everywhere except in the country which was supposed to have issued them. The desperate economic situation was driving more and more German Jews, with the exception of the old and sick, to emigrate. Large-scale arrests had not yet begun in the summer of 1938, but certain events were casting their shadows: the sad fate of the Viennese Jews during the weeks following the *Anschluss,* or the series of new rules excluding the Jews from an ever-growing number of occupations. It was at that time that by official edict all Jews had to change their first name to "typically Jewish names", such as *Chava*

(as a man's name), *Kaiphas, Sirach, Gelea, Tana* and *Rause.*
A ridiculous situation, but no one was moved to laughter.

A Jewish cultural association had been founded in 1933.
"Admission for Jews only on presentation of pass"—and here
the unemployed Jewish actors, singers and other musicians
found a modest field of activity. My father once took me
to the synagogue where I listened to Joseph Schmidt or
perhaps Alexander Kipnis (I cannot quite remember who it
was), singing arias by Donizetti and Puccini and from *The
Postillion of Longjumeau.* Though the acoustics were far
from ideal, there was warm applause. In the summer of
1938 one could attend lectures on "Jewish Emigration—
Whither?", "A Biedermeier Evening with Meyerbeer," "The
Origin and Nature of the Golem" (a mystical figure of clay
endowed with life, who had been the subject of much
speculation since medieval times), "Jewish Hellenism as a
Cultural Problem," "What Meaning Can Books Have for
Us?" There were also topical revues such as "From Romeo
to the String Quartet," "Poor as a Churchmouse" and "All
Aboard Please—a Travel Revue in 21 Tableaux" with Max
Ehrlich and Willy Rosen, or "Winterhilfe of the Soul" (*Winterhilfe* = an officially-sponsored German relief organization).

Hotel Frohsinn at Bad Harzburg, it said in a Jewish newspaper, was still offering *all mod. cons.* Football result:
Hakoah I *v.* ISK I—17:0. Small ads in the Jewish press
offered an "assured income" and "excellent prospects." A
Mr. Simeon Victor, of Frobenstrasse 5, Breslau 18, promised
a carefree old age by means of an annuity insurance paying
high benefits: "Pension arrangements to suit every individual requirement."

So here I was, several decades later, trying to take a snapshot of the University from across the river. I found it difficult to hold the camera steady because of the vibrations

from the heavy traffic crossing the bridge. A few passers-by turned their heads, wondering what I could see worth photographing. On the right, the cathedral with its ruined towers, on the left a small island in the Oder. I suddenly remembered Anders and Kallenbach, and I told N. of the many hours I had spent on this island in that summer of 1938. "On this island?", she asked. "In this weather, in this water?" But the weather was not always so bad, nor the water so dirty, and in those days the island had looked so much bigger to me. For bathers there was a rectangular wooden raft in a tributary of the Oder river, a few lockers and cabins, and an outsize "Nivea" ball. Access to the small island was free of charge. Jews had not been allowed to use the municipal pools for years, and the older generation had no penchant for swimming. So for most of the time, we were by ourselves—a few dozen boys and girls in the same age group and some younger children who were being taught to swim by the bathing superintendent at the end of a line, while others were moving cautiously along the edge in their first attempts to float unaided. If the sun was shining, we arrived early in the morning and stayed for hours; I usually brought some books, but never managed to read them. From the water itself you could only see the island—nothing of the people, the houses or the traffic on land. It was easy to succumb to the illusion that civilization was far, far away. But not for long; conversation inevitably returned to the same theme—emigration. Someone had a brother in a *kibbutz* in Palestine; someone else had discovered a rich relative in America who was willing to help; a boy talked of the difficulties he had to overcome if he was to be accepted at a hotel catering college abroad. E., whom I had known since our days at nursery school together, turned up during his holidays. He was being trained on a farm in Southern Germany where a fairly large group were preparing themselves for work on a *kibbutz*. He told us that at first he had found agricultural work very hard, and that his knowledge of the declension of Latin verbs had been no use to him at all. But he was almost aggressive in his optimism.

I had a girl-friend, L., whom I met here practically every day unless we decided to go cycling together. She had a tyrannical father who had been an officer during the War and was proud of his decorations. He was a member of the *Reichsbund Jüdischer Frontsoldaten* (Association of German-Jewish War Veterans). His constant refrain was that the German Jews simply had to stick to their posts "like good soldiers." Soon things would get better. The present measures were mainly directed against the East European Jews. He had forbidden his daughter even to think of emigrating. She rebelled and decided to run away from home, but her mother was in poor health and she did not want to leave her behind. I tried hard to persuade her, but to no avail. Once we went to the pictures—the *Delitheater* or the *Gloria Palast*, I cannot quite remember now. It was a film about Paris at the turn of the century. L. whispered: "If only one could . . ." An unattainable dream. Romeo and Juliet in the backyard.

L. was deported in 1942.

Twenty-five years later I saw—in what was now called Wroclaw—the Ida Kamenska Ensemble of Warsaw, in a comedy by Goldfaden in the same cinema which had been rebuilt as a theater. The performance—in the Yiddish language—was impressive, though I missed some of the finer points. Still, I could not bear to sit through the comedy to the end. The doorkeeper was concerned enough to ask whether the play was so unpleasing. It would have been difficult to explain.

The months went by, waiting, waiting. In February I had passed the *Abitur* for my higher school certificate, a year earlier than usual; the introduction of compulsory labor and military services had resulted in the abolition of the upper sixth. I did not mind; the last few years at school had seemed to me utterly superfluous. At one stage I had wanted to become an athletics coach, then again a textile engineer. I received a written confirmation from my school that I was "eminently suitable" for both occupations; they would probably have given me a similar testimonial for any other career I cared to mention. But opportunities for career training were diminishing day by day. Originally I had wanted to study History but this was now out of the question. One evening in the spring of that year I went to a lecture with a friend; a professor from the Hebrew University of Jerusalem was to talk about excavations in Samaria. I had no particular interest in Archaeology, but my friend who had heard this speaker on a previous occasion, was full of praise; it could have been that I had nothing better to do that evening. The lecturer's German was not perfect, but he knew how to make a fairly dry subject attractive to his listeners. I was not in a position to judge his eminence as an archaeologist, but he was obviously convinced of the great importance of the excavations, and he succeeded in infecting the audience with his own enthusiasm. He was an entirely different type from the German professors I had heard. After the lecture we accompanied him to his hotel; as we were walking along the promenade in the municipal gardens, we passed a monument. I ventured the remark that it was Bucephalus. "Nonsense," he said, "this is Pegasus. Bucephalus did not have wings." He seemed surprised to hear that we did not know of Xenophon's book on horses. Still, he went on to inquire with genuine interest about my plans for the future. "Study History? Like my eldest—if only playing at soldiers would leave him sufficient time . . . Why don't you come and study with us?" I explained to him that I was not yet 18, that we had no money, that I had heard there were very few places available at the Hebrew University . . . "Dear L.", he replied, "there will always be difficulties, but unlike you German Jews, we are not so easily discouraged. Do apply, I will put in a word for you —who knows, it might help? What is there to lose?" Indeed, I had little to lose. I took my leave of him outside his hotel very late that night.

Twenty years later, while attending an Orientalists' Congress at Moscow University I turned up by mistake in the study group for Near Eastern Archaeology. A lecture was given illustrated with slides; the hall was packed to overflowing. The speaker was reporting on the discovery of papyrus scrolls in caves near the Dead Sea—as is well known, one of the most important archaeological finds of our time. His father had begun the work, he had continued it. It was one of the liveliest lectures I had ever heard; sitting next to me was a Korean, though apparently unable to understand a single word, appeared to be spellbound. There was great applause. At the conclusion of the lecture, I waited for the usual cluster of inquirers to disperse and finally approached the speaker to tell him that it was thanks to the father that I was able to listen to the son. About the dangers of "playing soldiers," the old gentleman had not been entirely mistaken: the son had been Chief of Staff of the Israeli Army before returning to academic life.

But then—in the spring of 1938—my student days were still a long way ahead. Time passed slowly, waiting for the postman and queueing at various offices. (A little while ago my daughter asked me why I wait so impatiently for the postman at home in London, when I know full well that he calls regularly as clockwork three times a day. I tried to explain that it was a "conditioned reflex"—perhaps she had learned about this at school.) In 1938, the post was the link with the outside world and a gateway to the future. The finer points of the postal service were carefully studied. Airmail letters were very expensive, especially if they weighed more than 5 grams. One had to use very thin paper which sometimes made the writing illegible, and tore easily. Letters destined for abroad had to be posted at a certain time—for sea mail to Palestine one depended on the D-126 which left the Central Station on a Tuesday; for air mail it was necessary to post in special boxes by 8 o'clock on a Wednesday night, to make the connection to Berlin for a KLM or Imperial Airways plane. I used to wait for the postman outside our front door or, if it was raining, by the bay window of our flat from where I could overlook the whole street. I knew he would turn round the corner into the Rossmarkt from the Schlosstrasse at four o'clock or five past at the latest. If he had nothing for me, in my disappointment I would look enviously at the letters in his hand, bearing foreign stamps, addressed to the bank next door or to the city library. Never before or after have letters played such an important role in our lives; while there was mail, there was hope.

My parents' financial situation went from bad to worse. Father hardly spoke, mother who was in poor health, grumbled a lot. The business was being gradually wound up, and when my parents moved into a small flat, part of the furniture was sold. Of all this I wanted to see as little as possible —after all, I could hardly be of any help to them. In April and May of that year, I spent very little time at home; I was an unpaid trainee in a big textile mill at Reichenbach. One of the workers with whom I had become friendly initiated me into the mysteries of dyeing techniques. In my time off I tried studying chemistry, but it did not come easily; my heart was not in it. I was living with an uncle at Schweidnitz, nearly an hour's train journey from the mill; I had to get up early in the morning and did not get home till late at night. My grandfather had bought a house in the Ring at Schweidnitz, now my uncle was selling spirits from the premises. He was a tiny man, and I especially admired his courage and skill in dealing with drunken haulage workers. His cultural interests were limited, but he possessed a dry sense of humor and a feeling for music. In the old days, he used to play chamber music with his friends at least once a week; now the other members of the quartet had been "unable" to come to see him for some considerable time. One of them was a lecturer, the second a tax inspector, and the third worked in the police department. In this small town everybody knew everybody else. They would certainly have got into trouble had they continued their music-making with a Jew. As public servants, with pension rights, they had to be careful. Occasionally, one of them would steal into my uncle's flat after nightfall, and talk to him for a few minutes. Sometimes my uncle would ask me to accompany him on his evening walk. I did so reluctantly; it seemed a bore, and I had better things to do; the acquaintances we met during these walks were of no interest to me. Nice elderly folk whose conversation was mainly about whether they had saved up enough money to enable them to retire to an old people's home in Berlin. These people were too old to emigrate, and I heard them say occasionally that they envied me. I, for my part, envied my friends who had already managed to get out of the country, and their number was mounting from day to day. Behind my uncle's house there was a steep drop, and it used to be said that his neighbor, a baker, had fallen down there and died instantaneously. I often thought of death and of dying. But the depression did not last long. At night I was always so tired that I fell asleep at once.

The train arrived at Reichenbach shortly after seven o'clock every morning, and so I used to spend some time in the station waiting-room reading the paper: "TAKE-OVER OF AUSTRIAN NATIONAL BANK BY THE REICH," "TERUEL RECONQUERED." The *Berliner Il-*

lustrirte was serializing a new novelette: "Must Men Be Like That?" The advertising slogans still remain with me: *"Sei sparsam Brigitte, nimm Ultra-Schnitte; das ist der neue Name der altbwährten Ullsteinschnitte"* (an advertisement for dress patterns) *"The dead can be brought back to life if one lives with them in the spirit"* (Hans Schemm). *"Make Trilysin the essence of hair care . . ."* After work, we used to play soccer in an open field. Sometimes I stayed overnight; another apprentice had a motorcycle and we would spend the night riding round the mountains. The nights were clear, the weather was nearly always perfect, there was a ghostly silence. We passed through Langenbielau and Peterswaldau (the two largest villages in old Prussia) right up to the Waldenburg Mountains. This was the setting of, *The Weavers,* Gerhart Hauptmann's radical social drama. This area, though boasting the largest textile mills in Eastern Germany, had never acquired the genuine status of an industrial region. It was no more than a collection of overgrown mountain villages. Once, in the dark, we nearly ran into an army column on the march . . .

Our rides through forests and clearings, through abandoned villages, past factories and castle ruins, were an obvious kind of escapism, a fleeting illusion of a freedom to travel wherever and whenever we pleased. Its only tangible result was that, back in the factory next morning, I was sleepy and weary and even less attentive than usual. After a few weeks of this sort of life, the *Arbeits-front* foreman considered my presence a nuisance, and that was the end of my term in the dye shop. My uncle asked me what I intended to do, but how could I give him an answer? I took my leave from a few acquaintances; one of them, named, Urban, had been a friend of my father's, and a devout Catholic. In his spare time he attended to his bees, and when I was a little boy he sometimes took me along with him. His family was full of sympathy and advised me that

if ever I were in trouble, I should place my trust in the
Church which would help me in word and deed. When I
objected that I was not a member, they said this didn't
matter a bit; "the Church would help everybody. . . ."

Twenty-five years later I drove along the same road and
found Central Silesia scarcely altered (apart, of course, from
the new inhabitants). At Schweidnitz I found the houses
around the Ring freshly spruced up, even my grandfather's
old house had been renovated. With great effort, it was still
possible to decipher his name at a side entrance. I looked
for the cemetery, but neither the tourist bureau nor the
municipal administrative offices were able to assist me; they
said they only knew of Catholic cemeteries. Finally I entered the first churchyard I could see and enlisted the aid
of the watchman, a Ukrainian, who led me across some field
paths to an army camp enclosed with barbed wire. And
next to it, there was the cemetery. Some of the gravestones
had been piled up in a corner, most of them had been over-
turned. I turned them over till I found one I had been
looking for. . . .

Reichenbach was more neglected than Schweidnitz. I
could not find any of the big textile mills and soon gave
up the attempt. At the Ring, looking for a bite to eat, I
was unable to find a restaurant. The access roads to the
Ring or market square in these towns were rather narrow;
now they had been turned into one-way streets. They all
led away from the Ring; in Waldenburg I had to go round
and round three times before I managed to find a road
leading to it. I heard some French spoken, a few thousand
Polish miners from Northern France had settled here after
the war. We drove past the "Maurice-Thorez Pit"; the soccer club was also named after him. In the hills of the
Eulengebirge I lost my way. All the names had been
changed, and the new inhabitants of this area had never

heard of Lindenruh or the Sieben-Kurfürsten hut. All the houses were occupied, but there was not a soul to be seen, and we drove on for hours without meeting another vehicle.

After my abortive start as a textile engineer, there was an interlude in a carpenter's workshop in Frankfurt. Several applications for emigration were under way at different consulates, but it might take weeks if not months before I would know anything definite. I did not want to hang around at home. At the end of my first day I knew that I would never really become a carpenter. On the third day the workshop was closed; there was an outbreak of polio in the city. We started exploring Frankfurt and its surroundings, cycling to Wiesbaden and into the Taunus mountains. I got to know K., who was a few years older than myself, and a "semi-Aryan," according to the Nuremberg laws. He was a dedicated Zionist who could hardly wait to become a member of a *kibbutz*. We went for walks along the Kurpromenade in Wiesbaden, visited the Kronberg Castle, climbed the Grosser Feldberg, and discussed the latest events in Palestine, the partition plan, and the Arab terrorist attacks. I can still see him, broad-shouldered, invariably cheerful. His dream of a *kibbutz* life was not to be fulfilled; the last time we met was on a hot summer's afternoon in Palestine, on the road leading through the Jordan valley. He had brought over a group of children from Germany and was going back in order to get yet another group out. I tried to persuade him to stay, argued that he had done his duty, that war seemed unavoidable and then it might well be too late. He remained stubborn: one simply could not leave those children in the lurch. As a "half-Jew" he would be able to move about more freely in the Third Reich than his other comrades. I waved good-bye to him on August 20, 1939. Years later I heard from friends that throughout the War he had helped to organize an escape route from Holland and

Belgium through France to Spain: and by this underground route many hundreds had found their way to freedom and salvation. He lived a life of hourly danger as an "underground man." Shortly before the Allied invasion his group was trapped by the *Gestapo*, but in the general chaos of those months his personal dossier went astray—and he survived the War in prison. A few weeks after the end of the War he was run over by a car in a Paris street and killed on the spot.

A haze lies over those weeks in Frankfurt, and a feeling of unreality pervaded the whole of my last summer in Germany. We cycled along the Rhein and the Main rivers, ate the local cheese, drank the local cider, when we could afford it, and argued about ways and means of setting the world to rights. At night we returned back to the hostel, too tired to do more than glance at the headlines from which we learned that once again a crisis was in the offing.

In the middle of September I received a telephone call from the *Reichshauptstadt*—I had been accepted as a student at the University of Jerusalem, the entry permit was on its way, it would only take "a few more weeks now." Meanwhile I was to present myself at various offices in Berlin: I would also need "a medical." I left the next day. At the *Hauptbahnhof* the police were looking for juveniles under eighteen (on account of the polio epidemic, they had been strictly prohibited from leaving Frankfurt). Fortunately, I looked rather older and passed the barrier unmolested.

I do not mean to give a hectic impression; in fact until the end of September, things were rather quiet; it was as if time stood still. The situation seemed to be at an impasse, and I was living without plan: somehow I never felt under pressure. There were idyllically calm days, especially the week I had spent in the Riesengebirge.

We had met by the fountain in front of the Freiburger

station. The Monday morning train was packed—a few winter sports stragglers, officers and soldiers returning to their barracks, country people who had spent the weekend in the capital. Our journey went off without a hitch and we reached the frontier in the early afternoon, reporting first to the German, then the Czech border guards. The customs officer glanced at our rucksacks—"*In Ordnung,* just be careful with the Czechs. They are in a nasty mood because of Austria—they feel that it will be their turn next. . . ." The Czech official did not even bother to look at us; he stamped our passports, and we were free to go. We proceeded on towards our destination, a farmer's house at Ober-Kleinaupa where we had booked a room. We walked past snow-covered slopes and through fir forests. For as long as I could remember, I had spent summer and winter holidays in the Riesengebirge, first with my parents, later with friends. In our geography lessons at school, we were taught that "the Sudeten range runs from south-east to north-west like a rampart separating the North Bohemian basin from the Silesian plain . . ." The highest part of this rampart is the Riesengebirge, its peaks and ridges rising far above the tree-line. Mountain anemones and Alpine flowers could be found on the high plateaus; tough knee-pines struggled for survival between the gigantic blocks of granite. At the foot of the mountains which formed the frontier there were many summer and winter resorts catering for all tastes and able to satisfy the most exacting demands. The air was pure, there were chalybeate springs, traditional German hostelries, good old-fashioned cooking, white slopes and ski instructors.

On a rainy weekend, almost exactly twenty-five years later, I revisited the Riesengebirge. As we were driving up the steep climbs, our car started to steam like a locomotive, and we just managed the way back to a garage at Hirschberg. A swarm of children clustered round our *Volga* car, gleefully shouting *"Russki kaputt."* But there was no international "incident." A policeman chased the children away, the mechanic opened the hood and pronounced his diagnosis in measured tones: we should wait an hour and then fill the radiator with cold water.

All this took place in front of the monument to Zamenhof, the inventor of Esperanto. For the first time, I regretted the fact that the synthetic world language had not become sufficiently established to overcome our difficulties. While the engine was cooling off, we entered a food shop in the Ring, which still lay partly in ruins. I asked the elderly assistant, in Russian, whether he could open a bottle of wine for me as I had no corkscrew. He had forgotten his Russian since his days of service in the Czar's army, he said, but he could open a bottle of wine *po polski* without a corkscrew. No sooner said than done: placing the bottle firmly between his thighs, he slapped the bottom of the bottle with his flat hand, and the cork popped out, much to the entertainment of an appreciative audience of customers. Having retrieved our car, we drove along the streetcar lines to Warmbrunn and then further on up into the mountains. In one village people waved us down, the road was closed for the great international cycle race "Across the Riesengebirge," and the first competitors were due any moment now. And there they were, first the leaders in a small group, followed by the main body and finally a few stragglers. The villagers cheered them on, with a special round of applause for the last few.

The road snaked alongside a torrential stream shaded by tall trees; there was heavy traffic round the many bends, and I had hardly had a chance to enjoy the landscape before we reached the outskirts of Schreiberhau. A tourist department official took us to the "Snezka" Hotel—I remembered a Hotel Schneekoppe where I had stayed as a little boy with my mother. It was of course the same hotel; the forest began only a few yards away. If one followed the river Zackel, one came to the Josephinenhütte where glass-blowing was still a speciality.

Next morning, the sun was brilliant, and from our window we could see the crest of the mountain range, still covered with snow. The season had started: one could hear Polish, Czech, and a little German. For an hour or two, we stretched out in a clearing by the Zackel, where the roar of the water drowned human voices. Towards noon the rain started again; we drove to Flinsberg and on to Krummhübel. How the distances had shrunk! Both resorts were fairly quiet; only a few hardy holiday-makers were braving the rain for a walk on the promenade. In Berutowice (Brücken-berg) a huge dog was looking out of a second-floor window. When I got my camera out to take a snapshot of him, a local policeman advised me against it. A gentleman from Lodz asked me how he could convert *Zloty* into dollars; we made it clear that this was a subject in which we were not interested. We gave a lift to a young woman waiting at a bus stop. After grumbling about the lack of buses on a Sunday, she inquired why my Polish was so bad. Reassured by my reply, she took us into her confidence and told us she was of German origin married to a Pole. She had relatives in both the Eastern Zone and in the Federal Republic of Germany, and she had visited them once or twice. "And what was it like over here?" So-so, it was getting bearable now. In the summer, the whole district was crammed with holiday-makers, coming from all over Poland. There were not enough hotels and sanatoriums and many tourists had to find private accommodation. Groups of week-enders often came from Czechoslovakia and even from the German Democratic Republic. "And what was it like in comparison with the old days?" She couldn't say, she was hardly more than a child when the War ended. . . .

In the evening we went for another walk in the forest. We met groups of people going for strolls, a few drunks, some courting couples; one could hear folksongs and Polish jazz. Little remained of the peace and quiet of the Riesengebirge as I remembered it before the invention of the transistor radio. Perhaps we ought to have gone on a bit further *à la recherche du temps perdu*. But I had seen what I had come to see, and we were weary. I did not go to the Czech side of the mountain range; but a few weeks ago I received a picture postcard from my elder daughter who had gone to Prague on a school excursion and had visited Spindlermühle. It was very pretty, she was well, she was very busy—but everything was quite different from the description I had given her. She was nearly the same age now as I had been then, yet how different must be her impressions of a journey through mountains in a far-away country of which most English people—as Neville Chamberlain had said 25 years ago—knew nothing.

The Consultant in Berlin had insisted on a tonsillectomy. "Nowadays," he said, "this is only a matter of three days." He talked of focal infection and chronic septicemia, of throat inflammations which would have more than nuisance value once one had left the parental home. I felt like objecting, but then I thought of the hot and cold compresses round my neck, the gargling with various chemical substances, the frequent visits to ear-nose-and-throat specialists, the swabs, inhalations, and other unpleasant childhood memories. Anyway, opposition on my part would have been useless; he insisted on the operation. Thus I presented myself at the Jewish Hospital in Breslau on September 19, 1938, handed in my clothes and was allocated a bed in the surgical ward. M., a youngish doctor who was hoping to marry a cousin of mine, visited me that evening, and talked of wedding plans and emigration, but the ward sister turned off the light at ten o'clock. A little boy talked in his sleep, an elderly man was groaning, another was telling his neighbor dirty jokes, and two were playing cards by the weak rays of a flashlight.

The operation would be ridiculously simple, M. had said, it was "just a routine matter these days." But there were complications, and I had to stay in hospital longer than anticipated. In the morning we were awakened early—every hospital has its own routine, but on one point all these institutions seem to agree: and that is the conviction that it is harmful to health, if not downright dangerous, to allow patients to get sufficient sleep. In the semi-darkness, the nurses would start walking about, talking to each other in loud voices. Temperatures were taken, tea was handed round. M. came to see me briefly after breakfast: "You are not missing anything outside. The hospital is easily one of the healthiest places to be in at the moment. Have you heard the news?" Everybody in the ward was talking politics. Snatches of conversation drifted over to my bed: *"Chamberlain will surely find a way . . . Benes is in a very strong position . . . Ultimatum . . ."* With a bit of an effort, I managed to find out what was going on. Before my illness, I had been preoccupied with preparations for my departure and had only glanced at the newspaper headlines. There was a "crisis," this much I knew, but there had been a succession of crises since the spring almost without pause. At the beginning of September the situation had become more critical, Hitler had declared at his annual Nazi congress that he would solve the Sudeten question "one way or another." On September 15, Chamberlain had gone to Berchtesgaden. And I was lying in bed in the surgical ward, running a temperature.

My parents arrived later in the morning, looking very worried. Father said piously that I must get better as soon as possible. Mother told me the latest news about my schoolmates and friends, who were already abroad, what they had written to their parents, and she mentioned the bedding she had prepared for my emigration. The half-hour was painful. And what a time for an operation! Would there be war? My parents had brought me a newspaper in which I read about the "Czech-Jewish-Marxist blood terror," about German mothers-to-be who had been beaten with rubber truncheons by the Czech police. The headlines ran: BLOOD LUST AND HATE PSYCHOSIS RIFE, INCREDIBLE BEASTIALITIES BY CZECH SOLDIERY, UNPARALLELED BRUTALITIES BY CZECH MURDERING BANDITS. Czech children had thrown bottles of petrol on innocent German children, old people had to run the gauntlet past rows of bayonets. A report from Annaberg said that a Sudeten German mother from Komotau had tried to flee to Germany; at the frontier she was discovered by Czech officials who tortured her; the poor woman went out of her mind. "Prague threatens Europe with war . . . The blood of the victims cries for vengeance . . . Discovery of horrific murder plans by the Communists . . . Steel rods and rubber truncheons used on German workers . . . Moscow assassination commandos with poison gas and explosives are preparing for a bloodbath at Reichenberg. . . ." And amidst the clash of arms, the Muses were not silent:

Kein Friede wird ihnen werden,
Die Gott zu Kindern uns gab.
Es gibt keinen Frieden auf Erden,
Es gibt keinen Frieden im Grab.
Nicht wollen die Hörner wir dämpfen,
Es schreitet die Zeit mit Gestampf,
Wir kämpfen. Wir kämpfen, wir kampfen
Um einen besseren Kampf. (Wilm Pleyer)
(No peace will ever be theirs. That God promised the young.
No peace is there on earth, Nor is there peace in the grave.
Let us not mute our trumpets, with heavy tread time marches on.
We fight and we fight and we fight on, To make the struggle supreme.)

I remember a photo of a Sudeten German woman with the caption: *"This tormented face of a German mother expresses all the misery of mankind."*—"We want war!," so the Czechs are said to have cried. The German Embassy in Prague had lodged sharp protests against Czech border violations at Seidenberg and at the frontier huts.

During the next few days, the mood in the hospital wards was one of utter dejection. Everybody, it seemed, had finally realized how things stood. Newspaper headlines and radio reports were reflected immediately in the mood and behavior of doctors, nurses, and patients. When Chamberlain arrived at Bad Godesberg, there was some tangible improvement in the general atmosphere: there was going to be a compromise, "everything would turn out all right. . . ." The doctors were genial, the patients no longer difficult. The man in the bed next to me said: "It's a put-up-job—they have prearranged everything—and they are staging the whole show just to confuse the masses. . . ." And he continued with his never-ending game of cards. I went for little strolls in the hospital garden. The end of that September month had brought warm, sunny days following weeks of rains and floods. The gardener was pottering about his asters and dahlias; in the morning we were awakened by songbirds. A deep calm reigned.

Then came the news that, after all, reports of an agreement at Bad Godesberg were premature: Czechoslovakia had rejected the German demands. Hitler made a speech in the *Sportpalast* and said that the handing over of the Sudeten region was the final German demand. Demonstrations of loyalty everywhere, *"Führer, befiehl—wir folgen* (give the order and we will follow you)!" The propaganda machine was running in high gear:

This caricature of a State must come to an end . . . children in indescribable misery . . . Czech women as sharp-shooters . . .

In rooms requiring a great deal of lighting, the windows and skylights must be covered in such a manner that no light can be seen from the outside; this may be done with shutters or roller blinds made of wood, fabric, paper or other materials . . . Bohemian Woods a living hell for victims of Hussite murderers . . . Announcement of the Happy Event of the Birth of a Son to Henriette von Schirach, née Hoffmann . . . This is the Czech: lazy, cowardly and impertinent. . . .

The mood in our hospital ward sunk to new depths of depression; the patients suffered relapses and crises; the doctors were curt, the nurses irritable (some of them with eyes red from tears). A screen had been placed around the bed of the groaning old man, and now the card-player was lying in his bed in complete apathy, staring at the ceiling for hours.

In the bed opposite me, there was an accountant who had undergone a stomach operation. His wife and children came to visit him—the wife looked haggard, care-worn and badly dressed, the two little girls, obviously twins, were spruced up in white dresses, patent leather shoes and colored barettes in their hair. He told me his story: he had been employed by a large Jewish firm in Upper Silesia who had dismissed him without notice over a year ago, under pressure from the "Labor Front." They had moved to Breslau where they were living somehow in a one-room flat at the Odertor. During this past year they had gone through all his savings and were now dependent on charity. When his family had left, he said nothing a long time, but lay silently, his face turned to the wall. After supper he started to talk again; he did not know how it could go on, his wife didn't have a single pair of serviceable shoes left, and now he was lying here sick, unable to help. Had he not thought of emigrating? That was impossible for "little men" like himself, he had not even enough money to travel to Berlin, let alone to far-away countries. If he were twenty years younger and unmarried, then of course he would try. But for people like him there was only one way out—the gas tap —that is, if the gas had not been cut off already. . . . But for the children they would have ended it all long ago. On the Saturday, a friend phoned me: "*Mensch*, the mousetrap might be sprung any moment now. I am getting out of here —on my motorbike—to Constantinople!" Did he have a visa? No, he would get through one way or another. Next day again, in the paper: "Sudeten German youth caught in the pincers of Czech-Jewish blood terror . . . The masses of persecuted Germans raise their voices in protest . . . Rubber truncheons against weeping mothers . . . All Germans are going to be liquidated, say Czech policemen . . . Germany's world struggle against lies . . ."

On that Monday, war seemed inevitable. Had I missed the last train? I envied my friend who was at this moment riding his motorcycle through Czechoslovakia or Hungary. My parents arrived, tried to comfort me, pretended that in the outside world nothing had happened, discussed final preparations for my coming journey. They had bought a special pair of buttonhole scissors for Aunt M. in Haifa, and I was to take them for her. Several minutes were spent discussing the little scissors. The nurse who brought me my supper had been crying (her fiancé was in South America, she had booked a passage on a boat sailing mid-October, now she would never see him again). It was a long night, even with sleeping tablets. The old man was louder than ever, and his groans were mixed into the radio's request program called "Nights of Old Vienna."

Nothing seemed to matter. The old man had died during the night, and nobody in the ward felt like talking. Towards noon we heard the news that Chamberlain was, once again, on his way to Germany, this time to Munich. (His wife had accompanied him to the door of No. 10 Downing Street, the crowd had shouted "Good old Chamberlain, God bless you!"

And the old gentleman with the umbrella had made a short speech: "When I was a little boy, I used to repeat, if at first you don't succeed, try, try, try again. That is what I am doing . . . When I come back I hope I may be able to say as Hotspur says in *Henry IV:* " 'Out of this nettle, danger, we pluck the flower, safety' . . .")—The ward sister came in and attended to the little boy who had been seized with a fit of coughing: "Everything will turn out all right. . . ." There was much visiting between patients from different wards. All of a sudden, everybody was in a happy mood. There would be no war. We were not trapped. We would all get away. I started to write a hopeful letter, but couldn't quite manage it and put the pencil aside. On the radio, there was martial music, poetry recitals, and timely reminders: "Nations of Europe, this is the beginning of a Holy Spring. . . ." A foreign radio station reported that people in Prague were weeping in the streets. But who cared? Good old Chamberlain!

All was quiet during the night of Tuesday, and on Wednesday morning I was discharged from the hospital.

I saw the Jewish hospital again on my visit. On our way back from Poludnia Park we had to drive past it, the main street being closed to traffic, and we took the long route along the old water tower, opposite that large building of ugly dark red brick. I had assumed that the hospital had been destroyed during the wartime siege of Breslau, but I was mistaken; it was still standing, at least in part, and some public offices had been installed there. I asked my wife if she had been able to read the sign. No, I had been driving too fast. Should one go back? I hesitated for a moment. Was it really worth the trouble?

Six weeks after my discharge from the hospital, my train stopped at Munich en route for Trieste. It was the eighth of

November, and the papers reported that Herr von Rath, a German diplomat in Paris, had been assassinated by a Jew. There were a few young people of my age group in the carriage, and I made friends with a girl from the Rhineland. In Trieste no one knew anywhere to stay for the night, but we didn't mind. The Lloyd Triestino ship was due to sail the following day, the evenings were still warm, we would pass the time somehow. The days spent on the boat were a delight. Among my fellow passengers I met a few who were going to study at the University like myself, and others were going to a *kibbutz.* I went to the cinema in the evening; I have forgotten the name of the film, but Zarah Leander was singing *Der Wind hat mir ein Lied erzählt.* The ship's radio informed us that there had been "pogroms" in Germany. We felt concerned but, curiously enough, not intensely so. Surely it couldn't be all that bad? Then we sighted Cyprus, and the boat dropped anchor at Famagusta. I tried to tell a girl the story of Othello—but she was not the literary type. Late that night we packed our things, for it would only be a few hours more. We stood on deck long before land could be seen. An old hand told us that ships used to land at Jaffa in former days, but now they were diverted to Tel Aviv because of the terrorist attacks. Our ship was one of the first to berth in the new harbor. As we approached the shore, the minarets of Jaffa could be seen and finally the white buildings of Tel Aviv. A motor launch came to meet us, and a British police inspector climbed aboard. Evidently the harbor installations were not yet completed, for our ship had to drop anchor off the shore and groups of us were brought to land in small boats.

In my boat, a student from Cologne had been clutching an old battered case, and when he took out his violin, he started to play gaily, *Bei mir bistu schain* and then, more formally, standing up, the *Hatikvah.* One of the Jewish port workers pushed him: "Sit down, you idiot!" The boat rocked, he fell on to the seat, his violin soaked. It was November 14, 1938. We had come out of the ruins of Europe, and an old world was already half-forgotten.

(1963)

UTOPIA PLUS TWENTY

ONE AUGUST AFTERNOON in 1943 I was standing beside the road in front of the kibbutz gate, waiting for the truck to take me to town. It was very hot and the donkeys in the neighboring Arab village were braying like rusty pump handles. I remember the distant water towers in the valley of Jezreel and the cypresses lining the road. Someone was shoeing a horse in the stable just inside the gate. It was my last day in the kibbutz, the last hour, to be precise. A friend who was seeing me off remarked that each man had to plow his own furrow, that he could sympathize with my decision but not approve of it; and he said a number of other things that people usually say on such occasions. I don't think I made any reply; but we parted very cordially, agreeing to "keep in touch" and promising to meet again within a couple of years.

The truck arrived, rather late, as usual, and the driver was still swearing at the flock of sheep just passing by. I threw my small case on to the roof-rack,, jumped on to the running-board, and we drove off.

In the two decades that have elapsed since I left the kibbutz, I have often looked back on my years there. Others who trod the same path have surely done the same. Some, I know, look back regretfully on their sojourn there as the best years of their life, whereas others remember the "lost years" with unalloyed bitterness. My own recollections, let me say at the outset, are less clear and unambiguous, possibly because I severed my links with the past more completely, or perhaps because my work in later years has left me insufficient time to draw up a balance sheet of the period.

When I revisited the kibbutz recently I knew only a little more about the place and its inhabitants, old and new, than did my daughters, who had never been there before and wanted to see where their parents had first met. I had not seen any member of the kibbutz for many years, and any personal news I had received reached me very belatedly. I had heard that one member had lost his life in an accident, another had been sent to Teheran to instruct the Iranians in systematic methods of cattle-breeding, a third had remarried. I had also been told that things had "entirely changed" and that I "wouldn't recognize the place." Although my work in the intervening years took me far afield, I occasionally saw landscapes and people that somehow reminded me poignantly of life in Palestine, as it used to be—in Rhodes and the Caucasus, for example, where the cloudless blue sky, scorching sun, small white rectangular houses, flocks of sheep and scent of burning grass awakened a host of memories. One winter I spent a few days in Kano, south of the Sahara. The women with pitchers of water on their heads, the black tents and the local dyers' primitive techniques strongly recalled many scenes which I had witnessed in near-by Arab villages in the old days. True, this had nothing directly to do with the kibbutz, which was a unique and unparralleled phenomenon, but it was reminiscent of the general atmosphere in rural Palestine during the years around 1939. Recently N. reminded me of how I used to look round for my work-hat almost every morning because it had been mislaid, and of how I had successfully survived snakes under my bed, scorpions in it, foul-tempered horses and donkeys—even a few surprise raids during the riots in 1938–39—only to break a leg one day while trying to shave in the shower. Family anecdotes like these, which have naturally become more and more embroidered with the passage of time, refer to a quasi-heroic era which now lies in the distant past.

Fifteen or twenty years ago, the West indulged in a sort of vogue for the kibbutzim, which were "discovered" by intellectuals after the founding of Israel in 1948. American social psychologists started to write theses on collective child education; young Jewish intellectuals from Britain, France and America set off on grand tours which included an obligatory visit to a kibbutz; and a little while later non-Jewish pilgrims from Germany and Scandinavia began to arrive, intent on admiring the achievements of the kibbutzim. Professor Henryk Infield, an American sociologist, wrote a book on agricultural co-operatives in which it was alleged that, on average, married couples in the kibbutzim sleep together once a month (*Corporate Living in Palestine,* p. 99). My respect for sociology and sociologists has never been the same again. Then silence enveloped the kibbutz once more. Visitors from abroad continued to arrive, but intellectual fashions change every few years, as everyone knows, and the generation that had since grown up in America and Europe was not unduly interested in the way of life pursued by some 80,000 people in 220 agricultural settlements in a remote land. I occasionally heard sceptical or, at best, patronizing views expressed. The kibbutz, I was told, had long since passed its hey-day and was now stagnating. It might be the most suitable mode of life for the people over there, but not for anyone else. It was out of touch both with the problems of the modern industrial society and Western mass-culture, and with the vital questions posed by the underdeveloped countries. It was a hang-over from

Populism, a retarded youth movement—all very well in its way, a bit exotic and "different"—but it didn't really fit into the twentieth century. How much longer could it last?

My own interest in the kibbutz is governed by personal factors and, thus, less dependent on fashions in intellectual enthusiasm. Moreover, I am not a sociologist and find technical analyses of the kibbutz as an institution often erroneous and almost always boring. So it was that when I revisited Israel one summer, my sole object was to see a few of the settlements where I had lived between the ages of seventeen and twenty-two and to look up some of the people whom I had once known there. It was, if you wish, a sentimental journey, but it was not without intellectual implications of its own.

Shortly after my arrival in Palestine in the late 1930's I called on a number of friends who were living in kibbutzim. These trips by horse-drawn cart, bus or, more commonly, milk truck (fares were paid by helping the driver to load and unload churns) had an element of adventure about them. You never knew where you would land, or when. But time was not so important then, and you could always rely on finding a bed somewhere—or, if it had to be, a pile of straw in a haybarn. Tea and bread, with or without jam, were available in the communal dining-hall at almost any hour of the day or night. At that time there were about eighty kibbutzim. The oldest had been founded before the First World War, but the majority were composed of settlers who had not arrived in Palestine until the 1920s or (more usually) the '30s. A large proportion of the kibbutzim sympathized with the extreme non-Communist Left, while others either refused to have anything to do with socialist parties or had a distinctily religious bias. However, settlements differed from one another in more than political orientation. There were also differences of opinion over the form and content of communal life. At that time, most kibbutzim held that a settlement with more than a hundred or so members could not live according to the original kibbutz ideals. These ideals, it was unanimously agreed, consisted of practical Socialism, a return from the Diaspora to Zion, and a life dedicated to the Soil. All were agreed that this form of community represented a new and more exalted form of human co-existence: or, as one ideologist expressed it, "even the weakest collective has an infinitely richer and more meaningful content than life in the towns. . . ."

Once, when I wanted to travel to America during the Joe McCarthy era, the consul made difficulties and murmured something about "Communism." I denied that I had ever belonged to the Communist Party, but he quickly went on: "It's got nothing to do with the Party. But you can't deny, can you, that you were a member of a collective settlement which lived in a communistic manner? . . ." I couldn't. Strict equality reigned in the communal settlements, where a member's sole possessions comprised a bed, cupboard, table and chairs, a table-cloth, a vase and a few books. Until the mid-'30's, individual members did not even own their personal clothing. It was not until later that, as a result of a revolutionary innovation, the holiday clothes which they collected from the laundry at week-ends were the same as they had worn the previous week. As for working clothes, everyone received different sets each week, even in my time. They consisted mainly of patches of cloth, clumsily stitched together. It goes without saying that kibbutz members had no money, and luxury articles such as radios or privately owned phonographs did not, to the best of my recollection exist. We had neither the money nor leisure to indulge in spare-time hobbies. Food was poor, and generally eaten on tin plates. (Since there was a shortage of crockery, the main course was served first and the soup served on to the same plate afterwards.) Meat and fish appeared on the table once a week only. Two prerequisites had to be fulfilled before any kibbutznik saw a piece of chicken: both he and the bird had to be ill. Half a glass of wine was issued once a year, at Passover, and cigarettes (the cheapest variety, of course) were strictly rationed. I will not dwell on the sanitary arrangements, or their absence. As usual, women suffered more in this respect than men.

Naturally enough, individual kibbutzim varied considerably. In the older establishments, people were slightly better off than I have just described, but in the newer ones, which constituted the majority, conditions were often much worse. Families in the older settlements were each allotted a small room in a concrete house, whereas in more recent ones the members had to live for years under canvas or in wretched wooden huts, often in groups of three. When the unit comprised a family and an outsider (known, for some obscure reason, as a "Primus"), difficulties arose. Many of the newer kibbutzim did not have enough to eat for years on end, and the diet consisted principally of bread, tea, and oranges. The general level of health was poor, and malaria and other diseases claimed many victims. A number of settlements were so indigent that they could not afford to pay membership dues to trade-union sickness benefit schemes. One day, I remember, we were cut off from medical aid. On another occasion, we had to tie the soles on to our shoes with string because there was no money for new boots. I once worked in the vicinity of a British army camp, and I still remember with some shame the half-empty tin of Woodbines which I foraged from a deserted tent. Newspapers, of course, were to be found only in the communal reading room. In the evenings, members would cluster round the solitary radio in the mess-hall and listen to the news. Work in the newly-found settlements was generally unrewarding and their financial position was often disastrous. They were all in debt, a kibbutz secretary's main task being to obtain short-

dated loans on unfavorable terms—not that he always succeeded. Since there was not enough cultivable land, many
members were employed on outside jobs in the towns,
mostly in housing and in public works projects such as road-
building or, at best, forestry, for which a minimal wage was
paid. Fields were usually scattered among Arab villages and
so had to be guarded day and night, which tied up a great
deal of manpower in unproductive work. The girls were
detailed to extract rusty nails from abandoned buildings or
to darn trousers which only had one more week's wear in
them. Most settlement members had worked on the land for
a year or two before their arrival, but qualified agricultural-
ists—not to mention technical experts of any kind—were very
rare. Proper planning scarcely existed, and many mistakes
were made. There was, for instance, a belief in the virtues
of absolute self-sufficiency, of baking one's own bread and
tailoring one's own overalls. Available manpower was not
employed in a rational manner, and projects were undertaken which were not, and could never have become profitable. Anyone who wanted to leave the kibbutz was naturally at liberty to do so, but he could not count on the community's help. If he left he was given four or five pounds,
the clothes he wore on his back, and possibly a bed and a
mattress. And yet, looking back on those difficult times, I
can remember hardly any expression of ill-temper or dissatisfaction, let alone despair.

Members in most settlements were between twenty and
thirty years old, young, idealistic and carefree. Often, on
Friday nights in particular, there was singing and dancing
in the dining-hall or outside in the open air. The kibbutz
movement was small, but this had its advantages. One knew
all that was going on in one's own settlement and made
many acquaintances among the members of other kibbutzim.
I think I must have visited most of the existing settlements
at one time or another during those years. We used to walk

or drive across to nearby settlements to see a movie or a play. A family atmosphere prevailed. The kibbutz movement carried considerable weight within the Jewish population, which then numbered only half a million. Reinforcements arrived from abroad almost every week—groups of pioneers and parties of young people from Eastern and Central Europe and the Balkans—all destined to found their own kibbutzim in the near future. There was a universal sense of progress and, despite the bad news from Europe, a certain mood of optimism. No one then dreamed that the physical extermination of Central and East European Jewry was imminent. We heard of the outbreak of war, of the German armies' victories in Europe and their advances in North Africa, but none of this seemed to prompt acute depression or fear. The successful defense of the many kibbutzim that had been attacked during the Arab disturbance of 1936–39 had instilled a sense of security. Strange as it may sound, we felt safe. Unlike the Jews of Europe, we could at least defend ourselves against the aggressor.

I recently re-read some letters written by friends in spring 1939, also a letter which I myself wrote in the winter of 1938–39 but never sent off because the number of letters which one was allowed to send abroad was strictly rationed. They reflect the state of mind which prevailed among young people most of whom had left their sheltered homes at the age of sixteen or seventeen, and looked upon the kibbutz as a sort of continuation of the summer camps they used to attend as members of youth movements. The older people may have thought and acted more seriously and responsibly; we youngsters were slow to recognize the gravity of life.

Twenty years later I couldn't find the entrance to the kibbutz. The settlement had expanded so greatly that I could check my bearings only by the main road which led

from Haifa into the interior. As in the case of almost all
the kibbutzim I visited, the drive-way was neglected—in
sharp contrast to the *kolkhozy* we had seen in Russia, where
the drive-way was often the only decent road in the place.
Once past the barns, stables and workshops, however, the
picture changed abruptly, and for a moment I imagined myself in some prosperous American garden suburb on the
West Coast. Gone were the tents and wooden huts, gone
the horses, donkeys and sheep, gone the khaki shorts and
denim shirts. The only reminder of the old kibbutz was the
tall fence round the perimeter. Not far from the entrance
stood a dozen parked cars, and a little further away was a
large two-storied building, evidently the dining-hall, surrounded by trees and expanses of lawn. The sound of splash-
ing and children's voices came from a large swimming pool
across the way. It might have been a country club, not a
kibbutz.

It was late afternoon on the *Shabbat*, or day of rest, and
an idyllic scene met our eyes. On the playing-field, two
basketball teams were being cheered on by a couple of
dozen spectators. Family groups were sitting on the grass
beside the swimming pool, and children cycled along the
narrow paths between the various houses. ("Uzi!" I heard
one mother shout to her little boy, "Fill the bottle with soda-
water, right to the top, and mind you don't fall!") As we
strolled along, we saw men and women sitting in deck
chairs and on garden benches in front of almost every
house. In one group the lady of the house was fetching a
jug of fresh coffee while her husband cut into a large *Apfel-
kuchen*. They were obviously kibbutz members entertaining
guests from town, but there was no difference between the
dress of guest and host and one could even detect the influence of Western *boutiques* here and there. A number of
acquaintances from the old days accosted us and invited
us into their rooms. Gone were the iron bedsteads and

straw-filled mattresses, the tables and chairs hammered together out of packing-cases and the primitive table cloths. In their place were modern couches with foam rubber mattresses, modern furniture, carpets, radios, phonographs and pictures. In one room we saw a parrot and a canary, in another an aquarium filled with decorative tropical fish. The rooms had considerably increased in size and were sometimes arranged as two-roomed flats, each with a kitchenette, shower and W.C.

I felt rather overcome by the heat, so my host invited me to lie down and switched on the fan. He said that they would shortly be getting electric refrigerators but that there was a hitch over air-conditioning, which was rather expensive, both to install and run. However, a start had been made on the living quarters of old and infirm members in some of the Jordan Valley kibbutzim. He offered me a cool vermouth or brandy and soda. "There have been a few changes here, you know," he said with a smile, noticing my evident surprise. "Did you expect to find us still living in tents? . . ."

What impressed me most was the fact that members could now wash at home after a day's work. In the old days we had to make the long trek to the communal showers, returning bathed again in sweat in summer and soaked with rain in winter. Amenities in those corrugated iron sheds had been primitive in the extreme. The water was never warm enough in winter, clogs were in short supply, and everyone tried to avoid the mad rush between five and six o'clock. However, like the well in the neighboring Arab village, the showers had been an important community center, a place where deals were transacted between different branches of the kibbutz economy, political and social problems discussed and items of news exchanged. Had the communal life of the kibbutz ever recovered from this change, I asked my host? Well, he replied, people's needs at forty-five are not what they were at twenty-five. They set more store by private life. Anyway, he added, one still met the others at work and meal-times, so there were plenty of opportunities for conversation.

More surprises awaited us in the dining-hall. The evening meal was excellent and the kitchens as well-equipped as the ones in our hotel at Herzlia. We were in a so-called "small" kibbutz, but everything was on a much grander scale than anything I had seen in the largest kibbutzim twenty years earlier. As in former times, not even the oldest and most respected members of the settlement were exempt from the duty of helping to serve the food; but the huge trays with their aluminum plates and cutlery had vanished. Instead, there was a choice of several courses and dishes, which were wheeled around on small trolleys designed to keep the soup, meat, and vegetables warm.

At the entrance to the dining-hall we saw a cloak-room where everyone had his own pigeon-hole for mail. In the old days, incoming letters had been scattered indiscriminately on a table or on the piano in the dining-hall. Snatches of conversation drifted across to us from other tables: "I've had a letter from Giora in Paris. He says he'll be back next month."—"Could you get something for breakfast from the kitchen?"—"Shall we go to a cinema in H. tomorrow evening? My car should be in commission again by the afternoon—the garage promised me . . ." One of the kibbutz painters strolled past. I hailed him, but he didn't recognize me, although we later had our little reunion.

Our host's children had returned from the swimming pool and were listening, without much interest, to a conversation which revolved mainly around what had become of X, what Y was doing now, and whether one would ever have dreamt, in the old days, that . . . When we had temporarily exhausted personalities, I tried to find out something about the economic basis of this new-found prosperity. It seemed that people had indeed learned from their early mistakes, agriculture had been rationalized and mechanized, and productivity had risen fourfold in the past twenty years. "And how are the people in S. doing?" I inquired. "Pretty well," I was told. "They cleared two million dollars last year." (S. was the settlement in which we hadn't been able to pay the doctor or repair our boots.) Unprofitable lines of activity, such as sheep breeding, had been discontinued years before, and people had long ago abandoned the attempt to be "self-supporting" at any price. A systematic division of labor had grown up between the individual kibbutzim and between them and the towns. Many settlements had built large fish ponds or were growing cotton, and banana plantations had spread from the Jordan Valley to all parts of the country. Almost every kibbutz boasts some form of industry. While I was still in Israel, a political economist announced at a conference that, according to his calculations, only half the total income of the kibbutzim is derived from agricultural sources. This caused great surprise, although people should have been aware of this development. Mechanization frees manpower from the land, and employment has to be found for the older and less robust members of the community. Apart from that, industrial development is doubtless essential to any appreciable rise in living standards. This means of course, that little now survives of the original Tolstoy-Gordon "back to the land" ideals which used to dominate at least one section of the kibbutz movement. It also means that many kibbutzim have to employ paid workers from the towns, a fact which naturally conflicts sharply with the old kibbutz ideals and would have been quite unthinkable twenty years ago.

Most kibbutzim are still in debt to a considerable extent —on average, to a sum three or four times the value of their net annual income. I should also mention that loans are harder to obtain and terms less favorable to borrowers in

Israel than in any other country I know. On the other hand, no one loses any sleep on this account. Living standards are on the upgrade, and the man who leaves a kibbutz today —provided he parts with the community on good terms— seldom goes empty-handed. We were told that the kibbutz had bought a flat in town for an acquaintance of ours who had recently left the settlement. Comparatively few members over the age of forty-five still do agricultural work, except in positions of responsibility. Just as the "tertiary sector" (or public services) has expanded in the outside world, so the same process appears to have occurred—and with equal rapidity—inside the kibbutzim. Everything has become much more complex than it was. More secretaries, planning officials, and accountants are needed. Many of my old co-workers have become teachers; others are engaged in various political and economic institutes outside the kibbutz, locally, in Tel Aviv or even abroad; two are writing books, another produces plays, and yet another is working on a list of the major archaeological discoveries made in the neighborhood. Women tend to find their work less congenial and satisfying, and the difficult years have left more of a mark on them.

It was growing dark, but there was no lessening in the comings and goings outside the dining-hall. A film was being shown in the House of Culture. In the old days this used to happen perhaps once a quarter, but now every kibbutz has its own projector and there are two shows a week. The younger children were taken off to the children's dormitory by their parents, while the older ones, who attended boarding school in the neighboring kibbutz but were on holiday, sat around in little groups.

Twenty years earlier there had been much talk about the problems of mixed communities and collective child education. In many kibbutzim, parents were forbidden to keep toys in their rooms, let alone share a bedroom with their children, for fear the links between child and parent would become too strong. Many townspeople winked slyly and talked about "free love" in the kibbutz, about the "communal bath" which was supposed to have existed somewhere, and Jehovah knows what other unbridled excesses. In reality, there was as much sex in the kibbutzim as there is in Plymouth or Poughkeepsie—that is to say, a lot or a little, depending on the eye of the beholder. Today, the family is the focus of social life in the kibbutz, and the links between child and parent no weaker than in the towns. Leafing through a symposium on sex education which had just been published by the Kibbutz Teachers Association, I detected little of the enthusiasm or illusions entertained by the sex reformers of the 1920s and early '30s.

As time passed, the heat abated. In the distance we could see the lights of near-by settlements, where similar scenes were probably being enacted at the same hour. Have I painted too rosy a picture of life in the kibbutz? Admittedly, people still work longer hours there and enjoy far fewer holidays than in the towns. My description probably applies more to settlements which came into being before the founding of the State, or more than twenty years ago. In the newer kibbutzim in more remote and less fertile parts of the country especially to the south, such prosperity is far from being the rule. Finally, I ought perhaps to emphasize once again that I have described the kibbutz as it was on the Sabbath. The atmosphere on weekdays is far less leisurely. And yet, despite all these reservations, I found a vast and scarcely credible improvement. While meditating on this, it suddenly occurred to me that the bench on which I was sitting stood on the spot where our tent had once been situated. I remembered how we used to troop off, clad in our tattered working clothes, to the ancient and unprepossessing mess hall to feast on bread and awful jam.

As our host rightly said, times had changed with a vengeance.

One evening, two girl-soldiers returning to camp after a spell of leave thumbed a lift from us as we were driving along the high-road not far from one of the oldest kibbutzim in the country. I asked them how their generation differed from that of their parents in the kibbutz. The answer came back promptly: "Our lot are far better workers and take less of an interest in Zionism. . . ." By Zionism, they were referring less to the international Zionist movement than to the forms of indoctrination to which they had been subjected from an early age—the everlasting speeches, newspaper articles, and classes of instruction devoted to the mission of the Israeli people in their new home, to Marxism-Leninism (or, alternatively, Ethical Socialism), the history and function of the kibbutz movement, and similar subjects.

Most observers agree that members of the younger generation, which already forms the backbone of the oldest kibbutzim and those of medium age, are much less complicated than their parents were. While their fathers may have burned the midnight oil debating the issues of the Spanish Civil War or The Chinese Revolution, the youngsters of today are mainly interested in local affairs. In some respects, they reminded me of young people in post-Stalinist Russia: they accept parts of the official doctrine without question, but their interest in politics is generally slight. This may not be a bad thing. Anyone familiar with the history of the kibbutzim will be aware of the devastating effects of over-politicization, a process which resulted, for reasons that now seem quite incomprehensible, in the downfall and disintegration of many settlements. Education of the young must have been a success within its own terms, since most of them still live in the kibbutz. Kibbutz schools did not aim at producing Fausts or Einsteins, but efficient workers, and here again they appear to have succeeded. On the other hand, young boys and girls have shed many of the attributes which made their parents' generation so interesting and attractive. The price of normalization is a high one. When I asked the two girls from M. whether they themselves would have opted for life in a kibbutz (as their parents did) or merely felt that they had been born into it, they replied: "Actually, sir, we don't give much thought to the problem. . . ." Many people might consider this a reassuring answer, but I am not so sure.

Nothing is riskier than to generalize about the attitude of young people who are, in the nature of things, still in process of development. Even kibbutz teachers told me that they were often vague as to their pupils' real views. Outwardly, collective education produces a uniform type, but that makes it even harder to gauge underlying thoughts and feelings. Thus it is quite possible that the young people of the kibbutzim will give their critics a pleasant surprise in years to come, though others fear that when the youthful charm and freshness which at present conceals or disguises many of their failings finally fades it will reveal them to be an even duller and more uninteresting generation than they now appear. I can only repeat what I heard.

I find it simpler to describe the position of my middle-aged contemporaries in the kibbutzim. I had an opportunity to speak with friends who had recently left the kibbutz. They complained bitterly about the parochial intrigues and back-biting, and argued that, in the final analysis, it depended on how the individual adapted himself (they used a verb for which only Dual Monarchy German has an equivalent), on whether his "bargaining power" in relation to the collective was strong enough to help him get what he wanted. Others I met were far from satisfied with their communal existence but dreaded the transition to urban life ("We're not twenty any more") or were reluctant to leave the kibbutz because their children liked it there. Finally, I spoke to many people who referred scornfully to life in the towns and then went straight over to the attack: "We've built something here. We can live here as we think fit and teach our children a sense of values. Can you say the same?"

My impression is that most kibbutz members today are either reasonably contented or have ceased to ask themselves why they still belong—which in itself proves that they are not dissatisfied. Their original decision to live in a kibbutz frequently stemmed from political or, in the widest sense, ideological motives. Today, these motives play a very minor role except in kibbutzim which subscribe to Marxist ideology, and even there politics are waning in importance year by year. Even there, in the past decade, people have begun to realize not only that developments in Eastern Europe, Russia, and China have failed to follow the rule-book, but that changes have occurred in the world at large which must also be taken into account. The process of enlightenment is a slow and painful one, and it is understandable that some now aging politicians and ideologists decline to share in it. It is strange to see people who would regard any suggestion that they should buy thirty- or forty-year-old agricultural machinery as ludicrous—indeed, unthinkable—calmly accepting the validity of a political outlook which virtually ignores all that has happened in the world during the past thirty or forty years. Many attribute this to the specific nature of the kibbutz as a closed community and one which is not susceptible to new influences; but I find this explanation only partially satisfactory. After all, production methods in Japan, too, are at least a human lifetime in advance of the political ideas espoused by Japanese intellectuals. But perhaps this is signal confirmation of the Marxist theory that ideological "superstructure" always lags behind material development!

What keeps people in the kibbutzim today is not politics but principally, it seems to me, the satisfaction they derive from their work. It is an accepted fact that it is harder to find such work for women in the kibbutz than for men, and that the woman is usually the driving force behind the decision to leave. In addition to contentment with one's work and pride in individual achievement there is the sense of security that accrues from living in a collective. I have already mentioned that members tend increasingly to go home after work, and that the family plays a far more important role within the kibbutz than it did originally. But, although the intense community life of the early years is now a thing of the past, members have gotten used to each other, much as married couples grow accustomed to one another after years of living together and come to regard such companionship as the only conceivable mode of life. The material prospects of the individual townsman are uncertain and the living standard of the average kibbutznik is comparable with that of the urban worker. Apart from that, the sense of identification with the community which grows up in every individual after ten or fifteen years is a factor which in most cases discourages the would-be leaver. To say that man is a creature of habit is as trite as it is apt; a man must have fairly cogent reasons for deciding to make a radical change not only in his place of residence but in his community and whole way of life. Such things do happen, but only rarely.

It was late when we said goodbye to our friends in the kibbutz and drove off up the narrow, winding road that leads across the mountains. I was so deeply engrossed with my thoughts that I almost failed to spot a truck parked in the darkness on the verge of the road. I handed over the wheel to my wife so that I could reflect at leisure on our last day in the kibbutz. What would become of it, I wondered? The settlements had been stagnating numerically for quite a while now, and in some years departures and deaths actually outnumbered the total of new arrivals by birth or acquisition. There were no "reserves" to draw on abroad. Even if a fresh mass migration to Israel took place, *e.g.* from South America or Eastern Europe, few of the new immigrants would join kibbutzim. It also seemed unlikely that many new agricultural collectives would be formed. Israel is already suffering from agricultural over-production, and increasing mechanization will mean that fewer and fewer people are needed to fulfil national requirements in this sector. It is questionable, however, whether this denotes the end of the kibbutz. The kibbutzim are numerically much stronger and have a far more consistent and definite character than utopian settlements like New Lebanon or Ephrata in the United States, which have been in existence for 150 years or more. There is no reason to suppose that the kibbutzim will prove any less durable. Of course, it would not surprise me if the character of the kibbutz undergoes substantial changes, even in the coming generation. Private ownership of consumer goods will doubtless expand still further, and I suspect that members will eventually be paid, partially at least, in cash.

What can we learn from the Kibbutz Experiment? Aldous Huxley (not noted for his love of utopias) once wrote that we can learn something even from the stupidest experiment in organized human co-existence—if only how *not* to set about it. The kibbutz was not a stupid experiment, but it grew up under unique conditions such as prevail nowhere else in the modern world. If only for that reason alone, it can never serve as a pattern, let alone be imitated. Nevertheless, the experience of ordered human co-existence gained by individuals living in such a community—experience both positive and negative—is extremely wide in its scope and merits detailed examination, whether in regard to child education, kibbutz democracy, or a dozen other equally important and interesting problems.

So far, despite the best sociological intentions, few such investigations have been carried out. Most existing studies are not very satisfactory, and descriptive works, though mostly well meant, are either ill-informed or quite as uncritical as the Webbs' celebrated book on Russia, which also set out to depict "a new civilization." Similarly, the occasional attempts to portray kibbutz life in the novelist's idiom have with one or two exceptions fallen wide of the mark. The world has become aware that such a thing as the kibbutz exists, but people know little more about the essential quality of life there than they did when the first kibbutzim were founded more than fifty years ago.

It was just before midnight when we reached our large seaside hotel. A sizeable party of teen-agers had just arrived. I couldn't tell at first glance whether they hailed from the Bronx or Golder's Green, but their behavior suggested that they were hell-bent on enjoying themselves in the next three weeks. Some bemoaned the fact that the bar was already closed, others complained that the air-conditioning in their rooms wasn't functioning efficiently. The girls were too heavily made up, and I found the boys equally unappealing. They were probably about the same age as the party of leather-jacketed pioneers whom I saw disembarking at Haifa more than twenty-five years earlier. Those immigrants hadn't expected luxury hotels, air-conditioning or whiskys and soda. Instead, they were bubbling over with dreams of a New Jerusalem and a utopian idealism which probably seems, in retrospect, touchingly childish. To the majority of the party in the foyer, products as they were of our modern industrial mass-culture, the present-day kibbutz would doubtless seems an antiquated relic from a forgotten world—something to be visited on a sight-seeing tour, like a museum. But then, who wants to live in a museum?

Few would dispute that these young visitors from London or New York were decent enough fundamentally, or that they would shed some of their crudities within a year or two. But what a gulf separated them, "angry" and conformist alike, from the denim-shirted, khaki-shorted youngsters of 1936 and 1938, who were inspired by Hermann Hesse's *Demian* and Rolland's *Jean Christophe*, by Martin Buber and the "Communist Manifesto"; it was a curious mixture, some of it was bogus, and disappeared rapidly in the harsh Palestinian realities. Anyway, it was very different from more recent fashions. Whether the pioneers of the 1930s were better human beings is a moot point, but one thing is certain: they had the sort of chance that comes very rarely, the chance to make a radically fresh start and to try to mold their lives as they chose. Perhaps they failed; certainly, the pioneers of 1936 did not succeed in lifting the world off its hinges. If the kibbutz has any future, it is probably only as a way of life for those who now live there and for their children. I am not so sure, however, that the question of success or failure is of such vital importance: *in magnis voluisse sat est.* The post-1945 generation has had no such opportunity. It will—if I may, in this context, disregard war and the bomb for a moment—lead a more normal life, if a less exciting one, but the same can be said with equal justification of the second- or third-generation kibbutznik: his life is more or less mapped out. Life seems to have grown less interesting everywhere in the world—or is it simply that we are all twenty years older now?

(1963)

PRAGUE REVISITED

IT IS ABOUT 300 kilometers from my native town in Silesia to Prague—a few hours by car, twenty minutes in a jet. It had taken me almost twenty-seven years since that day in March 1938 when I last tried to reach Prague, but failed. The name of the city beyond the mountains had been a magical word in my childhood, *Zlata Praha*, "Prague the Golden", lots of coffee-houses, enormous portions of whipped cream, good soccer clubs (especially a goalie named Planicka), people who spoke German with a funny accent. After 1933 there were additional attractions. Hitler had taken over in Germany and we were glued to the radio in the late afternoon for news from non-Nazi sources. During the Winter holidays and in the Summer, one went to Prague to meet friends who had left Germany; I remember, at sixteen, buying up three months of emigré literature and spending the whole night in a dingy Prague hotel religiously reading all of it, from Otto Strasser to the Trotskyists. At the time it was tremendously exciting; it didn't make exciting reading when I looked through some of it the other day. In 1938 it was undoubtedly very wholesome; an act of mental hygiene, after exposure to massive doses of Nazi propaganda.

I had been to Prague a few times between 1935 and 1937

and in March 1938 I set out with L. on what was to be just another trip. We caught the milk train on Monday morning, crowded as usual with officers and soldiers returning from the provincial capital to their garrisons. There were also a few ski enthusiasts. It was an uneventful trip; in the early afternoon we reached the customs shed at the border pass. That part of the Giant Mountains (Sudeten) was very attractive; in the forests at the foot of the mountains were spas, for every taste and for almost any purse. They were free of pollen, had chalybeate springs, and *Bierstuben* in a fake old German style; the food was excellent. But we preferred the big wooden huts on the ridge of the mountains, the *Bauden*, which were much cheaper. Originally these had been stables with roofs of shingles, which were later turned into mountain rest-houses. This was a unique local institution; the very word *Baude* is found nowhere else in Central Europe.

The people in the nearby villages were not well-off. The soil was poor, the little glass works, the lumber and spinning mills, could not compete with the industry in the big cities of the plains. Tourism became the chief source of income. Some of the villages, especially on the Czech side of the mountains, were now quite fashionable and moderately prosperous; hundreds of tourists went up the ridge to admire sunset or sunrise and to feed the trout in the little ponds. The woods were full of children with their mamas. The tourist association had marked the narrow paths through the forests in the colors of the rainbow; one could no more go astray here than in the Champs Elysées or in Oxford Street.

This region had been known to me as a very peaceful place indeed, in which neither politicians nor economists had ever shown interest; the only journalists here were all taking skiing lessons. Suddenly, in 1938, it had become one of the world's main danger zones; a world war was about to break out over Ober-Kleinaupa. It all seemed very incongruous.

Next morning we continued on our way to Prague. The man who gave us a lift subjected us to a long political harangue. The individual Czech, he told us, was lazy, impertinent, and a coward *(faul, feig, und frech das ist der Tschech)*. Yet this dwarf nation of domestic servants, village musicians, and concierges wanted to rule a great *Kulturvolk* like the Germans—wasn't it utterly ridiculous? For decades now the Germans had had to fight every inch of the way for their elementary rights—the German language, customs, their autonomy in general. They had been steadily losing, but now the tide had turned. At long last people in Berlin were speaking the one and only language that was understood in Prague. He was proud to be a National-Socialist, proud that there had been a Nazi party in the Sudeten even before there had been one in the *Reich* . . . It was a very unpleasant half hour.

In Trautenau, the next city, we met a friend who, after long peregrinations through Europe, East and West, was about to leave for overseas. We had agreed to meet in the coffeehouse; he was there, but at first pretended not to know us. Later he gave us a sign to follow him. Outside the town, he told us he had been followed in Prague. In his cheerful tone, he made the gloomiest political forecasts: "Hitler was about to conquer all Europe . . . Stalin would make a deal with him . . . the western democracies would not resist the Nazis until it was too late" . . . Later we went back to the café and ate a lot of fruit cake and whipped cream; the dark prospects did not affect our appetites.

That evening, I fell ill and we returned to the mountain village where we had stayed the previous night. For a few days I had a high temperature. Prague was out, for we had to be back by the end of the week.

In writing about Prague, one should really go back to Libussa, the lady who allegedly founded the city, the Hussites, the Thirty Years War (which put an end to Czech independence), or to Mozart directing the first performance of *Don Giovanni*. These bygone ages have all left their imprint. Medieval Prague was one of the finest cities in Europe and had one of the first universities. But meaningful parallels may be drawn with Prague as it existed in 1905 or in 1935. This, too, is now past history; but there is some continuity, if only because some of those who knew Prague before World War I are still with us. They can be found in New York, London, Jersualem, and some, perhaps, in Prague itself. They take an interest in the literature of many countries, in philosophy, music, and the arts; it was easier to be a polymath in 1910 than in 1965, but it still never fails to impress me. They write to each other in an antiquated system of shorthand which will be as difficult to decipher for the cultural historians of the 21st century as Linear B.

To describe a city without the benefit of illustrations is a frustrating venture; if this were a movie, a flashback to 1905 would be called for. It would show, I imagine, groups of uniformed German students with their banners, marching down the Graben (named after the ditch which once divided the Old from the New City), singing *Deutschland, Deutschland über alles*, attacking and being attacked by the irate Czech crowd which had launched a counter-demonstration, singing *Kde domov muj*. These clashes had begun in 1880, were renewed in 1897, and became, so to speak, a weekly fixture between 1904 and 1909. They were the most spectacular, though not the most important manifestations of the bitter struggle between Germans and Slavs that had broken out during the second half of the nineteenth century.

In 1848 Marx and Engels believed that the Czechs were "a dying people"; they would survive only as part of Germany. But things were already moving in the very opposite non-Marxist direction. The Czechs clung to their language, customs, and national traditions* until legal sanction was given to their national aspirations in the declining phase of the Austro-Hungarian rule. Vienna made increasing concessions to the Czechs; the Germans felt betrayed, and some of them reacted by supporting a movement that became a precursor of Nazism. Here, in a pub, Jaroslav Hašek, who had not yet written the book about Schweik which made him famous, founded his own political party of moderate progress within the framework of the law; it was more a skit on his own people than on the Germans. The national antagonism in these parts largely overshadowed the social strife; there was poverty, but the extreme exploitation, the contrasts between rich and poor, were less pronounced in the Czech towns than in the rest of Western Europe at that time. The Czech regions of the Austro-Hungarian empire were among the most highly developed industrially, and they had a comparatively high living standard, a fact often forgotten now. In this, as in some other respects, Prague firmly belonged to Central, not to Eastern Europe.

The entry under *"Prague"* in a guide book around the turn of the century would have read approximately as follows:

Prague (635 ft.), Bohemian: crownland of Bohemia, the seat of the imperial government and residence of a prince archbishop, lies picturesquely in a basin on both banks of the Moldau. Population 183,000: ⅘ Bohemians, ⅕ Germans,

---

* Paul Claudel, once Consul in Prague, wrote about *"le Tchèque obstiné."*

20,000 Jews, a garrison of about 7,000 men. (The Jews and the soldiers did not apparently count.) The leading hotels were the Hotel de Saxe, the Blauer Stern, and the Schwarzes Ross. There were six street car lines and several cable street cars, but most of the travelling was still done by one-horse cabs and two-horse carriages, the *fiacres*. Beer, the guide-book would say, was "generally good" at all the hotels, restaurants, and cafes. Of the five theaters, three were German. The *Altneuschul,* the oldest Synagogue, would be described as a strange looking, gloomy pile of the 12th century. (The ghetto had been pulled down a few years before.)

Prague as it was then has been described frequently and competently. Contemporaries and scholars agree that there were really three different Pragues, the one of the Czechs, the one belonging to the Germans, and the one that was Jewish in character. The three met, of course, in daily intercourse, and influenced each other to a considerable extent, but they developed along separate lines. Physically, the Czech Prague has survived, but literary scholars nowadays are more interested in the Prague of the Jewish intelligentsia. Germans and Jews were minorities, and theirs was a psychological, if not a physical ghetto. Each had its own psychology, language, way of life. Franz Werfel once said about Kafka that no one beyond Teschen-Bodenbach was ever likely to understand him; others believed that this was already an unduly optimistic assumption.

Most of the Jews lived in the Josefstadt, a very small quarter in the Old City. The first thirty years of Kafka's life were passed within a radius of about a quarter of a mile. There he was born, went to school, went to work, frequented his favorite coffee-house—the Prague of the Niklasstrasse, Karpfengasse, Ziltnergasse, and of the Grosser Ring. But Kafka's name has been mentioned perhaps too often already; he was a genius, but not the only one of his time. It was a remarkably gifted generation; merely to list its main representatives and their achievements would require a long essay. We do not know what produces such an accumulation of talent in one generation. There are certain prerequisites, of which the confrontation of different cultures is no doubt a very important one. But the prerequisites by themselves do not produce great masterpieces; they produce, at most, a certain cultural ambiance.

This Prague was not, however, a happy and contented place—Kafka called it "the accursed city that should have been set on fire." Meyrink, author of *The Golem,* wrote that he was more eager to leave Prague than any other city (adding, however, that there was no city to which he longed so much to return). Germans, Jews, and Czechs all had different reasons for complaint. The Czechs felt unfree, oppressed by the non-Czech rulers. (This unfreedom may not appear quite so intolerable fifty years later—but that is a different matter altogether.) The Germans felt cut off, isolated from the *Reich,* and neglected, *"auf verlorenem Posten."* Prague, after all, had once been a predominantly German city and Marx wrote that it would be a "major tragedy" if it were lost to the Slavs. It played a great part in German literature and the arts, down to the end of the nineteenth century. Mozart lived here and Beethoven; Gluck and Liszt, Weber and Richard Wagner. Stifter dedicated his *Witiko* to the city of Prague. It was German *Kulturboden,* but two generations of extreme nationalism lost it all.

In the nineteenth century the Jews moved from a religious into a sociological ghetto. Formerly one of the most devout cities, Prague became in the eyes of its critics quite irreligious and rootless. Rabbi Loew, with his tall hat and long flowing cloak, still stood in front of the new town hall, but his descendants, with a few notable exceptions such as Martin Buber, were not greatly interested in Jewish mysticism. Berlin or Paris Jews believed in and worked for assimilation, but the Jews of Prague were a minority within a minority—what future was there in store for them except in a cosmopolitan city? All but a few of the better known members of the generation of 1905 had left Prague long before the *Wehrmacht* marched in. As for the fate of the other Czech Jews, 77,297 of them, they have a memorial: their names are engraved in small letters on the inner walls of the Pinkas Synagogue.

Now this is all distant history, as the guides will not fail to point out. The *Altneuschul* and the old Jewish cemetery are today must sights for the tourist, as important as the *Karluv most*, the Karlsbruecke. Ten years ago this was not so, but now there is a steady stream of visitors, particularly from West and East Germany, who listen to the tale of that famous Rabbi who created an artificial being which then went out of control. If interested in the history of ideas, they will be told that the *Golem motif*, which originated in the Talmud, has provided countless novelists with inspiration including some very good ones from E.T.A. Hoffmann to Karel Čapek, not to mention the plays, the operas (Rubinstein and Eugen d'Albert), and the films. It is probably an eternal theme—what with the emergence of the science of cybernetics and the new vistas that have opened up for our present-day Rabbi Loews.

When I first knew Prague in 1935, it was already a very different city. The capital of Czechoslovakia, Greater Prague now had some 700,000 inhabitants (some 95% Czechs); it was the seat of the government, had two universities, and it played a fairly important part in Central European politics. It was still a very beautiful city. There were still some Germans in the city, there were German newspapers and a German university, but public signs in German were strictly forbidden (with the exception of the billboards of the German theater). It was the era of Masaryk and Benes.

Prague was the main pillar of the Little Entente. There was constant coming and going between Paris, Prague, Bucharest and Belgrade; few people knew that these activities were not really of great consequence, and that in the long run only military power would count. America, to whom the country largely owed its independence, was still very much in fashion. There was a President Wilson Railway Station, a Wilson Hotel. The shops on the Příkope and the Hybernska were well stocked, the *vinarna* (wine shops) and *cukari* (confectioners) were full; Janacek was writing his operas, Nezval his poems; there were some interesting constructivist influences in the new houses built in the suburbs.

True, there were dark clouds on the political horizon. Hitler had come to power in Germany and was beginning to press his territorial claims; the Henlein movement had just emerged as the strongest political party among the three million Sudeten Germans. But on the whole, Prague was a prosperous city, the European order seemed fairly stable, and the town had suffered remarkably little from the world economic crisis. Much of the excitement and the sense of intense cultural life that had made Prague so interesting before the first World War had disappeared; the city had become more solid and provincial. But with all its deficiencies it was an island of civilization in a not-so-civilized Central and Eastern Europe. Few people realized it at the time; only now (one world war and thirty, mostly very unpleasant, years later) has the conviction gained ground that Habsburg rule and the first Republic were not that intolerable after all. Discontent, it seems, is an inalienable part of the human condition, seldom moderated by the lessons of history that the future might be considerably worse than the seemingly intolerable present.

The entry for "Prague" in a guide book of 1965 would run as follows:

More than one million inhabitants, almost all Czechs; capital of the Czechoslovak Soviet Socialist Republic; political, cultural, economic center of the country. Important center of trade, banking and the machine industry. According to the Constitution of 1960, all citizens have equal rights and duties, including the right to work and to receive proper remuneration for their labor. Czech industrial production has trebled since 1938, every second family has a television set, and the average Czech buys four pairs of shoes a year (the highest per capita footwear consumption in the world). There is one doctor for every 550 inhabitants.

At first, nothing seemed changed, except that there weren't so many people about before the war. Huge crowds are seen milling around *Vaclav Namesti* (Wenzelsplatz) and *Na Prikopi* (Graben). The foreigner soon gets the idea; it is quite hopeless to move against the stream. But there is no problem about finding one's way. Most European cities I know have changed very much during the last twenty years; some because of war damage, others because they have grown. Prague was not destroyed and has not been rebuilt. (There are, of course, many housing projects in the suburbs, but in Prague, more than in any other city, it is the center of the old town that counts.) Having crossed the Vltava on the way from the airport, one soon gets into a traffic jam near *Prasna Brana*, the "Pulverturm", the sole remaining fragment of the old fortifications. Opposite there was a big bank, which has changed its name. Next door there used to be the German Institute, and within a radius of about 200 meters, all the famous cafés of old Prague: "Continental," "Arco," "Central," "Edison," "Louvre," and the like. The function of the coffee-house as an institution of higher learning equal and frequently superior to a university, has been described by writers on Vienna; it was exactly the same in Prague:

Es brodelt und kafkat und werfelt und kischt . . .

The baroque palaces still stand, as do the 113 churches; in Smichov they produce very good beer called *staropramen*. Karl IV and Franz Joseph, Heydrich and Henlein are forgotten, as are the Masaryks. There is a column in front of the cathedral dedicated to the memory of the founder of the Czech republic, but his name has been erased. The leading hotels are now called "Alcron" and "Yalta," the interest in ice hockey and soccer is undiminished, and a Sunday afternoon, passing near a sports ground, one is likely to hear the old *"Do toho* (Go on)! . . ."

The part of Prague that matters is a fairly small section. In ten minutes one reaches the Charles Bridge; another ten or fifteen minutes brings one to the Hrad, the old Burg. There are always hundreds of visitors in and around the Cathedral and the little street nearby that once belonged to the Alchemists. In the evening there is music in the Waldstein Palace. In recent years many Western visitors have shown great interest in a modern writer whose name was not really widely known in Prague and whose novels were not available in Czech. But the authorities are quite willing to cater for all kinds of tastes. They are not yet ready to admit that Kafka may be as important for world literature as Egon Erwin Kisch, but they have certainly made concessions. There is an interesting illustrated volume, *Kafka's Prague,* but it is not in Czech. There was a Kafka conference a year ago, despite the fact that the East German Marxist-Leninists maintained that Kafka had not been a Socialist-Realist.

At the entrance to the new Jewish Cemetery there is one sign-post, which shows the path to Kafka's grave, between Marie Reiniger who, it says, was the wife of a professor, and Adolph Levy, the owner of an oil factory. Rilke, too, has no monument in his native city.

So much for the tourist's Prague which, needless to say, is not the Prague of the crowds milling through the streets downtown. Seen from the West, Prague is now a somewhat drab city, all the three-star sights notwithstanding. The economic statistics are interesting, but not that impressive. The standard of living should really be much higher, for Czechoslovakia was among the very few lucky countries that did not suffer much material damage in the second World War; on the contrary, the Germans transferred important industries to this region because during much of the war, it lay outside the reach of the Allied air forces. But Prague, alas, is not another Stockholm or Zurich, nor can it compare any longer with Vienna or Munich, with which it was once more or less on a par.

It is a story of lost illusions. The Czech Communists, of whom there were many after 1945, really believed that all problems could be easily solved and that under communism everyone would be happy. At a recent conference in Prague on family life and divorce, the lecturer, a well-known philosopher, said that 15 to 20 years ago he and his colleagues had thought that "nothing could stand any longer in the way of the People's Happiness." With the disappearance of class distinctions, morale would improve and family life would become more harmonious: "These were all very attractive illusions and there are many among us who regret that we lost them." It is a fairly typical admission.

The Czech party leaders have tried to steer a middle course between the pitfalls of "dogmatism" and "revisionism."* In view of the country's recent history and their own involvement in these sad events, it has not been at all easy. The purges and trials raged more fiercely in Czechoslovakia than in any other Eastern bloc country, including the Soviet Union. The Slansky trial, with all its trappings, marked an era in Czech history; it was then that President Novotny and most of the other party leaders of today came to the fore. In view of the gravity of the crimes committed

---

* The situation I am describing refers to the period several years before the so-called "Prague spring" with its "Dubcek experiment."

in those years the Czech party leadership was more reluctant and needed more time than the other East European parties to tackle what the Russians called the period of the cult of the individual. Some of the most compromised Stalinists, such as Bacilek, Siroky, Koehler, and the chief prosecutor, Urvalek, were given the sack only in 1963, ten years after Stalin's death. Novotny tried to follow a new, more pragmatic and flexible, policy; it was reformist rather than revisionist in inspiration, but many old party cadres were either diehard "dogmatists," or almost totally disillusioned.

The cultural scene, too, is dominated by the middle-of-the-roaders. There were two distinct stages in cultural de-Stalinization; the first, inspired by the Soviet example, began in 1956 and was of fairly short duration, though the literary journal that spearheaded the struggle *(Kveten-May)* somehow managed to survive until 1959. During the years that followed, in particular up to 1961, Czechoslovakia was in the rear guard of the communist camp, not only in comparison with Poland and Hungary, but even with the Soviet Union. Then the movement for a further relaxation of controls gathered momentum; in 1963, a second wave began which, against tough opposition, lasted until a short time ago. At the third congress of Czechoslovak writers, a spokesman of the young generation asked his elders:

"Where have you been—and what have you been?"

The question was obviously a rhetorical one, for everyone knew the answer. The spirit of the criticism spread from Slovakia, where it had been much more pronounced than in Prague (perhaps under Hungarian influence) to the capital; these years witnessed the publication of some remarkable books, the production of several interesting films, and significant new developments in music and the arts. The cultural magazines became eminently readable and there could be no doubt that these stirrings were supported by the great majority of Czechoslovak intellectuals. Although not removed, the cultural commissars of the Stalin period, the Stolls and the Skalas, had to share their posts with "revisionists" and middle-of-the-roaders such as Bublik, Karvas, and Mnacko. The advance was spectacular, though hardly anywhere did it proceed beyond the achievements of the Poles and the Hungarians. It was more dramatic simply because the advances that had taken years in Warsaw and Budapest were telescoped in Prague into a few months.

Tremendous changes have taken place in Czechoslovakia since 1948, yet one does not feel at all sure whether in a long range view 1918 or 1945 will be the more important date in Czechoslovak history. Perhaps the same can be said of most other countries in East-Central Europe and the Balkans. That independence was bound to come to these countries was obvious, but it is only now, in a perspective of almost fifty years, that it has become quite clear what price had to be paid for it.

In 1910 there was no state, only a Czech national movement. The case for national independence was, no doubt, irrefutable. Ten years later the Czechs had their republic; so had the Poles, the Hungarians, and the others. They established many new universities, schools, academies; Czech was the only official language. The dream of centuries had been realized. But very soon Europe began to lose interest in the Czechs, a process that gathered momentum after the second World War. Prague had been at the intersection of some of the world's leading civilizations; this made it a great cultural center in the middle ages and again in the eighteenth and nineteenth centuries.

In recent decades all this has changed. The centers of

gravity have moved West and East. To give but one example: among today's Czech writers there are no doubt some very good ones, but who, except for a few specialists, has ever heard of them? Czechoslovakia, says the official guide book, is a peace-loving country in Eastern Europe, which many in the West know from its exports of Pilsner Bier, Jablonec bijouterie, and motorcycles. I am a great fan of Pilsner Bier, and Jablonec bijouterie, but Prague made even more important contributions to world civilization at the turn of the century. A writer in a recent issue of a Czech literary magazine (*Plamen,* March 1965) noted that Czech literature of 25 years ago showed more wealth and creative genius than it does today. The same, one suspects, could be argued in comparing 1910 and 1935.

This may be an unfair comparison, but the great past of the city makes it almost inevitable. No doubt Prague still has more to offer to the tourist than Bucharest or Sofia. It is still a beautiful and interesting city, but what major cultural impulses have recently emanated from the Czech capital? The price of national independence plus communism has been higher than anticipated for a country that, unlike its Eastern neighbors, had already reached a fairly advanced state of cultural, political, and economic development. Gradually Prague became a backwater. There will still be international sport meetings and industrial exhibitions, and if a great composer should arise in our generation he will no doubt be appreciated in both West and East. But by and large the Czechs and the Slovaks have been cut off from the mainstream of European culture. Which, needless to say, is a matter of profound regret.

(1965)

II
IDEAS AND POLITICS

REFLECTIONS ON
YOUTH MOVEMENTS

I CAN well imagine that on Saturday nights across the
country, at hundreds of faculty parties where a year and a
half ago the main subject of discussion was the war in Vietnam, thousands of professors and their wives now passion-
ately debate the pros and cons of the student movement,
the tactics of the *SDS*, and the significance of the generational conflict. I myself have attended several such gatherings, and have been struck not so much by the intensity
with which the actions of the students are either approved
of or condemned by their elders, as by the baffled consensus
among those elders that the movement is both unprecedented and totally inexplicable in terms of what the university has historically represented. When I am asked, as
I invariably am, for the European view on these matters,
I rarely manage more than a few words, to the effect that
the American situation is unique and that anyway history
never repeats itself—which, needless to say, is of no great
help to anyone. And yet, I believe there *is* something to be
learned from the European experience, even if the lesson
is an ambiguous one. Not the least thing to be learned is
that the Western university has by no means always represented that tranquil meeting-ground, so fondly misremem-
bered now by American professors, of those who would
gladly learn with those who would gladly teach.

Quite the contrary. Organized youth revolt has for a long time been an integral part of European history. That, on the one hand. On the other, the idea of the university as a quiet place, devoted to the pursuit of learning and unaffected by the turbulence of the outside world, is of comparatively recent date. The medieval university certainly was no such place. As Nathan Schachner has pointed out, it was a place characterized more by bloody affrays, pitched battles, mayhem, rape, and homicide: "Indeed by the frequency of riots one may trace the rise of the University to power and privilege." In his monumental study, *Universities of Europe in the Middle Ages,* Hastings Rashdall relates the violence of the medieval university to the violence of medieval times in general, when the slitting of a throat was not regarded even by the Church as the worst of mortal sins. Thus, a Master of Arts at the University of Prague who had cut the throat of a Friar Bishop was merely expelled, while in the case of other offenders punishment consisted in the confiscation of scholastic effects and garments. The police were openly ridiculed by students, and the universities did nothing to exact discipline from their own scholars. In dealing with the subject of students' morals, Rashdall is constrained to write in Latin. According to Charles Thurot's history of Paris University in the Middle Ages, masters frolicked with their pupils and even took part in their disorders. The university was a great concourse of men and boys freed from all parental restrictions; morality, as Schachner notes, was a private affair, as were the comings and goings of the students. Nor was the trouble localized; the same complaints were to be heard from Oxford to Vienna and Salamanca.

As for the professor, his position in the medieval university was not what it became in later days. He was, first of all, paid by the students. A professor at Bologna needed his students' permission if he wanted to leave town even for a single day; he had to pay a fine if he arrived late in class or if he ended his lecture before the chiming of the church bells; should his lectures not meet with favor, there was a good chance that he would be interrupted, hissed, or even stoned. Supported by King and Church, medieval students enjoyed almost unlimited freedom. It was an unwritten rule, for instance, that they were always in the right in their clashes with towns-people. Of course, from time to time the citizenry would get even by killing a few students; the Oxford town-and-gown riots of 1354 were one such response, if a major one, to student provocation—provocation that took the form, in the words of a contemporary chronicler, of "atrociously wounding and slaying many, carrying off women, ravishing virgins, committing robberies and many other enormities hateful to God." To be sure, the real troublemakers were a minority, some of them not even students but young vagabonds enjoying the immunities of the scholar, drifting from master to master and from university to university. For every scholar involved in felonious offenses there were dozens whose story is unknown.

> "They studied conscientiously, attended lectures and disputations, worked hard, ate frugally, drank their modest stoup of wine, and had no time for the delights of tavern and brothel. The annals of the virtuous, like the annals of a happy people, are short and barren" (Schachner).

Nevertheless, it is a fact that only in later ages did the university begin to impose stricter discipline on its students.

If student violence in the Middle Ages can be ascribed mainly to the high spirits of youth, by the 18th century a new figure had appeared on the scene: the student as freedom fighter. *Die Raeuber* ("The Robbers"), the play that made Schiller famous, tells the story of a group of students

who, disgusted by society and its inequities, take to the mountains to lead partisan warfare against the oppressors.*
Sturm und Drang, the first real literary movement of youth revolt, combined opposition to social conventions with a style of life that is familiar enough today: wild language, long hair, and strange attire. Within a few decades after its inception, the romantics had made this movement fashionable, if not respectable, all over Europe. Suddenly there was Young England and Young Germany, Young Italy, Young Hungary, and Young Russia—all up in arms against the tyranny of convention, tradition, and outworn beliefs. One of the very few places untouched by the cult of youth at that time was America, itself a young country, unencumbered by the dead weight of tradition: *Amerika,* Goethe apostrophized, *du hast es besser. . . .*

Some youth groups in the modern period have done much good, while others have caused a great deal of harm. It has been the custom in writing about them to divide them into the progressive and the reactionary, the wholesome and the decadent, so that, for example, the revolutionary Russian student movement of the 19th century, the Italian *Risorgimento,* and the Chinese *May 1919* movement fall in one camp, and the fascist youth movements fall in the other. But this scheme is at best an oversimplification, since almost all movements of youthful revolt have contained in themselves both elements at once. The historical role a movement finally played depended in each case on political conditions in the society at large, the gravity of the problems the movement faced, the degree of its cultural development, and the quality of the guidance it received from its mentors.

The dual character of youth movements is illustrated with

* In the 1920's when Piscator staged the play in Berlin, he had Spiegelberg, one of the leaders of the gang and incidentally a Jew, appear in the mask of Trotsky.

particular clarity by the example of the early German student circles, the *Burschenschaften*. In his recent book, Lewis Feuer characterizes the members of these circles as "historicists, terrorists, totalitarians and anti-Semites"—all of which is perfectly true.* But they were also genuine patriots who dreamed of German unity and set out to combat the tyranny and oppression of the Holy Alliance. Most of them, in addition, were democrats of sorts and their movement was regarded by the liberals of the day as one of great promise. Their story is briefly told.

The leader of the group was Karl Follen, a lecturer at Jena, of whom a contemporary wrote that "no one could be compared with him for purity and chastity of manners and morals. He seemed to concentrate all his energies upon one great aim—the revolution." In 1818, a certain Karl Sand, an idealistic and highly unstable student of theology who had come under Follen's influence, assassinated a minor playwright by the name of August Kotzebue who was suspected of being a Russian agent. Sand genuinely expected that this action, undertaken in the service of a holy cause, would trigger off a revolution. But the choice of victim was haphazard, and the consequences regrettable: the government seized the opportunity to suppress the *Burschenschaft* as well as the whole democratic movement. Follen escaped to America, where he became professor of German literature and preacher at Harvard (he later drowned at sea in a shipwreck). It took almost thirty years for the movement he had led to recover from the blow dealt it by the authorities.

The idealism, spirit of sacrifice, devotion to one's people, and revolutionary fervor that marked the *Burschenschaft* have been an inherent part of all youth movements over the last hundred years. It is a mistake to assume that the

* Lewis Feuer, *The Conflict of Generations* (1969).

fascist youth movements were an exception to this rule, that their members were mainly sadistic, blindly destructive young thugs. To be sure, they preached a doctrine of violence, but as Mussolini said, "there is a violence that liberates, and there is a violence that enslaves; there is moral violence and stupid, immoral violence."*

The ideological forerunners of Italian fascism, men like Corradini and Federzoni, were second to none in their condemnation of capitalism and imperialism and in their defense of the rights of the "proletarian nations." Early fascist programs demanded a republic, the abolition of all titles, the redistribution of private income, and the confiscation of unproductive capital. They also placed great stress on youth. Giovanni Gentile, the philosopher of fascism, considered the sole aim of the new movement to be the "spiritual liberation of the young Italians." The very anthem of the fascist regime was an appeal to the young generation: *Giovinezza, Giovinezza, primavera di bellezza.*

Similarly in Germany, where the student movement after the First World War was strongly nationalist; the Nazi student association emerged as the leading force in the German universities (and in Austria) in 1930, well before Hitler had become the leader of the strongest German party. With 4,000 registered members out of a total of 132,000 students, the Nazis easily took control of the chief organization of German students several years before the party's seizure of national power. The declared aim of the Nazi student association was to destroy liberalism and international capitalism; point two on its program was to "purge the university of the influence of private capital"; point nine called on students to join the ranks of the workers. The slogan of

---

* Compare Marcuse: "In terms of historical function, there is a difference between revolutionary and reactionary violence, between violence practiced by the oppressed and by the oppressors."

"student power" made its first appearance at the *Goettingen Studententag* in 1920. Later on it was linked to the demand that the university be made political, a real "People's University," and that all the academic cobwebs and so-called "objective sciences" be cleaned out. Even before Hitler came to power, leading German professors attacked the "idea of false tolerance" of the humanist university. Invoking Fichte, Hegel, and Schleiermacher, they held that liberal democracy was the main enemy of the true scientific spirit, and demanded that henceforth only one political philosophy be taught. The Nazis, needless to say, were still more radical· academic life, they said, had largely become an end in itself; located outside the sphere of real life, the university educated two types of students—the only-expert and the only-philosopher. These two types produced a great many books and much clever and refined table-talk, but neither they nor the universities which sustained them were in a position to give clear answers to the burning questions of the day.

Criticisms like these were common at the time all over Europe. An observer of the French scene wrote in 1931 that the main characteristic of the young generation was its total rejection of the existing order: "almost no one defends the present state of affairs." One of the most interesting French youth groups was *L'Ordre Nouveau,* whose manifesto, written by Dandieu and Robert Aron, had the title, *La Révolution Nécessaire. Ordre Nouveau* stood for the liberation of man from capitalist tyranny and materialistic slavery; Bolshevism, fascism, and National Socialism, it declared, had assumed the leadership of the young generation and for that reason would prevail everywhere. The young in France were deeply affected—to quote yet another contemporary witness—by a "tremendous wave of revolutionary enthusiasm, of holy frenzy and disgust." When several prominent young socialists seceded from the *SFIO* in opposition to the rule of the old gang and established a movement of their own, this too was welcomed as one more manifestation of the rebellion of the young generation. All these people were deeply troubled by the existing state of affairs and no doubt well meaning in their intentions; together with Jean Luchaire, the leader of *Ordre Nouveau,* some of them ended up as Nazi collaborators during World War II.

The tactics adopted by these youth groups vis-à-vis the universities were the tactics of agitation. Even before the First World War, members of the *Action Française* had made it a custom to disrupt systematically the lectures of professors at the Sorbonne who had provoked their ire for political reasons. Nazi students perfected the system, forcing universities to dismiss Jewish professors, and even one Christian pacifist, well before 1933. But the question must be asked again: was this rowdyism, or an action undertaken in the genuine conviction that one's country was in grave danger and that the professors were enemies of the people who had to be removed? Among the fascist youth movements in the late '20's, one of the most sinister was the Rumanian terrorist band, the *Archangel Michael,* which later became the Iron Guard. Yet even the members of this group were not devoid of sincerity and idealism; Eugen Weber recently wrote of their leader:

> From a mendacious people he demanded honesty, in a lazy country he demanded work, in an easy-going society he demanded self discipline and persistence, from an exhuberant and windy folk he demanded brevity and self-control.

Whoever describes a youth movement as idealistic only states the obvious. Youth movements have never been out for personal gain; what motivates them is different from what motivates an association for the protection of the interests of small shopkeepers. The fascist experience has shown that the immense potential which inheres in every youth movement can be exploited in the most disastrous way; but the potential itself must be seen as neutral.

Almost everything that is great has been done by youth, wrote Benjamin Disraeli, himself at one time a fighter in the ranks of generational revolt. Professor Feuer would counter: many disasters in modern European politics have been caused by students and youth movements. The exploits of the *Burschenschaften*, he argues, set back the cause of German freedom thirty years. Russian student terrorism in the 1880's put an end to progress toward constitutionalism in that country. But for the terror and stress of the First World War (inaugurated by a bomb thrown by yet another student hero, Gavrilo Princip), Russia would have evolved in a liberal capitalist direction, and European civilization would not have been maimed by fascism and a second World War. According to Professor Feuer, the qualities needed to bring about peaceful social and political change are not those usually found in youth movements, and he accuses students of almost always acting irrationally in pursuing their objectives. Unfortunately, however, peaceful change is not always possible in history, nor are patience and prudence invariably the best counsel.

Take the Munich students who revolted against Hitler in 1943 and the student rebels who were recently sentenced in the Soviet Union. Had they acted entirely rationally, they might well have convinced themselves that as a consequence of long-term political and social processes, the dictatorship would disappear anyway or at least be mitigated in its ferocity. Why therefore endanger their lives? To their eternal credit, such rational considerations did not enter the students' minds. The impetuosity, the impatience, and sometimes the madness of youth movements has been a liberating force in the struggle against tyranny and dictatorship. Tyranny cannot be overthrown unless at least some people are willing to sacrifice their lives, and those willing to do so usually do not come from the ranks of the senior citizens. It is only when youth movements have launched a total attack against democratic regimes and societies—in Germany, France, and Italy in the 20's and in other countries later on—that they have come to play by necessity a reactionary and destructive role.

Most of the basic beliefs and even the outward fashions of the present world youth movements can be traced back to the period in Europe just before and after the First World War. The German *Neue Schar* of 1919 were the original hippies. Long-haired, sandaled, unwashed, they castigated urban civilization, read Hermann Hesse and Indian philosophy, practiced free love, and distributed in their meetings thousands of asters and chrysanthemums. They danced, sang to the music of the guitar, and attended lectures on the "Revolution of the Soul." The modern happening was born in 1910 in Trieste, Parma, Milan, and other Italian cities where the Futurists arranged public meetings to recite their poems, read their manifestoes, and exhibit their ultra-modern paintings. No one over thirty, they demanded, should in future be active in politics. The public participated actively at these gatherings, shouting, joking, and showering the performers with rotten eggs. In other places, things were not so harmless. "Motiveless terror" formed part of the program of a group of young Russian anarchists, the *Bezmotivniki*, in their general struggle against society. The *Bezmotivniki* threatened to burn down whole cities, and their news sheets featured diagrams for the production of home-made bombs. Drug-taking as a social phenomenon, touted as a way of gaining new experience and a heightened sensibility, can be traced back to 19th-century France and Britain. The idea of a specific youth culture was first developed in 1913–14 by the German educator Gustav Wyneken and a young man named Walter Benjamin who later attained literary fame. In 1915, Friedrich Bauermeister, an otherwise unknown member of the youth movement, developed the idea of the "class struggle of youth." Bauermeister regarded the working class and the socialist movement (including Marx and Engels) as "eudaimonistic"; the socialists, he admitted, stood for a just order and higher living standards, but he feared that once their goals were achieved they would part ways with the youth movement. Bauermeister questioned whether even the social revolution could create a better type of man, or release human beings from their "bourgeois and proletarian distortions."

The ideas of this circle were developed in a little magazine called *Der Anfang* in 1913–14. Youth, the argument ran (in anticipation of Professor Kenneth Keniston), was *milieulos*, not yet integrated into society. Unencumbered by the ties of family or professional careers, young people were freer than other elements of society. As for their lack of experience, for which they were constantly critized by their elders, this, far from being a drawback, was in fact a great advantage. Walter Benjamin called experience the "mask of the adult." For what did the adult wish above all to prove? That he, too, had once been young, had disbelieved his parents, and had harbored revolutionary thoughts. Life, however, had taught the adult that his parents had been right after all, and now he in turn smiled with condescending superiority and said to the younger generation: this will be your fate too.

For the historian of ideas, the back issues of the periodicals of the youth movement, turned yellow with age, make fascinating reading. The great favorites of 1918–19 were Hermann Hesse, Spengler's *Decline of the West*, Zen Buddhism and Siddharta, Tagore's gospel of spiritual unity (*Love not Power*), and Lenin. It is indeed uncanny how despite all the historical differences, the German movement pre-empted so many of the issues agitating the American movement of today, as well as its literary fashions.

Some youth movements in the last hundred years have been unpolitical in character. Most, however, have had definite political aims. Of this latter group, some have belonged to the extreme Left, others have gravitated to the extreme Right; some have sought absolute freedom in anarchy, others have found fulfillment in subordinating themselves to a leader. To find a common denominator seems therefore very nearly hopeless. But the contradictions are often more apparent than real, not only because many of those who originally opted for the extreme Left later moved to the Right, or vice versa, or because the extremes sometimes found common ground as in the National Bolshevik movement which gained some prominence in various countries in the 1920's. Whether a certain movement became political or unpolitical, whether it opted for the Left or the Right, depended on the historical context: it hardly needs to be explained in detail why youth movements were preponderantly right-wing after the First World War, while more recently most have tended toward the Left. But beyond the particular political orientation there are underlying motives which have remained remarkably consistent throughout.

Youth movements have always been extreme, emotional, enthusiastic; they have never been moderate or rational (again, no major excursion into the psychology of youth is needed to explain this). Underlying their beliefs has always been a common anti-capitalist, anti-bourgeois denominator, a conviction that the established order is corrupt to the bones and beyond redemption by parliamentary means of reform. The ideologies of democracy and liberalism have always been seen as an irretrievable part of the whole rotten system; all politicians, of course, are crooks. Equally com-

mon to all youth groups is a profound pessimism about the
future of present-day culture and an assumption that traditional enlightened concepts like tolerance are out of date.
The older generation has landed the world in a mess, and
a radical new beginning, a revolution, is needed. Youth
movements have never been willing to accept the lessons of
the past; each generation is always regarded as the first
(and the last) in history. And the young have always found
admiring adults to confirm them in their beliefs.

This leads us to the wider issue of *Kulturpessimismus*.
The idea that the world is in decline—an idea that is about
as old as the world itself—had an impact on modern youth
movements through the mediating influence of neo-romanti-
cism. The themes of decadence and impending doom can
be traced like a bright thread through the 19th century
from Alfred de Musset *("Je suis venu trop tard dans un
monde trop vieux")*, to Carlyle, Ruskin, and Arnold with
their strictures against the universal preoccupation with material gain. So widespread a fashion did *Kulturpessimismus*
enjoy that one can scarcely find a single self-respecting
19th-century author who did not complain about the dis-
junction between mankind and the world, between idea
and reality, or about the spiritual bankruptcy and moral
consumption of his age. In Germany, as *mal du siècle* turned
into *fin de siècle,* a whole phalanx of Cassandras raised their
voices, denouncing mass culture, crass materialism, and the
lack of a sense of purpose in modern life. *Kulturpessimismus*
induced in some a sense of resignation and gave rise to
decadent moods in literature and the arts; at the same time,
however, it acted as a powerful stimulus to movements of
regeneration. Whereas dissatisfaction led some to ennui
and perversions (*La jeune France,* an all-out revolt against
social conventions, was decadent and wholly unpolitical in
character), elsewhere and in other periods boredom gave

birth to activism. Thus, on the eve of the First World War, a whole generation of young Europeans, having pronounced themselves culturally suffocated, welcomed the outbreak of hostilities as heralding a great purge, a liberation that would somehow put things right. The close connection between *Kulturpessimismus* and boredom deserves more study than it has received so far, as does the connection between boredom and prosperity. Max Eyth, the German popular writer, astutely diagnosed the illness of his age in the autobiography he wrote during the Wilhelminian era: *"Es is uns seit einer Reihe von Jahren zu gut gegangen* (We had it too good for a number of years). . . ."

One of the main problems facing the decadents was that of combining their hatred of modern civilization with their love of the refinements that civilization had made possible. (This is still very much of a problem, although some of today's revolutionaries seem to have solved it on the personal if not on the ideological level.) The decadents also faced the dilemma of squaring their *langueur*—Verlaine: *Je suis l'Empire à la fin de la dècadence*—with their fascination with violence and revolutionary action. The indiscriminate assassinations and bombings carried out by the French anarchists found many admirers among both the decadents and the right-wing futurists. "What matter the victims, provided the gesture is beautiful," Laurent Tailhade wrote. D'Annunzio's career as a writer progressed from descriptions of courtesans in modish clothes, luminous landscapes, and villas by the sea, to the most lavish praise of the freshness and joy of war. Having begun by calling on youth to "abolish all moral restrictions," he ended as the prophet of moral regeneration and the poet laureate of fascism. The list could be lengthened: Maurice Barrès made his way from the decadent movement to the *Action Française;* Johannes R. Becher, who in the early 20's was known in Germany as the mad expressionist poet who had killed his girl friend, was to become in later life Minister of Culture in Walter Ulbricht's East Germany.

If the youth movements of the early 20th century arose, then, in a milieu in which the sense of decadence was widespread, they represented at the same time an attempt to overcome it. Their leaders were moralists, forever complaining about the evils of corporate guilt. Like all moralists, they exaggerated those evils, speaking out of the anti-historical perspective which is a hallmark of the moralist. For the study of history teaches that other periods have, broadly speaking, not been much better than one's own. This is why the moralist and the revolutionary regard history as a reactionary discipline, the story of big failures and small successes. The study of history is a breeding-ground of skepticism; the less the moralist knows of it, the more effectively will he pursue his mission with an untroubled conscience. Thomas Mann, pleading in a famous speech to German students in the 1920's for "aristocratic skepticism in a world of frenetic fools," was sadly out of touch with the mood of an audience longing for firm belief and certain truths.

If in what I have said up till now my remarks have indicated a certain ambivalence of feeling toward youth movements in general, it is because I have been trying to distinguish between the various ideas which they have espoused—ideas which are certainly deserving of criticism— and, what I take to be of even greater significance, the depth of emotional experience which they have provided their members.* (I say this as one who shared that experi-

---

* Although I originally intended this as a statement about youth movements of the past, I now read in Martin Duberman's review of Christopher Lasch's new book, *The Agony of the American Left:* "I think what is most impressive about the radical young people is not their politics or their social theories, but the cultural revolution they have inaugurated—the change in life style."

ence at one stage in his life.) The politics and culture of
youth movements have always been a reflection of the
Zeitgeist, a hodgepodge, often, of mutually exclusive ideas.
A proto-Nazi wrote about the unending and fruitless discussions of German youth movements in 1920:

> Look at those *Freideutsche* leaders and their intellectual leap-
> frogging from Dostoevsky to Chuang-tse, Count Keyserling,
> Spengler, Buddha, Jesus, Landauer, Lenin, and whichever lit-
> erary Jew happens to be fashionable to the moment. Of their
> own substance they have little or nothing.

There was, let's face it, more than a grain of truth in this
criticism; a list of the main formative intellectual influences
on the American movement would look even more incongruous.

But what was essential about the German youth movement, at least in its first phase, was not its "intellectual
leap-frogging" and confused politics but something else
entirely. The movement represented an *un*political form of
opposition to a civilization that had little to offer the young
generation, a protest against the lack of vitality, warmth,
emotion, and ideals in German society. (Hoelderlin: "I can
conceive of no people more dismembered. . . . You see work-
men but no human beings, thinkers but no human beings,
priests but no human beings, masters and servants, youth
and staid people, but no human beings. . . .") It wanted to
develop qualities of sincerity, decency, open-mindedness, to
free its members from petty egoism and careerism, to oppose artificial conventions, snobbery, and affectation. Its
basic character was formless and intangible, its authentic
and deepest experience difficult to describe and perhaps
impossible to analyze: the experience of marching together,
of participating in common struggles, of forming lasting
friendships. There was, of course, much romantic exaltation
as well, but although it is easier to ridicule the extrava-

gances of this state of mind than to do it justice, the temptation should be resisted. Experiences of such depth are very serious matters indeed.

The non-political phase of the German youth movement ended roughly speaking with the First World War. Summarizing the early phase, I wrote several years ago that "if lack of interest in politics could provide an alibi from history, the youth movement would then leave the court without a stain on its character."† In retrospect, this judgment seems a trifle misplaced; the truth is that the movement was simply not equipped to deal with politics. Being romantic and opposed to "arid intellectualism," its thought was confused and its outlook illiberal. Oriented toward a mythic past and an equally mythic future, it was darkly suspicious of the values of the Enlightenment—an attitude that did not have much to commend it in a country where the Enlightenment had not met with conspicuous success anyway —and it was easily swayed in different directions by philosophical charlatans and political demagogues preaching all kinds of eccentric doctrines.

All this appeared very clearly in the second, political phase of the German youth movement after the First World War. By 1930, the youth movement was displaying an incontinent eagerness to rid Germany of democracy. Almost all its members shared the assumption that anything at all would be better than the detested old regime. Lacking experience and imagination, they clearly misjudged the major political forces of their time. One of their leaders wrote much later:

> We had no real principles. We thought everything possible. The ideas of natural law, of the inalienable rights of man, were strange to us. As far as our ideas were concerned we were in mid-air, without a real basis for our artificial constructions.

† *Young Germany: A History of the German Youth Movement* (1962).

It was, in brief, not an intellectual movement, and any attempt to evaluate it on the cultural and political level alone will not do it justice; it moved on a different plane. The movement arose in response to a certain malaise; it attempted, without success, to solve the conflicts facing it; and it was, in retrospect, a splendid failure. With all its imperfections, it did succeed in inspiring loyalties and a deep sense of commitment among its members.

I am not sure whether today's youth movements can achieve even this much. "People who screw together, glue together," claims the Berkeley sds, but if that were true, the Roman Empire would still be in existence. Some time ago, I happened to meet with members of a radical pacifist communal settlement in upstate New York. This settlement had had its origins in the early German youth movement; its members were believing Christians who took their cue from the New Testament: "Ye cannot serve God and Mammon," and "the love of money is the root of all evil." Setting out to realize the ideal of social justice in their own lives, they established two settlements in Germany, moved to England in 1934, then to Paraguay and finally to New York State. Still convinced that their way of life is the best of all possible ways, the surviving members have recently been trying to find supporters and active followers. On their tours of college campuses they are invariably met with tremendous enthusiasm and a great show of willingness to join. Then, a few days after each appearance, they send a bus around to take prospective candidates for a tour of the settlement. No one shows up. One could argue that it is unfair to compare the depth of commitment and the ardor of present-day revolutionaries with that shown by those who challenged less permissive societies in by-gone days. Where the 19th-century revolutionary risked the gallows or a lifetime in Siberia, the rebel of the 60's risks a warning from a disciplinary committee. In these adverse circumstances a breed of devoted revolutionaries is unlikely to arise. That may be finally all to the good, but I for one confess to a certain nostalgia for the breed.

It has been said of youth movements: blessed is the land that has no need of them. For a long time, America was such a land. In the 19th and early 20th centuries, it alone among the major Western countries did not experience a widespread movement of generational conflict. The reasons for this are not particularly obscure. For one thing, the burden of the past was not felt as heavily in America as it was in Europe. Less distance separated parents and children, teachers and students; adventurous young men went West, the country was forever expanding; society as a whole was far less rigid. Then in the 20th century, when these factors had ceased to be quite so important, America was spared a movement of youth revolt by a series of economic and foreign political crises. For it is a rule of youth movements that, like *Kulturpessimismus,* they prosper only against a background of rising affluence. Another rule appears to be that they cannot strike deep roots in a country whose general mood is basically optimistic.

America in the 60's was a prosperous society, but it was no longer optimistic: the American dream has been lost on the way to affluence. It was thus in a sense inevitable that when the world-wide wave of youth revolt broke earlier in that decade, American youth should assume a leading role.* But the American situation is a complicated one, not only because it is accompanied by such factors as a general breakdown of authority, a crisis in the universities, and a widespread sense of cultural malaise, but also because of

* I am not speaking here of the black student revolt, because this is not a generational conflict but part of a wider movement for full political and social emancipation, and the success or failure of this movement will depend ultimately on the blacks themselves.

the response it has elicited in the society at large. Youth movements have come and gone, but never before has one been taken so seriously. Never in the past has an older generation been so disconcerted by the onslaught of the young. Previous generations of adults, more certain of their traditions and values, less ridden by feelings of guilt, have shown little patience with their rebellious sons and daughters. The middle-aged, middle-class parents of today clearly do not feel themselves to be in any such position of certainty. The milieu in which the youth of America have grown up bears striking resemblance to the European 1890's as described by Max Nordau:

> There is a sound of rending in every tradition and it is as though the morrow would not link itself with today. Things as they are totter and plunge, and they are suffered to reel and fall because man is weary, and there is no faith that it is worth an effort to uphold them. Views that have hitherto governed minds are dead or driven hence, meanwhile interregnum in all its terrors prevails and there is confusion among the powers that be . . . what shall inspire us? So rings the question from the thousand voices of the people, and where a market-vendor sets up his booth and claims to give an answer, where a fool or a knave begins suddenly to prophesy in verse or phrase, in sound or color, or professes to practice his art otherwise than his predecessors and competitors, there gathers a great concourse around him to seek in what he has wrought, as in Oracles of the Pythia, some meaning to be divined and interpreted. . . . It is only a very small minority who honestly find pleasure in the new tendencies, and announce them with genuine conviction as that which is sound, a sure guide for the future, a pledge of pleasure and of moral benefit. But this minority has the gift of covering the whole visible surface of society, as a little oil extends over a large area of the surface of the sea. It consists chiefly of rich educated people, or of fanatics. The former give the *ton* to all the snobs, the fools, and the blockheads; the latter make an impression upon the weak and dependent, and it intimidates the nervous. . . .

Nordau's *Degeneration* is an exaggerated, polemical tract, but much of what he wrote about the malady of his age was pertinent. He realized correctly that ideas, books, and works of art exercise a powerful, suggestive influence far beyond the small circle of the avant-garde: "It is from these productions that an age derives its ideals of morality and beauty. If they are absurd and anti-social they exert a disturbing and corrupting influence on the views of a whole generation." The moral and aesthetic ideals of today's avant-garde theater and cinema have certainly had their effect—as have the works of Jean Genet and Frantz Fanon. The deliberate gibberish of recent movies and novels finds its reflection in the involuntary gibberish of certain strands of youth politics; the message of John Cage's "Silent Sonata 4.33" (in which a performer sits in front of a piano for precisely that amount of time, poised to play but never playing) has its parallel in certain aspects of the wider cultural revolution; the theater of the absurd is not unconnected with the politics of the absurd. Indeed, the crisis of rationality has had a powerful impact. Affirmation replaces analysis and argumentation; *fin de siècle* revolutionaries arrange happenings and call it a revolution, or discuss *salon*-Maoism before enthusiastic audiences and call it radical commitment. Afraid to appear unfashionable or out of step with the avant-garde, those who ought to know better seem willing to take every idiocy seriously, trying to "understand" if not to accept.

Corruptio optimi pessima. The American youth movement, with its immense idealistic potential, has gone badly, perhaps irrevocably, off the rails. For this, a great responsibility falls on the shoulders of the gurus who have provided the ideological justification for the movement in its present phase—those intellectuals, their own bright dream having faded, who now strain to recapture their ideological virginity. There is perhaps some tragedy to be glimpsed in this endeavor of the old to keep pace with the young, but at the moment one cannot permit oneself the luxury of a tragic sense. The doctors of the American youth movement are in fact part of its disease. They have helped to generate a great deal of passion, but aside from the most banal populism they have failed to produce a single new idea. Most of them stress their attachment to Marx. But one need only read *The Eighteenth Brumaire* to find Marx's opinion on the value of bohemianism in the revolutionary struggle; and his polemics against Bakunin leave little doubt as to his feelings with regard to the idea, first propagated one hundred years ago, of a coalition between *lumpen-proletariat* and *lumpenintelligentsia*. Students should not be criticized for ignoring the lessons of the past and the dangers of chiliastic movements. They always do. The historical memory of a generation does not usually extend back very far, and the lessons of historical experience cannot be bequeathed by will or testament. But their mentors do remember, and their betrayal of memory cannot be forgiven.

The American youth revolt was sparked off by Vietnam, by race conflict, and later on by the crisis of the university. At any point along the line rational alternatives could have been formulated and presented. Instead, the movement preferred a total, unthinking rejection, and so became politically irrelevant. Yet a revolution is in fact overdue in the universities. There is nothing more appalling than the sight of enormous aggregations of students religiously writing down pearls of wisdom that can be found more succinctly and profoundly put in dozens of books. There is nothing more pathetic than to behold the proliferation of social-science non-subjects in which the body of solid knowledge proffered stands usually in inverse ratio to the scientific pretensions upheld. Whole sections of the universities could be closed down for a year or two, and the result, far from being the disaster to civilization which some appear to anticipate, would probably be beneficial. Unfortunately, this is about the last thing that is likely to happen, for it is precisely the non-subjects, the fads, and the bogus sciences to which the "radicals" in their quest for social relevance are attracted as if by magnetic force. As for the consequences of all this, one thing can be predicted with certainty: those to be most directly affected by the new dispensation in the universities will emerge from the experience more confused and disappointed than ever, and more desperately in need of certain truths, firm beliefs.

An American youth movement was bound to occur sooner or later; youth revolt is a natural phenomenon, part of the human condition. But the particular direction the American movement would take was not at all foreordained, and it is therefore doubly sad that in its extreme form it has taken a destructive course, self-defeating in terms of its own aims. It seems fairly certain at this point that the American movement will result in a giant hangover, for the more utopian a movement's aims, the greater the disappointment which must inevitably ensue. The cultural and political idiocies perpetrated with impunity in this permissive age have clearly gone beyond the borders of what is acceptable for any society, however liberally it may be structured. No one knows whether the right-wing backlash, so long predicted, will in fact make its dreadful appearance; perhaps we shall be spared this reaction. It is more likely that there will be a backlash from within the extremist movement itself, as ideas and ideologies undergo change and come into conflict with underlying attitudes. Insofar as those attitudes are intolerant and irrational, they will not quickly mellow, and for that reason America is likely to experience a great deal more trouble with its *enragés*.

The American youth movement of the 60's, infected by

the decadence of the age, missed the opportunity to become a powerful agent of regeneration and genuine social and political change. But decadence, contrary to popular belief, is not necessarily a fatal disease. It is a phase through which many generations pass at various stages of their development. The boredom that gives rise to decadence contains the seeds of its own destruction, for who, after a time, would not become bored with boredom?

In 1890, the prevailing mood in France was expressed in the term *fin de siècle;* the most popular sport was national self-degradation; and everyone was convinced that the decay of the country had reached its ultimate stage. Charles Gide, the economist, compared France with a sugarloaf drowning in the sea. Fifteen years later the crisis was suddenly over. Almost overnight, pessimism was transformed into optimism, defeatism into aggressive nationalism, a preoccupation with eroticism into a new enthusiasm for athletics. No one knew exactly why this happened: French society and politics remained essentially the same, the demographic problem was still in full force, moral and religious uncertainties were as rampant as before. I do not mean to suggest that recovery is always so certain; indeed, the form the cure takes is sometimes almost as bad as the disease. But generations seldom commit collective suicide. As they rush toward the abyss, a guardian angel seems to watch over them, gently deflecting them at the very last moment. Nevertheless, even the patience of angels must not be tried too severely.

THE ARCHAEOLOGY
OF YOUTH

THIRTY YEARS after its demise, the German youth movement has become a subject of academic study and, more than ever before, of controversy. The reasons are obvious; it is no longer seen as a baffling, unique phenomenon but as a specific manifestation of the generational revolt which, in one form or another, has erupted recently with great intensity in many parts of the globe. It was of course "typically German" up to a point, unthinkable in any other country; but whereas its specific traits were shaped by circumstances of time and place, certain aspects of its basic character are of much broader significance. While it was still in existence few people in either Britain or America knew about it or took any interest; D. H. Lawrence was one of the few, but he too believed that a youth movement would not gain adherents, for (as he said in a letter) "the English have so little togetherness, or power of togetherness. . . ."

When a group of young Germans came to England in 1927 to meet some of their contemporaries, they were told by a senior member of the Foreign Service—in his private capacity, needless to say—that he was not impressed by their acutely self-conscious nationalism:

> To be intensely self-conscious seems to us to mean that we are not sure of ourselves—a kind of inferiority complex. . . . A youth

movement in England would have the flavor of being for the
doubtfully young, and a patriotic movement for the doubtfully
patriotic.

It was a remarkably astute observation, but the speaker
seems to have been oblivious of the fact that there was
after all in Britain a youth movement of sorts, albeit politically and culturally less ambitious than its German coun-
terpart, and that it was precisely its doubtfully young character which made the Germans so critical of the Boy Scouts.
For one of their basic tenets was that youth should be led
by youth, if they were to fulfil the "mission of the young
generation."

In England, unlike Germany, youth movements did not
become a vehicle of political protest. This is usually explained by reference to the relatively stable conditions in
English society. On the other hand, the British youth movements were themselves important agencies in the creation
of the moral and psychological resources which helped the
young generation to take the strains of the depression:

> The successful English youth movements were not simply move-
> ments of protest by the young. Rather they were carefully de-
> signed attempts to respond to their needs and demands, to har-
> ness their energies for great causes approved by their adult
> leaders—imperial defense, national defense, international co-
> operation, national efficiency and so on. . . . Tactically they were
> restricted to the pace permitted by their patrons among the
> political, ecclesiastic and military elites. Through their agency
> many demands of the young were contained, absorbed, and re-
> directed, with astonishing success.*

The smaller rebellious groups of the 1920s were much
closer in their romantic inspiration to the German move-

* Paul Wilkinson: "English Youth Movements 1908–30", *Journal of
Contemporary History*, April 1968

ment. They rejected the authoritarianism of the Boy Scouts, with its orientation towards the establishment and official Christian doctrine. The Woodcraft Folk gravitated towards socialism, and the Kibbo Kift eventually joined Major Douglas's Social Credit Party. But these were small groups and it was precisely because of their romantic and utopian character that they remained isolated.

The early history of the Wandervogel is that of a group of highschool students who went hiking through the German countryside unaccompanied by adults. But hiking and the rediscovery of nature were not the main purpose of the movement, which quickly spread throughout Germany. One went on such excursions to escape the control of teachers and parents, to experience the togetherness, the new *Lebensgefühl*. This emerged even more clearly during the second phase of the youth movement, when the ideologists took over. A study of the literature of this period involves reading a great many romantic effusions, a great deal of nationalist bombast and plain gibberish—an undertaking liable to tax the patience of even hardened students of history. But it is nevertheless a worthwhile effort, likely to provide food for thought for a whole generation of historians, sociologists, and psychologists with an interest in youth revolt. The German youth movement experienced most of the problems and expressed almost all the ideas which continue to preoccupy students of generational conflict to this day. For this reason the study of the movement cannot be recommended warmly enough. Even though the conclusions reached cannot be simply transferred to a later period, such a study still is more illuminating about recent events than the various ad hoc theories recently advanced by baffled western psychologists and sociologists, ranging from misplaced references to the Oedipus complex to the revulsion-against-affluence and revolt-against-technologization-of-man concepts.

Former members of the German youth movement, far from being flattered by the attention it has of late been receiving, have been deeply disturbed, and it is no doubt to this feeling of apprehension that we owe two massive new collections of documents, which are to be followed by others. The youth movement produced an enormous literature, including many hundreds of journals, most of which are inaccessible today; the *Grundschriften* provides a collection of some of the basic writings of a movement which was composed of a great many different political, religious, and social ingredients; *Wandervogelzeit* is a documentary survey of the internal development of the *Bünde* in their early stages.* The purpose behind these publications is no doubt to defend the youth movement against its detractors, but the selection has been made fairly; there is no attempt to embellish or to gloss over those of its features which now make for embarrassing reading.

Professor Flitner clearly says in his introduction to *Wandervogelzeit* that the youth movement reflected all the defects of the German *Staatsbürgertum*—the romantic hangover, the excessive irrationalism of its political thinking, the lack of democratic experience. Former members of the *Wandervogel* and the *Bünde* have been willing to admit that much since 1945, but they feel that the attacks made by some writers in recent years have been out of all proportion to whatever sins their movement may have committed. They claim that its aims and activities have been misunderstood or wilfully distorted, not only by foreigners but even

---

* Werner Kindt (Editor): *Grundschriften der Deutschen Jugendbewegung.* (Cologne, 604 pp., 1968).
 Die Wandervogelzeit: Dokumentation der Jugendbewegung. (Cologne, 1,098 pp., 1969).

more blatantly by a new generation of young German historians. To be misunderstood is a common enough complaint among Germans, but in this instance it is not altogether groundless. While the movement still existed it attracted wide publicity only after Hans Blüher published his history of the *Wandervogel*, and later on as the result of the writings of Gustav Wyneken, the preacher of youth culture.

Blüher was a muddle-headed pseudo-philosopher with great but totally unwarranted intellectual pretensions. *Wandervogel* was his most readable book, but it owed its success to the sensational revelations about homosexuality in the movement. Wyneken was an educator of genius who claimed that German youth had neither the right to, nor the opportunity for self expression until he appeared on the scene. He was not a modest man, and though he must have heard of Comenius, Pestalozzi, and a few other predecessors, these names do not figure prominently in his writings. Wyneken was in many respects a typical representative of the idealist school in German philosophy. *Geist* and *geistig* are the key words in his writings. Tending towards the Left in politics and glorifying youth, as representing "mankind's eternal hope", Wyneken had the misfortune to have been born too early; very much of an outsider during his lifetime, he would no doubt have become in our age one of the culture heroes of the New Left—somewhere between Herbert Marcuse and Che Guevara.

Neither Blüher nor Wyneken was in any way typical of the youth movement, its character and ideals. The *Wandervögel* was anything but a philosophical or literary movement; its early leaders were modest men who had no interest in abstract ideas. These two were intellectuals, and the intellectual was wholly out of place in a movement which came into being in reaction against anemic and arid intellectualism and which reflected a fresh awakening to life, spontaneity, human warmth. There was much resentment among the rank-and-file *Wandervögel* about outsiders like Blüher and Wyneken, who tried to explain the youth movement by introducing categories profoundly alien to its spirit. But there was worse to come.

After 1945 a new school of historians and sociologists appeared on the scene which was interested only in one aspect of the youth movement—its relationship to National-Socialism. Since the Nazi era has been the central event in recent German history, this interest was neither unhealthy nor unwarranted. These historians wanted to establish to what extent members of the youth movement had been precursors of National-Socialism (or at least auxiliaries to the *Völkische**. Their approach was not exactly welcomed by the former members of the movement, who claimed that books like Howard Becker's *German Youth—Bond or Free* (1946) or Harry Pross's *Jugend, Eros, Politik* (1964) falsified the past. The youth movement, they argued, was made up of groups of boys and girls who were unpolitical; one could not fairly read into their youthful romanticism a purpose and meaning which simply was not there. Many of them had admittedly been influenced by the nationalist and *völkisch* concepts prevailing at the time, but others had resisted them. The whole issue had not been central for the activities of the youth movement.

There is something to be said in defense of this line of argument. It was inevitable that historians in their search for the roots of National-Socialism should subject the youth movement to critical re-examination. But such investigations are difficult; they require not only a thorough knowledge of the various youth movements, but judgment, historical perspective, and a feeling for the period in which they developed. It is dangerous to stick too closely to an analysis

---

* George Mosse. *The Crisis of Germany Ideology* (1966).

of the manifestos of the youth movement and its mentors. Exercises of this kind are likely to produce the most astonishing discoveries: Martin Buber, for instance, may well appear as a predecessor of Alfred Rosenberg. Need it be said that Buber's concept of the "voice of the blood" was not quite identical with that of the Nazi philosophers?

Such obvious mistakes unfortunately occur quite frequently nowadays. A study of the history of the Jewish youth movement in Germany, published in a recent issue of *Germania Judaica,* maintains in all seriousness that the Nazis derived their idea of *entartete Kunst,* book-burning and all, from Max Nordau's *Degeneration.* The author, a young German, cites an enormous range of sources and writes not without sympathy for his chosen topic. And yet the impression likely to be gained from his account, and even more from his selection of documents, by readers unfamiliar with the subject is that the Zionists really belonged to the *völkisch* camp, with their emphasis on race, blood, and soil, and the other components of their mystique; while their opponents, the assimilationist Jews, were hopeless simpletons joining in the general German hurrah patriotism in the obviously mistaken belief that they would be accepted as equals by their German contemporaries. The quotations are all correct, the textual similarity is startling, the evidence seems overwhelming.

If a friendly historian of the Jewish youth movement can be misled to such an extent, it is not surprising that less well-meaning historians of the German *Bünde* should have reached even more hair-raising conclusions. This is not to deny that there was a substantial element of lunacy in the youth movement, that the romantic orgies appear from this distance incomprehensible and at times comical. Even if one leaves aside the lunatic fringe of the movement, it is difficult to make any sense of the talk about redemption,

the Holy Grail, the myth of the *Reich,* the cult of the
Samurai, and the other strange concepts which had their
fervent believers during the 1920s. But no age has a
monopoly of madness, and it may do no harm if those
baffled by the antics of the *Wandervögel* and the *Bünde*
occasionally wonder what future generations of historians
will make of the higher idiocies of our own times, the
youth movement of the late 1960s with its ecstatic confessions and millenarianism, its cult of witches and astrology,
its hopelessly muddled ideology and the gibberish of many
of its appeals and pronouncements.

The temptation to condemn and deride the youth movement of an earlier age is only natural but it should be
checked by a sense of history. This is not to advocate an
attitude of *tout comprendre, tout pardonner,* but it implies,
for instance, understanding that it is neither fair nor realistic to expect from boys and girls in their late teens
greater political judgment and foresight than from the intellectual leaders of their age. If blame and guilt have to
be apportioned, it is the mentors, not the disciples, who
should get the greater share.

The historian of the youth movement has to be aware of
the magnitude of the task facing him. It is comparatively
easy to unravel the intricacies of diplomatic negotiations
provided copies of the relevant documents are accessible.
But how to do justice to an inchoate movement of generational revolt, with its conflicting, often rapidly changing
views, its intangible but very real dynamism, the quality of
life distinguishing it from its surroundings, the quasi-religious emotional experience shared by its members? The
mood of a generation is only rarely reflected in historical
documents, and even then they do not necessarily provide
the most reliable guide.

A youth movement has a certain resemblance to a love

affair, and the difficulties facing the outside observer are similar: the intensity of a love affair cannot always be reconstructed from the communications exchanged between the partners; the writers of great love letters may not necessarily be great lovers—and vice versa. The dominant feature of the youth movement was not its manifestoes, its programmatic articles, its published views about politics or sex, but its way of life, and this is more likely to find its reflection in a good autobiography or a great novel. Such novels, unfortunately, do not exist. There were a great many poets and writers in the ranks of the movement, but none seems to have been inspired in his later years by his youthful experiences. It is nonsense to claim, as some old *Wandervögel* have done, that the history of the youth movement can be written only by someone who shared their experience. But it is true that more than a thorough knowledge of archival sources is needed to understand what it was all about.

The world of the *Wandervögel* of the years before 1914 has now receded into the distant past and seems unreal. Perhaps the historians of some future period will find that world of Fidus drawings, folk songs and dances, with its unquestioning religiosity and patriotism, a more interesting and rewarding subject. Today it appears merely quaint— much farther away in historical time than the sixty or seventy years dividing us from the age which came to an end with the outbreak of the First World War. It may have been a happier world, but its problems seem now altogether irrelevant. The war was the great divide. If the pre-1914 *Wandervögel* appears unbelievably antiquated, the movement of 1919 seems almost uncannily modern. The war had radicalized it and given it a political bent. True, there had been a few groups even before 1914 advocating the destruction of the old school and university and dissociating itself in toto from the world of the adults with their mendacious conventions. But these radicals were not typical; nor was the demand for sexual freedom as voiced by the young people who edited the periodical *Der Anfang*. The cultural malaise of the pre-1914 decade found different channels of expression all over Europe, and the typically German manifestations were certainly less radical than those of, for instance, Italian Futurism.

For the great majority of the *Wandervögel* it was the war that spelt the end of their innocence. The reports of Ehmer, Busse Wilson and others in the *Grundschriften* convey the atmosphere of the early post-war meetings and the issues discussed with such vehemence. Part of the movement joined the extreme Left, others the radical Right, and some were in favor of opting out from this sinful world altogether. Both Left and Right were hostile to soul-destroying capitalism, materialism, the alienation of man; everyone agreed that the old world was beyond redemption, and many thought that nothing less than total revolution would put things right. The cure suggested was the class struggle, the dictatorship of the proletariat, and world revolution. Speakers claimed that the great aim of the liberation of mankind could be achieved only if Western culture was destroyed down to its roots. This demand, too, enjoyed great popularity on both the Left and the Right, and Ernst Jünger found many to admire his dithyrambs about the joys of destruction, an idea that goes farther back and has been re-echoed in our day. It should be added in parenthesis that while everyone was in favor of socialism a genuine socialist youth movement emerged only in Austria; the reasons why the Austrians succeeded where the Germans and other Europeans failed remain to be investigated by the historians.

On the fringes of the German movement all kinds of eccentric theories and activities were discussed and prac-

tised in 1919. With the *Neue Schar*, the predecessors of the
hippies appeared on the scene with their ecstatic dances,
Asian mysticism, and flower power. Elsewhere the first urban and agricultural communes were established. The revolutionaries of 1919 were much fewer in number than their
grandchildren of fifty years later, the higher education
explosion had not yet started and there was no television
to promote their cause. But so far as essentials are concerned, all the basic ingredients of present-day youth politics and youth culture already existed fifty years ago. The
innovations made in the 1960's are minor in character and
not very significant, with the possible exception of drug-
taking as part of a new way of life. The *völkisch*, racialist
element has disappeared, which of course is all to the good;
but youth movements are not entirely based on all-embrac-
ing love and new targets had to be found for the aggressive
instincts. The Maoism of 1969 is probably less dangerous
than the anti-semitism of 1919 simply because it is so absurd and its appeal so limited.

The ideologies of youth movements are interesting in so
far as they reflect the spirit of their age, and as such they
deserve careful study. But there is a danger of taking them
too seriously. Youth movements have a great many sterling
qualities, such as sincerity, idealism, the spirit of sacrifice,
but they usually lack historical sense, political sophistication, and originality. The metapolitics of youth movements
are always more significant than their declared aims. In this
context the parallels between then and now are most striking. As Wilhelm Stählin wrote in 1922, in his essay, "Fever
and Salvation in the Youth Movements",

> Behind the big words of a high-faluting *Kulturkritik* there was
> hidden a touching helplessness, a feeling of bitter spiritual
> poverty and emptiness, and a great and deeply moving longing.

Kulturpessimismus was the basic formative influence, the

sense of being both witnesses and active participants in a crisis of universal historical dimensions. Whether in such a situation a generation in its politics turns to the extreme Left or the radical Right, whether the crisis of rationality manifests itself in open anti-intellectualism or pseudo-rational doctrines—these are fascinating questions but they do not touch the core of a problem which can be understood only on a deeper level both of consciousness and of the unconscious. The real assignment of the future historian of the youth movement lies in this direction.

If the generation of the *Wandervögel* and the *Bünde* has been saddened by the way the history of the movement has been written, they are even less happy about today's young rebels. They are horrified by the lack of self-discipline, the obscenities, the total rejection of all authority. They think that a generation which has never experienced real repression may well with their fight against mainly imaginary dangers destroy all the achievements of post-Hitler Germany. The generation of 1919 forgets that even if they were more sparing in their use of obscene words, they too were once considered dangerous rebels by their elders. They too once preached moral relativism and total revolution. But the more thoughtful among them recall the heavy price their generation, and their country, had to pay in the end for the nihilism that once seemed so attractive. And they fear that history will repeat itself, that the young will learn their lesson only as the result of a disaster of perhaps greater magnitude.

Such criticism of the young may not be altogether free of resentment and envy, of idealism turned sour; the conflict of generations is hardly ever a one-sided affair. But it is equally true that the old youth movement, with all its absurdities, was on the whole a saner and (to use a highly unfashionable term) more wholesome affair. The elements of madness, the suicidal impulses were present, but in our time they have become more pronounced and threatening, and they cannot be explained by the usual references to the moral bankruptcy of the older generation, the sickness of the age, and the injustice of the social order. The frightening aspect of the contemporary movement is not its political extremism, its rejection of historical experience, not even the largely verbal cult of violence. The real danger is collective regression under the banner of the fight against repression.

However, the recuperative powers of a young generation should never be underrated: the Jena debate of 1919 did not after all end in a cataclysm. After having discussed the revaluation of all values, the unleashing of the soul *(Entfesselung der Seele)*, Taoism, destruction of Western culture, and having agreed in principle on world revolution, all the participants—according to their chronicler—retired to a *Konditorei* to devour enormous quantities of ice cream, coffee, and fruit-cake with whipped cream.

The temptations of the consumer society are now even greater and more corrosive. It is not at all certain that the present romantic exaltation, the boredom and the enthusiasm will outlast the next decade. The movement will no doubt leave its traces, shaping the spirit and way of life of the 1970s, until—this much seems certain—a new generation will challenge and condemn it as rotten and corrupt.

LITERATURE AND THE HISTORIAN

HISTORIANS sometimes forget that they have no monopoly in their own field of study. The reading public, perhaps unfortunately, has a preference for amateurs over professionals, and outsiders over academics. The book trade is hardly likely to agree with Ludwig Börne's dictum (admittedly 140 years old) that no one ever profited from the study of history with the exception of some publishers and booksellers. Novels do not merely sell better; *War and Peace* and *Le Rouge et le Noir* ought to figure at least as prominently in the education of the student of Borodino and Waterloo as the works of Kolyubakin, Horsburgh, or Navez. The writings of Balzac and Dickens do not abound in statistics, but they are as essential for an understanding of 19th-century social history as even the best conventional histories. Eugene Sue and Spielhagen are not in the same class and their rating in the annals of literature is not now very high, but they remain invaluable for understanding the *Zeitgeist* of the 1840s. About the life of the proletariat around the turn of the century there are now many interesting monographs. Does anyone give a fuller, a more gripping picture than Zola and Gorky, Andersen Nexö and Blasco Ibanez? No period in recent history has been more thoroughly studied by historians than the first World War. There are military accounts, diplomatic analyses, and economic surveys, many of them of the greatest value. And yet, to realize what the war meant for millions of participants, to understand the quality of life during those years, teachers will refer their students above all to Barbusse and Remarque, to Siegfried Sassoon, Jules Romains, and the dozens of others who took it as their theme.

The historian, by a venerable tradition, used to be a man of letters: "History begins in novel and ends in essay", Macaulay wrote. True, the number of badly written histories is legion. But the Muses had *one* father; and Calliope and Erato were Clio's elder sisters. If tragedy was born out of the spirit of music, history descends from epic and lyric poetry, from tragedy and comedy, not from Euclid. The relationship between Clio and her sisters in the age of quantification has become a distant and tenuous one, but it ought to be recalled from time to time as, so to speak, part of the family genealogy.

The strict division between writers and historians occurred only in the second half of the last century. Before that, historians had often dabbled in *belles lettres,* and poets were not disqualified from writing history. Schiller wrote "straight" history, but this is not what he is famous for. Of the well-known historians of the pre-scientific age, many were by modern standards profligate characters; their extra-curricular activities would do them little good now in terms of academic promotion. Gibbon wrote on the theory of literature, Guizot on Shakespeare, Michelet on nature and nightmares. Voltaire could be classified both as a historian and as a writer, and what about Carlyle and Macaulay, Renan and Taine? The literary approach came under attack following the growth in influence and prestige of the German school of historians—not only in Germany, but also in England, the United States, and elsewhere. Later this trend was reinforced by the emergence of the scientific school of historiography. This was the era when many historians felt they were on the verge of some discovery that would do for history what Darwin had done for nature (as a famous president of the American Historical Association once observed).

The break-through, alas, never came. The historical school stuck closely to the sources and hardly ever went beyond preparatory spade work, as some of its earliest critics had predicted. Imagination became a dirty word, though it was later brought in through the back door as "associative imagination"—in contrast to poetic fancy. Some brave attempts were made to restore Clio as a Muse. The belief in scientific history waned, but there was no revival of the literary school in the academies. Of the new technical historians some wore their learning lightly and were blessed with grace in expression; others less gifted produced papers and monographs destined to be read by a small circle of professional colleagues only. The whole trend was not conducive to books of wide appeal. The progressive specialization characteristic of industrial society was reflected in the universities in a strict division of labor according to which every scholar was classified and put into a compartment. There was an unwritten convention as to how history should be written, and it became unwise to stray too far from it. Unwise from the academic point of view, but not if the taste of the reading public was considered; they continued to ask for readable history. The great historians of the 18th and 19th centuries had produced best-sellers; none of their successors (with the exception of Toynbee and one or two others, similarly suspect in professional circles), had done so. The average scholarly work became more and more specialized or esoteric; the appeal of even the best books of this kind was in inverse ratio to the critical acclaim they received. As Lessing said about Klopstock: Everyone praised his books but who bothered to read them?

It was not, however, only a matter of style and literary approach. The public was deterred by the reluctance of many historians to deal with broad and important subjects, by the perverse attraction that historical footnotes held for the professionals. The image of the ivory-tower historians emerged, "the rag pickers of Clio who take their subjects from the garbage heap, who make napkin rings to pass the time like a retired customs official" (Lucien Fèbvre). "We protest when the public takes XYZ for historians. But what do we offer them to read that is readable?" XYZ have been doing well in recent decades. For if the historians have not produced best-sellers, the appetite of a public, much larger in numbers than in the last century, for historical literature has grown by leaps and bounds. Lytton Strachey and Emil Ludwig had their vogue in the 1920s. There has been a whole spate of literature, much of it of value, in our own time. Mr. William Shirer's book on Nazi Germany has sold many hundreds of thousands of copies despite the almost universally negative attitude of professional historians. More recently Mr Cornelius Ryan has done even better. The comments of the historians did not greatly matter; this literature answered a definite need which the historians had been unable or unwilling to satisfy. In France there is a whole galaxy of highly successful journals devoted to popular history of the *histoire historisant* kind; *History Today* in Britain (a journal by no means popular in character) succeeded beyond all expectations.

This great interest in history, biography, the historical novel, has not diminished even under the impact of a new literary genre, science fiction. Technical history could not compete with popular biographies and instant history— these are legitimate activities moving on different levels; to this extent the relative unpopularity of the professional historians was inevitable. But was it not at least in part often due to a deliberate neglect of style and an absence of imagination on the part of the academic historians themselves?

Style and imagination are the great preservatives in history, and the world at large, as a contemporary historian has reminded us, will sooner forgive lack of scientific solidity than lack of literary charm. Competence, scientific solidity, should be a prerequisite for writing history, not a synonym for boredom. A limpid style is invariably the result of hard labor. As Trevelyan put it:

> The idea that histories which are delightful to read must be the work of superficial temperaments and that a crabbed style betokens a deep thinker or conscientious worker, is the reverse of the truth. What is easy to read has been difficult to write.

Writers of historical novels—and what 19th-century author did not try his hand at this genre at one time or another?—have had it easier than the historians. They can pick and choose, extracting the most dramatic incidents, ignoring everything that lacks wide appeal. They are attracted by great men and women, their ambitions, intrigues, confrontations. Above all, they search for the motives behind the action: why did Philip II kill Don Carlos? Why did Peter the Great have his son Alexi executed? What was the real identity of the false Dimitri and of Kaspar Hauser? What made Thomas-à-Becket act as he did? What impulses motivated Jeanne d'Arc and Mary Stuart? Was Masaniello a criminal or a patriot? Who is more worthy of our sympathy—Charles I or Cromwell?

These and other heroes have attracted hundreds of writers and playwrights over the years and, to a certain extent, continue to do so. In a few decades a more sophisticated Lanny Budd will no doubt report his meetings with Hitler and Goering. Where historians feared to tread writers of historical fiction have moved with far less restraint, unfettered by any of the rules and taboos which historians have to observe. There have been novels and plays that merely transfer into the past contemporary problems and conflicts. In the medieval romances Charlemagne or Edward IV appeared as living characters; in the modern psychological novel Julian the Apostate and Antigone become 20th-century figures. It is interesting, but it has nothing to do with history. But there were others, the purists of the historical novel who, like Walter Scott, based their work on solid historical research, retracing the course of events with much insight and knowledge. Their reconstruction of the past may often be, for all we know, as near the historical truth as the work of the professional historians. Even so, historians have usually regarded the historical novel as unfair competition and have not, on the whole, taken it seriously. Were not the heroes of even the most successful historical novels like guests at a masked ball—contemporaries of Bulwer Lytton, Sienkiewicz, or Manzoni in Greek, Roman, or Papal garb? Were not most of these novels *romans à clef* in which prominent contemporaries appeared and could be identified without undue difficulty? But the same charge can frequently be made against eminently academic historiography, in the sense that all history is contemporary history. There is not that much difference between the historical novel and orthodox historiography where the assessment of key figures is concerned. Surely it is no coincidence that in the struggle between Charles I and Cromwell the sympathies of almost all the historians and the writers up to the early years of the nineteenth century were on the side of the King. There is a similar parallelism in the approach of both historians and novelists to Charles XII of Sweden; the adventurer of the eighteenth century became the great romantic hero of the nineteenth. Napoleon, so bitterly attacked during his lifetime outside France, after his death was presented by historians and writers alike as a genius to whom ordinary standards could not be applied.

History and literature meet on many different levels, and

there is a large area of no-man's-land into which both sides have made forays. Some of the writers who have written history have already been mentioned; there were many more who had no intention of writing history, but have done so if only indirectly, and often unconsciously. For their works reflect the issues of their times, and thus constitute a source of great importance for the historian. An account of the Vormaerz that does not refer to Heinrich Heine and *Das Junge Deutschland* is at best incomplete; a survey of the Second Empire that omits Victor Hugo is unthinkable. A discussion of the politics of Thomas Mann and Sartre, of Graham Greene and Roy Campbell are relevant to the understanding of the *Zeitgeist* of the twentieth century.

Lastly, there are those writers who from time to time have not only written or reflected history but have made it. Some historians have belittled their importance for roughly the same reasons that made Stalin inquire about the number of divisions at the disposal of the Pope. But is political power really measured that way? The "literary intelligentsia" has been prominent in all political movements of the past two hundred years; they have played a decisive role in revolutions even if their function usually extended no further than blazing the trail.

Neither as individuals nor as a group have intellectuals held political power for long. Usually they are in opposition; indeed, it is widely thought that to be outsiders is their historical mission. To their political allies they may not be of great help, but as opponents they can be dangerous. More and more of them are politically committed.

On the news of the death in 1841 of Diego Leon, a now forgotten Spanish general, the German revolutionary poet Ferdinand Freiligrath wrote a poem that shocked and disturbed many of his friends: "Whatever I wrote", he asserted, "I wrote freely". The poet does not and should not care whether his verses please everyone. He knows that there has been evil in the world since the days of Troy. The poet bows to the hero Bonaparte, and is angered by the Duc d'Enghien's death cry, for he views the world around him from a higher vantage point than that of a political party:

> Er beugt sein Knie dem Helden Bonaparte, Und hoert mit Zuernen d'Enghien's Todesschrei: Der Dichter steht auf einer hoeheren Warte Als auf den Zinnen der Partei.

Georg Herwegh, Freiligrath's friend and his rival in popularity among the German Left, answered almost immediately in a poem called simply *"Die Partei."* Who could refuse to join the great movement in these stirring days? Who could shirk the question: Slave or Free? Were not the poets in duty bound to act, to break their lyres and to lead the people in the struggle for a better future? Not for poets the Olympian detachment; and had not the gods themselves descended from Olympus to take part in the partisan struggle? Poems are swords, poets are called to action.

> Ich hab gewaehlt, Ich hab mich entschieden, Und meinen Lorbeer flechte die Partei.
> (I have chosen, I have decided, and *my* laurels will be woven by the party.)

This controversy in the poetry columns of German newspapers more than a century ago anticipated in its main arguments current discussions about commitment and *littérature engagée.*

Individually, writers and poets have always participated in the political and social struggles of their time. But the idea of literature as a political force and the poets as the unacknowledged legislators of their age appeared only towards the end of the eighteenth century. It originated in France, where men of letters without wealth, social eminence, or the responsibilities of official status (as Tocqueville notes in a famous passage) took the lead in politics, as they were the only ones to speak with the accents of authority. The political ferment was channelled into literature, "the result being that our writers now became the leaders of public opinion and played for a while the part which normally, in free countries, falls to the professional politicians." These men of letters were now in charge of the political education of the French nation, shaping the national temperament and outlook on life. It was a great movement and it had a great impact. But was the importation of literary propensities into the political arena an unmixed blessing? Tocqueville, at any rate, did not think so; he did not like the broad generalizations coupled with contempt for hard facts, the abstract words, the gaudy flowers of speech, the sonorous clichés: "For what is a merit in the writer may well be a vice in the statesman, and the very qualities which go to make great literature can lead to catastrophic revolutions." It is almost literally Monsieur Raymond Aron castigating Sartre one hundred years later.

The French revolution marked the great water-shed. Ever since the literary intelligentsia has made a great and growing impact on politics, and 1848 was the revolution of the intellectuals *par excellence*. This involvement did not proceed everywhere in equal measure, and it was not to everyone's liking. Least of all to Goethe's, who wrote to his friend Luden that it was not necessary for him to take up public affairs when they were adequately handled by excellent men, "and so I could stay in my closet and think of my innermost self." On another occasion, to the same correspondent: "Let the world go its way, and do not mix yourself up in the quarrels of kings." And when his advice was ignored and Luden decided to go into politics after all: "I hate all bungling like sin, especially bungling in affairs of state, from which nothing but misery results for thousands and millions." Goethe's reasoning is unexceptionable—

the effects of bad politics are usually more fatal than those of a bad poem. But the men of letters in France and Germany, in Italy and Austria, were convinced that affairs of state were not in the hands of excellent men, and that the bunglers at the top needed to be replaced by intellectuals. England was the one country whc.e these ideas had no impact. It was teeming with revolutionary ideas but there was no revolution. It has been argued, *e.g.* by Belloc, that in England at the time literature and the arts were far more extreme and revolutionary than on the continent—Blake's and Turner's paintings, for instance, in comparison w. 'h David's pseudo-classicism, "Kubla Khan" and Shelley in comparison with André Chanier: "English Romantics, English Liberals, were not public men making a republic but poets, each seeing a vision." In the Victorian age even the visions disappeared; social criticism there was, but on the whole the divorce between public affairs and writing became more pronounced. The aftermath of the first World War caused despondency and withdrawal but no major call to action as on the continent. The great debate about commitment and literature came to England only in the 1930s, almost a century later than to the continent.

Russia, on the other hand, was the country of *littérature oblige.* When Chernyshevsky wrote that novels, essays, and poetry "have a far greater significance for us Russians than they have in any other country", this was a statement of fact, not merely the credo of the extreme Left. As in 18th-century France (only more so), literature was the only outlet into which revolutionary energies could be channelled. It had replaced religion as the main inspiration of the intelligentsia, and since the censorship made open discussion of political questions impossible, literature became the obvious forum for such debates. Philosophical, aesthetical, literary essays and surveys were almost invariably political tracts in disguise; indifferent novels like *What Is to Be Done?* educated generations of revolutionaries. The Russian *littérateurs* in their enthusiasm were all in favor of abolishing literature. When Bazarov said that he believed not in principles but in frogs, and that a decent chemist was twenty times more useful than a poet, the caricature was uncomfortably close to realities. The leading critics at the time wanted to ban private, individual problems from the novel and from poetry —for were not public issues much more important? The extremism, and above all the nihilism, of some of these enragés annoyed even Herzen in his London exile:

> What struck me about them was the ease with which they despaired of everything; the ferocious joy of their denial and their terrible ruthlessness. Despite their excellent spirits and noble intentions, our "bilious ones" can by their tone, drive an angel to blows and a saint to curses. They exaggerate everything in the world with such aplomb and not as a joke but out of such bitterness, that they are quite unbearable.

These observations refer to young mid-19th-century Russian bohemian revolutionaries; it is purely accidental if they have a familiar ring on some university campuses in the western hemisphere.

The nineteen-thirties were the classic age of political involvement, of writers' congresses, manifestos, and politico-literary tracts. The social convulsions in the wake of the world economic crisis, the rise of fascism, the emergence of Stalinism, brought home the lesson that politics did matter. There was much talk about the responsibility of the writer, his obligation towards society, his duty not to withdraw into the proverbial ivory tower. The idea of the writer as a man of action was not altogether new; in practice most of such adventures after the first World War had not been successful, whether on the Right (d'Annunzio in Fiume) or on the Left (Eisner, Toller, Muehsam in Munich). But in the

30's there was a collective call to arms; a partial retreat from politics came only in the '50s with the emergence of a new literary generation.

The responsibility of the writer is twofold. As a writer he has, if he is any good, a wider forum and more authority for his views than most other men. But is he always aware of the responsibility which such a position implies? Would the political views of Thomas Mann or of Jean-Paul Sartre have attracted the same measure of interest but for their eminence in the field of *belles lettres?* Would the leaders of the extreme Right in France have found enthusiastic followers for their ideas but for the fact that many of them had a witty, elegant, and effective style? Have we not seen playwrights of genius in whose expert hands a primitive political message assumes great sophistication, in which perverse moral judgments become a new categorical imperative? There is a danger of eminence in one field imparting more or less automatic authority in another—politics in this case. If here we are concerned with letters, the danger is no less great in the case of physicists, theologians, and above all television personalities.

If historians had a wider public they would probably be faced with the same dilemma. Even the choice of subject may invite criticism. A discussion of the views of Chernyshevsky in a Russian historical journal of the 1860s would no doubt have encountered criticism by its contemporaries —what has this to do with history? A great deal, even if it was not always immediately obvious. History will never be the exclusive preserve of the historians; literature should not be the monopoly of the literary critics. Poetry is under no obligation to take notice of diplomatic or economic history. But in a wider sense history and literature need each other. They must make constant forays beyond the borders established a long time ago by well-meaning pedants.

RUSSIA THROUGH
WESTERN EYES

For life moves out of a red flare of dreams
Into the common light of common hours . . .

W. B. YEATS, *Land of Heart's Desire*

IN the preface to his *Histories of the Latin and Germanic Nations from 1494 to 1514,* Ranke wrote that to history has been assigned the office of judging the past and instructing the present for the benefit of future ages. The passage that follows is perhaps the most famous in all historical literature: "To such high office this work does not aspire. It seeks only to show what actually happened *(wie es eigentlich gewesen).* . . ." Most historians since then have been more ambitious, though not necessarily more successful than Ranke. They *have* sought to instruct the present for the benefit of the future. The writing of Soviet history is a case in point. It is contemporary history, and the difficulties in writing it are twofold and well known; those who try to write *Zeitgeschichte* have as a rule less of the essential source material at their disposal than their colleagues dealing with the more remote past, and they lack distance from their subject, are prone to be more involved emotionally than is thought becoming by the purists.

Such obstacles do not obviate the necessity of writing contemporary history. The disparaging attitude towards it on the part of some members of the historical profession is of comparatively recent origin; Ranke, after all, wrote not only about the middle ages but also about the aftermath of the French revolution—events that happened in his own lifetime. Michelet and Thierry, Guizot and Mignet were all very much concerned with the France of their own period, and Lord Acton was preoccupied with the disputes then being fought out in the Catholic church. They would all have agreed with what a later day historian, Trevelyan, said about the virtue of detachment: "dispassionateness—*nil admirare*—may betray the most gifted historian into missing some vital truth in his subject." To Mr. E. H. Carr, whose *History of Soviet Russia* is undoubtedly a very remarkable achievement, the same criticism applies as Trevelyan made with regard to Creighton's treatment of Luther—what he says is both fair and accurate, and yet from him alone one would hardly ever guess that he is dealing with a momentous and stirring movement in which great passions, much idealism and self-sacrifice—and their opposites—were involved. It is not the only criticism; Mr Carr is the antithesis to Cato, of whom it was said that *Victrix causa deis placuit sed victa Catoni.*

It is necessary to stress that dispassionateness in a historian is not the supreme value, for the impression may easily be gained that a greater measure of detachment would have resulted in a smaller measure of mistakes in so far as the Western image of the Soviet Union is concerned. This is not necessarily true, for it was not so much passionate involvement that produced error, as the inability or unwillingness of the writer to apply his critical faculties.

There is no time like the present to pause and re-examine some of the landmarks in Western writing about the Soviet Union. Not all the passion generated in the 1920s and '30s has been spent, but the memories are beginning to fade as a generation grows up for whom not only Trotsky but even

Stalin is past history. Some of the essential facts, bitterly contested only yesterday, are to-day no longer disputed—the purges of the '30s and the Moscow trials, for instance. In the following some of the books published between the October revolution and Stalin's death that attracted much attention at the time have been subjected to critical analysis. This is not an exercise in historical one-upmanship; with the advantage of hindsight, nothing would be easier than to hold up to ridicule the false prophets of yesteryear. Some of the commentators were remarkably correct in their prognostications, and where others went wrong there is usually a lesson to be drawn for our time. The 20th, and to an even greater extent the 22nd Soviet party congress have opened fresh vistas. This, then, is the time for a backward glance.

Russia belongs to the group of countries to which students of metaphysics have attributed a historical mission and a destiny. This goes back to the days when the idea of a Third Rome was first conceived. Some, like Gogol, compared it to a *troika* at full gallop of which nobody knew the destination; others, more specific, regarded Russia alternatively as the scourge of the West and its savior. Outside Russia, too, speculation about its historical role and future dates back at least three centuries: it occupied poets and pamphleteers in Britain, diplomats and essayists in France, and in Germany it became something in the nature of a popular sport on a national scale. Did Russia belong to the West or the East?

> *Briton and Russian differ but in name*
> *In nature's sense all nations are the same,*

Aaron Hill wrote in a poem in 1718 dedicated to Peter I, who was called by another contemporary, Jean-Jacques Rousseau, "le plus barbare de tous les hommes." In the nineteenth century Russia was the great bogy for most European democrats and liberals, though there were some dissenting voices. Heine regarded Tsarist absolutism as the best ally of the European revolution in its struggle against the old order. Ernest Coeurderoy, a Frenchman, wrote a remarkable pamphlet in 1854, *Hourra, ou la revolution par les Cosaques,* in which he welcomed the "proletarians of the North" as allies in the struggle against the decayed culture of the West.[1] Some recently rediscovered philosophers of history of the 19th century, such as Vollgraff and Lasaulx, developed most detailed theories about the decline of the West and the rise of the East, anticipating much that has been said in our time by Spengler and Toynbee.

Everybody is free to speculate on the future of one particular country or of the world in general. But unless he is proved right by the subsequent course of events even the most ingenious arguments and the most relentless logic will soon be forgotten by all but the professional historians of ideas. It is a risky pastime in which few reputations are made but many undone, and if political analysis and predictions are hazardous in days of peace and calm they become even more difficult in times of unrest and revolution. And yet it is precisely in times of revolution that people are most acutely confronted with the great issues of the day. The French revolution is the classical example: nobody in Europe could stay aloof. Eloquent witnesses have told us how it appeared to the enthusiasts—and who was not an enthusiast in that blissful dawn? Klopstock, no less sympathetic than Wordsworth, spoke for the majority of German *Dichter und Denker* when he wrote:

> *Frankreich schuf sich frei. Des Jahrhunderts edelste Tat hub da sich zum Olympus empor!*

[1] Dieter Groh, *Russland und das Selbstverstaendnis Europas* (1961); J. H. Gleason, *The Genesis of Russophobia in Great Britain* (1950); P. Scheibert, *From Bakunin to Lenin,* vol. I (1956).

Recently attention has again been drawn to the immense popularity in Britain of the French revolution in its early days, not only among literary and artistic circles.

> It seemed to mark the end of that medieval obscurantism in institutions and beliefs associated with the ancient regime. It symbolised the destruction of despots in Church and State, and the chance of an era in which human personality, freed from the shackles of the past, could achieve a new fulfilment.[2]

The discussions and controversies about the French revolution in England and Germany as well as in other countries bear a certain resemblance to the debates on Soviet communism in the 1920s and '30s. Burke had as little feeling and understanding as some 20th-century conservatives for the existence of a "revolutionary situation" and attributed all that happened to individual wickedness. The Declaration of the Rights of Man was a great historical event, and Thomas Paine was right in saying so, but it came to mean little under the Committee of Public Safety and under Napoleon. It is more difficult to understand how Sidney Webb (to name but one) could have accepted the Stalin Constitution at its face value. The Russian revolution had its Koblenz and its Rivarol as well as its Marat and Desmoulins. It too devoured its children, but by now the purgers of the purgers have also been purged and the émigrés never went back.

The French revolution was welcomed by public opinion in Europe in its overwhelming majority, though most of its admirers had had second thoughts by 1792. The Russian revolution was hailed by a minority only; it won enthusiastic support only much later, and under the impact of events outside Russia itself, in the "popular front" period and during the second World War.

The writing of history is by its very nature selective. No

[2] J. H. Plumb, *England in the Eighteenth Century* (1950).

work of research can possibly record every opinion uttered in connection with a certain event—nor indeed is it desirable that it should do so. I want here to concentrate on some significant views that were voiced outside Russia and outside the Communist parties; obviously there is not much point in re-examining the products of a lunatic fringe, or the deliberate lies that were spread (the story about "the nationalization of women" in Moscow, Kiev, and Odessa is probably the best remembered incident). But there is a world of difference between a deliberate lie systematically spread by the propaganda apparatus of a totalitarian country and the occasional misstatements of journalists writing for the more conrationalist proce organno in a domooratio world.

The Soviet Union was much sinned against in its early days, and Bolshevik propaganda has made full use of the inventions and distortions of its foes. The very first editorial on the revolution in the London *Morning Post* was headed "Revolution Made in Germany," and many other contemporary observers commented in a similar vein.[3] Most commentators did not stop to consider the revolution outside the narrow framework of the shifting day-to-day fortunes of the first World War and thus altogether missed its enormous political and social significance.

Much of the early criticism was based on misinformation on Russian affairs and a total ignorance of even the elementary principles of Marxism, and betrayed a total lack of political imagination. The Soviet experiment, it was said,

[3] Cf. M. M. Karlinder, "Oktyabrskaya Revolutsiya i angliskaya burzhuaznaya pechat" in the *Festschrift* devoted to the memory of F. A. Rotshtein, *Imperializm i borba rabochevo klassa* (Moscow 1960), and Stephen R. Graubard, *British Labour and the Russian Revolution* (1956). The *Morning Post* blamed "Russian Jews of German extraction," *The Times* blamed Kerensky for lack of firmness, the British Liberal newspapers blamed the British government for hostility to the Russian Provisional Government, and H. N. Brailsford, writing in the *Herald*, said that Lenin's in perpetuating an epoch of violence." See Richard H. Ullman, *Intervention and the War* (1961).
and Trotsky's "real crime against Russia is that they have followed Kornilov

could not work; an editor of the London *Daily News* (not a very hostile paper) returned from Moscow and reported (3 June 1924) "Communism fails because it is an impracticable ideal". This was but one voice of many and the arguments in support of this thesis make strange reading thirty or forty years later. Communism was "bound to fail" because it was too egalitarian, everybody earned the same, there was no incentive to produce." Planned economy was a chimera that could never be realized; Russia would soon return to its old nationalist tradition. Ustryalov in Harbin and his friends of the *Smena Vekh* in Prague were already packing their bags to return. At one time it was believed that the Soviet government would soon orientate itself towards the new NEP bourgeoisie. Meditating in front of the Kremlin in 1927, M. Alfred Fabre Luce reported that Stalin was regarded as *"le roi des kulaks"*. Right-wing extremists regarded the whole affair as a conspiracy by the Elders of Zion carried out by the three Jews, Lenin, Stalin, and Trotsky. The public image of the Bolshevik was fairly accurately depicted in some of the novels of John Buchan and Sapper's Bulldog Drummond—communism was a synonym for anarchism, a conspiracy to throw the whole world into a state of chaos.

This early period of know-nothingism not unnaturally played into the hand of the communists. As time passed the "Soviet experiment" achieved some spectacular economic and military successes, as it was realized that Russia was neither a paradise of free love nor a heaven for the anarchists, the inclination grew to dismiss criticism of Russia and Soviet communism altogether. As a result, the Soviet Union under Stalin began to attract more support than it did under Lenin.

The fascination exerted on so many Western intellectuals by Stalin, and by Russia under Stalin, is a complex phenomenon which cannot be explained by any single formula; different people were attracted by different aspects. Lion Feuchtwanger, a sensitive writer and the author of a number of eminently readable historical novels, was not a communist, certainly not a Stalinist, before he went to Moscow in 1937. What did he see, how was he impressed at the height of the purges?

"The whole big city of Moscow breathed satisfaction and agreement, more than that, happiness"—Feuchtwanger wrote. And again: "Whoever has eyes to see and ears to hear, to differentiate between the genuine and the spurious, feels at every step that the phrases about the happy life are no more idle talk."

What about Stalin and the Stalin cult?

"The people feel the urge to express their gratitude to Stalin, their boundless admiration."

Not that Stalin really wanted so much adulation:

"He is particularly reserved . . . It manifestly annoys Stalin to be deified."

How to explain the purges and the show trials?

> Some of my friends, otherwise not unreasonable people, find the trials from beginning to end, in both their content and their form tragicomic, barbaric, incredible, and monstrous . . . But when I attended the second trial in Moscow my doubts dissolved like salt in water under the impression of what Radek and his friends said. If these were lies, or somehow prearranged, then I don't know what is truth.

To those obstinate Western intellectuals who nevertheless, persevered in their doubts and maintained that Stalin's despotism and terror were but the expression of his lust for power, Feuchtwanger said reprovingly:

> Such rigmarole shows ignorance of the human soul and lack of judgment. One need only look at any book, any speech by Stalin, one need only recall any specific step he has taken in connection

with the reconstruction of the USSR, and it emerges beyond any shadow of doubt that this wise, superior man cannot possibly have committed the colossal stupidity of staging such a clumsy comedy with the help of countless collaborators.[4]

Lion Feuchtwanger was not the most extreme case; there were many like him in Paris, London, and New York willing to give Stalin not merely the benefit of the doubt but the most enthusiastic support. It was a voluntary abdication of critical faculties, a *trahison des clercs* comparable only to the attitudes revealed by so many German intellectuals in 1933. If mitigating circumstances can be found for intellectuals in a totalitarian country, it is difficult to find an excuse for those who had the opportunity to choose.

Admittedly, one is always tempted to underrate the role of stupidity in human affairs. But Harold Laski (to name but one) was a highly intelligent man, and in contrast to Feuchtwanger the *litterateur*, he had made a lifelong study of politics, national and international. And yet Laski could report after a visit to Stalin's Russia in the middle '30s.

> Basically I did not observe much difference between the general character of a trial in Russia and in this country [*i.e.* Britain].

The Soviet courts, he observed, were much more concerned with prevention and cure than with deterrence and punishment. Nobody was more concerned with the prevention of crime than Andrei Vyshinsky, with whom Professor Laski had a long and amicable conversation:

> I was predisposed to think of him essentially in his capacity as prosecutor. . . . I found him a man whose passion was law reform. No one I met was more clear about the steps he wanted to take for their improvement. He was doing what an ideal Minister of Justice would do if we had such a person in Great Britain— forcing his colleagues to consider what is meant by actual ex-

---

[4] Lion Feuchtwanger, *Moskau 1937,* pp. 14, 20, 77, 82, 141.

perience of the law in action. He brought to the study of the law in operation an energy which we have not seen in this country since the days of Jeremy Bentham.[5]

Vyshinsky-Bentham as the ideal Minister of Justice in Great Britain—it was a daring and original suggestion, but no more so than many of the statements of the Webbs and Professor Cole and many others in the West at the time.

These then were some of the intellectuals, who in the name of progress and idealism declared their support for Josef Stalin. But there were others who were neither highbrows nor progressives and yet reached similar conclusions. Walter Duranty, for many years correspondent of the *New York Times* in Moscow, expressed the views of many when he wrote: "I don't care a whoop for socialism or totalitarianism, or any of their isms. . . ." But on Stalin he said:

> I backed Stalin the way you back a horse until you think of it as "your horse", though it may belong to Whitney or Widener or someone; you think of it as your horse, because you always backed it. That's how I felt about Russia, that's how I feel about Stalin.[6]

One such realist who did not care a whoop for socialism (because *inter alia* he was a multi-millionaire) and who yet regarded Stalin as his own horse, was Joseph E. Davies, American Ambassador in Moscow in the late '30s. He was a lawyer, and sitting in at the trials he reached the "reluctant conclusion that the state had established its case":

> On the face of the record in this case it would be difficult for me to conceive of any court, in any jurisdiction doing other than adjudging the defendants guilty of violations of the law as set forth in the indictment and as defined by the statutes.[7]

[5] Harold J. Laski, *Law and Justice in Soviet Russia* (1935), p. 21.
[6] Walter Duranty, *The Kremlin and the People* (1942), p. 15.
[7] Joseph E. Davies, *Mission to Moscow* (1942), vol. I, p. 39.

If at the time of the Radek-Pyatakov trial the situation still had Ambassador Davies guessing ('the simple fact is that ordinary psychology does not apply in this situation', p. 117), his doubts were dispersed by the Bukharin trial.

All the fundamental weaknesses and vices of human nature, personal ambitions at their worst, are shown up in the proceedings. They disclose the outlines of a plot which came very near to being successful in bringing about the overthrow of the government. This testimony now makes it clear what we could not understand and what happened last spring and summer. . . . But the government acted with great vigor and speed. . . . Then it came out that quite a few of those at the top were seriously infected with the virus of conspiracy to overthrow the government and were actually working with the Secret Service organizations of Germany and Japan. . . . Quite frankly we can't blame the powers that be much for reacting in this way if they believed what is now divulged at the trial. (p. 177)

Thus Ambassador Davies to his daughter Emlen on 8 March 1938. Three years later Mr. Davies gave a talk to the University of Wisconsin Club:

It was just three days after Hitler had invaded Russia. Someone in the audience asked, "What about Fifth Columnists in Russia?" Off the anvil I said: There aren't any—they shot them. (p. 179)

Neither Feuchtwanger nor Laski nor Ambassador Davies had any background knowledge of Russia; they did not speak the language and had not spent any length of time in the country before. But such background knowledge was absolutely essential, as Professor Pares once pointed out:

One can always see at once whether anyone talking of Russia has really lived there; it is a kind of freemasonry independent both of class and views.[8]

[8] Bernard Pares, *Russia* (1940), p. 256.

Professor Pares certainly knew Russia from his frequent visits, beginning as a student at Moscow University in 1898. He was the author of many historical studies and towards the end of his life generally recognized as the leading British expert on Russia and the Soviet Union. This Russian expertise had only one major flaw; it did not care a whoop (as Duranty would have put it) for socialism or Marxism or any other ism or ideology (though he hardly ever put it so bluntly). It was good old-fashioned empiricism, interested in actions, not in words.

> If we regard his actions rather than his words (one of Professor Pares' favorite sayings whenever dealing with Stalin) it appeared that he [Stalin] has changed his course steadily and radically [away from Leninism].

Russia under Stalin appeared to Professor Pares:

> as a nearer approach to true democracy than the liberal movement before the revolution; for then liberalism was a theory where the sense of its responsibilities was lacking, and now we are beginning to see that material of character and purpose out of which true democracy can be made.[9]

Of the trials and purges Pares took the conventional view:

> Zinoviev was now finally brought to book and died, still fawning, like the coward that he had always been. . . . Nearly all the accused admitted having done so [conspiring] and on this point it is not necessary that we should doubt them, in whatever way their evidence was originally obtained. The bulky verbatim reports were in any case impressive.[10]

[9] *Russia and the Peace* (1944), p. 33.
[10] *Russia*, p. 262. Pares was so impressed by Radek's "confession" that he had it reproduced in *The Slavonic Review* (April 1937). Sir John Maynard also shed "Light on the Trotskyist Trials" (*Political Quarterly*, July 1937): ". . . the confessions have not been of the defiant kind. Rather they have been of the penitent kind, of a sinner making a clean breast of his sins and extenuating nothing."

Of all the stupid comments made at the time this one surely deserves to be repeated and remembered: "The bulky verbatim reports were in any case impressive." Such a pearl of wisdom was the outcome of fifty years of study of Russian history, of the Russian people, its country, its language.

About the post-war world and Russia's role in it Professor Pares was very optimistic. After all, did not the three Allies have certain principles in common? "All three have alike had to grapple with the inescapable problem of reconciling a federal system with regional independence." One could have imagined a great many other similarities, such as the common need to build schools, to grow tomatoes, or to produce toilet paper. As for Stalin and his policy in the post-War world, Professor Pares thought

> that his deeds have been much more enlightening than his words. He has already travelled very far in very definite directions. To judge by his past, my forecast of his future action would be: He has shown that his heart is in his own country, that he has set his reputation on a purely practical object of vast scope, its radical transformation for the benefit of all. Then he will need world peace. . . . He can be credited with the good sense to see that he too must play his part in the building of world peace. . . . It would not be sense to bring Poles or Czechs under Russian rule[11]

Sometimes, like the priest in Don Quixote's library, one gets tired of taking down from the shelves one book after another, to pass judgment on each, and feels inclined to pronounce sentence *en masse*. But that is hardly the way to do justice to those that cannot be classified by accepted norms and standards—Rosa Luxemburg, for instance, a "Westerner" and yet very close to the Bolsheviks, who, in her little book on the Russian revolution, written in 1918, was acutely aware of what was in store for the young Soviet republic. At that time these were solitary voices in the multitude that

[11] *Russia and the Peace,* p. 192.

looked at Russia either with utter incomprehension or with uncritical and reverent adulation.

What then is the state of affairs a half-century later?

All things considered, the general level of comment on and understanding of the Soviet Union has risen since the 1930s. Partly this must be attributed to the late Josef Stalin who, especially in his later years, compelled even the most starry-eyed and reluctant to re-examine their attitude. Partly it is the result of the collection by specialists over twenty or twenty-five years of a great amount of factual material, from the working of the Soviet railway system to the details of Soviet primary education. It is easy to scoff at these sometimes over-specialized studies, for taken alone, none greatly contributes to our understanding of the "Socialist Sixth", but, taken together, they constitute an impressive body of knowledge. True enough, too little of this has so far filtered down to the general public, or even to many students of world affairs who should know better; but it makes a cumulative impact that should not be underrated. Many more people now read Russian (including Soviet newspapers and magazines), and the study of Soviet affairs, in general, has spread widely. Before the second World War, the study of the USSR, its institutions, economy, and cultural life, did not exist as a scientific discipline. Today, of course, all this has changed, and as a result de-mythologization is by now fairly advanced. There still is a great deal of ignorance in newspapers and books and on the radio and television where Russia is concerned, and some of the old warhorses are still with us, though with a smaller public in Europe. In the newly independent countries of Asia and Africa, too, public opinion is becoming sophisticated at a surprisingly fast pace. Granted that Western expertise on Russia every few years brings forth a strange crop of amateur commentators (ranging from Dr. Fromm and Viscount Montgomery to the Birch Society), but they have little influence on informed public opinion. Some of the grosser acts of folly, at any rate, are unlikely to be repeated.

Whole libraries have been written on the Soviet Union since 1917. All I am trying to do here is suggest a reassessment of some of the more important and widely read books of the last 50 years. Some still retain a special interest for the current student; Kautsky and his exchanges with Trotsky and other Soviet leaders in the early '20s; Otto Bauer: the Russian emigration with its various factions and theories; the debates of the late '30s, when a great measure of ingenuity was invested in attempts to define the political, social, and economic character of the Soviet system (Hilferding's famous essay). Men and women of different political philosophies have reached and will continue to reach different conclusions about various aspects of the Soviet regime. This is as it should be. My only intention here was to show that a political engagement based on prejudice, illusions, wishful thinking, and, sometimes, as in the case of the Moscow trials, on willful perversion of the truth, has little value and will not endure. In a wider perspective, it is even self-defeating.

For it is surely comforting that, in an otherwise cynical age, truth does come to light sooner or later; however great the success of Webb's book at the time, it has since become something of a joke, and even the most hardened apologists of the Moscow trials do not now feel very proud of what they said and wrote at the time. Historical truth advances at an agonizingly slow pace, but, taking it all in all, it does make progress. In this sense the study of Western writing on the Soviet Union during the last 50 years offers a lesson and a challenge, to be ignored only at considerable risk. Ignorance in this respect (as in others) is not innocence but sin.

THE THIRD WORLD

CASSANDRA, daughter of King Priam of Troy, had (we are told) her ears licked by a serpent while asleep and so received her prophetic gift: forever after she was fated to foretell the evil results of successive events. All civilizations have had their Cassandras, but probably none more than 20th-century Europe. A symposium in *Le Figaro* in 1898 ("What's wrong with France?") reads uncannily like an American *Partisan Review* symposium 70 years later. Visions of doom have been fashionable for a long time, and their prophets sometimes address large audiences. Brahmanism taught that the world was in decline, Horace and Livius are full of dire predictions following the general relaxation of Roman discipline, and every self-respecting writer in the tenth century began his chronology: "While the world is approaching its end. . . ." Henry and Brooks Adams wrote long ago about the decline of Western man, and Baudelaire hated Paris (*"centre et rayonnement de bêtise universelle"*) as much as do Sartre and Simone de Beauvoir. Between the two World Wars fascism proclaimed the impending demise of the senescent West—and the rise of the young nations.

Since World War II prophecies of doom have come from many quarters and on the basis of different political convictions. Usually, these are frightening visions. Arnold Toynbee regards Western civilization as an apostasy of Christian civilization, the fatal plunge from faith into the barren grounds of secularism. Western civilization, he says, exhibits authentic symptoms of breakdown and disintegration, and the only thing that can save it is a fresh religious revolution.

Such reasoning is not shared by many. Toynbee has been chided by (among others) Geoffrey Barraclough, a British historian now at Oxford, Barraclough criticized the "breathtaking oblivion to the enormous genocide involved," as well as the lack of accuracy and consistency in Toynbee's historical judgment, the wishful thinking and dubious speculations in his reflections on the prospects of Western civilization.

Yet Barraclough himself is the author of a recent introduction to contemporary history which could, with equal justice, be entitled "New Light on the Decline of the West." In one of his essays he wrote that in 1943, when Stalingrad was relieved by the Russians, he suddenly awoke to the fact that he had mis-spent his life dealing with such recondite subjects as the machinery of papal chancelleries in the thirteenth and fourteenth centuries. Such an awakening to the winds of change by people educated in an Eurocentric tradition should only be welcomed.

That Europe is no longer the center of the world is hardly in dispute any more. The realization of this fact, however, came too abruptly for some who were led to believe that Europe was finished altogether. What did Hitler and even Stalin matter in a world whose history was only to begin? For how could one be blind to the wave of the future personified by Mao and Sukarno, by Nasser, Nkrumah and Ben Bella? Politically and economically the European age was over, and with it the predominance of European values. Culturally, too, Europe had had its day; new peoples were arising, new energies seeking expression, a definite view of life set in conscious counterpoint to the weary disillusion of

Europe. These, at any rate, were Professor Barraclough's conclusions, and he was not alone in holding them. Toynbee rejects Western civilization on the basis of religious-mystic convictions. Barraclough, on the other hand, is a radical, a left-wing liberal. The politics of Frantz Fanon are different again; his rejection of Europe is total.* *The Wretched of the Earth* ends with a passionate appeal to all the downtrodden in the ex-colonial world to leave this Europe where they are never done talking of man yet murder men everywhere they find them:

> The European game has finally ended. . . . We, today, can do everything so long as we do not imitate Europe, so long as we are not obsessed by the desire to catch up with Europe. . . . Europe now lives at such a mad, reckless pace that she has shaken off all guidance and all reason and she is running headlong into the abyss. . . . When I search for Man in the technique and the style of Europe, I see only a succession of negations of man and an avalanche of murders. . . . What we want to do is to go forward all the time, night and day in the company of all men.

The Third World is here assigned the task of starting a new History of Man. The number of these prophets of doom is legion, and they have all seen the writing on the wall: Europe is a spent force, America incurably ill. But despondency is a mood, not a way of life. If the old idols have been shattered, men need new ideals and new gods. For two pre-

---

* "Europe" for Fanon includes the United States: "Two centuries ago a former European colony decided to catch up with Europe. It succeeded so well that the United States of America became a monster, in which the taints, the sickness, the inhumanity of Europe have grown to appalling dimensions." Professor Toynbee would disapprove of the language but likewise regards the United States as an extension of Europe. Barraclough, on the other hand, seems to consider America a case *sui generis*: the positive European heritage (he wrote) has become embedded in both the Russian and American civilizations.

vious generations Soviet Communism was the great beacon illuminating the darkness, showing the road to a better future. But Russia's attraction in the West as the standard-bearer of progress has diminished in the same measure as its economy has advanced. Some former admirers now believe that the price that has been paid for this progress was too high; others find the Soviet preoccupation with production and things material uncongenial, the emergence of a new autocracy and all-powerful bureaucracy distasteful. Others, while not denying the "progressive" character of the Soviet régime if seen against the background of Russian history, doubt the validity of the Russian lesson for the rest of mankind.

During the last decade more and more of the sympathetic attention formerly devoted to Russia has been transferred to China and Indonesia, to Ghana and Guinea, to Algeria and Egypt, and to some other countries attempting against heavy odds to carry out national revolutions on the basis of Marxist-Leninist concepts differently interpreted and applied. It is now believed that only in these countries (to quote Frantz Fanon) is there the opportunity "to do everything," to advance a step further beyond Europe, to learn from the mistakes committed elsewhere, "to bring the problem of mankind to an infinitely higher plane." These régimes have been in existence only for a comparatively brief period, but long enough to draw an interim and tentative balance. It is not too early to ask whether their progress has been encouraging, and to what extent others could benefit from the example set by them.

What lesson can the outside world draw from recent events in China? China has become strongly isolationist, almost entirely preoccupied with internal affairs; it has virtually cut itself off from the outside world. As these lines are written the cultural revolution is still in progress. There is little

doubt that some of the antics of this extra-ordinary movement will be revoked in coming months and years: this is
the dialectic of history. But it has happened, it cannot be
explained away. It took place, not at the beginning of the
Communist era, not during a civil war, but 18 years after
the establishment of Communist China. It came as a
surprise not only to the friends of Communist China, it
surpassed the expectations of its worst enemies. No Sinolo-
gist expected such outbursts; area experts, however critical
of their subject of study, are motivated by a certain ambivalence. In this case they clearly exaggerated not merely the
depth of Mao Tse-tung's thought but the general intellectual
level of Communist China. They overrated (it now appears)
the element of rationality in Communist China—and they
underrated the impact of such elements as obscurantism,
nationalist passions, the struggle for power between various
factions. They were aware that China was economically
backward, but they underrated the extent of *cultural* backwardness in 20th-century China. They read into official pronouncements and speeches hidden meanings and a sophistication that never existed.

Insofar as this second Maoist revolution has a rational
purpose (and it may be wise not to overrate this aspect), it
aims at the perpetuation of the revolutionary fervor of both
the Chinese elite and the masses. This aim can only be
achieved by frequent changes in the leadership on all levels,
by combating specialization and "bureaucratization," and by
preventing the emergence of a "new class," the technical
intelligentsia. There is a certain logic in these aspirations.
Equality, after all, is one of the basic socialist aims even
though historically the most neglected. But the inner contradictions of Maoism are glaring, and, in all probability, self-
defeating. From a Marxist point of view it is a major heresy.
There are, of course, Marxist elements in Maoism, but the
"utopian" element, not to mention the nationalist motivation,

seems to be stronger. The idea that Chinese man (equipped with Mao's thought) can overcome all obstacles, achieve all aims is an attractive one, but what has it in common with a political system concerned with the study of the laws governing historical and social change?

Mao's second revolution is a romantic-idealist movement, a primitive reaction against the trends inherent in a modern industrial society that make it more and more difficult to stick to the way of life established in the case of Yenan during the 1930's. It is interesting that such a movement finds support, temporarily at any rate, among the very young in China. But it conflicts with another basic aim of the Chinese revolution—to modernize the country, to increase industrial and agricultural production, to raise the standard of living. Constant change is the one way to defeat the danger of revisionism in China, whereas the opposite—stability—is the prerequisite for the economic development of the country. Such a movement is unlikely to be more successful than the Luddites; it either adjusts itself to historical forces stronger than itself or it is swept away. There are no precedents for Mao's second revolution, but it can be said on the basis of much historical experience in other parts of the world that movements with a fervent belief in the omnipotence of a great leader and that "everything is possible" often end by pursuing policies very different from, sometimes diametrically opposed to, those they originally set out to accomplish.

The cultural revolution may be a temporary aberration, a setback, from which the country will eventually recover. What has been the balance sheet if we ignore the upheaval and the confusion of 1966–67? On the credit side there is the fact that China is united, that the country received a great national uplift after 1949, that there are few unemployed, that China has produced the bomb. In foreign affairs China has been less successful—perhaps it does not bother; why should a country of 700 million be unduly worried about the opinions and susceptibilities of others? Its foreign policy has been clumsy and arrogant. It has lost ground in the battle for influence in the Communist camp. It has antagonized most of its well-wishers in Asia and Africa, despite the great sympathy for China that originally existed and the "objectively revolutionary situations" in many sections of the Third World. China's promises to give aid and its subsequent default have antagonized even such a well-disposed régime as Castro's. The antics of the "cultural revolutionaries" have made China the butt of ridicule almost everywhere outside Tirana.

What is the internal balance sheet? During the 1950's there was very considerable progress. But the great leap forward ended in a fiasco; about seven years were needed to recover. Broadly speaking, Chinese industry and agriculture were only slightly ahead of where they were a decade before. These estimates do not take into account the effects of the "cultural revolution," the extent of which cannot be assessed for some time to come. Since the population continues to grow at a rapid rate, the standard of living is now no higher than it was 10 years ago. Real earnings in industry and agriculture may have slightly declined since 1958. Chinese industry can only expand on the basis of "primitive accumulation." But agriculture during the next five years will hardly increase at a faster rate than the population. Where will the industrial investment come from? Mao's little red book may be a source of spiritual comfort to many Chinese, but it does not offer an answer to the very basic questions facing the régime. Achievements in nuclear weaponry and the building of missiles are impressive but not matched by similar development in the national economy.

A country of the magnitude of China will always remain a very important factor in world politics, which no one will be able to ignore. The Chinese are patriotic and exceedingly hard working; perhaps they will be able to overcome the present convulsions in a comparatively short period. Given moderately favorable conditions, the Chinese will continue to make headway. But there is no indication at present that it will serve in the forseeable future as a model to anyone outside China, except perhaps by the industry and the dedication of its inhabitants and other such features of national character that antedate 1949.

If we ignore for a moment the "cultural revolution," China has held its own during the last decade. Not so Indonesia. "Is there anything real in Sukarno's Indonesia?" one observer asked shortly before the coup—and the counter-coup of 1966. And he provided this answer: "This huge and heavily armed country full of sound and fury and decay ceased years ago to belong to the world of today." The combination of verbal extremism in foreign affairs, political mysticism, and utter incompetence in domestic affairs which was so typical of Sukarno's rule, created a state of permanent chaos.

Indonesia received considerable aid from both Russia and the West—the foreign debt is $2.7 billion. But foreign aid made no difference in respect to the economic situation; funds were spent on military equipment and prestige buildings the country could ill afford. There was no serious attempt to tackle industrial development or the country's very basic problem: agricultural resettlement. So far, 80 per cent of all Indonesians make their living from agriculture, but 60 per cent of the population is mainly concentrated on the land area of Java. A land redistribution scheme in Java and Madura was passed in 1960, but it provided land for less than 10 per cent of the landless and moreover was inefficiently applied. A real resettlement program would involve the removal of substantial sections from Java to Sumatra and Borneo. But the present resettlement rate is considerably lower than the normal population increase in Java.

Inflation under Sukarno assumed fantastic proportions, the price of rice, for instance, going up six-fold within a few months of 1965.

Meanwhile "Indonesian socialism" was propagated. But beneath its veneer of revolutionary activism (to quote a close observer of the Indonesian scene) there was a deeply conservative policy idealizing a regression toward a natural economy and the social structure of the Javanese village. Basically, Sukarno was far more interested in foreign affairs, where successes (New Guinea) were after all possible—very much in contrast to the domestic front. From Mussolini he adopted the principle of living dangerously *(vivere pericoloso)*. But in Italy the fascist bombast was spread by a régime that, however abominable, somehow functioned. In Indonesia these were just words that had no relation to reality.

Sukarno's personal responsibility was grave; but the failure was also that of a whole élite. The problems inherited from Dutch colonialism were grave; objective conditions such as the demographic structure of the country were, to say the least, not propitious. But was the country bound to fail? There was no inevitable logic in the retreat from rationally coping with the situation to magical incantation. Demagogic politics, human frailty and incompetence caused the breakdown in 1965–66; not predestination. Indonesia, after all, is potentially a rich country. Around the turn of the century it had been the world's main exporter of raw materials. The preconditions for an economic take-off—for primitive accumulation—existed. Indonesia had once been known as the country of Bandung and *pancha sila,* its prestige in the early 1950's had been high. Within a decade, under Sukarno, it had become a textbook illustration of how to ruin a country.

In the 1950's and early 60's, a new political force emerged

—the bloc of the national-revolutionary countries of Asia and Africa. In addition to Sukarno's Indonesia there was Nasser's Egypt, Nkrumah's Ghana, Sekou Touré's Guinea, Ben Bella's Algeria, united in the struggle against imperialism and neo-colonialism. By 1967 this bloc had disintegrated, not merely as the result of outside pressure, but mostly as a consequence of inner weakness. There have been some instances of solidarity such as Sekou Touré's assistance to the fallen Nkrumah. Egypt, in a similar way, showed concern for Ben Bella after his overthrow. Attempts are still being made to reassemble the national revolutionary régimes; but since a chain cannot be stronger than its component links, these efforts are at present not very promising.

Among the leaders of the national revolutionary camp no one enjoyed greater prestige than Ben Bella. His country had won independence after a bitter and heroic seven-year struggle against France. The leaders of the FLN were a group of devoted revolutionaries, a "band of brothers." They had been trained in the French left-wing political school and had a clear anti-capitalist program. Surely, Algeria faced great structural economic and social difficulties which the protracted civil war had aggravated. But on the whole, the state of affairs was not without promise when Ben Bella took over. There existed, owing to French initiative, the basis of a modern industrial infrastructure. The return of almost a million French settlers to France and the seizure of their property enabled the Algerian government to engage almost immediately in a socialistic transformation of agriculture—not on a basis of poverty but on a relatively highly developed level. This was a chance which no other Asian or African country had. Not only were industries nationalized, but also the trade, small hotels, and cinemas. Self-management was introduced in both agriculture and industry.

A year sufficed to show that "socialism" could not be in-

troduced by decree, that the revolutionary phraseology bore
no relation to reality. Within a short time Ben Bella had
deposed, exiled, or imprisoned his erstwhile comrades and
established one-man rule. Within an even shorter time an
enormously inflated, grossly overpaid, and parasitic bureaucratic machine developed which for all practical purposes
ran internal affairs. Production in most industries fell to
about one-third or one-fourth of what it had been before
independence. (Oil production was the one exception but
this was entirely in French hands.) Output in agriculture
fell, especially of wine which is so vital a product for export. (Ben Bella nevertheless declared that Algeria was an
advanced country, that self-government in Algerian agriculture was more progressive than in Yugoslavia!) The net
agricultural revenue which had been over 100 billion fr. in
1961 fell to 10 billion fr, in 1964.

At the same time Ben Bella decided (to quote his successor) simply for reasons of personal prestige to spend 15
billion fr. on the Afro-Asian Conference that was to be held
in Algiers in 1965. While pursuing political schemes far
beyond the power of his country, both in the Maghreb and
all over tropical Africa, his government neglected elementary social reforms at home; unemployment in Algeria was
estimated between 60 per cent (Soviet sources) and 80 per
cent (Western observers) of the total labor force. Again, it
cannot be too strongly stressed that disaster was not inevitable. It was the result of theoretical confusion, of demagoguery and verbal radicalism, of a régime in which there
was far more corruption than sincere will to build a new
society. About Ben Bella's political orientation his successor
has said: "For him socialism was only a means to avenge
himself on those who opposed his personal power. One day
he would proclaim Castro's type of socialism; the next day
he would call himself an Algerian socialist; on other occasions a Muslim socialist. . . ."

Ben Bella set out to realize his aims in a particularly inept way. But the schemes themselves were unrealistic. A meaningful socialist transformation is impossible with an intelligentsia lacking the technical know-how as well as patriotic spirit and selfless devotion to serve the country. There were individuals, some of them known, others nameless and faceless, who were inspired by genuine idealism, even if their ideas all too often turned out to be mere chimeras whenever they collided with the harsh realities. But by and large it was an unedifying rush by a new élite to escape austerity, to establish itself as a privileged class, materially as well as politically.

The story of Nkrumah is not dissimilar to that of Ben Bella or Sukarno: a national leader of strong if confused left-wing convictions acquired genuine respect and admiration in the struggle for the independence of his country, but whose subsequent rule had disastrous consequences. There is in some ways more ideological consistency in Nkrumah than in Sukarno or Ben Bella. He began as a Christian Socialist but moved steadily toward fairly orthodox Leninism (Marxism-Nkrumahism) adapted by him for African conditions.

Nkrumah's ideas have been developed in his two most recent books *Consciencism* (including an attempt to describe "positive action" in mathematical formulas) and *Neo-Colonialism*. In these books Dr. Nkrumah comments at length on philosophical questions, on world affairs and world economics in general, and on the need for African unity. He hardly ever deals with his own country's problems; the Ghanaian stage clearly was not big enough for him.

Nkrumah was handed over by the British colonial administrators a country that, with all the ill effects of colonial rule, was the most developed in tropical Africa. It had the highest literacy rate by far. It received very substantial sterling holdings. But it also inherited an agriculture geared largely to monoculture and thus subject to the vagaries of world prices. (210,000 tons of cocoa in 1954–55 yielded Ghana about $240 millions; 590,000 tons ten years later actually yielded Ghana less—about $210 million.)

Instead of lessening this dangerous dependence on cocoa crop exports by diversifying agricultural production, Nkrumah's government encouraged new planting which eventually led to flooding the world market. The state farms turned out badly. While 32 big state corporations were established in industry, trade, and communications, all but one steadily lost substantial money; mining and the timber industry contracted. At the same time tremendous sums were spent on prestige projects such as Nkrumah statues, sports grounds, and conference halls for meetings with African heads of state. Many millions were allocated to promoting Nkrumah's prestige abroad and the training of political agents to be used in other parts of Africa, in pursuance of ambitious schemes for a pan-African government. The cost of living rose by 30 per cent in one year, financial resources were dissipated; holdings of about $600 million when the country attained independence in 1957 had turned into a debt of fantastic size when Nkrumah fell in February 1966.*

Not all this money had been squandered by mismanagement and corruption, though the famous golden bed of Mrs. Edusei was certainly not an exceptional case. Ghana

---

* The extent of the debt (and the general plight of the country) became known only after Nkrumah's fall. The misinformation about the real state of affairs in Ghana was to a considerable extent the fault of certain European and American residents—journalists, scholars, and others—unfortunately a recurrent phenomenon in many African and Asian countries. Journalists and scholars are admittedly under indirect pressure not to publish unfavorable reports about their area of study. Any violation of this unwritten rule may cause their *expulsion,* and thus cut them off from the subject of their specialization. As a result, the coverage of the African and Asian scene both on the scholarly and the journalistic level is often unreliable.

had been the pace setter for tropical Africa before 1957, and it tried to live up to its reputation after independence. Nkrumah's government built many new roads and did much to develop education in Ghana. There was a real attempt to industrialize the country, and achievements such as the Volta dam scheme ought to be mentioned. The little fishing village Tema was transformed into a big modern harbor. But most of the development schemes were undertaken in the mistaken assumption that the outside world would pay for them in the end.

What is, or was, Nkrumahism?

In his saner moments Nkrumah realized that without the transformation of Ghana into a strong industrialized economy and society, "socialism" would remain a slogan and all talk of socialist progress empty chatter. And he also understood that one could not build socialism without socialists. But instead of concentrating on the basic tasks, he engaged in overambitious schemes in many directions at one and the same time. Not a very brave man at the best of times, he isolated himself in his castle, became the "Redeemer" depicted together with Jesus Christ—the man who would live forever. He surrounded himself with self-seeking courtiers and established a dictatorial regime that antagonized the country's technical intelligentsia.

Conor Cruise O'Brien wrote that proportionately no African country had more of such people than Ghana and none lost more. Those who left or gave up did so not because they were anti-socialist or pro-colonialist—"on the contrary, they had contributed more than their share to the real progress which Ghana has made—but they experienced conditions in which it proved increasingly difficult to work effectively." The official model was a strong, disciplined party, with "democratic centralism" as its guiding principle of organization and leadership. In fact, the one-party system was simply a means to communicate commands from the top leadership to the masses—and not a very efficient and reliable means at that, as the crumbling of the party after Nkrumah's fall has shown. Only then did it emerge how little idealism and genuine conviction there had been behind the staged mass adulation of the great leader and his invincible party, how narrow his "mass basis." Nkrumah was motivated by a strange mixture of "scientific socialism" and black magic (his trust in Kankan fetishes and, to a certain extent, in witchcraft).

There was nothing specifically left-wing about this regime; one political observer has said that Nkrumah possessed more of the hysteria of Hitler and the vanity of Mussolini than of the cold genius of Lenin. Nkrumahist Ghana was "an ideological state without an ideology, a one-party dictatorship without a party." The rise of the régime meant in sociological terms the "eclipse of a bourgeoisie *manqué* by a new petty bourgeoisie of the new municipalities and local market centers" (Dennis Austin). Nkrumahism was an "indiscriminate hotch-potch of sadly familiar concepts, usually ludicrously exaggerated and invariably unsuited to Ghanaian realities. The parentage of most items is easily recognizable; manic industrialization for its own sake; the glorification of autarchy and self-help; the official slogan of 'One leader, one Party, one Nation'; the egregious cult of personality; the abuse of Western plutocracy, the doctrine of proletarian nations." (T. Szamuely)

Almost every African country has made socialism its declared policy and everyone agrees that boundless confusion has been created as the result of the indiscriminate and, on the whole, misplaced application of a Western term to African realities. "All kinds of strange notions are peddled in many parts of Africa as to the nature of a socialist society," a British Communist has written. There is Muslim socialism, Arab socialism, Neo-Destour socialism, pragmatic socialism (in Nigeria), African socialism, and so forth. But if modern history has had any lessons at all, it is that socialism presupposes a fairly high level of development—social, economic, and political. In its absence all talk about a socialist society is either meaningless or a perversion of the term.

African countries, especially those which have inscribed revolutionary socialism on their banners, have learned this to their detriment. Congo-Brazzaville, for instance, is extremely radical; it follows a pro-Chinese foreign policy, but there is nothing revolutionary about the domestic policy of a government whose power is based exclusively on a palace guard of several hundred men, many of them foreigners.

Guinea engaged in an ambitious socialist experiment in 1959–60, promising a rate of growth superior to the Soviet Union and China. Illusory plans were drawn up which failed within a very short time. Most of the national Guinean companies that had been established went bankrupt or were dissolved. Those who prepared the plans were not all aware what kind of effort was needed to carry them out. French observers of the Left (René Dumont and Charles Bettelheim) have noted the extreme disparity between the institutional superstructures and the degree of political morality: "Guineans have not been willing to bend themselves to the efforts and discipline necessary to carry out the measures they adopted even when they were advised by Communist countries (whose nationals have left Guinea quite discouraged). . . ." These are strong warnings, all the more telling, because they came from close friends and sympathizers. "To some extent, a lack of knowledge can be compensated for by complete honesty and vice versa; but a country cannot do without both."

The preconditions for development in Mali were somewhat better than in Guinea because its leaders had a better grasp of economic problems and because the peasants of

Mali are among the most industrious and progressive in West Africa. However, to quote Dumont again, "when political leaders and particularly civil servants, address the Mali peasants, they give them orders in much the same way as the colonial administrators do. They do not understand rural problems and therefore cannot help the peasants efficiently." The result has been stagnation in agriculture (with the exception of cotton production which has been boosted at very high cost) and very small advance in industry.

Tanzania was one of the more hopeful countries of Eastern Africa. Like Guinea and Mali it has a one-party system and the economic sector has been gradually nationalized; about 75 per cent of the exports are government controlled. Yet the country is beset by the same difficulties as the other "socialist" African countries; considerable—and growing—unemployment, shortage of materials, allocation of resources to unproductive purposes, lack of trained personnel. True, the population is treated to radical socialist speeches and ambitious plans as if these had any bearing on reality. As in most other African countries, enormous sums are squandered on prestige projects, expensive embassies abroad, the latest models of aircraft, etc. Far more money is spent on administration than on productive development. President Nyerere has called for hard work and austerity on the Chinese pattern, but the local élite has shown a marked lack of enthusiasm in following this appeal.

Compared with Algeria, Ghana, and Guinea, Nasser's Egypt (the United Arab Republic) was, with all its weaknesses, a model of purposeful achievement. From a position of a somewhat vague "Arab socialism" President Nasser had moved toward a platform of "scientific socialism." All the main industries and the banks were nationalized in the early 60's; agricultural reform, which began hesitatingly in the middle 50's, has been speeded up. Cooperatives have been developed in the Egyptian village, work on the Assuan dam was completed in time. The rate of growth in key industries, in mining and oil production has been substantial over the last few years. Yet despite this progress Egypt found itself in a state of permanent crisis even before Nasser tried his luck in brinkmanship. Most of the progress was achieved owing to massive economic help (both aid and free gifts) from West and East. The country has vastly overspent, its foreign currency reserves are exhausted, and this in turn has caused stoppage of work in certain industries. Since Egypt is unlikely to receive such huge gifts in the future, and since the war with Israel was also an economic catastrophe, its crisis has immeasurably deepened. The cost of living has risen rapidly, much faster than productivity. The population explosion continues, the cotton crop is mortgaged on arms sales for years to come.

Some of the reasons are, for the time being, beyond human control; Egypt is one of the poorest countries in the world. The odds facing Egypt in this respect are much heavier than those which the other, more primitive African countries have to overcome. Yet, Egypt has been, of course, all along far more developed: it never really was a colony. It has technical experts in almost all fields needed, so much so that it exports teachers to many Arab and African countries.

Some of the setbacks can be explained by miscalculation and over-ambitious schemes on the part of the government, lack of enthusiasm and willingness to work on the part of the masses. Like other Asian and African leaders, Nasser had tried to play a role in world politics out of proportion to the real strength of his country. The unsuccessful attack by Britain and France in 1956 gave him enormous political credit, which in some ways has lasted to this day. On the other hand, there have been severe setbacks in the Sudan, in tropical Africa, and Yemen; it is too early to say whether anything may come of the schemes to unite the Arab world under Egyptian leadership. The outcome of the war with Israel, deliberately provoked by him, has shown all the weaknesses of a régime, the inner strength of which had been grossly overrated by many outside observers.

Basically, Egypt is as poor as it was, though poverty has been spread more evenly. Economics apart, to what extent has Egypt under Nasser advanced toward a socialist and democratic society? The attempts to establish a state party, never very energetically tackled, have not been successful: the country has been ruled by a new class, army officers (including those who were subsequently given civilian assignments), and the secret police. Among the bureaucracy and the intelligentsia there are conflicting trends: Islamic, orthodox Communist—and those favoring Marxism-Nasserism, *i.e.*, "military socialism" which has absorbed economic and social techniques from Leninism and which in foreign affairs steers close to the Soviet camp but socially is no nearer to Soviet Communism than to France under Napoleon III or to Fascist Italy. Following the defeat in the war and the ouster of so many officers who had to serve as scapegoats, the mass basis of the régime has further narrowed. Since no Egyptian ruler can be certain of the loyalty of the new class, he has to rule through his party— which hardly exists as an effective body—and, to an increasing degree, through the police. Egypt under Nasser was a more modern state than it was under Farouk and the Pashas 20 years ago. If there is a harsher dictatorship and less political freedom now than two decades ago, it is difficult to see how any semblance of parliamentary democracy could have prevailed under any effective régime. The bulk of the population, vegetating on subsistence level, totally incapable of influencing politics in Cairo, has not basically changed since Farouk—the people have no more at stake in this country than their ancestors 50 or 200 years ago. Under Nasser, Egypt has survived; but it is grotesque to think that this police-socialism, now wholly dependent on outside help, could or should serve as a model for any other country.

An interim balance sheet of the 60's of the national revolutionary régimes of the Third World shows, to put it cautiously, that the expectations of some of their prophets mentioned here have not or not yet been realized. It is one thing for the *literati* of St. Germain des Prés (and their colleagues in other parts of the world) to declare that the Third World is starting a new history of man. But facts, as Lenin among others used to observe, are a stubborn thing. Facts and figures show that the industrialized countries of the West (including, of course, Eastern Europe) have forged ahead, while the distance between them and the national revolutionary régimes of Asia and Africa has widened, not lessened.

Seen from this angle there are no major differences between the national-revolutionary régimes of Asia and Africa and those that do not proclaim a radical-nationalist policy; the problems of backwardness are common to all of them. Comparisons are always risky and often unfair; if other North African countries have done better than Algeria, it is only fair to add that Algeria, regardless of its political system, faces greater problems than its neighbors. If, on the other hand, the performance of China is compared with the mounting crisis in India, the reason is not merely, and probably not mainly, the greater inefficiency of a democratic government. Geographical, climatic, and historical factors are at least of equal importance. Can one reasonably expect labor productivity in a tropical country like India to be equal to that in a moderate climate? Indonesia and Algeria under Sukarno and Ben Bella have failed, but not simply as a result of their national-revolutionary and quasi-Marxist orientation; generalizations along these lines are almost impossible because conditions vary so much from country to country. But it can no more be doubted that what was hailed as a panacea—namely radical slogans—has, by and large, not worked better than other forms of government. The general trend in Asia and Africa is toward military dictatorship. Some observers have regarded this as a retrograde step, others welcomed what they consider the "progressive character of military socialism." The truth is simpler; when civilian rule breaks down, the military remains as the only force capable of preventing chaos. Military rule which seems likely to prevail in Asia and Africa for a very long time is thus an *ultima ratio*. It is hardly the dawn of a new civilization that Fanon or Sartre imagined.*

Since these developments come as a disappointment to everyone, their causes ought to be discussed frankly and dispassionately. Some have already been mentioned; they are "objective" in character—geographical and climatic. So far, industrial societies have developed only in the moderate regions of the northern hemisphere and they were not plagued by a population explosion at the time of their take-off. With further technological progress this handicap may eventually be overcome, but this may take many decades if not centuries. Nature has made Egypt much poorer than Kuwait (so long as petroleum is needed), or than Syria and Iraq. Given the nation-state, inequality will persist. Nor is

---

* There is little sense in discussing in this context other predictions that are manifestly absurd—such as the assumption that Asian and African society would be regenerated by a series of peasant wars, more or less on the Chinese model. That such *Jacqueries* may occur is extremely likely and they may be wholly justified. They may possibly be successful in one country or another owing to local conditions. But the idea that they will be able to achieve anything other than a redistribution of agricultural property is fanciful. Even in China, where the peasants provided the mass basis of a revolutionary movement, it has ended, it would seem, in a military dictatorship. Populist ideas have their attractions, but they are even less relevant now than 100 years ago.

there much point in blaming neo-colonialism for the failing prices of raw materials on the world markets; world demand for most commodities is limited and cannot be artificially boosted. Something ought to be done to remedy the situation—but it is a problem likely to recur regardless of the world order.

There has been a strong inclination in Asia and Africa to blame colonialism and neo-colonialism for most, if not all, the present misfortunes. Much emotion is involved and it is difficult to separate myth from reality. That the colonial situation was an unnatural and an immoral one goes without saying. Nor does one have to repeat the whole register of colonialist crimes of commission and omission. Perhaps the most fatal omission was the failure of the colonialist powers in education—with the result that in the Belgian Congo or Indonesia, for instance, there was hardly a native intelligentsia at all to take over when these countries became independent. And in most other countries the élite was deficient both in number and quality. The political failure of Asia and Africa is therefore to a large extent the responsibility of the West.

But the proponents of the new Afro-Asian ideology go much further. They claim that the Western powers have exploited Asia and Africa all along, that modern societies in the West could only be established on the basis of this stolen wealth of the colonies. The riches of London and Paris belong therefore to the damned of the earth as well as to Englishmen and Frenchmen. Western economic aid is therefore simply a partial restitution of stolen property. These are sweeping claims, but do the facts bear them out? That the colonial powers did not acquire colonies for humanitarian reasons need hardly be elaborated, and that individuals and companies have greatly enriched themselves from them is undeniable. But in the overall balance and from a Western point of view, colonies were a prestige operation, and an expensive one at that—most of them cost the metropolitan country more than they contributed to its wealth, especially during the last 50 years.

The economics of the former European colonial powers were not ruined as a result of the loss of colonies; they prospered more than ever before. According to the classical theory of imperialism, colonies were needed by the metropolitan countries for the export of capital and the import of raw materials. The first part of the formula is not true— Western capital has never been really attracted by the colonies. And to obtain raw materials in the modern world there are cheaper ways than the establishment of colonies. The most telling charge against the Western imperialist countries is not that they robbed Asia and Africa, but that they prevented indigenous economic development.

But would these countries be more highly developed today if there had not been Western domination? The answer is by no means clear. It is in the self-interest of the West to help the countries of Asia and Africa transform themselves economically and politically into viable countries. Much of the economic aid given during the last two decades has for a variety of reasons not had the intended effect; but this is no reason at all to discontinue it. The new Afro-Asian ideology, however, is dangerous because it tries to provide the ideological justification for what is, not to mince words, a parasitical relationship, as harmful in the long run for the self-respect of the Asian and African peoples as was the colonial relationship. It has, above all, the effect of blinding the countries, and especially their élites, to their own responsibility for the present shortcomings and failures.

The Asian and African élites are overwhelmingly "socialist" in political aspiration. Yet even the most sympathetic outside observers have had to admit that more often than not this is based on the assumption that a radical socialist phraseology is sufficient to build a socialist society. That there is a relationship between socialism and work is not at all clear to those who believe that a revolution is like a magic table in the fairy tale. In the private life of these people, revolutionary phraseology is often coupled with a horror of work and an exaggerated urge for the good things in life. In this respect the African and Asian revolutionaries could no doubt learn from the Chinese example but for the fact that Peking's motivations seem not to have been altogether altruistic. (Potentially dangerous intellectuals have been sent to work in the communes; one has not heard of the party *apparatchiks* taking part in similar exercise.)

This is not to say that the national revolutionary régimes ought to copy Sparta or the Puritans in every detail. But unless there is some work ethos, unless these élites begin to understand that socialism is not only high-flown oratory but that it has some direct bearing on their own lives, that selfless devotion, sacrifice, and hard work are needed, they will not make any real progress. Unless they give up their aspiration of a life of luxury, all the talk and all the literature about socialism and socialist society will remain meaningless phrase-mongering.

(1967)

THE WORLD AND
MR. BARRACLOUGH

WHOEVER wishes to write history, Martin Luther once said, must have the heart of a lion. Geoffrey Barraclough is one of the bravest of the brave. A medievalist by training, he has written a long essay on the course of global history in our times.* In it he covers, to name but a few of his topics, the impact of scientific and technological advance, the rise of mass democracy, demographic developments, the role of Marxism-Leninism in West and East, alienation, the African personality, T. S. Eliot and Kafka, Schoenberg and Mondrian. It is, in brief, the kind of subject which in this age of the narrow specialist few historians would dare to tackle.

Mr. Barraclough puts up a very sensible case for the writing of contemporary history, which is not, as so many historians believe, a newfangled notion, a subject of doubtful provenance and uncertain academic standing. This prejudice evolved only in the late 19th century; almost all great historians from Thucydides to Ranke wrote contemporary history without any doubts or qualms of conscience. What in our age is meant by "contemporary history"? Most historians think contemporary history should begin in 1918—or at most in 1914—but Barraclough believes that the watershed lies

---

* Geoffrey Barraclough. *An Introduction to Contemporary History* (1965).

further back: many current problems can be traced back to the 1890's.

I find this point of view convincing and I sympathize equally with the author's criticism of those fellow historians who are more concerned with continuity than with change in the modern world, perhaps because they believe that all change is change for the worse, and who are more preoccupied with the disintegration of old attitudes and patterns than with the formation of new ones.

Mr. Barraclough's central argument is that contemporary history, in the strict sense of the phrase, (i.e. "post-modern history"), begins at the end of 1960 or at the beginning of 1961. At about this time there was a decisive break with the past, even more important than the one in the 1890's. Power in the United States passed into the hands of a generation that had not been conditioned by pre-War experiences; in the Soviet Union the change that had taken place since the death of Stalin had reached the stage of crystallization; the conflict between Russia and China introduced a new element into world affairs, and there were throughout Asia and Africa the tremendous economic and political problems of independence.

This new era, Mr. Barraclough maintains, is marked by the collapse of Europe, which "counts for less now than at any time during the last four-hundred years." It is marked at the same time by the rise of the "emergent forces" to a place of new dignity in the world. In contrast with the old political systems, the weary spirit of dissolution and the general cultural fatigue of Europe there are "new people arising, new energies seeking expression, a definite view of life set in conscious counterpoint to that of Europe." According to Mr. Barraclough, we have witnessed the end of the European age which extended from 1492 to 1947 and with it the end of the predominance of the old European scale of values. It is being replaced not by a new "'Atlantic era," but by a new age in which all the continents will play their parts and in which the chief impulses will come from outside Europe (and the Americas).

At this point we have moved from the realm of contemporary history to that of noble fantasy. That World politics and European politics are no longer identical has been common knowledge for some time. Nor has it escaped our attention, as Mr. Barraclough seems to think, that all but a handful of former colonies have become independent, that the United Nations now has a neutralist majority and that China has about 700 million inhabitants.

Since the early years of the century, whole libraries have been written about the great and growing importance of Africa and Asia. The efforts of the "emergent forces" to build up their countries ought to be followed with sympathy. But neither the cause of historical truth nor that of the emergent nations will be served by fanciful statements about their economic prospects, their cultural promise and their political futures.

Europe has been written off many times before but it has shown a surprising power of recovery. (My own concept of Europe is admittedly somewhat broader than Mr. Barraclough's; it includes the Americas and, ultimately, the Soviet Union.) Culturally, its pull on the rest of the world is at present stronger than ever before.

When Mr. Barraclough talks about the "collapse of traditional forms of art, and a wave of experimentation in every branch of artistic expression"—what does he have in mind but ancient, degenerate Europe? I am not aware of a "wave of experimentation" in China, Russia or perhaps Indonesia. When he mentions the breakthrough in scientific knowledge, the increase in productivity—where has this been achieved but in America and in Europe? The renewed stress which

Eastern Europe and the Soviet Union are placing on the common European heritage is one of the most significant trends in recent years. To deny these peoples their stake in Europe is now the worst insult one can inflict on them. The talk about the teeming millions of Asia, and about the demographic "dwarfing of Europe" sounds very impressive even if Mr. Barraclough adds, as an afterthought, that the significance of mere size is often disputed. I wonder whether he has discussed the social and economic complications of a population explosion with those in authority in Peking, Cairo, and New Delhi. Mr. Barraclough also thinks that technical skills and productivity are easy to transfer from one country to another. We all wish this were true, but most economists, I suspect, will not agree with the author.

No one in the West, to the best of my knowledge, spends sleepless nights out of fear that Indonesia and Egypt might catch up with us. The real danger surely is that the backward countries may fall back even further behind the developed countries of the northern hemisphere. Mr. Barraclough, in brief, greatly underrates the extent of the present and future impact of the West on the rest of the world. So far as there is no retreat into chaos and neo-barbarism among the newly emergent nations, Western political ideas, Western cultural impulses, Western scientific and technological discoveries will be the agents of progress in the foreseeable future.

Mr. Barraclough's *tour de force* is based on much erudition and a wealth of reading. His is a challenging book and interest never flags even though its central themes are unconvincing. I hope it will not strengthen the fashionable neglect of Europe in American social studies, in which, I am told, support can be received for almost any project if it pertains to a continent other than Europe. The unhappy, old-fashioned few who pursue their European interests cannot now even publish their studies. There are many periodicals on Africa and Asia, on Russia and the Far East, but there is at this moment not a single journal devoted to present-day Europe. Soon it will be the turn of some Columbus in reverse to initiate a crash program for the rediscovery of that neglected and, I still think, most promising of continents.

TWO AGES OF
CONFUSION

TO UNDERSTAND their own troubled times, to find comfort and guidance, men and women always look to the past. The American revolutionaries turned to 17th century England, the militants of 1793 drew inspiration from revolutionary episodes in Roman history, the 19th-century decadents were fascinated by the decline of the Roman Empire. Such immersion in the past is only partly motivated by a thirst for knowledge. At least equally strong is the desire to find proofs and arguments to support political beliefs already held. As Anatole France said about one of his heroes that he looks in the history books only for the *sottises* which he already knows. But the invocation of the spirit of the past is no less interesting for the special myth-making involved.

Seen in this context, the growing attention paid in America in recent years to the culture and politics of modern Germany between the defeat in World War I and Hitler's accession to power is not surprising. It was a fascinating period in almost every respect; but this is not why it figures so prominently in recent discussion. Some writers have detected striking parallels with present-day America; but even those who deny this feel sufficiently troubled to devote much time and effort to disprove these analogies. For the debate is a manifestation of deep *malaise*, common appar-

ently to both ages, and reflected in the disintegration of
established authority, the contempt shown for the "system",
the cult of violence, unreason, and intolerance, the belief
that almost any political and social order would be preferable to the present, and the alienation of large numbers
of the young generation.

This is not to say that the political situation in America
today resembles that of Germany after 1918. Germany had
been defeated in war, the Kaiser had been expelled, a harsh
peace treaty had deprived the country of substantial parts
of its territory and had imposed reparations which it was
clearly unable to pay. Power was at first in the hands of
the Social Democrats, but at no time did they have an absolute majority. Nationalist passions were running high, millions of Germans were firmly convinced that their armies,
victorious in the field of battle, had been "stabbed in the
back" by the enemy within. The confidence gained in the
years of normality after the currency breakdown of 1922–23
was destroyed by the impact of the world economic crisis
(1929–32), and support for the radical parties of the Left
and the Right became overwhelming. Their mounting
strength effectively paralysed the democratic process. Both
Left and Right referred with utter contempt to an outmoded
liberalism which did not express the popular will, to the
rottenness of parliament, the sickness of society. "In the
liberal man German youth sees the enemy *par excellence*",
wrote Moeller van den Bruck, who coined the phrase "the
Third Reich." Most students favored a socialism of sorts
and demanded the overthrow of *das System;* many of their
elders were proud of their fighting spirit and their revolutionary ardor. There were some dissenting voices. In a
speech in October 1930 Thomas Mann warned against the
new wave of barbarism, fanaticism and ecstasy, the monotonous repetition of slogans "until everyone was foaming
at the mouth." Mann with all his scepticism had grown up

in the humanist school of the nineteenth century with its optimistic view of human nature and of progress; to him and others of his generation the retreat from reason seemed not only utterly abhorrent but totally inexplicable.

The political history of the Weimar Republic is a tale of almost unmitigated woe; culturally, with all its tensions and despair, it was a fertile period, a "new Periclean age" (as a contemporary called it). These were the sound years of the revolutionary theater and the avant-garde cinema, of psycho-analysis and steel furniture, of modern sociology and sexual permissiveness. It was a time of exciting new ideas and cultural experimentation, of the youth movement and youth culture. German literature and the arts, the humanities and science, were generally considered the most advanced and most authoritative in Europe. Christopher Isherwood's Berlin appeared to be the most exciting city in the world.

Weimar culture had an impact that outlasted the Third Reich and can easily be discerned in America today. The rediscovery of Bert Brecht and Hermann Hesse, of George Grosz, the *Bauhaus,* and Dr. Caligari, of psycho-analysis and modern Marxism (to mention only some of the more fashionable imports) are obvious cases in point. Certain cultural parallels are almost uncanny: the chic radicalism of New York clearly evokes memories of the drawing-room communism of Berlin-West. The phenomenal revival of astrology and various quasi-religious cults, the great acclaim given to prophets of doom, the success of highly marketable *Weltschmerz* in literature and philosophy, the spread of pornography and the use of drugs, the appearance of charlatans of every possible description and the enthusiastic audiences welcoming them—all these are common to both periods. Yet at this point the resemblance ends, for with all its perversities Weimar culture had a creativeness and a depth without equal in present-day American radical culture (and counter-culture), which is largely eclectic and second-hand. The difference in the general cultural level, to put it bluntly, can be measured by the distance between *Portnoy's Complaint* and *The Magic Mountain.* This is all the more remarkable since what is now commonly defined as "Weimar culture" was produced (and consumed) by a small group of people; some tens of thousands, rather than the millions who today constitute the American intelligentsia.

Political comparisons between the Weimar Republic and contemporary America are not, as I have said, very helpful. The United States was not defeated in a world war; aggressive nationalism and revanchism are not the main issues at stake today; democracy in America is not a foreign importation of recent date, as it was in Germany after 1918, where it failed to strike roots. The extreme Right in America is not a great dynamic force, and racialism is on the retreat. The American crisis, such as it is, is not the result of the major economic crisis; on the contrary, it is the outcome of a long period of unprecedented prosperity. And yet with all the differences Germany serves as a useful object lesson in one vital respect: to show what happens in a country where reason abdicates, where democratic authority disintegrates, and political freedom is sacrificed as those who should know better are afflicted by a failure of nerve.

The German radical intelligentsia of the Left showed little wisdom in face of the Nazi onslaught. Following the Communist lead, they regarded the Socialists, not the Nazis, as their main enemy. They claimed (as some of their American successors do now) that there was "no basic difference" between fascism and liberal democracy. In 1931, when Germany was a parliamentary democracy, they asserted that fascism was already in power, so that as far as they were concerned Hitler's take-over came as an anti-climax. The German Left-wing intelligentsia (unlike the French) jettisoned in its politics not only patriotism—which by itself would have been suicidal—but too often common sense as well. The main weakness of the moderate Socialist and the German liberals was that they lacked not just inspired leadership, but the courage of their convictions. They were incapable of decisive action when the advent of fascism could still have been averted. Unlike the Nazis and the Communists, they had no ideas, no faith or promise to offer to the young generation, only the sober, reasonable, unemotional, and tired explanation that democracy was probably the least oppressive of all political systems. This was not very satisfactory for a young generation in search of the Holy Grail. The German democrats, of whom in any case, there were not too many, suffered from a paralysis of the will to survive.

Individual Jews took a prominent part in the radical movement of the Left. Some were in key positions in the mass media and suffered from the delusion that their calling was to act as the conscience of the nation—as they understood it. They never realized how much out of tune they were with the mood of the nation. Having lost their own moorings in history, dissociating themselves from the Jewish community but not fully accepted by the Germans either, it was easy for them to deride national symbols—always, of course, on behalf of a great messianic idea. The majority of their co-religionists had nothing to do with them, but in the eyes of the public they represented the urge to negation and destruction, and their tactless behavior increased the latent anti-semitism. Lacking political instinct, they did not realize that they were harming the very cause they wanted so much to promote. In the end even the extreme Left deserted them.

The Right-wing intelligentsia behaved disgracefully at its time of trial. Communist workers and monarchist landowners occasionally showed courageous resistance, but only a handful of intellectuals opposed Hitler. There were still many simple, uneducated people in Nazi Germany whose scale of moral values had not been perverted and who felt in their bones that Nazism was evil and that there would indeed be a day of reckoning. The young intellectuals, on the other hand, trained to provide an ideological apologia for every abomination, were in the vanguard of the Nazi movement. Hitler's party won a majority in most universities well before it gained strength in the country at large. The clamor for a "political university," teaching only one political doctrine, met no resistance from weak-kneed professors and administrators. The old humanist traditions and the idea of the inalienable rights of men were rejected as irrelevant. The conformism which overtook the academic world was frightening; the great majority plunged into "the wave of the future", some out of cowardice and opportunism, others from sincere conviction.

Having said all this, one must point to certain extenuating circumstances which explain, though they do not excuse, this weakness and confusion. Germany was facing a crisis of unprecedented magnitude. Since 1914 it had experienced only five years of relative stability and prosperity (1924–29). In 1932 industrial production was only 60% of what it had been three years previously, and more than one-third of the labor force was out of work. The government seemed utterly unable to deal with the crisis, and the conviction rapidly gained ground that only a strong leader could save the country from chaos. The German intelligentsia was numerically small and politically uninfluential; Hitler would have come to power whatever its behavior.

After 1945 those who had voted for Hitler disclaimed all responsibility. They had meant (or so they pleaded) to support a movement of national and social revival, not a terrorist régime and a relapse into barbarism. How could they possibly have known what Nazism in practice would be like? Equally those who supported Communism in 1930 could claim that the Soviet experiment, still in its early stages, was much more promising than the movements for piece-meal reform. The realization of Lenin's dream of a revolution that aimed not merely to seize political power but to share it among the people, a vision of a far more progressive and democratic system, seemed just around the corner. Four decades and a dozen revolutions later, history has shown that the outcome of any attempt to establish a socialist régime which by-passes democracy, is bound to be a dictatorship, oppressive, fundamentally reactionary in character, and not unrelated to fascism.

The last years of the Weimar Republic were a period of almost unmitigated gloom. But there is, I believe, one basic difference between 1932 in Central Europe and present-day America. Whereas the German disease was immanent and in all probability incurable, the confusion and loss of balance in America are, in my view, to a large extent self-inflicted. There are, to be sure, serious problems: Vietnam, the race question, the growing realization that traditional liberalism may no longer have the answer to the problems besetting the country. But serious problems are not usually solved by apocalyptic predictions about Babylon the Great, the mother of harlots and abominations.* The retreat from reason is gathering strength; a distinguished Princeton professor recently wrote in an equally distinguished journal that the moderate majority on campus now sees the world in much the same way as it was seen by the New Left only

---

* The language of American radical literature, let it be noted in passing, seems to owe more to the *Revelation* of St. John the Divine than to the *Communist Manifesto*.

a short while ago. It has absorbed many of the New Left's ideas but has impatiently pushed the SDS leaders to one side, rejecting their tired rhetoric. Which takes us right back into the world of the German cinema of the early 1920s, to the dreams of Dr. Caligari and Dr. Mabuse, of lunatic asylums where the psychiatrists take on the role of the psychotics, determined to show what learned madmen are capable of doing provided they jettison restraint and good sense.

Periods of grave mental confusion are less infrequent in history than is commonly thought, and they have to be studied with detachment and sympathy rather than with anger and moral indignation. Intellectuals are not necessarily the most reliable guides in such unhappy periods. By long tradition they are second to none in their sensitivity to the inequities of the world. At the same time many of them lead a sheltered life. Even the students of society and politics among the academics all too often have little contact with real life; questions about next year's curriculum are the most important they have to decide. In their seclusion there is a constant temptation to devise political constructions firmly rooted in mid-air, in which everything seems possible, in which governments and political authority in general are replaced by communes of free and equal individuals, in which society exists without repression, and domestic policies require no sanctions, diplomats always tell the truth and nothing but the truth, and a foreign policy is pursued in which the wolf lies down with the lamb, and the leopard with the kid, all presumably under the strict supervision of Professor Noam Chomsky. Such utopianism may be needed as a corrective to the cynicism of the professional politicians and to unthinking conservativism. But once the divorce from reality becomes too pronounced, the results are ludicrous or dangerous, or both. Nowhere is this danger greater than in America, which has never accepted Max Weber's memorable dictum, namely, that he who seeks the salvation of the soul, his own and others, should not seek it along the avenue of politics, for whoever engages in politics lays himself open to the diabolical forces lurking in all violence.

The present wave of cultural discontent and protest has appeared in all democratic countries, but some societies are more vulnerable than others. Certain causes are sociological; the expansion of the universities with a heavy preponderance on subjects which no longer prepare their students for any specific job in society, the emergence of the intelligentsia as a class with its own unfulfilled ambitions in the struggle for political power. Some aspects of the present unrest are familiar to students of youth movements (of which fascism incidentally was also one). Others confirm the findings of those who have investigated the pattern of aggression found among young adolescents in society, both primitive and modern.*

Beyond these general features there are some specific ones which make America especially vulnerable. Measured by absolute standards, America is no doubt full of repression: compared with other periods and countries it is one of the freest societies that have ever existed. It faces enormous problems; yet compared with those confronting other countries they are to the outside observer not exactly overwhelming. How then to explain that for so many young Americans

---

* This can be seen in the communal riots in Ireland and India or the Charrot factions of Byzantium. A student of war wrote the other day in the London *Times:* "It involves confrontation with taunts, grimaces, 'pointing' and war cries, while the adversary is called animal names, usually monosyllabic. Long hair and aggression often go together, *e.g.* in Vikings, Sikhs, and Chindits . . . The war urge comes first and the *casus belli* after, instead of the other way round . . . If one cause of grievance is removed or shown to be non-existent another is quickly found. The act of removal is merely a further irritant and may even of itself be dangerous.

and for some of their elders, their country has become the epitome of repression, a country unfit to live in, a society doomed to perish?

To the outside observer this is perhaps the greatest riddle. It may be connected with the traditional exaggeration in American speech which Dickens derided more than a hundred years ago, and which in recent years has reached new heights of absurdity. The use of terms such as *genocide, Gestapo, Auschwitz,* is disturbing, for it betrays a lack of historical perspective, a provincialism and narrow-mindedness so monumental as to make rational discourse impossible. It may be partly rooted in the traditional American hypochondria (also reflected in the enormous number of pharmacies and surgical operations), the state of mind in which any physical or social affliction, real or imaginary, immediately turns into a fatal illness. Perhaps it has to do with the traditional American naiveté and the surfeit of idealism, engaging qualities in themselves but potentially dangerous. For they reflect a predisposition to be taken in by demagogues and their slogans. How else to explain the enthusiastic support given by so many well-meaning young Americans to causes and movements which, below a thin veneer of "progressive," anti-capitalist, anti-imperialist verbiage, are unmistakably proto-fascist in character and which, if given power, would establish a rule of terror and oppression such as America has never known? Which demagogue in history has not demanded "Power to the people," and has not promised freedom and social justice? Yet such is the confusion and the blindness that no one wants to hear about history and the experience of other countries. It is this unthinking acceptance of slogans which constitutes perhaps the closest and most frightening parallel to the lost generation of the 1930s in Europe.

Commenting in his French exile on the suicidal policy of the governments of the day, Trotsky once wrote that he felt like an old physician with a lifetime of experience behind him who was not consulted at a time when someone dear to him was mortally ill. Europeans who lived through the 1930s and who have not been infected by the disease will react in a similar way. Whether they have any cure to offer is less certain, and anyway it will hardly be accepted. The historical memory of a new generation does not reach back very far and the lessons of historical experience cannot be bequeathed by will or testament. Each generation has to commit its own mistakes and will have to pay for them.

Unlike Europe, America has never experienced a ruthless dictatorship or foreign invasion. Precious civil liberties are taken for granted by the middle-class radicals; there is a great deal of loose talk about creeping dictatorship, but few of them have the faintest idea what it would really mean. It will be (if it should ever come to that) a rude awakening and it may be—as a generation of Europeans realized at the time to its detriment—too late for second thoughts. For this much seems certain: society does not suffer anarchy for very long. It is impossible to predict whether authority will be reimposed by the right or the left if the crisis should deepen further, or by a Populist mixture of both; but in any case democracy as we know it may not survive the process.

In contrast to widespread popular belief, history does not repeat itself; luckily, therefore, a repetition of the German catastrophe is not a foregone conclusion. But in one essential respect serious damage has already been done. World peace, the independence of Western Europe, security in the Middle East and other parts of the world, depend at present on the balance of military power between the United States and the Soviet Union. It is a highly unsatisfactory situation; it would be vastly preferable if it depended instead on the wishes and hopes of men of goodwill all over the globe. Regrettably this is not the case. No particular gifts of pro-

phecy are needed to predict the future course of world politics if this balance is radically upset by a paralysis of American foreign policy, an inevitable by-product of the trend
towards neo-isolationism. The first results can be seen in the
Middle East; yet this may be only the beginning of a disastrous process which could eventually affect other parts of
the world. Such a prospect may not give rise to alarm among
those in America who welcome a defeat of their country,
because, as they see it, it would mean the victory of "revolution." But those not living in the fantasy world of what is
called the "New Left" know that the only revolution likely
to prevail is that which now rules in Czechoslovakia and the
thought can hardly fill their hearts with joy. If America's
position in the world were that of Sweden, the present crisis
could be regarded with greater equanimity; sooner or later
it will no doubt run its course, and, for all one knows, the
country may emerge stronger from it. But America, for better or worse, is not Sweden, and it is not the future of
America alone which is at stake.

It is unfortunate that the role of leadership should have
been thrust at the end of the second World War on a nation
unprepared for the role. It is largely Europe's fault; unable
to make a concerted effort, it has not asserted its true role
in the world and taken on itself part of the burden which
has become too heavy for the United States. It is the foreign
political aspect of the American crisis which now looms most
prominently in the eyes of outside observers, for it is this
which makes it potentially more dangerous than the European crisis of the 1930s. These concerns and fears will not be
shared by those deeply immersed in their debates on repressive desublimination and the demerits of vaginal orgasm,
not to mention other subjects of topical and cosmic relevance.

Kurt Tucholsky, that extraordinary German writer who in
many ways was the epitome of the radical intelligentsia of

the Weimar Republic, wrote in 1935 from his exile in Sweden that "we have to engage in self-criticism, in comparison with which sulphuric acid is like soapy water." A few days later he committed suicide.

III
RUSSIA

IN SEARCH OF RUSSIA

SOONER OR LATER it was bound to happen—the emergence of the student of Soviet affairs as a fictional character. "Who stole Punnakan?" a long short story (a "pamphlet," as the author prefers to call it) in *Oktyabr** the Soviet literary periodical, is a fascinating account of the work and, above all, the *moeurs* of Western students of Soviet affairs. It is the story of a Thai Court Chamberlain who finds himself caught up in the gang warfare between various Western institutions of higher learning. I do not want to say much more about the tale, not wishing to spoil the enjoyment of others. I had looked forward a long time to its appearance, for the author was known as a man of powerful imagination. True, I had not been quite sure whether he was a bacteriologist or a writer, since the only other work of his that I knew was published some twelve years ago, describing how the Americans waged germ warfare on the people of Korea and China. Roman Kim, we are told, has done much research work for his new *opus* in a number of places, including Africa. Ideologically, the Western student of Soviet affairs as he emerges from this novel can be placed somewhere between Porfirio Rubirosa, Allen Dulles, and the late Madame Blavatsky, but ideology is of very little impor-

* *Oktyabr* (Moscow, 1963), No. 10.

tance really. Most of his time is spent in the bars of luxury hotels, beautiful women abound, and only the poorer members of the profession drive a Jaguar E; but all of them are experts on drinks, perfumes, French cooking, men's clothes, and generally speaking the better things in life. Arguments among experts and research centers are settled not in scholarly journals but with the help of a Beretta 25. This glamorous image of the student of Soviet affairs, James Bond and Lemmy Caution rolled into one, will make him the envy of academic colleagues toiling away in less favored domains, such as patristics or medieval economic history. And yet the picture painted by Mr. Kim does not seem quite complete. To fill in the necessary details one has to go back rather far in time, and the point of departure should preferably be a major library, not the Stork Club. I do not know whether at the end Mr. Roman Kim will be with us, but this for once cannot be helped.

The traditional fascination which Russia has had for the West has not always been matched by exact knowledge. Regular contacts between Russia and the West date back to the seventeenth century. Yet fifty years or so later, one of Peter the Great's envoys to a West European court reported that he found it exceedingly difficult to enlist specialists for work in Russia; not only was it generally believed that the country bordered on Red Indian territory; it was thought to be, quite literally, the end of the world. Most Russians' notions of Europe at the time—and for many years to come—were even more fanciful.

Many foreigners went to Russia in the seventeenth century—British traders, French and Austrian diplomats, Italian churchmen, and some of them wrote useful and entertaining accounts of their stay there. But it was only after the Petrine reforms and the influx of more foreigners in the eighteenth century that Russia became an object of systematic study.

Most of the foreigners who had settled in Petersburg and Moscow were Germans, and this, and its geographical nearness, made Germany the center of early Russian studies. It is a sobering thought that almost 200 years ago there was a German periodical which provided a critical bibliography of *all* books published in Russia; there was no such compilation in Russia itself at the time, nor for many years after, and there is none now in the West.

The early nineteenth century was the heyday of historical-philosophical theories and constructions, formulated not only by travellers and historians, but also by men of s, ch widely different background, outlook, and interest as Donoso Cortes, Moses Hess, Victor Hugo, and Nietzsche, who all commented at length on the present state and future destiny of Russia. Most of them had never been near the country, but what they wrote was not necessarily more misleading than the accounts of the experts, for even their knowledge was slight. What Herzen knew about Russian agrarian institutions he had learned from the account given by a well-known visitor, the Baron from Westphalia.

Russian language and literature were taught in very few European universities. The first great expansion in political-historical studies, what would now be called "area study" or *Zeitgeschichte,* came only around 1880. Mackenzie Wallace's *Russia,* subsequently translated into many languages, first appeared in 1877; the following year saw the publication of Rambaud's *Histoire de Russie* and Brueckner's *Culturhistorische Studien;* and soon after the first volume of Anatole Leroy-Beaulieu's famous work was published. The first modern periodicals devoted to the study of Russia and Eastern Europe appeared only on the eve of the first World War. The Germans were first off the mark with Schiemann's *Zeitschrift für Osteuropäische Geschichte,* which did not, however, strictly speaking, deal with contemporary Russia; there had been such a journal, the *Russische Revue,* but it

folded up in the early '90s Bernard Pares' *Russian Review,*
launched in Liverpool in 1912, was less academic, more
lively, and far more concerned with contemporary affairs.
It should therefore be regarded as the first of the modern
journals devoted to the study of Russia—as distinct from the
study of Russian history.

Great Power rivalries contributed much to the development of Russian studies. The other day I read a long memo-
randum dated 1912 or 1913, submitted by Professor Hoetzsch to the German Foreign Ministry, in which he urged the
need to establish a German society for the study of Eastern
Europe. One of his main arguments was the reference to
Bernard Pares' activities in Liverpool, which he somewhat
exaggerated.* Obviously, Germany could not possibly lag
behind Britain.

It is instructive to compare the editorial statements in the
first numbers of these journals. There was the brisk, optimistic, no nonsense attitude of Bernard Pares, who announced
in the first number of the *Russian Review* that

> 'the Russian people does not as a whole share the idiosyncrasies
> whether of extreme reactionaries or extreme revolutionaries, and
> seeks both the steady and normal progress of the Russian empire
> and the goodwill of our own country'.

This was in 1912; when, ten years later, the *Russian Review*
was reborn as the *Slavonic Review,* the same writer had lost
most of his illusions, and had at least stopped projecting
British mental attitudes on the unsuspecting Russians. In
his new preface he simply stated that it was important to
know about Russia, because through the World War England had come into closer contact with that country. He
also promised an impartial hearing to all schools; but this

---

* (German Foreign Ministry Archives 1867–1920, University of California microfilm 159).

apparently did not extend to the communists themselves, for as he put it elsewhere, "It was never a question whether the vain experiment of Bolshevism could succeed in Russia." He complained (as he had done in 1912) about the abysmal lack of knowledge in England of things Russian, as revealed in debates in Parliament, in the press, and elsewhere.

The *Monde Slave* was founded during the first world war in 1917 to be precise; it is not surprising to find in its first editorial statement, fuller and more elegant than the British, many references to the German danger. *Osteuropa,* the German monthly devoted to Russian affairs, came into being at the time of the Soviet-German rapprochement, and soon became the leading periodical of its kind in any language. Its editor, Otto Hoetzsch, was a pro-Russian conservative, not unlike Bernard Pares in the scope of his interests, which were by no means limited to academic life. Usually a most prolific writer and speaker, he preferred on this occasion to be very brief; there is nothing quotable at all in his short introduction. Soviet-German relations were still a very fragile plant, and Hoetzsch probably thought, no doubt correctly, that whatever he said was likely to be misconstrued and give rise to suspicions.

Perhaps even more anti-climatic was the emergence of a journal of Russian studies in the United States—one day it simply existed. A project had been afoot in 1939 to establish an American review, but when preparations had almost been completed, a cable from Sir Bernard Pares from blitzed London induced the American editors to play host to the *Slavonic and East European Review* during the war. If America found itself without due preparation drawn to play a leading role in world affairs, its initiation into the field of Russian studies was similarly abrupt.

The study of Russian and other East European languages was, of course, the precondition for all other research. There was no lack of teachers in Germany or the United States;

instruction in Russian was first given at Harvard in 1896, then at the University of California in 1901. In England, on the other hand, there were very few men or women with the necessary qualifications; Forbes at Oxford and Goudy at Cambridge were well known, but the list of teachers and translators of Russian in the whole of Britain could still be printed on a single page of the *Russian Review,* and it included a reference to the Russian vice-consul in West Hartlepool. These linguists and students of literature were not as a rule deeply interested in contemporary Russia, being more attracted to language than to politics. But there were a few who had chosen recent history, economics, or Russian institutions as their field of study, and who were themselves actively engaged in politics. Archibald Coolidge, Prince, Harper, Pares, all spent years in government service. Theodor Schiemann, the Nestor of Russian studies in Germany, was an adviser to Kaiser Wilhelm on East European affairs, and an editorial writer on the arch-conservative *Kreuzzeitung.* Of Baltic origin, he was violently anti-Russian, very much in contrast to his successor Otto Hoetzsch, who likewise played a prominent part in German politics. It is no exaggeration to say that all leading students of Russia at the time advised their governments in an official or unofficial capacity, though not all rose as high in rank as their erstwhile colleague Thomas Garrigue Masaryk.

Whether historians are superior to other observers in judging current political situations is open to doubt. The Russian experts, almost without exception, underrated the importance of the revolutionary movement. After the revolution their difficulties increased; they had now to deal with a country that in many essential respects had undergone radical change. Little had been known in the West about Russian socialism and communism; the comments on this subject published by German and British experts during the first World War must be read to be believed. One of them

translated "Trudoviki" (a small but important faction in The
Old Russian Duma) as "The Weary Ones" (this was
not intended as a joke); another introduced Trotsky as a
Ukranian nationalist. In Germany, Staehlin, the leading historian of modern Russia, interpreted the Bolshevik revolution and subsequent events in terms of religious philosophy;
Pares, after prolonged and bitter opposition to Lenin's Russia, came to display as much enthusiasm for Stalin's Russia
as he had for Nikolai II's; in America Samuel Harper, the
only American scholar to deal with contemporary Russian
affairs, began by declaring the Sisson papers, that crudest
of anti-Bolshevik forgeries, authentic, and twenty years later
described the big purge as a necessary stage on Russia's
road to constitutional government.

Such naiveté was unfortunately very widespread; the
judgment of intelligent journalists, from Mackenzie Wallace
onward, has on the whole been more reliable than that of
the academics. The real merits of men like Pares or Hoetzsch lay in a different field altogether; they tried to explain
to their governments and to the reading public that Russia
was a very important country, that detailed information on
things Russian was urgently needed. They fought an uphill
struggle, and in doing so laid the foundations for the extensive and systematic study of Eastern Europe at a time when
its need was scarcely recognized.

Today it is easy to underrate the difficulties faced by these
men; financing Russian studies, for instance, was a major
problem. Universities in the Western world were as a rule
marked by an attitude of detachment from the life around
them. Fashions might come and go, but why change the
syllabus? Why study Russian, why not Assyrian? In Germany most of the money for Russian studies came from
business men, particularly from exporters from the iron and
steel concerns, who were interested in accurate economic
and political information in connection with their trade. In

America, after the second World War, the foundations
stepped in and made the rapid expansion of Russian studies
possible. There were no such foundations in Britain, and
big business showed little interest. As a result Russian
studies in Britain were constantly faced with financial
difficulties; it was a foreign government (Czechoslovakia)
that paid for the building of the permanent home of the
School of Slavonic Studies, and even rich American universities needed Polish and Czechoslovak subsidies until well
after World War II to maintain chairs for the study of the
literature of Eastern Europe.

The inter-war period was not a happy one for Russian
studies in England or the United States. The institutions
that had been founded before the first World War continued
to exist, but did not really grow. In America the academic
experts were enlisted into government service for long
stretches of time, while those who continued to teach, such
as Patrick, Noyes, and Karpovich, had few students. Russian
studies were moreover impeded by an unfavorable political
climate which reinforced the prejudice and resistance in the
academic world to area studies. Nor were there enough
qualified men at the time in the United States; despite the
presence of so many millions of immigrants from Eastern
Europe and their descendents, interest in Russian and East
European affairs was selective and strictly limited.

In Britain there was similar stagnation, though a School of
Slavonic Studies had been founded in the 1920's. There were
close relations with many East European countries (owing
to the contacts of such men as R. W. Seton-Watson), but
there was much less activity in the Soviet field. There were
individual historians, economists, philosophers, theologians,
and linguists studying specific aspects of Russian history,
philosophy, etc., but their work was uncoordinated and
taken all together did not add up to "Russian studies." In his

efforts to introduce Russian studies in Britain before the first World War, Pares had had the active support of leading personalities and friends of Russia outside the academic world like Mackenzie Wallace, Aylmer Maude, Constance Garnett, Maurice Baring. After the War, these old friends dropped out; the new friends of Russia were not interested in making the country they admired a subject of study and detached investigation. As a result Russian studies were pursued on strictly academic lines, that is, with hardly any reference to contemporary affairs.

The Slavonic Review went through a similar development; originally founded to study contemporary Russia and its institutions, it became less and less interested in topical problems and was gradually transformed into an eminently respectable academic journal. Much of the stagnation in Russian studies in the West was due to the difficulties of communication with Russia, of obtaining Russian books and newspapers, not to mention the obstacles to visiting the Soviet Union for many years after 1917. Not that this prevented the Germans from forging ahead; the years 1920–33 were the heyday of Russian studies in Germany. A society of sponsors similar to the English in scope had already been founded before the first World War; subsequently a number of Russian and East European research institutions came into being at German universities at Breslau (1918), Koenigsberg (1922), and Leipzig (1928). Hoetzsch pursued very actively his policy of cultural exchange; *Osteuropa* frequently published contributions by Soviet experts; German students of East European affairs often went to Russia. There were more "Russian experts" in Germany than in any other country, and more publications—by and large on a fairly high level. The Germans before 1933 were on the whole the best informed people on Russia, meaning that those few thousands who had an interest in foreign affairs had a fuller and more realistic picture of the state of affairs in the Soviet Union than their counterparts in other countries.

After 1933 this changed very rapidly. Some leading students of Russian affairs were forced to emigrate; others (including Hoetzsch) had to resign their academic posts. With the progress of Nazification, the conditions for objective, scientific study disappeared. Some valuable research was still done in more specialized fields such as economics, but even those who did not believe in official Nazi doctrine on Russia and the Slavs had to pay lip service to the new dogma. Many German students of Russian affairs became involved in activities of a non-academic kind that they were later to regret. Even so, the orthodox Nazis were never quite satisfied with the state of affairs in the field of *Ostforschung.* They criticized their colleagues for not paying sufficient attention to racial factors in Eastern Europe, for regarding Russia as a national entity, neglecting the minorities, and, generally speaking, for being too well disposed towards Russia. Even Schiemann was posthumously hauled over the coals.

By the end of the 1930's, with the growing involvement of the Soviet Union in world affairs, the demand in the West for information on Russian affairs expanded rapidly but the universities and other academic research institutes were quite unable to meet it. In consequence what information was available came largely from communists, or ex-Communists, or from journalists who had been stationed in Moscow. Some of these men and women wrote excellent books, but their work could not replace systematic study, especially on the more technical aspects of Soviet development. Only the Second World War brought a decisive change in this respect, following the old adage that war gives (or used to give) a powerful impulse to discovery and technical advance. It certainly did so in the field of Soviet and East

European studies, for hundreds of experts were now needed, and since only a few existed, they had to be produced as quickly and expediently as possible.

It is not my intention here to provide a catalog of Russian research, or even a review of the main stages of its development; those interested can refer to the detailed studies published in recent years.* The study of Russian, East European, and communist affairs has made great progress since the second World War, large research centers have come into being, libraries and other facilities have been developed, and the list of members of the various professional organizations have become longer and longer.† This growth has levelled off in recent years: the Soviet Union, however important, is not the only field of interest in today's world; Africa, Latin America, and the Far East have also figured prominently in area studies. Even so, the growth of Russian and East European studies has been astounding, especially in the United States, considering how ill-prepared academic institutions were for such an expansion before the second World War. Unfortunately, this quantitative growth has not always been matched by a parallel advance in quality. There are some basic shortcomings in contemporary Russian and East European studies, and in some respects developments over the last decade or so seem to have gone in the wrong direction. This has been due largely to prevailing customs and intellectual fashions in the academic world. Universities

* See: Harold Fischer on *American Research on Russia;* Manning's *History of Slavic Studies in the United States;* Seton-Watson's and Bolsover's essays on Russian studies in Britain; Jens Hacker's surveys of East European and Russian studies in West Germany and Austria; Berton-Langer-Swearingen on Japanese research in the Russian field; and the briefer notes on work in Italy (Hartmann), Spain (Ronay), and France (Kerblay and others).

† Between 1850 and 1950 some 200 doctoral dissertations on Russia and the Soviet Union were approved in American universities. The number accepted since 1950 is estimated at 1,000 and has probably already exceeded this figure.

try to inculcate a spirit of objectivity and detachment, and put a high value on thoroughness; these are admirable qualities, but against this there are at present some very serious drawbacks, which sometimes provoke the question whether the universities are the best place to pursue Russian studies.

One of the most striking developments since the second World War, particularly in the United States and in Germany, but to a lesser extent also in other countries, is the gradual disappearance of the full professor as an active participant in these studies. Most of the articles and books published these days are dissertations or parts of dissertations, or "papers" written by young lecturers aspiring to higher positions in the academic world. Since a brilliant writer is not necessarily a good teacher, and vice versa, and since both teachers and writers are needed, the system which, as in America, insists that everyone shall publish seems both mistaken and wasteful. In the past the most important contributions to learning came from men at the height of their mental powers and experience; today the publication of a book or even an essay by a leading member of the profession is an event, and unfortunately not always a joyful event. Administrative responsibilities of various kinds have grown to such an extent that substantive work is often impossible. Trapped in countless board meetings, committees, and other extraneous activities, those who could and should be leaders in their field do not always find the time even to keep abreast with current developments. Hoetzsch was a scholar, a public lecturer who drew large audiences, a member of the German parliament, a well known editorial writer; he not merely found the time to follow current events but wrote for many years a monthly political survey in *Osteuropa*. Sir Bernard Pares' many public activities hardly affected his output as an historian and a student of current affairs. Today it is exceedingly difficult to imagine a professor anywhere in the world with enough time (and the urge) to achieve half as much as his predecessors; and since there is no reason to assume that academicians today are inferior to those of the 1920's, it can only be concluded that something is very wrong with the whole system.

Partly it will be explained as the inevitable result of specialization and fragmentation in the study of international affairs. It is certainly true that it has become much more difficult to master all the important material than it was forty years ago, what with the multiplication of books, journals, and other sources. Yet for all that, the need to do so, the need not to lose sight of the broad lines of development in each field, is no less pressing than it was. Unfortunately, the fashions prevailing in the groves of academe have aggravated the situation. There is a widespread belief that the study of contemporary problems is not a suitable subject for academic research. This is supposed to be the traditional approach, yet leading philosophers and historians of the eighteenth and nineteenth centuries would certainly not have assented to this doctrine. Today it has become accepted; a scholar who publishes a book on some present-day topic will frequently retreat in his next work to safer ground in order to re-establish his academic respectability. The trend towards specialization is not combated but encouraged; it is much easier to obtain support in the academic world for a highly specialized project of doubtful value than for a work of a more general character. Obviously, there is no such thing as an 'all-round, all-purpose Soviet expert'; there is no earthly reason why a student of Soviet poetry should be well informed about current developments in Soviet agriculture. But it is disconcerting if the student of poetry is totally unaware of developments in the other arts, or if the student of agriculture approaches his subject in isolation from other socio-economic developments. This lack of broad perspective is frequently coupled with a false image of scholarship. The "sound scholarship" praised in a book review often simply refers to the number of footnotes; no wonder that students want to conform and think it necessary to quote an authority for the bold statement that the first world war broke out in 1914. This concept of the scholar puts a premium not on fresh insights, on independent thought, on a contribution to knowledge, let alone on a clear intelligible style; its ideal figure is more likely to be the author of a monograph on an obscure subject, written in a professional jargon that will be intelligible at most to a small group of like-minded people, and of course plentifully supplied with footnotes. As a result, scholarship and academic standards have often become synonyms for sterility and irrelevance.

Often there is a breakdown in communication between the expert and the wider public; many academics these days seem to be capable of producing books that are read only by fellow professors and occasionally by their students. But there is perhaps no more urgent job to be done; intelligent popularization and generalization is needed not only to combat the dangerous trends towards over-specialization; it would in many cases be a most useful intellectual exercise. Unsheltered by professional jargon and accepted methodology, those trying to expose their findings in intelligible terms may find themselves rethinking some of their basic assumptions.

Innovators have been at work during the last decade and one feels reluctant to criticize attempts to experiment with new methods and concepts. Yet the sad truth is that the contribution to the field of Soviet studies of the more modern trends in sociology and political science has been on the whole negligible. Some of the early straight historical accounts, such as Louis Fischer's book on Soviet foreign policy or W. H. Chamberlin's *History of the Civil War,* have retained their value for thirty years or more. It is difficult to think of any book published in the 1950's by a sociologist or a political scientist whose prospects are equally bright. Some sociological studies have broken fresh ground by marshalling and analyzing new material on various aspects of Soviet life; but the contribution they have made to our knowledge comes from their broad factual content, not from their methodological approach, their model-building, theory of communication, quantification, and what not. One recalls even among the best samples of the species those great projects with their weighty emphasis on methodology and their even weightier discovery of the obvious. One recalls, on a different level, the sterile endeavors to find sundry operational codes and unravel rituals, or, in different fields, ill written pages upon pages of unmitigated trivialities, of pseudo-academicism and bogus scholarship, of a pomposity that passes for profundity. It has been a very sheltered world in which a professor's word carried great weight and an outside critic's very little, for he had neither academic standing nor academic patronage. This lack of a critical approach was often reflected in book reviews. Most irritating about much of this literature was not so much its content as the aura of academic respectability which concealed the poverty of its substance.

Seen in a broader context the picture is admittedly far less bleak; most of the shortcomings noted are common to many other fields of study, which suffer in addition from a number of disorders from which Soviet studies are free. And no one will deny that in comparison with the immediate post-war period tremendous progress has been achieved, particularly in the United States but also in England. One recalls that not so very long ago the late Professor Baykov's *Development of the Soviet Economic System* and Dr. Schlesinger's *Spirit of post-war Russia* were considered the most authoritative works in the field of Soviet studies in Britain.*

That Eastern Europe has attracted less interest than Russia as a field of study is not surprising; Bulgarian foreign policy is intellectually not a very important topic and Albanian cultural life not a very stimulating one. Yet it is not only a neglected field of study; the lacunae are more glaring than in Soviet studies, standards seem to be lower, and, to put it very bluntly, the likelihood that outrageous nonsense may be produced considerably greater. The field of East European studies is to a considerable extent manned by friends and enemies of a certain country rather than by students who approach it with an open mind; personal considerations seem to play an important part. Nationalist passions in Eastern Europe have always run high and their impact on academic life has usually been disastrous; to see some of the old battles fought out over again on a new continent is a strain to which the uninvolved public should not be but is often subjected.

Soviet and East European studies in the United States require a fairly extensive appraisal, for since the second World War America has unquestionably taken first place in this field. In Britain, by contrast, new academic fashions have had singularly little effect. Individual writers have fortunately not hesitated to tackle large subjects; over-specialization certainly has not been a major danger in this country. At one time in the 1950's it appeared as if uncritical attitudes were to prevail. The one periodical existing at the time might be thought to resemble an English-language edition of *Voprosy Ekonomiki*. As such it had its merits. But subsequent events have not borne out these fears; prolonged

---

* Dr. Schlesinger, it will be remembered, wrote: "Our interpretation would put the 1936 Stalin Constitution into line with the Declaration of Rights, the American Declaration of Independence, and the French Rights of Man' (p. 86).

exposure to the facts of life has a corrosive impact on all but the most tightly closed minds. Some of the old habits may linger on in certain quarters but this has to do with the general political and intellectual climate in Britain; it is certainly not peculiar to students of Soviet and East European affairs alone. More disconcerting, perhaps, is the narrow basis of Soviet and East European studies in Britain. The fact that some leading members of the profession are very much in demand as lecturers and writers abroad tends to make one forget that the number of students is very small indeed, and does not appear to be growing.

West Germany faces the opposite problem; a far greater proliferation of Soviet and East European studies, but an undistinguished performance with some exceptions by the leaders in the field. There has been some encouraging specialized work—for instance on Soviet medicine, and in legal studies—but at the same time the once so prolific German professors on the whole have stopped publishing. The burden of organizational and administrative duties weighs heavily there as it does in other parts of the world. But there may be other reasons as well; a certain reluctance to express opinions on recent or current affairs; for the recent past has taught them the great advantages of caution. Apart from some general textbooks and some compilations of documents it is difficult to think of any outstanding work done by Germans in a field in which they were once the undisputed masters. The visitor to the magnificently equipped West Berlin *Osteuropa Institute* cannot help comparing it with the discomfort and the cramped conditions elsewhere. Yet the intellectual output seems not to be of equal excellence.

Many French intellectuals have shown interest in communism and some have studied Marxist and Marxist-Leninist philosophy. Yet this interest has not extended far into

Soviet and East European affairs; Frenchmen have traditionally been less interested than other people in foreign countries; what interest there was has been restricted to immediate French preoccupations. Individual Frenchmen have made valuable contributions to our knowledge, but it is doubtful whether one can as yet talk about a French school of Soviet studies.

In Italy publishers and newspapermen have shown more awareness and initiative than the academics. While the Italian press has had for some years now the best news coverage from Moscow, and while Milan and Rome publishing houses have brought out, in Italian translations, Soviet writers whose names were not even known to all the specialists in England and America, few comparable contributions have been made by Italian universities. Italy may be an extreme example, but its case raises one most important question, namely the impact of Soviet studies on public opinion. Does informed public opinion, do governments, take any notice of its achievements? To what extent do those with a general interest in politics now have a fuller and more realistic picture of things Russian and East European? Prevailing fashions in the academic world have made such communication difficult if not impossible.

Some recent critical comments of mine on the state of Western coverage of things Soviet have been approvingly quoted, mostly out of context, in Soviet publications. This has not deterred me from returning to this subject in greater detail. However grave the deficiencies of much that is published in the West, there is no doubt that the preconditions for unfettered study and publication exist in the countries I have mentioned. In other words studies in the West could improve. One does not have to say more.

I am not sure whether Mr. Roman Kim has followed us all

the way. He may have found the theoretical digressions somewhat boring; they may not tally at all with his image of the student of Soviet affairs. Nicholas II, it will be recalled, believed the *Protocols of the Elders of Zion* to be gospel truth. We know, and the Barghoorn case merely confirms it, that Mr. Kim's fantasies are shared by others in the seats of power in the Soviet Union. In their eyes, too, the study of Soviet affairs outside Russia is still part of a conspiracy.

FROM A
RUSSIAN NOTEBOOK

MY FIRST RUSSIAN holiday began at the Moscow airport Vnukovo; but it is at the railway stations in the capital where the crowds are, and a raucous (and unintelligible) loudspeaker constantly blaring instructions. At the airport I saw only a few elderly people: apparently the older generation still have their doubts about air travel and prefer to leave flying to the more enterprising young.

It was in July of 1959 and half of Russia seemed to be setting out on journeys, to Leningrad and the Ukraine, to the Crimea, to Lake Seliger and the Caucasian health-resorts. Some, I noted—the more adventurous, I suppose— were departing for such far-away places as the Urals, the Altai Territory, and Siberia. Travelling is comparatively cheap in the Soviet Union; four weeks at a Spa on the Black Sea cost considerably less than a worsted suit of medium quality, and it is a good deal cheaper to take a room for a week in a Moscow hotel than it is to buy a pair of shoes. On the other hand, it is much easier for a foreigner than for a Russian to obtain a room. In a city of five million, visited by hundreds of thousands every year, there are altogether twenty hotels (and no boardinghouses). The official and recently-published Russian reference book, *In Moscow*, also lists seven guest-houses but these are mainly reserved for foreigners attending the permanent Agricultural Exhibition. The various ministries and specialist organizations also have a number of private hotels at their disposal for their own members. In any case, it remained a mystery to me where the masses of visitors are actually accommodated. Many of them probably stay with relations or friends (despite the acute housing shortage, to do this is far more common than in the West). The Russian loves company, and he is offended if his guest does not eat and drink furiously. The Western desire for "privacy" is, I suspect, quite beyond his comprehension. I kept on asking Soviet citizens whether they wouldn't prefer "a room of their own" rather than sharing one with others. Without exception they replied that they did not go on holiday to be bored. They wanted company. Especially while they were away.

Some of the Moscow hotels are enormous; the *Ukraina* has thirty floors, with over a thousand rooms and suites. In the new hotel which is being built on the banks of the Moscow river there are to be 2,500 rooms, several cinemas, a theater, and even air-conditioning (by no means a luxury in the Moscow summer). On the whole, however, the ostentatious and extravagant architecture of the Stalin era has now been abandoned. The simple and convenient hotels around the exhibition ground in the northeast of the city differ favorably not only from the neo-Victorian *Peking* (built quite recently), but also from the average London or Paris hotel. The railway stations are crowded (even at three in the morning), and there are enormous queues in front of all the booking offices.

My first impressions were paradoxical and conflicting. The people *are* badly dressed, their shoes *are* poor, and their suitcases wretched. But many of the travellers have cameras which are not at all bad (the Russian imitation of the *Leica* now costs less than 500 roubles); they nearly all have watches of fairly good quality (a rarity only ten years ago); they smoke cigarettes which are much cheaper than in the

West, and they drink good vodka. They have larger air-planes than the Americans, but landing-grounds (like their toilets) that are far too small. Jet aircraft and turbo-jets (such as the IL 18) are used on nearly all the airlines; I imagine that the Soviet Union probably has the quickest as well as the largest air fleet in the world today. But during the first twenty minutes before the aircraft is allowed to take off, we are submitted to a sort of Turkish bath; with no ventilation, men strip to their trousers and wring their shirts out in the toilet. *"Kulturni"* or *"njekulturni"*—nobody here likes it hot.

Our travelling companions passed the time pretty much like travellers throughout the world: reading books and periodicals, playing chess or cards (forbidden curiously on railroads), talking, yawning. A baby cries; the stewardess brings round papers and magazines. From what I could gather by a little over-the-shoulder research, the books people were reading were mostly "holiday literature": historical novels, Soviet detective and spy stories by Sheinin, the series called *Bibliotheka Prikliutchenija,* and, finally, the *Roman Gazetta* (cheap editions of best sellers). But, above all, they were anxious to talk—even with the foreigner, above all with the foreigner. Conversation between a Russian and a foreigner is nearly always dominated, however, by two fairly routine gambits.

1. Ah, you are a foreigner? But how very nice. In recent years the conditions have been created for a fruitful cultural exchange between our two countries, with a view to developing neighborly relationships, maintaining world peace, increasing trade relationships, etc., etc. At this point it is usually advisable to butt in, politely but quite firmly, and mention that one has also read with varying interest, the leading articles in *Pravda* over the years. With that interjection, a serious conversation generally becomes possible.

2. In some slight contrast to the tedious declarative, the second gambit is the torrential interrogative. Ah, you come from abroad? How do you like the Soviet Union? Why are there so many unemployed in other countries? Why are the Negroes persecuted in America? What is the average wage in the West? . . .
These questions recur, in somewhat different sequence, again and again. The only variation I have come across is: "Forgive a silly question—but have you a personal interest in the outbreak of a third World War? . . ." Politely suggest to the questioner that the question is in fact rather stupid; circumnavigate skillfully various other conversational rocks; and "the conditions for a fruitful exchange of opinions" will at long last have been created.

At the American exhibition in Sokolniki I heard the very same questions put to the seventy-five American guide-interpreters dozens of times. These students executed their assignments honestly and with considerable acumen. They did not at all deny the existence of the race problem but tried to explain "the background," stressing the efforts now being made towards desegregation in the Southern States. The opening questions were always controversial, if not blatantly provocative; but controversy soon gave way to the sheer thirst for knowledge—and the visitors embarked on a mass of questions about washing machines, refrigerators, color-television, automobiles. The notion that the Soviet citizen is considerably more interested and educated in politics than citizens in the West seems to me quite romantic. Soviet students may be more taken with politics, but the adults (especially the women) are definitely not. Anyway, not as they set out on their holidays.

Nobody knows how many foreigners visited the Soviet Union in 1952; at that time the authorities were shy about publishing statistics of any kind. Apart, of course, from official delegations, the number of visitors can hardly have amounted to more than a few thousands. But in 1957 it was already 550,000. This may not seem very large compared with the number of tourists who visit Switzerland, France, or Italy; compared with only a decade ago it represents an enormous increase and the Soviet organizations, above all *Intourist,* are finding it very difficult to cope with this sudden influx. The majority still come from Eastern Europe, but tens of thousands are now coming from the "capitalistic West" (including about 15,000 from America). *Intourist* has agencies in all the European capitals, and the visitor is offered a large selection of tours, ranging from six days in Moscow to the Grand Tour (Leningrad-Moscow-Stalingrad-Rostov-Sochi-Kiev). It's possible to go hunting in the Crimea, and one can get a room in a Sochi sanatorium fairly cheaply. The various classes of accommodation are: with a bathroom or shower; with or without a private car and an interpreter; with or without caviar.

It all began probably (Marxism is contagious) in the summer of 1957 when the Soviet Government introduced a new rate of exchange. The old official rate was four roubles for a dollar, about eleven for a pound sterling, a rouble for a Swiss franc. This rate made the rouble about four times dearer than its value in Russia; a private visit to the Soviet Union was impossible except for millionaires and their families. The new rate for tourists has more than doubled the value of foreign money. Still, the present rate of exchange does not bear the slightest relation to the real purchasing power of Western currency. The black marketeers near the large hotels are not only prepared to buy Dacron suits and Orlon pullovers but offer twenty roubles for the dollar instead of the official tourist rate of ten. (What do they do with these dollars?)

The head offices of *Intourist* are in the Red Square. This Soviet "joint-stock company" (why joint-stock?—another mystery) does everything it can to make the visitor's stay "as pleasant as possible." The headquarters officials and their representatives at the airports, railway stations, and hotels are hospitable, courteous, helpful. But the coupon system remains the tourist's nightmare: he has had to buy these coupons before coming to Russia and is now compelled to make up the equivalent of ten roubles for breakfast, twenty-two for lunch, three for tea, and fifteen for an evening meal. The service in the Moscow hotels is quite inadequate, and the result of an absurd system (every waiter has his own till in the anteroom where he has to solve fairly complicated mathematical problems before and after every order). The whole organization of *Intourist* is still based on delegations (*"Delegazja"* is the magic word in Moscow). It is no doubt simpler to organize thirty North Koreans or Czechoslovaks doing everything in admirable collectivity than thirty bourgeois Western individualists who insist on rising at different times, want to eat different food, refuse to join in group excursions, and are all just dying to "go off exploring on our own."

As the charming young Uzbek lady who accompanied our group on behalf of *Intourist* so rightly remarked: "You are not a proper group at all! You have no leader! There's no one I can talk to!"

One of her colleagues, a young girl who had just finished her studies at the Institute for Foreign Languages, sharply berated a corpulent and rather elderly politician of the Labor Party because he only wanted a light snack on a very hot evening and had politely refused a formidable meat dish. In a voice obviously used to issuing commands the *Intourist* interpreter said: "You must eat it! It is good meat and it will do you good!" The scene lasted about five minutes; and the Russian girl must no doubt have thought the undisciplined foreigners' laughter stupid, ungracious, and quite incomprehensible.

I had the feeling that the whole *Intourist* set-up is beginning to fall to pieces. One only needs to have seen the queues of impatient foreigners at the passport offices in the hotels: every visitor has to submit his passport which is then taken by hotel employees to a special department of the local Soviet for registration. The harassed hotel employees and the local Soviet do their best; but bureaucracy knows no magic; and if an unsuspecting visitor puts up for the night in a Soviet hotel and intends to continue his journey the next morning—well, he has a slight disappointment awaiting him.

Are the Soviet authorities prepared to reorganize and simplify, and possibly let thousands of foreign visitors loose in the Soviet Union without "organizational assistance?" It is, of course, perfectly possible to travel *de luxe* on one's own if one can afford thirty dollars a day for accommodation; and in any case one is still only permitted to visit a limited number of towns. There is a growing demand for more freedom for the individual visitor, and travellers from the West are not alone in making this request. Even Soviet tourists (returning from the West) have recently been criticising "group tourism" and attacking the assumption that when they travel abroad Soviet citizens are only happy when they are in a group. Thus the gifted Soviet writer Nekrassov has recorded, in an interesting account of a journey to Italy (published in *Novy Mir*), that the group should not be the only form of travelling possible in Soviet tourism—in spite of his ignorance of the Italian language, he at any rate had not felt at all "lonely" in the market places of Northern Italy. Soviet citizens (or at least some of them) are beginning to savor "the good life"; the more a man gets the more he wants.

In the travel brochures Sochi is usually called "the gem of the Black Sea," and few who have been there will want to quarrel with that.

From the seashore the slopes of the Caucasus ascend in the
form of steps, behind it lie the wooded mountains, and still
further in the distance the snow-clad peaks rise towards heaven.
On the shore, on the edge of the bathing beaches, the white
palaces of the sanatoria stand amidst the dark green of the sub-
tropical vegetation. . . .

I can only agree with the official handbook: Sochi is certainly beautiful, healthy, and popular. Four hundred thousand Soviet citizens spend their holidays there in the course
of the year, *"luchshie Ludyi nashei Strany,"* the best people
of our country, as Stalin used to say. (He himself used to
spend many weeks there every year.) Again the mystery is
where these hundreds of thousands are accommodated.
Sochi only contains two medium-sized hotels, and there are
only 12,500 beds in the sanatoriums. All the same, according
to my enquiries, most visitors stay there for three or four
weeks. Well over half the visitors must therefore find private
lodgings: how they manage to do so (and they certainly do)
baffles the outsider.

As a holiday resort, Sochi (the name comes from the Circassian) is almost exactly fifty years old. The first sanatorium, the "Caucasian Riviera," was opened in 1909. Aristocratic families (the Yussupovs, the Obolenskis, Lievens, Dol-
gorukis, Count Witte) had villas or country estates here. But
the chronicler of Sochi apparently finds little good to record
of its early history: dirty streets, two tumbledown cinemas,
and drunken orgies in the public houses of the "Caucasian
Riviera" are all that he has to report on this period. (But
this at least is registered as a fact: Fyodor Chaliapin won
half of Sochi at cards in a single night, and then lost it
again the same night.)

Sochi began to boom in the 1930's, and has evidently now
outstripped all its rivals in "social prestige." Sochi, I learned
from all sides, is to be "rated higher" than Yalta. Writers
and composers still prefer to withdraw to their dachas;
producers and actors have remained faithful to Yalta; but

the *élite* of the political and economic world, the Marshals and Generals, meet in Sochi. I wonder if "meet" is the right word. The sanatoria are almost hermetically sealed off from one another; and, needless to say, no "unauthorized person" is allowed to approach the villas of the party bosses. Stalin "made the place," and there are still many reminders of him. I often saw statues of him, alone and also "in conversation with Lenin," in the parks; one of the large sanatoria is called "*Svetlana*" after his daughter. (I wonder if, since Svetlana Allulieva's flight to India and America, the name has been changed.) In the post offices, however, his picture had been replaced by that of N.S. Khrushchev, and the main street is no longer called "*Prospekt Stalina*" but "*Kurortni Prospekt.*" It is not only the main street but almost the only street, more than thirty kilometers long, meandering along the shore from Adler, the airport of Sochi and its environs, to the northwest, and lined by cedars, lemon trees, yews, laurel trees, cypresses, box-trees, palm trees, cacti and bamboos, tulips, narcissi, gladioli, magnolia, hyacinth beds, and other luxuriant vegetation. There are also statues: young men and girls, fathers and mothers, apparently intended to symbolize the Soviet people at work and after.

Below the Kurortni Prospekt is the Black Sea: the descent to the shore is very steep and access is mainly by means of small cable cars staffed by girl attendants. Above are the various sanatoria—the ones owned by *Pravda* and *Izvestia,* "Rodina," "Donbass," "Moskva," "Chaika," "Novy Sochi," "Raduga," "Sokol," and so on. The Soviet Defense Ministry alone has half-a-dozen sanatoria, and the mines own one of the largest buildings—the "Ordzhonikidze." (I suppose it was Ordzonikidze who drew the attention of his fellow-countryman Stalin to Sochi in the mid-thirties.)

Many of the sanatoria are built in the massive, neo-

classical style of the Stalin era. I heard one foreign sociologist, apparently a student of Veblen, mutter something
outrageous about "conspicuous consumption." What I found
disturbing about them was not so much the ostentation
(much less conspicuous here than on the Moscow skyline),
as the fact that so much stress was laid on outward orna-
mental display rather than on comfort and convenience.
Elevators are very few and far between; air-conditioning
(a vital necessity for invalids in the hot and humid summer
months) non-existent; beach equipment very mediocre. In
one sanatorium (for sufferers from heart disease!) I counted
two hundred steps which patients have to climb, in the
sweltering heat, from the Kurortni Prospekt to the main
building. No wonder the doctors are notably successful with
patients capable of such exertions: get to the top and probably you need no doctor. The most recent buildings are,
however, considerably simpler and more practical; less impressive, more comfortable, inexpensive.

In the center of Sochi we strolled and looked at shops and
wandered in the "culture parks," drank tea, listened to a
concert, dropped in to see a new film, ate Viennese sausages,
had ourselves weighed. Large red streamers *("Forward to
Communism," "The Fulfilment of the Seven-Year Plan is the
Duty of Every Soviet Citizen")* and huge masses of statistics
offered some civic instructions. A public-spirited citizen on
a bench, in a burst of informal conversation, told me that
recently plans have been completed for supplying the town
with gas and that "it is hoped to supply gas to 15,000 house-
holders by 1965. . . ." I also discovered a botanical garden,
a nursery-garden, and a theater, the Leningrad Philharmonic
Orchestra, and gypsy bands. I made a circular tour of the
town in an open bus. It reminded me a little of Bourne-
mouth.

Apparently there is no night life in Sochi, at any rate no

public night life. The "culture parks" are closed at midnight. After that there are only a few lovers, and some drunks in the streets. Dipsomania is a very serious problem; it has apparently become worse. Last year a "workers' militia" was formed to combat the "drunken hooligans," and wearing red armlets they are all over the place every night. Their efforts have not been completely successful. The local paper *Krasnoye Znamya* still publishes a daily list of drunks who have spent the previous night in jail cells. Nor have the "amateur prostitutes" been overlooked. Their photographs, names, and addresses were published on large posters. But, lo! the stratagem had a rather different effect from what the city fathers had intended; and it was revoked without delay. All this is, however, untypical. Sochi is well-behaved and very orderly; its inhabitants are in bed by eleven, and its visitors all asleep by midnight.

For the "best people" in Russia, Sochi is today what Karlsbad was for Goethe and Vichy for Napoleon III, what Ischl was for Franz Josef and Kissingen for Bismarck, and what Baden-Baden, Bath, Aix-les-Bains, and Wiesbaden were for the European aristocracy of the 19th century. It is a political as well as a social center. Not a few resolutions of the Presidium have been drafted in Sochi, rather than in the Kremlin; some diplomatic notes (for example, during the Suez crisis of 1956) have been dispatched from Sochi, not from Moscow.

It has a magic and a mythology. In the brochure *50 Years of Sochi* (Krasnodar, 1959), I found, for example, a report on the case of patient M. from the Urals whose complaint was insomnia. "Whether I have gone to bed early or late, I have always had great difficulty in getting to sleep. A car only had to drive past and I was never able to sleep again till morning." It was decided to cure M. by a course of therapeutic sleep by the seaside. "Three days passed," he said, "and a miracle took place. My insomnia vanished. One night there was a storm but I went on sleeping quite soundly in spite of the noise."

Faith moves more than mountains, and there is here a touching belief in the infallibility of doctors and medical instructions. The impression I received was that although the Russians are by nature rather tough and healthy, they adore consulting doctors, taking treatment, and talking endlessly about cures and illness. A patient's "medical book" has to be seen to be believed. It prescribes an enormous daily program of baths and massages of all kinds, X-ray treatment and sunbathing, remedial gymnastics and walks, swimming and drinking and waters. I could not escape the feeling that only a very healthy person could possibly stand all this. I was told that often a husband and wife share the course of treatment between them—one will take the thermal oxygen baths while the other takes the mudbaths and mineral waters—simply because it is just too much for one person.

Even life on the beach is organized to the last minute. There is a notice at the entrance with precise instructions: seven minutes airbath in the shade; four minutes in the sun; then a shower; then five minutes swimming or paddling in the sea; then a few minutes in the sun; then a period for drying off, followed by another airbath in the shade, then, after a few intermediary stages (I can't quite make out my wilted, sundrenched notes), a second and somewhat longer period in the sea. To comply with all these instructions the patient needs an excellent memory and a waterproof watch.

At seven in the morning the first of the patients make their way down to the beach in the funicular, the men often in pajamas (though this garb has been attacked in recent years as "Njekulturni," apparently, without complete success). The men carry towels, books, magazines, the women little plastic shopping-bags. We found the sun was brilliant, the sea not too cold and not too rough, and motorboats cut through the water to Gagra and Adler, and steamers to Yalta, Odessa, or Suchumi were gliding by, and it all seemed quite idyllic, except for the noise of the loudspeakers. After an hour or two on the beach we all returned for breakfast. In the funicular everyone has to show his permit *(propusk)*. Soviet citizens show their medical book, and I flashed some brochure or other ("Visit the Beautiful Soviet Union") —regulations are regulations. In the dining-room a six-piece danceband plays, with much enthusiasm, the "Merry Widow" waltz and a variation on a Brahms Hungarian Dance. Also "Arrivederci Roma."

In the afternoon we tried to go shopping. The scene in the streets is not essentially different from that in any other Soviet town of approximately 100,000 inhabitants. The public buildings, stations, post offices, town hall are quite magnificent and well-fitted for their purpose, but the shops leave a great deal to be desired. Some of the shops were tiny wooden huts crowded with dozens of overheated persons all shouting *"Devochka, Devochka,"* to attract the attention of the one and only assistant. I imagine that similar scenes may have taken place in the "general stores" in the Wild West seventy or eighty years ago. But, as I was told, "we have solved the problem of heavy industry and in ten or fifteen years we shall also have put light industry on a proper footing. . . ." I tried to browse in the bookshop in the corner. But there is "a system," and it almost drives one to illiteracy. In all Soviet bookshops the customer has to tell the assistant his exact requirements (author, title, etc.). To examine the shelves on one's own is not only forbidden but quite unthinkable.

In the evening all the patients returned to the sanatorium, and the doctors (mostly women, as everywhere in the Union) appear on the scene again. The Russian patients, these lusty Hans Castorps, need doctors, but the salary the doctors are paid by the State seems much too low. The average income of a Soviet doctor is probably not more than 900–1,200 roubles per month—they are the worst paid section of the intelligentsia. (A few leading professors in Moscow do receive much more.) Many doctors have a few private patients—this is neither prohibited nor permitted, although the Soviet medical press often protests against the practice. A private consultation with a leading Moscow specialist is said to cost 150 roubles—less than in America, but as much as in Harley Street. Some doctors are said to have returned mainly or entirely to "private practice" in recent years. On a stroll through Sochi I did in fact see such notices as "*Zubnoi Vratch*" (Dentist) on some of the doorplates.

In some branches of medicine, especially surgery and ophthalmology, the Russians have achieved unique things, but elsewhere they seem to be where the Germans were in 1910—their outlook is mechanistic and they are more concerned with the individual organ than the whole human being. But we only heard praise. Praise for the doctors, praise for their diligence, devotion, and humanity, praise for their treatment and drugs and cures. As far as I could make out, the Sochi patient returns home, after four weeks, firmly convinced that every day, in every way, he is getting better and better. What more can one ask of scientific medicine?

I found members of this upper class to be astonishingly well-informed about events in Russia, especially those that are not reported in *Pravda*. Equally astonishing is their ignorance of the West. Many of them, to be sure, listen to foreign wireless stations and are well versed in "the news", but somehow they lack all appreciation of what political, cultural, and economic life is really like in the West. In many departments of the Academy of Sciences there are young men and women who have read all the Western books and journals on their special subjects; still, they had not the slightest glimmer of understanding of how things actually worked.

The new upper stratum seemed to me to be full of patriotism and pride. They appear to be firmly convinced that in ten years they will have "caught up with" and "overtaken" America. As far as China is concerned, I encountered much reticence. One thoughtful man commented merely that it is "a very big country."

If they are in agreement with the social system, it is also true that they would like "more freedom for themselves," but they do fear that any slackening of the authoritarian regime would have "bad results among the masses." All "the evils of the past" which are claimed to be happily overcome (lack of discipline, anarchy, dipsomania, etc.) would flourish again. There is here a natural, self-protective identification with the present régime. Most of them grumble about Stalin and say that "Nikita Sergeyevitsh is a much better man. There is no longer any need to be frightened when there is a knock on the door at three in the morning. . . ." Material conditions are improving; there is an increasing choice of consumer goods; the country is more powerful.

I left wondering whether there were not some parallels in the past: Victorian England? Wilhelminian Germany? America? But in some ways this new upper stratum is a fundamentally new phenomenon and comparisons with the past can offer no guide to its future development. I was fascinated to find such clear signs of *embourgoisement,* of addictions to "bourgeois tastes." But I will not venture to say how much political significance is to be attached to that. There were moments on the Black Sea, almost in the shadow of a statue of Stalin and Lenin, when politics seemed happily, surprisingly, grotesquely far away.

II

1961: Reading on a train in the Caucasus I find the following:

"Yesterday evening I arrived in Pyatigorsk and found lodgings on the outskirts of the town, fairly high up at the foot of the Mashuk; if a storm comes the clouds will hide my roof. When I opened the window at five o'clock this morning my room was full of the scent of the flowers in the small garden; cherry blossom gazes into the room and sometimes the wind covers my desk with white petals. The panorama is magnificent: in the west one sees the blue peaks of the five-headed Beshtau . . . in the north the Mashuk rises like a Persian fur cap; in the east below me there lies the clean new town; one hears the murmuring of the mineral springs and the voices of the cosmopolitan crowd. Further away the mountains form a kind of amphitheater, blue and hazy in the distance; and on the edge of the horizon one sees the silver chain of the snow-covered summits from Kasbek to Elbruz. It is a pleasure to live in such a place. . . ."

Thus Lermontov's Petchorin, in *"The Hero of Our Times,"* probably the most astonishing short story by a 25-year-old writer in world literature. The journey to Pyatigorsk has become faster, but the jet age has only recently reached the Caucasus. It takes 54 hours by train from Moscow, arriving in the town at midnight in bright moonlight, the traveller feels something of the old romantic magic of the place.

In the early morning such illusions fly away; the traveller opens the window at five o'clock, wakened not by the murmuring of the mineral springs or the scent of the flowers but by the infernal noise of the Kolkhoz market opposite. The crowd outside is cosmopolitan all right, but the fine gentlemen from Petersburg and Moscow are gone, as are their elegant ladies whom Lermontov saw and fell in love with. It consists of highlanders *(gortsi)* with their large hats, Kabardines, Georgians and Russians, Armenians and Ukrainians. There are no Westerners in this crowd: until recently they were not allowed in this area at all. Neither the mountains nor the magnificent panorama have changed, but there is a gigantic television mast on the top of the Mashuk and on a single day the indomitable Elbruz was recently climbed by 1,300 Alpinists.

Nowadays Pyatigorsk is a rather dull provincial town with 69,000 inhabitants, seven public libraries, 15 sanatoria, an Institute of Education and a pharmaceutical college, factories where bricks, reinforced concrete, machinery, butter, liqueurs and chemicals are produced, four cinemas, four large and several small bookshops, five restaurants, 15 nursery schools, a newspaper and a television station. The traveller can get this and other important information from the telephone book which, very much in contrast to Moscow, he finds in his room. There is a special quality about the only hotel in the place; it appears to date from the period of Pushkin and Lermontov, but the sanitary installations were probably in a better state then. A modern hotel in another part of the town is, however, to be opened shortly and the traveller cannot complain about bad service even in the old *caravanserai;* everyone is courteous, friendly and obliging. (One has to leave Moscow to become acquainted with Russian hospitality.)

In the entrance hall of the hotel there is a branch post office with large pictures of Lenin, Stalin and Kalinin. In the main post office which is a modern building there was, however, only a picture of Khrushchev; there are more portraits, busts and memorials of Stalin in the Caucasus than anywhere else in the Soviet Union. The local patriots are not prepared to give up the great son of Georgia.

Various queues form in front of the post office counters, including one for telephone coupons (or "talons"). In the Soviet Ur ion it is not at all easy to ring up somebody in another town even in the immediate vicinity; first of all one has to go to the post office (which is impossible at night) and buy coupons for a trunk-call. Armed with these one books the call at home or from a public phone booth; to avoid the complications many Russians prefer to send a telegram.

Pyatigorsk is not only a town with sanatoria and factories, it is also a cultural center. Notices on the walls of the houses announce performances by leading theatrical companies from Moscow, Leningrad and Saratov who appear in the summer months. Deborah Pantoffel sings arias from "La Traviata" and "Rigoletto." The "Great Waltz" appears twice —as a film and as a ballet. It is possible to see Leslie Caron in "Lili" and Gregory Peck in "Roman Holiday." Comrade Filimonov of the Society for the Propagation of Political and Scientific Knowledge is giving a lecture on "The Cunning Methods of Foreign Espionage Organizations."

Pushkin lived in Pyatigorsk and Tolstoy was stationed here as a young officer. Above all, however, the town is bound up with the life and work of Lermontov who was killed here in 1841 in a duel at the age of 27. In the presence of a lady, he had called a fellow officer a "highlander (gorets) with a big dagger." Martynov was in Circassian clothes and did have a big dagger, but he took offense and insisted on a duel. Lermontov, who was the first to shoot, fired in the air, but Martynov took good aim. An obelisk has been erected on the spot where the duel took place and beside it a large stone plaque on which the events are described which led to the duel; around the obelisk there stand four stone figures, symbols of mourning. One or two groups of pioneers and Oktyabryat, the youngest members of the Communist youth organization, with their red scarves, are here on a visit from their holiday camp. Their leaders tell them "the story of the great Russian poet and his tragic end . . ."

The scene in front of the Lermontov memorial in the town park is different. In the morning, at any rate, the place is quite empty and deserted apart from a young man who, leaning on the pedestal with one hand, recites poems in a loud voice. It is not quite clear whether they are Lermontov's or his own. Then there is a Lermontov Gallery, the Grotto of Diana, the "Restoration" House where the ball took place which is described in *The Hero of Our Times*, and finally the building in which Lermontov quarrelled with Martynov. *Habent sua fata libelli*—Petchorin, the "Hero of Our Times," was, to put it mildly, a wastrel—his problems were card-playing, the seduction of young girls and married women, duels and, above all, how to escape boredom. One might expect that a character like Petchorin would not mean very much to the Pioneers except as a warning. But no one likes renouncing a world-famous work of literature and so the Lermontov Cult is more developed now than ever before. A local writer has just published a long and learned treatise to prove that Lermontov did not die immediately after the duel but lived for another day or two; and his thesis has given rise to a great deal of discussion.

Pyatigorsk is the town of the five hills (the Kabardinian Beshtau); it was formerly the county town but now the administrative center is Stavropol, about 150 kilometers away. There have apparently been few building developments in the town in recent years; there is a housing shortage, though probably not so acute as in Moscow. In the town center and on the road to Essentuki one can still see houses destroyed by the Nazis or in the fighting which have not been rebuilt. Pyatigorsk and the other North Caucasian health resorts were taken up by Group A of the German Army under Field Marshal von Kleist in August 1942, but the *Wehrmacht* did not get much further, and in January 1943 the Red Army returned.

The destruction was light in comparison with the Ukraine or White Russia, but in Mineralnye Vody, the neighboring railway junction and airport, the corpses of thousands of Jews, Russians and people of other nationalities were found in a kilometer-long ravine. The victims included professors and employees of Leningrad University who had been evacuated here. The extermination task force D, led by Colonel Bierkamp, had been at work with its usual efficiency. No trace of Colonel Bierkamp could be found in 1945. The people of Pyatigorsk have no fond memories of the Germans.

III

Though it is the headquarters of the Party and the Government, Moscow adds nothing to the foreigner's knowledge of how Soviet policy is actually made. And as far as everyday life in Soviet Russia is concerned Moscow is certainly not at all typical, far less even than New York or Paris typify the United States or France. A walk through the streets of a provincial town like Pyatigorsk provides more vivid impressions and more significant deails of the life of the Soviet citizen than weeks in the capital.

The day begins very early in the provinces; people are already on their feet, or more precisely, in the streets, by seven o'clock. The crowds are greatest in the *kolkhoz* market and the wooden stalls surrounding it. Men and women with shopping bags stream through the gates of the great market-hall adorned with portraits of the Party leaders, and inscriptions about the coming victory of Communism. The Soviet authorities are very touchy about the *kolkhoz* markets and taking photographs there is very much frowned on.

They regard it as a relic of capitalist economy, since the hundreds of peasant women, on their little stools, offering their goods for sale, do so on their own initiative and fix their own prices: it is really a bit of a free market economy inside a completely different economic system. According to the Moscow guides there are "no longer" any such markets in the capital: but one can see with one's own eyes that this is not true. The Moscow telephone directory contains the addresses of no less than 29 such institutions. It is true, however, that the *kolkhoz* markets have ceased to play an important part in the provisioning of the capital now that supplies in the State shops are generally adequate.

In the provinces the *kolkhoz* market is often still the center of the small town—at any rate for some hours of the day. It is difficult for the foreigner to understand the touchiness of the authorities since it is obvious that the *kolkhoz* market is bound to disappear in the course of time. Anyhow, he cannot fathom the economic rationale of these undertakings: how can it possibly pay the women to travel a considerable distance by train just to offer for sale six or seven kilos of apples or plums or a few dozen eggs? They themselves or their husband will know best whether it is worthwhile; the prices of fruit, vegetables and meat are high and so long as they do not come down to any considerable extent, the markets are likely to continue. Incidentally, in spite of all its primitive fittings, the market hall is clean and there are no flies. There is no wrapping up either: the buyers bring their own nets or bags or buy a newspaper at the entrance for twenty kopeks, which they use as packing paper.

Not far from the market hall is the large State food shop (*Gastronom*). The choice and quality of goods is not bad, the prices are high and the purchasing system exasperating. To buy bread, butter and sausage, for example, you have to stand in seven different queues: first of all, you go to the assistant of the particular department, who indicates the price of the commodity; from there you proceed to the cash-desk where you are given vouchers for the desired amount, and finally you return to the bread, butter and sausage queues where, after waiting patiently for your turn, you get the goods.

Since in many cases man and wife are both out at work all day, the congestion in the shops is greatest in the early morning and late afternoon. People wait patiently in most of the queues, but sometimes there are altercations and even something of an affray. (Men, it seems, have a tendency to push themselves forward and are generally more impatient than women.) The police on the street corner, not keen on interfering, look the other way. There is an old Soviet joke about the militia being responsible for order but not for disorder. The passivity of the militia led in 1958 to the establishment of the *Drushiny,* a kind of Home Guard with a distinctive red arm band who appear in strength especially in the late afternoon and evening. These men and women enlist on a voluntary basis to fight holliganism and have done more to restore public order than the militia. Although they are unarmed, they are far more feared than the militia.

The Soviet traffic police are likewise well-known for their vigor and severity. They often stop drivers in the streets without previous warning and subject their vehicles to a pretty thorough inspection.

It is needless to mention a still further type of police which, although not in uniform, is fairly easily spotted even by the untrained foreign visitor. It is said that since Beria their methods have become "more humane." They endeavor (they say) to work by warning and persuasion rather than terror. People prefer, all the same, not to make their acquaintance. In the small towns, as opposed to Moscow, there are no secrets. Everyone knows where everyone else works.

Opposite the *kolkhoz* market is the public prosecutor's office and next to it a kiosk where one buys the local morning paper as well as the Rostov edition of the Moscow *Pravda*. By the side of the kiosk, watches are repaired in a small shop: the traveller sees more shoemakers and watchmakers in Russia than anywhere else in the world. Fifteen years ago a watch was still a rarity; today they are available in all price ranges, beginning at about 225 roubles (*i.e.*, $22). Part of the road is excavated and gas pipes are being laid. There has been talk of gas supply for years, and the local paper complains that the work is not going ahead fast enough. Demands are growing: until about 1950 there was hardly any public transport, and no private cars at all, yet today, one of the older inhabitants told us, people grumble if they have to walk a mile or two.

Many houses have been supplied with running water, another revolutionary innovation. A little boy proudly showed us his school; first impressions were very good. Then we learned that there are not enough school buildings in Russia, and some of the schools are run in two or three shifts. We asked the little boy whether the teachers are allowed to beat their pupils. He looked up at me pitifully and said, "No, they are not even allowed to give lines." Afterwards an adult confirmed that a teacher is liable to lose his diploma if he uses corporal punishment.

Among the adults, however, everything is conducted in strictly hierarchical fashion: the senior officer in an institution addresses his subordinate as "thou," whereas they have to address him as "you." There has been some opposition to this recently, however. Old Party members are an exception and always address one another as "thou."

Many of the women over 40 still wear the headshawl which here as elsewhere in Russia marks the older generation off from the modern young girls hurrying to their offices, shops or factories, many of them with a book under their arm.

On a large red roll of honor in the middle of the square are inscribed the names of citizens who have distinguished themselves at work. Not far away there is another pillar on which no one cares to see his name: the commander of the local *Drushiny* is accused of sleeping when he should have been on guard. Another caricature shows a woman (name and address given) with a venomous tongue: she is described as a hooligan and is said to have slandered her fellow-lodgers and written anonymous letters. In Khrushchev's Russia it became customary to mobilize public opinion against (unpolitical) evil-doers who cannot be prosecuted under the statutes of "Socialist legislation"; public denunciations at mock trials specially convened for this purpose are now very much the fashion.

A stay in a Soviet provincial town leaves the visitor with contradictory and conflicting impressions, and a picture that is not absolutely clear. What is certain is that the reality one sees with one's own eyes has little in common with the official propaganda put out especially for foreign countries.

It is equally certain that life is very different from what it used to be in the Stalin era. Russia is in the throes of developments which may lead in all kinds of directions but, as in Gogol's celebrated *Troika*, it is impossible for anyone to say where the road will end.

IV

Essentuki: fields of sunflowers on either side of the road; an imposing building, rather like a fortress, is in fact the mud bath establishment which Tsar Nicholas II had built for himself and which was finished in 1916. The layout of the new part of this little town is pleasant: the streets are lined with flower beds. There is a touch of the Orient about the old part of Essentuki: we are near the frontier between Europe and Asia. We pass a *stanitsa* (Cossack settlement) founded about the middle of the 19th century, with a newly painted church in the center.

The main road climbs to about 1,000 meters and it is not long before we reach Kislovodsk. For the Soviet citizen Kislovodsk means Narzan, the mineral water that is drunk all over the Union. There is a Narzan street, a Narzan Hotel, a Narzan bookshop, a Narzan art gallery and, needless to say, a Narzan sanatorium and countless other institutions where the name occurs. It comes from the Kabardian and refers to the carbonic drink of the legendary heroic tribe of the Nartens. Nowadays the mineral water is bathed in by unheroic patients suffering from circulatory or other internal complaints, but plenty of Narzan is still drunk. Round the original spring in the spa park, which is now mechanized and surrounded by glass, a few young girls in white Russian blouses stand pouring out the Narzan for visitors. The patients subject themselves to a strict regimen: for there are 15 different diets and baths and innumerable variations in 50 sanatoria. Not without good cause: Soviet doctors think highly of walking as a cure and there are three standard walks ranging from nearly a kilometer for the infirm to 11 kilometers for those with no organic disorder. On the way there are 20 check points where one can have one's pulse and blood pressure measured and where inquiries are made about one's general state of health.

There are references to the hot chalybeate springs of the North Caucasus in medieval times, but one of Peter the Great's physicians, a man called Schobert (or Schubert), was responsible for the first scientific description of them. At the beginning of the 19th century members of the nobility who had made themselves unpopular at Court were sent here. Patients only began to appear when the railway was opened in the 1880s. But then the place developed very quickly and revolution and civil war only interrupted activities in the spa for a few years.*

Nowadays 150,000 visitors come to Kislovodsk alone every year. The Academy of Sciences, the Usbek Council of Ministers and many other more or less important organizations have their own sanatoria here. A considerable number of visitors who come to Kislovodsk are, however, in the best of health. They come because so many of their friends and acquaintances spend the summer months in the Caucasus or because they want to get away from the heat of Baku, Erivan and Tiflis.

It is a mystery where they are all accommodated, since, apart from the sanatoria, there is only one large hotel and three boarding houses in the place. A key to the problem has been supplied, however, in an article published in the local paper, *Sovietskaya Zdravnitsa*, about a man at the railway station who offers to obtain accommodation for visitors in return for a small commission or 15 per cent of the charge for board and lodging. The area around Kislovodsk was described as follows by Lermontov in *A Hero of Our Times*:

> "Solitude pervades the whole place and mystery is everywhere: the deep shade of the avenues of lime trees which lean over the noisy foaming river rushing on from stone to stone through the verdant mountains; and the gorges, misty and silent, branching out in all directions; the fresh aromatic air, impregnated with the fragrance of the tall grasses of the South and the white acacias; the everlasting sweet, drowsy murmuring of

---

* It was here that Trotsky spent the politically decisive months before and after the death of Lenin, when he allowed Stalin a free hand. When he returned to Moscow he had already been excluded from the supreme command.

the icy streams which meet at the valley's end and race merrily along to their final plunge into the Podkumok."

Lermontov was also one of the first propagandists for Narzan, which he called a "boiling fresh water which restores the physical and mental powers," a statement which is naturally quoted by the spa administration on every possible occasion.

It is doubtful whether Lermontov would recognize Kislovodsk today. The solitude and stillness and the mystery are all gone. At the Khram Vosducha (the "air temple") there is a roundabout that never seems to close down; the gigantic rocks around the old castle "Intrigue and Love" are covered with such inscriptions as *"Long live peace in the whole world"* and *"Serge Ivanov was here."* Despite the cool weather hundreds of people bathe and row in the lake and one has to queue to get a free table in the *"Tourist,"* an excellent restaurant, a few miles from the town.

The best way to escape the crowds is to follow the little footpaths into the mountains: in the distance one can see the little mountain villages *(Aul)* of the Kabardian-Balkar Autonomous Soviet Republic. In 1944 Stalin had all Balkars deported to Central Asia and it is only in recent years that some of them have returned to the Caucasus. There are still wildcats, foxes, and wolves in these mountains. In winter they come right up to the edge of the town. Bears and lynxes were hunted here up to a few years ago.

The best place to undertake sociological studies is the spa park where thousands take the prescribed walk in the afternoon or evening. There are the Armenians and Georgians who come with their large families by taxi or in their cars, and there are professors from Moscow, Leningrad or Kiev with their wives. They used to be the best paid section of Soviet society. Some of them received more than one salary and were paid 10,000, 15,000 or even 20,000 roubles a month. This has now been changed: a professor can now only draw one salary (and one pension) and the maximum is around 5,000 roubles, except in the case of the very few full members of the Academy of Science. But it is possible to manage quite well even on 5,000 roubles which is six or seven times the average salary. Then there are actors from the great cities combining a starring part with a holiday at the spa. Finally there are visitors who really are ill.

What do all these people do in their spare time? In spite of the baths, showers, walks, diathermy and sunbaths, there is a lot of free time in Kislovodsk and not every Russian plays chess or reads a book all day. In recent times this problem has begun to be discussed in public. Even *Problems of Philosophy* has published an article which stated that spare time activities must be better organized, otherwise there is a danger that some young people may go astray. Whole sections of the population have been seized by a mania for games. Even in the park you can see them playing cards, dominoes, billiards and a game, unknown to me, called preference.

Russians have a traditional weakness for games: *vide* Pushkin, Tolstoy and Dostoyevsky. Some of them forget time and the world when they become absorbed in cards or billiards. It is not easy to modify this tradition but attempts are now being made to offer more light music and organize lectures, not only on the world political situation and the resolutions of the 21st Party Congress but also on such subjects as "Is There Life on the Stars?" and, more down to earth, "Problems of Married Life".

The day ends early in Kislovodsk. There is no night life. Dance music can be heard coming from one of the sanatoria, "Soviet jazz," a very widespread form of light music that is only grudgingly tolerated. The dancing is very slow and except for such recent hits as "Domino," most of the tunes appear to date from the period of "Alexander's Ragtime Band."

The last train from Pyatigorsk brings in a few visitors who queue up in the possibly vain hope of getting a taxi. The last shops have closed; in the food stores work goes on till late in the evening. The last visitors to the flower exhibition in the *pump room* have returned. Over a loud-speaker comes the beginning of the news: *"Govorit Moskva."* In spite of holidays, Narzan and billiards, the voice of Moscow is still audible in the Caucasus.

V

1960: The very skyline has changed. Forests of television aerials cover the roofs, up to 15 on a small two-story house. Large colored posters, some of them quite attractive, loom on the walls of the houses: *"Citizen, save time, use a taxi."* Which is easier said than done, especially at night. There are of course the ubiquitous *Shabashniks* (don't look for this word in a Russian dictionary) who will take you anywhere if you are in a hurry, for money and soft words, and especially for money. The taxi drivers are talkative as usual; and someone should write a dissertation sometime on the impact of Moscow taxi drivers on the formation of public opinion in the West. They are still the main source of information for foreign correspondents and some diplomats are said to—well, one should not give away any diplomatic secrets.

Many small things have changed since I was last here a year ago. They have even acquired the rudiments of installment buying. There was no speed limit in the Soviet capital but now it is set at a very firm 40 miles.

The Muscovites are full of praise for a new kind of vehicle seen more often now in the streets of the capital and even in the provinces: the "emergency aid," usually a doctor and nurse who are not only available for accidents but will also make urgent domestic visits and are on call at any time of the day and night. There are, generally speaking, more cars in the streets now than a year ago; it is said that a Soviet "compact" will be on the market at the end of the year. At the moment the only car in the very cheap category is a small vehicle from Czechoslovakia which seems to be available only to institutions. On a steamboat trip to Kuntsevo on a hot Sunday afternoon I saw one or two private motor boats; the crowd of bathers stared at them with astonishment and no doubt a certain amount of envy.

In recent years Moscow has outgrown the old Russian provinciality. This finds expression in many ways, great and small: the constant stream of foreign visitors from many parts of the world, of delegations of the most varied kinds, and of tourists who can, if they like, sleep in tents instead of *Intourist* hotels for the first time this year. The foreigner is no longer a rarity in Moscow and the native does not look around twice even when the foreigner in question is an American college girl in an outlandish getup. Letters to and from Western Europe only take four days now—instead of two weeks and at some newspaper stalls in Moscow it is now possible to buy the previous day's *Humanité, Unita* and *Daily Worker*—it used to take considerably longer.

London and Paris as well as Tiflis and Baku are clearly marked on the dials of the new radio sets and it seems that a lot of people are taking advantage of the fact. Trips abroad have also become possible, in theory at least; Soviet spokesmen refer proudly to the fact that hundreds of thousands of Soviet citizens have been or will be going abroad in 1960. Admittedly, "abroad" usually means such places as Bulgaria or Czechoslovakia. Relatively few people get to Western Europe and then generally as members of delegations. A fortnight's holiday in Paris and London costs the

Soviet citizen about 5,000 roubles ($500), which is beyond the means of the majority of the population.

There is a great interest in foreign countries, but the people of Moscow are curious not so much about political affairs as everyday life in the West, the schools, the health service and the shops. Hardly anyone wants to discuss politics and it is somewhat touching to see well-meaning foreigners trying to involve waiters, chamber maids and taxi drivers in arguments about the basic tenets of dialectical materialism. A new weekly paper has recently been started to meet this interest in life abroad; called *Za Rubeshom* (*Abroad*), it is a sort of *Reader's Digest,* offering the readers translations from the Western press in which the Soviet Union is praised or at any rate the West is criticized.

It may have been partly due to the summer holidays that the interest in politics seemed so slight in spite of American planes and the Congo; the *New Times,* the leading political weekly, struck me, at any rate, as the least read paper in the Soviet Union.

Men's shoes and hats have improved, but the appearance of the place in summer has been revolutionized by the clothes of many girls and young women. Blouses and skirts in pleasant bright colors, manicured hands, medium high heels, some jewelry, complicated coiffures and dyed hair, and even occasional low necklines. Wedding rings, which were very rare only a few years ago, are being worn more and more and in the larger towns there is now a *Dom Svadbi* where it is possible to buy all the necessities—for a solid middle-class marriage!

It is not without interest to observe how firmly established the institution of the family has again become in recent times, whereas in Communist China it is being constantly asserted that the family (and not merely the middle-class family) is doomed. In the Soviet press a discussion has recently begun on whether it would be a good thing if Soviet women were only to work half a day in some occupations so as not to neglect the home and family! One comes across necking couples again and again on benches in the Gorki Park and on the banks of the Moskva; the old shyness and reserve in public have gone and the preachers of morality (of whom there is no lack) who complain bitterly about the corruption of manners are apparently fighting for a lost cause. Asked about this the Muscovites usually talk of the new stream of foreign visitors, observing that since the Communist Youth Festival of 1957 the younger generation of the Soviet capital has never been the same again—they picked up their new ideas and manners from the French and Americans. Which shows that foreigners cannot be trusted, whether they are Communists or not.

All this goes for Moscow and also Leningrad and Kiev, and a few of the best summer resorts such as Yalta and Sochi. In Novosibirsk and Sverdlovsk, not to mention the countryside, a low-necked dress is still regarded as shocking and in this, as in some other more significant respects, Moscow is still not typical of the Soviet Union in general. But every year many hundreds of thousands of astonished provincials come to the capital and take home some of the changes in Moscow's way of life. Moscow certainly sets the style and in several years even Khabarovsk may have caught up with the capital.

There is by no means any lack of money in the provinces; the standard of life in Tiflis is probably higher than in the capital. There are goods in Kiev and Kharkov which are unobtainable in Moscow and everyone knows that in Siberia higher salaries are paid than in European Russia.

In the 1950's one often found that people in the shops and stores were ready to buy anything that happened to be available, whether it was teddy bears or sewing machines, because they knew from experience how restricted the choice of goods was, and that once a particular consignment had been sold out, it was impossible to reckon on another delivery. In the 1960's the Soviet buyer is already more particular; this is partly the result of the many Soviet trading agreements with overseas countries. Tinned food from Mexico and Southeast Asia, *Crême de Cacao* from Czechoslovakia and pineapples which have obviously not been grown in Bessarabia, have suddenly turned up in the shops. Soviet cigars (five roubles apiece—50 cents) are impossible, but Soviet smokers are hoping for an improvement as soon as Castro starts to deliver the goods.

A good deal could also be said about the service in many Soviet shops. The idea that the customer has certain rights is quite unknown. There is much truth in what a high official, the Party Secretary of the district of Voronezh, wrote in *Ogonyok* recently—some (meaning, many) employees in the shops behave as though they were suffering from an inferiority complex: the thought of having to serve customers does not please them and because they are not doing a productive job they imagine that they are not taken seriously. Whatever the psychological explanation may be, the Soviet customer is not to be envied, and in spite of the efforts which are now being made to improve the situation it may be many years before any real change takes place.

Moscow in the summer of 1960 is a city of prosperity. Measured by Western standards it is a modest sort of prosperity; it is hardly worth going into the official statements about the shortest working day and the highest standard of living. But the Soviet citizen does not measure by Western standards, he only knows that he is better off than he was a year ago and that in 1961 he will be able to buy even more for his money. This new wave of prosperity is not being enjoyed by all sections of the population to the same degree; where there is only one wage-earner in the family earning the average of 800 roubles ($80) or less, there is not much evidence yet of progress. With a monthly income of 3,000 roubles ($300) people begin dreaming of a small car, some go in for a poodle and many talk about wanting to lose weight. The fact that women's fashions are now the thing in Moscow is hardly likely to soften the Soviet stand on Berlin. From a longer term point of view, however, developments in the social and economic field should certainly not be ignored, even though one is not a Marxist. Soviet reality is much more complex than the leading articles of *Pravda,* and official speeches and statements are not the only driving forces in Soviet society. Both are realities: the Russia of the Party and the ideology, and Soviet everyday life, which is in some ways quite different—there comes to mind the old French distinction between the *pays légal* and the *pays réel.* Under Stalin the one was suppressed but it has never really ceased to exist.

There is a famous statement which Stalin made in the middle 1930's: *"Life has become easier and better, Comrades!"* That was shortly before the eruption of the great "Purge" and the saying is still remembered as a bad joke. In the 1960's Krushchev can claim with greater truth that "they never had it so good"—as Harold Macmillan once did in a British election campaign. After more than 40 years of deprivation many believe the good life is just around the corner. Just now, comparisons with the West are quite irrelevant; they may become important later on. Among Mr. Khrushchev's inexhaustible supply of old popular sayings, there must surely be one to the effect that the appetite grows while eating.

VI

1963: Red Square, an unending stream of visitors: guided tours, delegations, and even some individual travellers, buses from Huddersfield and Hamburg, Citroëns and Minibuses, Uzbek cotton-growers and Sverdlovsk steel-workers, Russians hurrying to work and foreigners photographing the entrance to the Kremlin.

The square got its present name (*Krasnaya Ploshshad*) in 1662; much of the time since it has been the center of Russian history. It is, of course, in no way red; the name *(krasny)* is probably derived from beautiful *(krasivy)*. In the Middle Ages it was a fair-ground and market-place; the Cossack rebel, Stenka Razin, was executed here, and Peter I established the first Russian theater around the corner. After the great fire of 1812 the square was completely reconstructed; Minin and Pozharsky, who saved Moscow from the Poles, were commemorated with a statue, and Lenin and Stalin with a mausoleum. After the revolution all the big parades and meetings took place in the Square. Stalin's name has since been erased; in the great red brick Lenin Museum they now have a picture of Martov, the Menshevik leader, but none of the late "Father of the People." At midnight all Russian radio stations switch to Red Square to transmit the chimes of the Kremlin.

Moscow is not exactly beautiful, yet it has always had a special place in the hearts of the Russians. Chekhov's three sisters dreamed day and night of "going to Moscow." Can one imagine English poets raving about London as Russian poets do about Moscow? Lermontov, for instance: "I loved her like a son, like a Russian—with a strong passionate, delicate love . . ." or Pushkin: "*Moskva, kak mnogo v etom zvuke* (Moscow—how much there is in this sound) . . ." Visitors from Voronezh, Murmansk, and Nizhne Tagil still come to Moscow to admire the tall buildings and the new fashions, the big open spaces and the shops. For them Moscow is the pattern of things to come. It sets the fashion, intellectual and otherwise; it is the center of Russia, and Red Square is still the center of the capital. (Curiously enough, it was a

French Communist, Pierre Courtade, who wrote the first novel about it.)

The Square is bordered by the Cathedral of St. Basil (now a bit decrepit and supported by much scaffolding), GUM (Russia's biggest store), and the Kremlin. Ten years ago there was a standard scene in Soviet fiction: on a rainy, cold, November evening the hero, with or without wife or girl-friend, crossed the empty Red Square and looked towards the towers of the Kremlin. Everything was shrouded in darkness but one window gleamed with light—the omni-potent, omniscient Father of the People was still busy, never relaxing in his work for the good of his children. Now, the Kremlin is open to the public during the day. Most of the political decisions are taken, I surmise, not here but at the Central Committee of the Party at *Staraya Ploshshad* (about half a mile away), or in Krushchev's own office nearby. The Kremlin is now mainly used for receptions and confer-ences, most of the real work being done elsewhere.

Standing in the queue in front of the mausoleum: Is de-Stalinzation likely to progress much further? The answer seems to be a qualified "no" for the near future. The genera-tion of the over-45's, in so far as it was politically active, was involved, one way or another, in the Stalin era, and it simply cannot disavow its own past altogether. In addition, there is some popular pro-Stalinist sentiment, a fact fre-quently ignored by foreign observers. "He did win the war . . . he started the experimenting with rockets . . . he built up our heavy industry . . ." After all, the purges and the trials mainly affected the political élite and the intelligentsia. Of course the peasants were hit by the collectivization, and Russian working-class life was drab and dreary under Stalin; but on the whole the workers suffered less than the rest. I am not, therefore, surprised to find a considerable residue of pro-Stalin feeling among the workers. The Stalin cult was all-persuasive and lasted for many years, and much of this propaganda was sincerely believed. De-Stalinization has been half-hearted. Generally speaking, the working class seems to be, in its cultural taste and its views on *byt* (one of those untranslatable Russian words—"way of life"?), a conservative factor in Soviet life. In pre-Revolutionary Russia the class-conscious worker was always described as the students' natural ally in the political struggle. Today, workers' brigades are used to re-educate obstreperous or wavering students and young intellectuals. The sterling qualities of the industrial workers are contrasted with the feckless intellectuals and their political shilly-shallying. The party leadership may be largely working class in origin, but a very large percentage now has higher education; their circumstances have changed much from those of the working class. It is a real problem and nobody believes that "leadership by rotation," as suggested in the last party program, will work. The working class is still the official *fons et origo of* Soviet power; it certainly is not a revolutionary factor in Soviet life. In addition, there is a great and apparently growing gap between the way of life of the working class and that of the intelligentsia. This is a general phenomenon and may be inevitable, but it must be of particular concern to political leaders in this country. The differential in wages and salaries is small; a young workman usually earns more than a young intellectual. But their interests, the way they behave, and the way they spend their free time are very different indeed. Communism, we are told, will overcome the differences between intellectual and manual labor; for the time being the two classes certainly develop apart. Khrushchev realized this when he demanded that every student work for two years in industry or agriculture in order to be accepted at the university. Some say that this scheme is now being gradually abolished because it did not work. Anyway, it did not make the students like the factories any better, and "intellectual" is still a derogatory name in many circles. The students, on the other hand, complained of the cultural desert experienced in factory life, and even more in the *kolkhoz*. The blue badge denoting that its bearer has graduated from an institution of higher education is worn defiantly by hundreds of thousands.

"Why should anybody want to draw attention to his education?" I asked a Russian friend. "And why not?" he replied.

Russians and Germans

Travelling by tram or trolleybus from the center to the airport, or westwards via Volokolamskoe Chaussee, one soon passes a pillar marking the furthest advance of Hitler's Panzers in the winter of 1941. The destroyed bridges have been repaired, the factories have been rebuilt, and there is little to bear witness to the bitter fighting that once raged here. But the War caused a trauma as far as the Russian attitude to the Germans is concerned. Stalin had consistently underrated Hitler; from 1933 to 1939 he was merely the "tool of German monopoly capitalism"—the aggressive nationalist and popular essence of National Socialism was never understood. Nor, indeed, is it to this day; not a single serious book on Nazi Germany has been published in the Soviet Union since 1945. As for the Germans themselves, this period remains for the Russians a piece of *unbewaeltigte Vergangenheit*. From 1939 to 1941 Hitler was almost an ally; small wonder that the invasion of 1941 came as a tremendous shock.

Even now Soviet propaganda is curiously schizoid on the subject of Germany. It is always stressed that in the age of the H-bomb and rockets, West Germany has been reduced to military impotence, that it would simply be wiped out by a few bombs. But on other occasions "West German revanchism" is described as a formidable danger to the security of the Soviet Union. A special anti-German library has just been established, sponsored by the State Political Publishing House. Dr. Adenauer is described as slightly worse than Hitler, and Herr Willy Brandt (whose anti-fascist record is rather more consistent than that of most Marxists around here) is called a "Gestapo agent."

The East Germans, admittedly, are hardly more liked. One misguided soul in charge of cultural exchanges between East Berlin and Moscow, had decided to bring an East German army choir and orchestra to the Soviet capital. It was not an outstanding success, to put it mildly. Russians appear to be allergic to German uniforms.

Most of this feeling, however, is limited to the older generation. Yesterday I went to Gorky Park and listened to some community singing. It ended with a song new to me: *"Nabat Buchenwalda* (The Buchenwald Tocsin)." But the boys and girls, mostly around seventeen or eighteen, sang it as if it was a very funny song indeed. One should not blame them, it doesn't mean anything to them—this, at any rate, was the explanation given by a Russian friend of mine.

"My generation would react differently," he said. He was born in 1924; only two of the boys from his class at school returned from the war.

Books

For the last decade one school of visitors has used the condition of plumbing as a yardstick to measure Russia's progress. It is a legitimate complaint, and it doesn't even have a funny side; a *Clochemerle* is unlikely ever to be written in Russia. But the tourist who looks down on the Russians because of their poor sanitation may, in turn, be held in contempt by people here for his lack of interest in the "higher things of life." How many books has he read during the last month? And what kind of books? The number of bookshops is truly astonishing and still growing. They hawk books, like fruit or vegetables, in the streets, and people queue in front of the stalls. All this, we are told, is the achievement of Soviet power, which historically is not quite correct. Russians were always avid readers; the number of titles published in 1913 was as great as that of France, Britain, and the United States combined.

Tremendous business goes on in the secondhand bookshops at the Kuznetski Most and the Arbat. A friend bought an early *Leninski Sbornik* the other day, edited by Kamenev, for a pittance. I saw books by Max Weber, Milyukov (!), and Henry James (in an American paperback edition) offered for sale. Absurd prices (up to £30) are fetched by such books as *L'amour est mon peche, Mademoiselle Fifi,* or a battered volume of Casanova's Memoirs. There seems to be considerable interest in Catulle Mendès and Octave Mirbeau and their contemporaries. But the most sought-after author seems to be a Frenchman by the name of Count Salias of whom, I am ashamed to confess, I have never heard. I am told he wrote novels on high life for domestic servants, and his books now fetch considerable prices. So does Elsa Marlitt (1825–87, *Das Geheimnis der alten Mamsell*), who fulfilled a similar function in Wilhelminan Germany and who gave her name to a whole literary genre (*Marlitteratur*). All kinds of people, all kinds of tastes. In Russian bookshops the prospective buyer cannot approach the shelves himself, he has to ask the saleslady, and the answer is usually *nyet*. In some Russian cities a revolutionary experiment is now being tried whereby the buyers are actually permitted to browse for themselves. This is evidently part of the gradual transition to Communism, in order to give the citizen a greater feeling of social responsibility.

In a shop on Teatralny Proyezd, I found a copy of Kliuchevski's post-doctoral work of 1865 on the reports of foreigners on the Moscow State. Kliuchevski was the greatest Russian historian and his book is, I believe, out of print. I paid only a few kopeks; clearly he is no match for Count Salias.

Foreigners

M. who has been here for almost three years, is getting very restive. Some other foreign residents are showing unmistakable signs of claustrophobia. Of course, they are free to take long walks (not always practical in winter), to go to the theater and cinema, and, only with permission, to travel outside the 25-mile limit. The diplomatic season will soon start; there will be frequent invitations to cocktail parties, dinner parties, and for the full global round of national holidays. Unfortunately, there are always the same faces.

True, Russians feel a bit freer now and may talk to foreigners on occasion; they will certainly not shy away from your table in the restaurant—especially if no other places are available. But a real conversation, let alone a close relationship, is still impossible. After all, every foreigner is a potential spy (or so they say in the little booklets put out with monotonous consistency by various publishing houses). Some distinguished Russian writers, composers, and scientists are invited to some of the Western embassies once or twice a year. But I suspect that it is done all too often simply in order to report home that so-and-so had been to dinner; motives on the Russian side may be similar. Perhaps I am doing them an injustice, but the value and importance of these meetings is somewhat doubtful.

The Russian suspiciousness towards foreigners is, of course, nothing new. Herberstein, Mayerberg, Possevino—in fact all the 16th-century diplomats and visitors complained of it. There were armed guards in front of the embassies then as now, and the diplomats were virtually held prisoner in their homes. "Whoever visited a foreign embassy for whatever reason drew very strong suspicion upon himself." When Mayerberg complained that all his letters to Vienna were intercepted and destroyed he got no answer. When Herberstein complained that he had been given an empty house without furniture or even beds, he was told that this was the usual procedure. Some of this, of course, has changed, and the Soviets feign a fastidiousness about diplomatic etiquette, though there are still difficulties as regards housing. The Soviet Foreign Ministry apparently has a limited number of flats at its disposal. Newcomers are often told to stay with their families in a hotel. There is a wall, albeit an invisible one, around the foreigner; if he does not want to run into trouble he had better not try to outsmart the authorities.

There are fifty non-Communist Western journalists in Moscow and in many respects they are, of course, much freer than they would have been under Stalin. And yet I do not envy them. They have to act as their own censors, but many would prefer the old system. Now, if somebody oversteps the boundaries he is warned, or attacked in the local press, or simply thrown out—as was the case with the *Newsweek* correspondent last summer. In the present "climate of uncertainty," as it affects both Russians and non-Russians, it is exceedingly difficult to stay on the right side of the unwritten law. Collecting news is not at all easy; everything has to go through official channels. An application to visit a Soviet school may take several months to be considered, and the reply may well be negative. In a way it is preposterous to expect detailed political coverage and analysis from Moscow. There is much room for social reportage of a different kind altogether; so many aspects of Soviet life are quite unfamiliar to the Western reader. By and large the Western press does not seem to be interested in this; some of the correspondents complained about this to me, often criticizing their editors or their readers, sometimes both.

In recent weeks there have been many attacks against journalists who came to the Soviet Union for short visits. Yuri Zhukov singled out Harrison Salisbury and a *Figaro* correspondent, whereas two lesser known Moscow journalists have belabored Patricia Blake (of *Life* magazine) in *Izvestia*. In Stalin's times all foreigners, and journalists in particular, were considered "spies"; foreigners noted the price of a pair of shoes or a pound of cucumbers and thus amassed economic intelligence. Today, the situation is more complicated and Zhukov has applied a new concept—the "semilegal collection of information"—in his article in *International Life*. What he means is this: Every foreign visitor is bound to notice certain things during his stay in the Soviet Union even if he does not speak to a single Russian. If the correspondent compares the quality and the price of Soviet shoes or cucumbers favorably with Western products, nobody is likely to take umbrage. If, on the other hand, he should draw unfavorable comparisons his activities become "semilegal," something in the nature of an ideological diversion— for do not his comments reflect unfavorably on the regime as a whole? The two writers in *Izvestia* have suggested that Western correspondents who have published critical accounts on the Soviet Union should not be readmitted. One can easily imagine what will happen if their advice is taken by the authorities—and if the West, as can only be expected, retaliates. Stalinism, one is constantly reminded, is not yet a thing of the distant past.

Youth

A procession approaches from Sverdlov Square—a trumpeter in the small car leading, followed by several buses of singing boys and girls in white blouses and red ties: out-of-town Komsomol—or more probably the Pioneers, its younger section—or an excursion through Moscow. "*Molodaya Gvardia Rabotchikh i Krestian*"—they are singing the old song of the Komsomol about the young avant-garde of workers and peasants, which brings back memories of the 1920s: the storming of Perekop and Kronstadt, how the Komsomol fought always and everywhere for the "general line"—collectivizing agriculture, working at Magnitogorsk, building the city named after itself, Komsomolsk-on-the-Amur. It reminds one of the generation of the children's republics, of Kostya Ryabtsev and the Rabfak (the workers' faculties) of endless discussions about free love, revolutionary literature, and art.

Pavel Kortchagin (in Ostrovsky's *How the Steel was Tempered*) was the great hero of that period. Paralyzed and incurably ill, he continued his political activity up to his last breath. Pavel Kortchagin's contemporaries are now grandfathers and grandmothers, if they were lucky enough to survive the War and the Purges. In the high command of the party there are now many who, born after the 1917 revolution, joined the party only during World War II. And the youngsters in the white shirts were just three or four years old when Stalin died—for them this period, too, already belongs to the distant past.

There is much speculation about the character of this new generation, "the Russia of tomorrow." Nothing perhaps is more dangerous than generalizations about this, for "youth" is not a finished product. The Soviet student of 1962 is very different in his mental make-up and outlook from his predecessor twenty, or even ten, years ago. "Too different," their elders complain. The teachers say that these youngsters are not at all accustomed to receiving an order without discussion. Parents complain that their sons and daughters want to enjoy themselves; they get very impatient when faced with the "what-was-good-enough-for-us . . ." argument.

They take Soviet reality (and to a certain extent Soviet ideology) to be self-evident; there are little jokes about "Diamat," one of those party subjects learned by rote, but in the end they will take over unthinkingly much of the doctrine, which does not mean that they are content with Soviet society as it is now. They are impatient with bureaucratic chicanery, they want a better life and more freedom, they don't think Russia is developing and changing fast enough. They earnestly believe that less control plus *izobilie* (abundance of goods) equals Communism; people who do not believe in Communism seem more than slightly daft to them. How can anybody be opposed to "the good life"? They are more interested in literature and the arts than in ideology, more in their professional training than in politics. "Only the less savory type," it is said, choose politics as a career these days.

Some of the manifestations of youthful ferment are by now well under control. The poetry recitals at Mayakovsky Square have now been discontinued. The youth cafés such as *Molodozhnoe* and *Aelita* have been taken over by the Komsomol, an organization that evokes no more enthusiasm among the young generation these days than the Ministry of Fisheries. But in the long run it will be difficult to control the stirrings of the post-Stalin generation, which are by no means limited to young avent-garde writers, composers, or painters; they do speak a "different language" from that of their parents. The decision, just taken, to discontinue the Russian-language edition of *Molodezh Mira,* the organ of the World Federation of Democratic Youth, as well as the magazine of the (Communist) International Union of Students, are two more straws in the wind. Soviet officials had sharply criticized the independent line of their subsidiaries who *inter alia* had dared to denounce Ulbricht's wall. And the editor of the I.U.S. organ has just stated that "for about ten years now the I.U.S. and the editors of *Vsemirnoe Studencheskiye Novosti* have been struggling against censors in various countries who dispose of our publications as they please. . . ."

A scene in the Moscow Writers' Club. Any *putyovka* available for travel abroad? Yes, certainly: Cuba 1,100 roubles, Ghana 850 roubles. Anything else? No. . . . The inquirer pulls a face indicating that he does not think highly of Castro's Cuba and Nkrumah's Ghana as holiday lands and withdraws. It is difficult for outsiders to imagine how much the Russian intellectual wants to go abroad, even if only for a short time; and he is not thinking of Prague either. Soviet tourism, never very developed and almost always partaken of in groups, has now been cut to between 10–20 per cent of what it was in 1961. According to the semi-official version, this is the result of lack of foreign currency; the real reason is not difficult to imagine. The few lucky people who get the passport and the *putyovka* are envied by their friends and neighbors and the whole neighborhood talks about their good fortune. They prepare themselves for many months beforehand, as people in the 18th century did for the grand tour, brushing up their English, French, or Italian; they are starved for fresh impressions and therefore less blasé and much more observant than the average Western traveller. Later they will have to report back in great detail to all their friends and acquaintances about "life abroad." There are some professional travellers—Ehrenburg was perhaps the best known. As for the rest, a trip to London, Paris, or Rome is a momentous event, equal in importance only to a flight to outer space.

The feeling of isolation from the West is very strong, and the authorities are aware of it. They provide various *ersatz* outlets: trips to Eastern Europe are now less difficult than they used to be; there are international Communist gatherings, like the Helsinki Youth Festival, which may provide at least the illusion of a real international meeting of minds. Non-Communist newspapers are unobtainable, but the new kiosks in the streets give an impression of great variety at first glance: how many papers there are, how many different colors, languages, alphabets! A closer look reveals the basic uniformity: it is the same newspapers, from Havana to Ulan Bator. True, the attentive reader of, say, *Unità*, *Drapeau Rouge* (of Brussels) or the Polish press will learn a great deal not contained in *Pravda, e.g.,* the explosion of a new Soviet H-bomb near Novaya Zemlya, the death of Hermann Hesse. People queue for these papers. The London *Daily Worker* (now known as the *Morning Star*), I am certain, could sell three or four times as many copies in Russia as it does in Britain; there is a great interest among the hundreds of thousands who now have a working knowledge of English. But the editors should not congratulate themselves too soon; these are not personal admirers of Palme Dutt or John Gollan; they want to know about literature and television in Britain, about new films, fashions, and sport. And even the London party organ conveys, at least to them, a glimpse of that hostile and decadent (read: strange and fascinating) world—"the West."

Patriotism

The Cosmonauts landed safely earlier today, and Yuri Levitan now reads out the declarations of the Soviet government. (During the war he used to read Stalin's more important orders of the day.) But hardly anybody seems to me to be listening; there is evidently sales resistance to the loudspeakers. Everybody is proud of the achievements; there has been an upsurge of patriotism over the last year or so. An adept of content-analysis would probably find that the word *Russian* is again more often used: "We Russian people . . . The great Russian scientist. . . ." This, in a way, is only natural. There is cause for pride, but it creates a number of problems. For there seems to be a resurgence of nationalism among the minorities too—in Georgia, the Baltic republics, and Central Asia—but not of "bourgeois" Nationalism. It is a new phenomenon altogether—the people in Tiflis, Riga, and elsewhere merely want to manage their own affairs, with minimum interference from Moscow. It is a development parallel to the centrifugal trend in the world Communist movement. Which brings me to the "Sino-Soviet conflict."

It takes some time to realize how little the Chinese are in evidence in Moscow. There are receptions for North Koreans, one meets a Mongolian army delegation and even visitors from North Vietnam. But where are the Chinese? The bookshop in Gorky Street sells the same cheap scrolls that were there two and three years ago; Chinese fountain pens and textiles are sold in Kirov Street. But there is little about China in the press; there are hardly any translations, no visiting artists, no Chinese films shown; there are few if any Chinese students around and one simply does not hear of anybody who has lately been to Peking or Canton. Moscow and Peking seem to have agreed to disagree. But how long is it likely to last? Meanwhile, some scarcely veiled ideological tug-of-war goes on. The last number of *Questions of Philosophy,* for instance, berated Mao for "some incorrect interpretation of the theory of antagonistic contradictions". There may be more serious trouble brewing under the surface in the less rarefied sphere of economic planners, military attachés, and intelligence agents.

Any report from Moscow, however cursory and impressionistic would be incomplete without reference to the most important problem of all. Yet nothing is more difficult than to comment on just this topic from the Soviet capital. The broad lines of Soviet policy are known from countless publications and statements which can be studied at greater leisure in Paris, London, and Washington. As for the actual decision-making, the internal discussions preceding it, the whole complex of Army-Party-State relationships, the formation of foreign policy goals and the deliberations as to how to attain these targets, that is a sealed book to all foreign residents and to most Russians as well.

I am not suggesting that all aspects of Soviet life can be studied more profitably from the outside; this, after all, is not 1952 when *Pravda* contained all one needed, or could hope, to know about the Soviet Union. Since Stalin died something in the nature of a popular opinion has gradually come into existence. It was, and continues to be, a long drawn-out process and nothing is easier than to belittle its political impact. If "public opinion" in the Soviet Union is not merely anti-war but opposed to even minor military adventures, this too could be explained as a reflection of the policy of the Presidium. Some foreign observers believe that Soviet policy has realized that there is no "military overtaking" in the nuclear age, and that it has given up any hope for further advances in Europe. But the feeling of a mission that has to be fulfilled, remains; so does the willingness to take greater risks than the West in the political struggle. Soviet foreign policy does not embark on foolish or suicidal adventures any more than the West does. But the only way out of the dilemma would be the establishment of an international order which would perpetuate the *status quo* in world affairs and thus undermine the universalist character of the communist historic mission. No doubt: there has been a certain amount of ideological erosion. The movement has become less missionary and certainly less universalist. But these are perspectives for the more distant future, meanwhile Moscovites, as everybody else, have to live not only with the bomb, but with the permanent danger of escalation and even the blind force of accident. "No human activity has a closer connection to accident than war," Clausewitz said. It is, to put it mildly, an uncomfortable thought and people here seem to be aware of it as much as anybody else.

Standards of living: It has increased during the last two years; the selection of goods in the shops is wider, prices, too, have gone up—between 10 and 20 per cent I would estimate. There were the usual shortages in Moscow in the spring, but one should not overrate this. The shortage in the supply of tomatoes will not affect the balance of power; steel production will—and Russia has, at any rate for one month this summer, produced more steel than the United States. The price structure is always difficult to understand; a child's hat costs as much as two fairly good cameras. For the price of a pair of ladies' sandals one can buy a whole library of L.P. records (thirty-five, to be exact).

Karl Marx: Since the twenty-second party congress the "cult of personality" has found a new victim. Okhotni Ryad has been renamed Prospekt Marksa, so has the Mokhovaia, Teatralni Proezd, and the underground station nearby. On Sverdlov Square a big statue of Marx has been put up, the first in Moscow. Stalin is now blamed for having neglected this. The new Marx-Engels Museum has just been opened, and the two founders of scientific socialism are now celebrated as precursors of space travel as well.

The father image has been replaced by the grandfather image.

(1959–1965)

THE END OF
THE MONOLITH

FOR world Communion 1961 was the year of the great
schism. "Polycentrism," a term apparently first used by
Palmiero Togliatti in June 1956, is not yet in the dictionaries,
but it has become a most important fact in world politics.
In 1948, when Tito broke with Stalin, it was no more than
a small cloud on the horizon; in 1956, after the Polish "October" and the Hungarian revolution, it had become a full-
size specter in Communist demonology. Five more years
sufficed to turn what was, at least outwardly, a united Communist camp into a battlefield for ideological supremacy
and political leadership between two major and several
minor centers. It even is no longer certain whether this
struggle will not break the existing polycentric framework
and move on to a lasting, irreparable rupture. Even if the
Sino-Soviet conflict were somehow to be resolved (a most
unlikely eventuality indeed), world Communism will never
be the same again, for meanwhile other Communist parties
in both Eastern and Western Europe have staked out their
claims to independence and self-determination, and the national Communists in Asia and Africa have gone even further. Communist ideologists had spent much time developing their theories about the emergence of Communism as
a world system, a social, political and economic community
of free and sovereign peoples united by close bonds of international proletarian solidarity, by common interests and

objectives. Their mutual relations were to be based on the principles of Marxism-Leninism. The argument rested on the denial of any objective reasons in the nature of the Communist commonwealth for conflicts between the states and parties belonging to it—very much in contrast to the conflicts between nations and states outside the Communist world.

Today (in 1962) all of this sounds like bitter mockery. Whether or not there are "objective" reasons for discord may be a subject for unending scholastic disputations. Meanwhile, relations between Moscow and Tirana, in so far as they still exist, are not exactly based on proletarian solidarity, nor can Sino-Soviet relations be defined by any stretch of the imagination as either close or friendly; Italian and French Communists have engaged in ideological controversy that reflects disagreement on basic tenets of belief, and M. Sékou Touré, guided presumably by the principles of complete equality, mutual advantage and comradely assistance (to quote the 1960 declaration of Communist parties), gave the Soviet ambassador just 48 hours to leave Guinea. It is a list that could be prolonged (Jugoslavia, for one, has not been mentioned), and it shows clearly that an entire era in world Communism has come to an end. Since about one-third of mankind lives under Communist régimes, any such dispute was bound to have the most far-reaching political repercussions on the world situation in general. It had begun as a family quarrel—as so many of the most bitter disputes do; for an understanding of the mechanism of fatal family quarrels one must turn not to Marx, but to one of the favorite authors of the father of scientific socialism, the one who wrote *Hamlet, Macbeth* and *King Lear*. There is a touch of Shakespearean drama in the present turmoil in the Communist world.[1]

---

[1] ". . . those were difficult, dramatic moments. It was not for nothing that Chisinevschi received the nickname of Iago, the prototype of the intriguer." (*Scanteia*, December 12, 1961. Speech by Petru Borila to the

Both Communists and non-Communists now seek an explanation for the disarray in what was once the Communist bloc. The Marxists-Leninists have gone on record with a number of most un-Marxist explanations. Instead of anaiyzing the political, social and economic roots of the conflict, they prefer to stress the deficiencies in the character of individual leaders of their intellectual incapacity to interpret correctly Marxist-Leninist theory. According to this analysis, everything is reduced to subjective factors—the ill-will or the stupidity of individuals. Similarly, most Communists have been unable or unwilling to discuss Stalinism in anything but the most superficial terms. Their doctrine prevents them from probing any deeper; Stalinism, they are told, was not a cancer in the body politic of Soviet society, but a non-malignant growth that could easily (and painlessly) be removed; they have been promised that it will not, indeed cannot, reappear. Polycentrism, likewise, is officially regarded in the Soviet Union as a temporary aberration by well-meaning but confused foreign Communists.

In theory, Communists have always admitted the existence of national differences and have made allowances for them in their tactics. In practice, however, this never amounted to much more than lip service; substantial differences in approach were actively discouraged if not roundly condemned. All this has been done in the name of the principles of Marxism-Leninism. But Marxism is essentially a 19th-century doctrine and even the writings of V. I. Lenin provide little authoritative guidance on such contemporary issues as whether the Chinese communes are preferable to the Soviet kolkhozes, or the Sovkhozes to the Jugoslav agricultural coöperatives.

The Communist "revisionists" alone have made a more

Central Committee of the Rumanian Communist Party on the activities of the local "anti-party" group.)

serious attempt to analyze and understand the tensions between the Communist parties and states—the Italians and
the Poles in 1956, and again, with renewed vigor, after the
22nd Party Congress. According to Togliatti, the polycentric system corresponds most closely to the new situation in the international Communist movement, to the
development in its doctrine and its changing structure.
Jugoslav observers, who have had more time than the rest
to ponder these questions, have stated in their theoretical
writings that Communism is not a magic formula which
will do away with conflicts and contradictions overnight.
Edward Kardelj has drawn attention to a point first made
many years before by the social-democratic critics of Bolshevism—that the starting point of each country on its "road
to socialism" was of paramount importance for its subsequent development. If the starting point was very low, it
was more than likely that political backwardness would be
perpetuated and perhaps even canonized as part of the
great heritage of the past. Such heretical comments, needless to say, provoked the sharpest criticism in both Moscow
and Peking.

There was no unanimity in the West with regard to the
emergence of several autonomous centers in the Communist
world. One school of thought was convinced that it was all
a question of productive forces, and interpreted Russia's
development from Stalin to Khrushchev and beyond mainly
in terms of "improving living standards" that would, more
or less automatically, lead toward a freer society; they now
argue that recent disputes merely reflect the great disparity
in the economic development of the different Communist
countries. There is a grain of truth in this argument. The
fact that the Chinese have their supporters in the more
backward areas of the world, and Albania as their only
European bastion, can hardly be quite accidental. Unfortunately, while backwardness breeds tyranny, it has yet to

be proved that a rise in the standard of living leads in it-self toward democracy. Czechoslovakia, economically the most prosperous Eastern bloc country, is now politically again among the most reactionary, and the economic progress achieved in East Germany in recent years has found no reflection in the political character of the Ulbricht régime. The "economic determinists" apart, expert opinion in the West has ranged from the prophets of an inevitable clash to those who deny the very possibility of conflict. Among those who foresaw Sino-Soviet tension at a very early stage was the late Wilhelm Starlinger, a German physician who wrote in 1951 that geo-political factors beyond their own control would soon set the Soviet against the Chinese Communists. He reached a correct conclusion on the basis of a wrong assumption (for the struggle for mastery in Siberia and Outer Mongolia is not at present the main bone of contention between the two Communist superpowers). Whereas the late Franz Borkenau, at about the same time, developed the more sophisticated theory that a conflict between Moscow and Peking was inevitable because totalitarian régimes were bound to establish their absolute control as far as they could; the unity of the Communist camp could be based only on domination, not on equality, and was thus bound to create discord. To this could have been added yet another apparent law of totalitarian societies—that there is no room at the top for more than one man or group of men.

At the other extreme it was contended until quite recently that a basic conflict between two or more Communist powers was impossible because, since all Communists agreed on essentials, any dispute among them could be of a tactical nature only. Some went even further and asserted that ostensible conflicts might be deliberately staged in order to "mislead the West." This exaggerated

view of the potency and validity of Marxist-Leninist doctrine led its proponents as far astray from realities as did
the views of those who denied the importance of ideological
motives altogether.

It has been suggested that we learn from a comparison
between the centrifugal forces in world Communism today
and those in the history of the Papacy, especially in its
very early days and again in the later Middle Ages. Some
of these parallels seem attractive, especially at a distance;
upon closer inspection they prove to be largely irrelevant
if not actually misleading. For each historical situation is
unique; Khrushchev and Mao bear no resemblance to Arius
and Athanasius; the present age of crisis in the Communist
camp and the era of the triple schism could not be more
dissimilar. As a non-Marxist Russian writer correctly observed, each unhappy family is unhappy in its own way.

. Historical parallels, then, will not take us very far in
the search for the causes of the split in the Communist
camp. Two questions above all remain to be answered: one
concerns the deeper reasons for the crisis; the other, Khrushchev's role in all this. What induced him to start it off?
Could he not have prevented it by displaying a more con-
ciliatory attitude?

A convincing case could perhaps be made to show that
the strife in the Communist camp was originally caused,
not by ideological disagreements, but mainly by what the
Communists call "national peculiarities." The Russians and
the Chinese, in other words, quarrel not over the correct
ideological interpretation of Marx and Lenin, but because
they are Russian and Chinese, dissimilar in national character, heirs to a markedly different cultural and social heritage, because their present political and economic interests
diverge, despite all their internationalist professions. Even
if Peking and Moscow had seen eye to eye with regard

to, say, the Stalin cult, peaceful coexistence and the organization of agriculture, other bones of contention would in all probability have appeared. The fact that Peking now claims to be closer to Leninist orthodoxy is of no great significance. Only five years ago the Chinese leaders took a more "liberal" view on some issues than their Soviet comrades; five years hence they may criticize Moscow from yet another angle. When Tito and his colleagues quarreled with Stalin in 1948, they were to the "left" of the world Communist movement, more militant and aggressive; today they are definitely to its right. The ideological orientation has changed; what remains is the insistence on their right to autonomy.

Doctrinal considerations play an important part in all this, but not a decisive one. The conflict in the Communist camp is caused by the clash between unifying and centrifugal trends. The latter are now proving the stronger—since membership in the camp is on a national basis, and since the differences between the various Communist states are much more important than most Marxists-Leninists imagined. These countries set out on their road to Communism at various times and from different starting points, and yet it is doubtful whether the conflicts could have been prevented if they had all started at the same time and from the same point.

Why did Khrushchev deliberately provoke a fight that many think might otherwise have been delayed, if not perhaps indefinitely postponed? Communist societies are not exempt from the effects of crises and shocks; they only manifest themselves in a different way. Stalin had ruled his own country and the rest of the Communist world (with two notable exceptions) with an iron fist. Gradually his régime had become a hindrance to progress; it impeded the growth of the Soviet economy and imperiled the physical safety of its ruling stratum. Stalinism had to be done away with—but it could not be disavowed without destroying at the same time the dogma of the infallibility of the Soviet Communist Party leadership. It was precisely this dogma on which the "unshakeable unity" of the camp was founded. Once it disappears, the most the Soviet leaders can hope for is to keep their leading role on the basis of their experience, and their economic and military power. There is a world of difference, however, between following the omniscient and omnipotent head of the only true faith and adherence to a worldly alliance, necessarily much looser in character, in which the members pick and choose when to follow the leader and when their own ways: an alliance in which leadership is no longer undisputed.

This transformation could at best have been only partially successful; the crisis, in any case, was of Stalin's making, not Khrushchev's. If Stalin, who was in so many ways in a stronger position, could not break Tito in 1948–49, Khrushchev could not hope to coerce a foreign party boss in 1962, short of applying military pressure. Khrushchev did not provoke the crisis but merely brought it into the open. The Communist states had ceased to be a united camp long before, and the Russians had apparently decided to make an end to what must have appeared to them as the harmful, perhaps intolerable, pretense of unity where no real unity existed. Khrushchev's outburst against Hoxha, and "Hoxha's supporters," was neither spontaneous nor unprovoked. It was comparable, perhaps, to the behavior of the head of a supposedly happy and united family who has been driven beyond endurance by some of its members, who has had to support, cover up and bear the cost of all their escapades and misdeeds, without having any real control over them. Some of the Communist parties and countries had apparently got accustomed to doing what they liked, taking Soviet support for granted. Mr. Khrushchev may have felt as President Kennedy must occasionally have felt, as he studied the dispatches from Paris, London, Bonn or *NATO* headquarters.

Sino-Soviet relations since the 22nd Congress have been marked by the desire of both sides to prevent an open break and by an equally pronounced inability to coöperate. An open break would be a major disaster and would cause irreparable harm to the prospects of Communism as a world movement; it would dwarf into insignificance all previous such disputes. But how can it be prevented except by an agreed division into spheres of interest that would be both unworkable and in utter contradiction to the basic tenets of Marxism-Leninism?

Until fairly recently it had been argued in Peking that the "bloc" needed a leader, and that such leadership could be provided only by the Soviet Union. But Mao always thought in terms of a special Chinese mission in East and Southeast Asia. Such ambitions have undoubtedly grown in the same measure as China's industry and military strength. In a long-term perspective Mao undoubtedly always assumed that "bloc" leadership would pass to China not only because China is the most populous country in the world but also because he believed his own interpretation and application of Marxism-Leninism to be much more orthodox, less afflicted by distortions and deviations, than the Soviet brand. A Chinese "co-prosperity sphere" in Asia is unworkable because most of China's neighbors are distrustful of Peking's territorial designs, and some of the neighboring Communist parties (such as the Indian and Mongolian) are openly hostile and would never voluntarily accept Chinese tutelage. China's friends are found further afield, and this makes geographical division impossible. Any attempt to create agreed blocs on ideological lines seems equally impractical; it would raise more problems than it would solve, for the pro-Chinese elements within the

Soviet sphere of influence would undoubtedly continue to look for guidance and support to Peking, and the pro-Soviet militants in the Chinese sphere would likewise maintain their allegiance to Moscow. If no solution is in sight for the conflict of the two Communist super-powers, the situation in Eastern Europe is somewhat less complicated, though reactions have by no means been uniform. The liberals have become more liberal, the diehards have become, if possible, even more hostile to liberalization. The Soviet leaders feared the possible repercussions of the 22nd Congress, and almost immediately after it they launched a concentrated propaganda campaign to "keep the ideological offensive." Men like Georgiu Dej, Ulbricht and Novotny were even more afraid of possible consequences than their Soviet comrades, as shown by the unwillingness of their press to publish in full the revelations about Stalin and Stalinism made at the 22nd Congress.

These leaders all accepted the Khrushchev line and sharply denounced Tirana and Peking on the one hand and the advocates of polycentric Communism on the other. But such support for Khrushchev was strictly limited to inter-bloc relations. In their own countries they now followed a path different from the Soviet road, deviating from the Soviet pattern as much as Gomulka or Togliatti.

In Czechoslovakia, the liquidation of the cult of the individual was at the outset restricted in the main to the decision to move the 6,000-ton Stalin statue and to "cartographic de-Stalinization" (a term actually coined in Eastern Europe). The Prague leaders also engaged in Bolshevik self-criticism in performances worthy of the good soldier Schweik. They were all misled by Slansky, Taussigova, Svab and the other victims of the 1952 trials, who were now accused of having been at one and the same time enemies and supporters of Stalin, foes and friends of Tito. Other Czech leaders, such as Gottwald and Zapotocki, have also come in for some criticism; fortunately, they are dead. As for the living, they never saw, heard or spoke evil. The Rumanian leaders, who were the last to react, were equally unwilling to commit political suicide by admitting their past "mistakes"; their local Stalinists (such as Pauker, Luca, Chisinevschi) were, it appears, purged long ago. But what about Georgiu Dej, the Party secretary-general—now, as under Stalin? Well, he could not do much, we learn, since his telephone was tapped by the Paukers and Lucas. The Bulgars behaved in a slightly more dignified way and decided to oust a man who had been in partial disgrace for some years past, Vilko-Chervenkov, one-time supreme Party boss. The Bulgarians also used the opportunity to rehabilitate fully Traicho Kostov, one of the chief victims of the régime, who had been partially rehabilitated in 1956. If Novotny delivered a 20,000-word report, and the Bulgarian Zhivkov needed 30,000, Ulbricht of East Germany was the most long-winded (35,000 words) and said less than anybody else. He gave the order to change the names of some cities, streets and factories, brought new accusations against some of his foes eliminated from the Party leadership long ago, and defended himself against allegations of having engaged in the cult of the individual. Being in the very front line of "imperialist attack," he had apparently persuaded Moscow that it would be unwise to weaken himself and his régime by misplaced self-criticism at this time. Kadar of Hungary, whose speech was the shortest, said, not without some justification, that the whole commotion did not really concern his country, since the leading Stalinists had been chased out of Budapest back in 1956. There was some relaxation in the cultural field in Hungary following the 22nd Congress, though less than in Poland. Gomulka had to dissociate himself from the open advocates of polycentrism, but he did so halfheartedly, declaring at the same time that there was no longer a "center" that could prescribe the policy to be followed by him, his Party and government. Jugoslavia and Albania, the old foes, found themselves outside the "camp"; the Albanians did not even wait for the end of the 22nd Congress to counterattack, whereas the Jugoslavs, the trail-blazers of polycentrism, could for once afford to watch the storm around them with a measure of equanimity.

Western European Communists, free of the burden and responsibilities of state power, diverged even more widely in their reactions. The ideological dispute was highlighted by the polemics between the Italian and French Communists, which go back to the year 1956 when Paris denounced Togliatti for his polycentric heresies. When the polemics were now resumed, the French predictably argued that unity was a precondition for the victory of Communism, that polycentrism would open the door to factionalism in the world movement. But the real quarrel was not about polycentrism, which is now an established fact, but about the use made of their new autonomy by the various Communist Parties. Togliatti, and even more the younger leaders of the Party, wanted to submit the Stalin era to a searching critique and to draw from it far-reaching conclusions for the present.

Why was it that the French Communists opted for a policy that, but for the support for Khrushchev against Albania and China, is neo-Stalinist in character, whereas the Italians joined the extreme revisionist wing of the world Communist movement? This can undoubtedly be traced to the composition of the two Parties. Both have strong mass support among industrial workers, but the French Party has always been far more Stalinist in character. At one time it attracted many intellectuals, but gradually antagonized most of them. Its top leadership has been subjected to many purges over the last decade. The Party has become ossified, though French domestic conditions apparently have a galvanizing effect even on fossils. The French Party is therefore little influenced by international affairs, whereas the Italian Party, being far more alive and sensitive, at once registered the shock. Its leadership is far superior to the French in political and general intelligence. Most of the other European Communist parties are somewhere in between these extremes of neo-Stalinism and "revisionism." For the time being the Italians are more or less in isolation. But there are signs that the tide is running in favor of Togliatti's views. The North African Communist parties, for instance, who had been for a long time under the guardianship of the French, have come to regard Rome as the place to turn for help and guidance in recent years.

The problems besetting European Communism appear strange and probably somewhat fanciful to the sister parties in other parts of the world. Most Communist Parties outside Europe have not expressed any strong views about de-Stalinization and polycentrism. They were established as parties only in the last decades, and the whole Stalin period belongs for them to pre-history. While Frenchmen and Italians quarrel about whether Trotsky should be rehabilitated, the Ceylonese Communists have already entered an alliance with the local Trotskyites; the leadership of the Indian Communist Party has likewise engaged in highly unorthodox activities. These Parties have had a comparatively large measure of autonomy for many years. In part it was conceded to them for tactical reasons, in part they simply took it in the absence of a central institution exercising control over the activities of the various branches of world Communism.

In recent years the formerly clear dividing line between Communists, National Communists, and sundry friends of the movement has been partly obliterated. In 1960, countries such as Cuba, Mali, Ghana and Guinea were elevated to the status of "National Democracies"—in contrast to other independent countries such as India, Indonesia and Egypt, still (at least at that time, and Marxian analysis can change swiftly) under the sway of the "national bourgeoisie." At the 22nd Soviet Party Congress, representatives of the Convention People's Party of Ghana, of the Guinea Democratic Party and the Union Soudanaise of Mali were treated as full-fledged comrades and were invited to address the Congress, a privilege bestowed only on Parties accepting all the changing articles of faith. Such practices, scheduled to create a reservoir of good will in the *tiers monde,* in fact contributed to the general confusion; only a month later, following the December 1961 "plot of the students and teachers," Sékou Touré had expelled the Soviet ambassador and accused Soviet and other foreign and local Communists of plotting against his rule. Mali is as unpredictable as Guinea from the Soviet point of view, and Ghana (then under its official ideology of Nkrumahism) looked like an even less likely candidate for membership in the "camp." Dr. Castro was Russia's safest bet in this class; believing himself under strong pressure from "American imperialism," he is unlikely to bolt. But in a wider perspective he may not merit absolute confidence; he came to power, after all, without Soviet help. The men in Moscow know from bitter experience that such self-made revolutionaries are prone to cause difficulties later on.

The Cuban leaders want the whole of Latin America to follow their example; and it would appear that only such a brand of National Communism stands any chance of making headway in this hemisphere. But this in its turn would contribute to the emergence of yet another regional "center," and thus contribute to the spread of polycentric Communism. It is perhaps somewhat ironical that any progress by world Communism can now be achieved only by strengthening the centrifugal trends and thus weakening the movement from within. However ardent their feelings of friendship and admiration, there is no room for Russia and China in the blueprints of most non-European Communists for the future of their continents. To hamper Soviet activities even more, Chinese Communist propaganda in these parts is less than coöperative, and the disruptive theories of the Jugoslavs, those first secessionists, have gained wide currency in many of these capitals.

The very success of Communism in the underdeveloped countries has been its undoing. It has been adulterated and yields a strange harvest: under a veneer of Marxist-Leninist ideology, of anti-imperialist slogans and state capitalism, influences and interests are at work which have nothing to do with Marxism-Leninism and sometimes nothing to do with any European doctrine whatever. Communism is Africanized and Asianized even faster and more thoroughly than Christianity, because it is a secular movement and therefore in greater need of adaptation. The outcome is a mixture of Communist elements and components alien to it. Political scientists undertaking some form of qualitative analysis will have a hard job to establish the exact composition of the mixture and the character of each régime, and whether it belongs to the bloc or not. As the bloc is transformed into a polycentric system, and that system itself endangered by sudden shifts of political allegiance, it will be exceedingly difficult to determine who belongs where, especially as those most directly concerned may not always know the answer themselves.

Will Communist countries and Parties be able to coexist with each other? Their internal differences are in some ways more intractable than West-East tensions, precisely because each believes itself to be the sole possessor of the means of grace, because they are more dynamic, because their sense of mission is so much more acute. In these circumstances the heretic must appear as a traitor and hence a worse enemy than the open foe. Stalin could enter into a working alliance with Hitler but never with "Judas" Trotsky. But have there not been changes in the Soviet world in recent years? Has Soviet policy not become much more elastic? Isn't there still a large measure of common ground and interest which may prevail over all the disagreements? Were there not similar "national deviations" in the very early days of the Comintern which were successfully overcome?

There are essential differences between the "National Communism" of the early 1920's (in Germany, Turkey, and some other countries) and present-day trends, just as the "revisionism" of 60 years ago is radically different in character from the contemporary trend of the same name. One was prehistoric, so to speak, the other is post-Communist, based on a confrontation with Communism in action. The earlier variety of National Bolshevism was an attempt from outside to water down Communism. Present-day National Communism is a disruptive trend within the camp and hence infinitely more dangerous.

To an outsider, the causes of the original dispute between Khrushchev and Mao, between Tito and Hoxha, between Togliatti and Thorez, may still seem negligible. A contemporary Hindu may have reached similar conclusions with regard to the quarrel between Luther and Leo X. Communists may coexist; a final and lasting break may be prevented if they find a *modus vivendi* on the basis of mutual tolerance. But toleration is a state of mind notably absent from missionary movements, and from their point of view the Communists may rightly fear it; a slackening of the dynamism of the world movement, of its revolutionary zest and fervor, would have incalculable consequences. If factions are officially recognized on the international level, it would not be long before similar factions were established in each Communist Party. The monolithic unity would be broken, party democracy would be restored, and the Communist Parties would gradually become the same as other parties; for obviously there can be no iron discipline at home if there is anarchy within the world movement. It would be the end of Communism as we have known it in our time: the Communist Parties might remain radical, even revolutionary in character, but they would cease to be totalitarian.

Such prospects may seem almost unthinkable today, but what are the alternatives? An open break, followed by a struggle in which all means short of war would be used. Looking to the more distant future, toward a China stronger in industrial power and self-confidence and foolishly unafraid of an atomic holocaust, even the possibility of war between the Communist super-powers cannot be entirely ruled out. Most likely, at least for the foreseeable future, is a state of "neither war nor peace," an uneasy coexistence based not on toleration of the rival but on the impossibility of overthrowing him. Thaws will alternate with freezes, attempts to iron out existing differences and resume closer contacts will give way to the fiercest political and propaganda warfare; in short, it will be a state of cold war.

There seems to be no short cut leading the Communists out of the predicament now facing them. A greater measure of organizational unity between them is now impossible. If even Stalin did not contemplate merging the East European countries with Russia into one Communist superstate, such a development is utterly impossible in other continents among the newly independent countries where nationalist passions play an even more important role. The degree of cohesion of the world Communist movement is reflected in the history of its international organization. The Comintern exercised a fairly close control over all its members. The Cominform (in the words of Togliatti) did only two things: it published a weekly newspaper and condemned Tito. Since the dissolution of the Cominform, an even looser form of coördination has prevailed: yearly meetings, not unlike the Councils of the Catholic Church in past centuries, convoked to publish lengthy manifestos. In the past, these meetings were apparently preceded by private discussions between the Soviet and Chinese leaders, agreeing as best they could and then bringing the resulting compromise before the assembly of the 80-odd Communist Parties. This practice too has now broken down. Instead, a tug-of-war ensued and a jockeying for positions in which small Parties, temporarily at any rate, have assumed an importance out of proportion to their real strength. It is a situation somewhat reminiscent of the United Nations General Assembly, and the big powers are showing signs of impatience.

What should Western policy be vis-à-vis these tensions in the Communist world? In a short-range perspective, Communist pressure on the West will certainly not lessen; it may even increase temporarily since the Parties concerned may have to prove their undiminished militancy and fervor. But in a more distant view the lines dividing the two present power blocs may well become more blurred—a prospect that need not necessarily dismay the West. The West should follow with cautious sympathy, as it has done, the endeavor of some Communist parties and states to shed the heritage of tyranny and totalitarianism; it should keep a line open to all the sides irrespective of their orientation at this moment, but make no effort to intervene at any point. World politics are moving toward a new stage which may be full of surprises and in which maneuverability will be an important asset.

(1962)

REMEMBERING STALIN

GREAT MEN, taken up in any way—surely we know this at least since Carlyle—are profitable company: we can hardly contemplate them without gaining something. Yet how to define greatness?

"Of course, history alone can show how important this or that public man has been." It was Stalin who said this. But history, we are told, usually passes final judgments only after people cease to care; meanwhile each generation does its revaluing according to its political lights. To forecast how "this or that public man" is likely to fare in the judgment of coming generations amounts to predicting the course of politics of the next century. Communists will hardly ever agree with non-communists about the role of Stalin; even among the former, differences of opinion will persist as to whether the late "father of the people" did more harm than good, or whether in that so-called last analysis he was "a progressive force" after all. Such fluctuations in the post-humous fortunes of historical figures can persist for a long time. Up till the middle 'thirties Russian historians took a dim view of the activities of Ivan IV ("the Terrible") who, they said, had been in a state close to mental illness. In the heyday of Stalinism (for obvious reasons) there was a wholesale reappraisal and Ivan became one of the great heroes of Russian history—cruel by neces-

sity, yet wise in his decisions. After Stalin's death,[1] the Tsar
was at once downgraded, cautiously at first, but recently
in a more sweeping way. Ivan IV has been dead for close
on four hundred years; Jenghiz Khan has not been with
us for even longer, and yet, as we recently learned to our
surprise, Marxists cannot agree as to his place in history
(some, in Mongolia and Peking, think he played a progressive role; those in Moscow disagree emphatically).

Such shifts and reversals in historical appraisal are bound
to be far more abrupt in a dictatorship, but of course they
do happen elsewhere: the historiography of the French Revolution and of Napoleon is an obvious example. Is it not
extremely likely that rival historians of the future will cham-
pion Stalin against Trotsky, and *vice versa,* re-enacting the
whole drama, in the same way that Aulard saw Danton as
the hero of the revolution, while Mathiez held it to be
Robespierre? The Michelet school already seems to be behind us: those who (as Pieter Geyl argues) described the
terror but did not allow the radiant beauty of their dreams
to be darkened by what they had so keenly observed. Patriotism and "loyalty to the revolution" the decisive criteria
then; the "strengthening of Soviet power" became the chief
test in a later age. Since Stalin did not reintroduce private
ownership of the means of production, he could scarcely
escape remaining progressive whatever he did. Had fifty
million people perished in the process instead of five or
ten, would "quantity" then have become a new quality? The
dialectic doesn't tell us.

Yet there are good reasons for thinking that Stalin will
fare worse than the heroes of the French revolution. "Public men," to use his own phrase, are, after all, appraised
in the context of their times. Some of Ivan's actions were

---

[1] JOSEPH VISSARIONOVICH STALIN *died in Moscow on 5 March 1953, and
was buried in the Kremlin. (He has since been re-buried.)*

deplorable, but then his age was not exactly a model of enlightenment. Stalin, on the other hand, will be judged as a twentieth-century ruler, not as a sixteenth-century despot—and against this background historians cannot fail to note the relapse into barbarity. It is surprising (and somewhat illogical) that some historians who believe that the golden progressive age is ahead of us should have any doubts about this, for a more civilized time is likely to judge Stalinism even more harshly than our own. Especially to Communist historians of the future, Stalin will be a major embarrassment. They may even do him some injustice, for the comparatively sane beginnings of a public figure in history are usually overshadowed by later wilder, more dramatic events. Who but a few readers of Suetonius remember that Caligula was universally welcomed as a moderate leader when he came to power and promised to restore the rule of law suspended under Tiberius? And who recalls that Napoleon was first hailed as the leader most likely to restore peace to France?

If history rarely passes unanimous judgments, still each generation of historians feels obliged to take a stand. Both Burke and Paine have survived as major commentators on the French revolution despite their passionate engagement. I wonder whether today's relativist and wait-and-see historians will fare as well. I read the other day that Mr. E. H. Carr has said that "to us Hitler, at the moment, seems a bad man, but will they think Hitler a bad man in a hundred years' time or will they think the German society of the 'thirties bad? . . ." Most of us think that Hitler *was* "a bad man" and that German society was in something less than good shape. It is quite likely that a hundred years from now some misguided people will put *all* the blame on German society; according to some evidence, this may even happen much earlier. Yet what concern is this of ours? Has the effort to anticipate the judgment of posterity ever really produced great works of historiography? Politically the suspension of moral standards is disastrous. It should be fairly obvious by now that the believers in "historical necessity" bear at least some responsibility for the rise of Hitler and Stalin; a great many more people would have resisted the dictatorship had it not been said to be irresistible, had they not been captives of some notion of a "wave of the future" or an "historic process." But as Leon Trotsky pointed out in his biography of Stalin (1939):

> *Nero, too, was a product of his epoch. Yet after he perished his statues were smashed, and his name was scraped off everything. The vengeance of history is more terrible than the vengeance of the most powerful General Secretary. I venture to think that this is consoling.*

We are, of course, all anti-Stalinists nowadays. The friends or relatives of many of his victims are still alive; in Russia the authorities have really only just begun to permit them to give expression to their feelings. It may take years before the anti-Stalin wave reaches its peak. Yet in a few decades the sufferings will have receded into the past and one can foresee with some certainty a revisionist school of historians who will reassess Stalin in historical perspective without emotional involvement. But who can believe that he will ever again be proclaimed as "one of the geniuses of world history?" Stalin dominated a greater stage and his actions had an impact on many more people than had either Cromwell or Napoleon: which makes him very important indeed. Everything done by the ruler of two hundred million people is important, however cruel, however stupid. Disastrous though the policies of the present Chinese leaders may be (unless they succeed in reducing the population of their country by some significant percentage), China is bound to remain a big and therefore an important country. It is apparently exceedingly difficult to ruin a big country, and only Hitler seems to have succeeded, but then it is too early to say whether his was a lasting success, and anyway Germany was too small to qualify as a super-power by twentieth-century standards. Any President of the United States after 1914 (even Hoover, even Eisenhower), any ruler of Russia after 1880, any leader of China since 1930, must figure prominently in future history books.

Stalin, as the hero and villain of the totalitarian age, will probably be compared not with Napoleon or Robespierre but with his most outstanding contemporary, namely Adolf Hitler. This, curiously enough, may be the best way of salvaging part of his reputation.[2] Hitler suffered from romantic delusions; he thought he could dominate the world as the leader of a people of seventy million and with a doctrine of racial exclusivity which made collaboration with other peoples impossible. This, in a way, doomed him from the very beginning. Stalin, the realist, was far more aware of the limitations of his land and the international Communist movement—his Marxian studies stood him in good stead here.

Within the framework of their own movements, Hitler was undoubtedly the more important and the more gifted leader. Without Hitler, National Socialism as we know it would not have come to power. The extreme right might have prevailed in 1933, but a Germany led by a Goering, (not to mention a Frick or Hugenberg) would have been a very different proposition. When Stalin came to power the course of the Russian revolution was already set. After 1921 there was no serious attempt at military intervention; Bolshevism would have remained in power with or without

[2] We know little about what Stalin thought of Hitler; he never publicly ridiculed him, as far as I know. Hitler thought highly of Stalin; in his *Table Talk* there are frequent references to him as one "of the most extraordinary figures in world history," . . . "Stalin too must command our unconditional respect. In his own way he is *ein genialer Kerl*" (oddly translated in the English edition as "a hell of a fellow").

Stalin. Hitler was an excellent speaker, absolutely dominated his subordinates by force of personality, and exuded
the charisma of a leader of men or, at any rate, of one
"possessed." Stalin was anti-charismatic; he came to power
by organizational scheming and plotting, and ruled by
means of an elaborate apparatus, but only after he had
liquidated the "Old Bolsheviks" almost without exception.
(Apparently Hitler had only contempt for his *alte Genossen;*
he was certainly not afraid of them, which may be the
reason why so many of them survived.) With the exception
of June 1934 there were no major purges in Nazi Germany:
Goebbels, Goering, Himmler, *et al.*, remained with him to
the end of the war.

Yet a comparison suggests that Stalin was more ideally
suited for the control of a totalitarian state. His critics have
made great play of his intellectual shortcomings. That he
was not a great thinker needs hardly to be emphasized today (though the distance between him and the other Old
Bolsheviks was perhaps less than some wish us to believe).
In this, as in most other respects, he was mediocre. But
an intellectual at the helm might not have lasted long; in
difficult situations he might have wavered, for there were
so many aspects to be considered, so many eventualities to
be taken into account. Stalin's mind was a simple one; there
were a number of basic truths which he had learned at an
early age, and these were all that mattered for his purpose.
Surely he understood them better than his rivals did: that
only power mattered and that all the rest was idle talk—
that the cadres decide everything—that heavy industry was
more decisive than light industry—and so on. His very limitations were an enormous advantage: they made it easier
for him to act. That he frequently took wrong decisions did
not greatly matter—somebody else would be paying for
them in any case.

Both Hitler and Stalin regarded themselves as indispensable; they would have found much common ground in their distrust and contempt of the people; nor was there much to choose between their views about such things as justice or truth. Hitler could afford to be cynically frank in his infrequent utterances about these subjects, whereas Stalin had to be described in official and unofficial writings as modest, sincere, truthful and deeply devoted to the masses. Hitler fancied himself to be a kind man, basically; whereas Stalin (according to the official literature) was merciless towards the enemies of the party but a paragon of humanity and solicitude in every other respect. Hitler acted and reacted quickly without much self control; Stalin was unhurried in his decisions. Stalin will be judged by rational criteria to a far greater extent than Hitler; yet what appeared to some of his contemporaries titanic achievements may appear to future historians as so much sound and fury. History is usually more willing to forgive cruelty (even senseless cruelty) than hypocrisy; surely Stalin was one of history's great hypocrites.

He shared with Hitler a great capacity for sustained work, though he was more painstaking, pedantic, plodding, and therefore better suited to direct a gigantic bureaucracy. Hitler was bored by the minute organizational work in which Stalin found obvious satisfaction. As strategists they were apparently equally gifted (which means that they understood no more about military science than possibly one or two million others). If they proved to be right on occasion against the advice of their generals, this reflects the quality of the judgments of professional soldiers. It is a' most comical how easily myths are created—and believed. Stalin's best-known Western biographer describes his image as a strategist: "a prodigy of patience, tenacity and vigilance, almost omnipresent, almost omniscient," and on another occasion: "He displayed extraordinary will power, tenacity and cool headedness." One should compare this with what is now said and written on the subject in Russia by those who ought to know. Hitler's ideas of the *Blitzkrieg*, it could be argued, proved very successful in the West—but disastrous in Russia. Stalin, in his military decisions as in his foreign policy, for many years mainly reacted to outside challenges; domestic affairs had for him absolute priority during the 'thirties. Once he had decided to "build socialism in one country" he was more or less on his own: nothing that Marx, and very little that Lenin, had written was of much help in the transformation of Soviet society. Hitler's position was much easier; he never envisaged radical social change; economics and domestic affairs were of little interest to him; his party never had a clear social and economic program. Yet is it really correct to say that German economy "stagnated" under Hitler? In fact it made considerable progress (in comparison with the low of 1932/3), even if the rate of growth was much smaller than that in the Soviet Union; it was bound to be smaller in a country that was already fully industrialized. Once the worst of the world crisis was over the German economy would have improved anyway—but so would the Soviet economy after 1929 under any sensible leadership. Much of the German industrial production was geared to armament (though less than is commonly assumed). It is one of the major riddles of the Third Reich that Hitler did not prepare more efficiently for his great war. Some historians now say that he did not "really" want a war; I tend to believe that his ignorance on all things economic was a decisive factor.

Stalin's real and lasting merit (or so it is often said) was the industrialization of Russia. He realized that it was a race against time, that Russia would again be overwhelmed as it had been so often in its past, unless it emerged as a strong industrial power within a decade or so. And so it did—there was "the tremendous advance in heavy industry in the 'thirties"; the Red Army was "strong and fully prepared" when the great test came in 1941; the Nazi menace was defeated; Russia became "the strongest industrial and political power in Europe"—all this owing to the man in the Kremlin who relentlessly pursued his aims, regardless of all obstacles and difficulties. This amounts, surely, to the most persuasive plea that can be made for Stalin. Yet this version has already received some bad knocks, and in the years to come not much of it is likely to survive.

The first World War, the Revolution, and the Civil War had interrupted Russia's industrialization. By the time the ravages had healed, in the late 'twenties, the stage was set for rapid industrialization—under any leadership. It was merely a question of the rate of growth; Five-Year-Plans were not Stalin's invention. Soviet industrial output between 1928 and 1940 might have only been doubled rather than quadrupled under a less brutal régime, but it is more than doubtful whether this would have had a fatal effect on Russia's ability to resist the German invasion. Stalin's mistakes and failures weigh heavily in the balance: the dislocation in industry and the weakening of the army caused by the purges, the widespread disaffection of the population caused by the forced collectivization (which even Soviet authors are beginning to admit was "a mistake" as carried out), Stalin's refusal to believe in, and to prepare his forces for, a Nazi attack when all the world knew it would come in spring 1941. When all the mistakes are added up, not much remains of the myth of the great leader who foresaw so much. That the terrible reverses during the first part of the war were unnecessary is now maintained by all Soviet authors; Russia, after all, was neither Denmark nor Holland, and a *Blitzkrieg* could not have worked. She had been a formidable military power even under the not-so-efficient leadership of the Tsars; her armies—with the advantages of vast numbers and territory—had defeated greater military geniuses than Hitler. The question whether, at such a high price, Stalin was "necessary" for the Communists has been debated in some detail. Necessity has been the tyrant's plea since time immemorial. Stalin's decision to achieve a high rate of industrial growth by holding down consumption and wages and by concentrating on high investment rates and the production of goods that cannot be consumed was dictated not by economic but by political considerations. Such a policy could be pursued only by a dictatorship, and (as an economic historian has recently emphasized) it provided a government with a social function and a justification for its existence:

> . . . a policy of rapid increases in the levels of consumption may, in the short run bridge the political difficulties, but in the long run is likely to create troublesome problems. Plentiful supplies of consumers' goods produce a climate of relaxation among the populace which is not congenial to dictatorships. Once the stress and strain have been reduced, the problem of political liberty is almost bound to arise. . . .

Necessary or not, the social impact of Stalinism on the Russians was far more lasting than Hitler's on the Germans. So was its impact on Soviet intellectual life. Isaac Deutscher concludes his biography of Stalin with an impressive comparison of intellectual life in the Third Reich and in Stalinist Russia. Hitler, we learn, ruined German cultural life; Stalin on the other hand gave a tremendous impetus to Russian intellectual life by sending the whole nation to school. "Its [Germany's] medical men were turned into specialists on the racialist purity of blood and into assassins of those whose blood was deemed impure. . . ." The level of German

---

[3] Alexander Gerschenkron in his book, *Economic Backwardness in Historical Perspective* (1962).

medicine suffered from the exodus of the Jews, and several hundred German physicians committed unspeakable crimes against humanity. Yet 99% of German physicians went about their jobs as they had before and as they have since, as did Soviet physicians under Stalin, doing some good and some harm (inventing, incidentally, the sulphonamides and making a few other discoveries). Mr. Deutscher also stated that "Stalin has not, like Hitler, forbidden the new generation to read and study the classics of their own literature whose ideological outlook does not accord with his." Closer investigation shows that much of Dostoevsky, some of Tolstoy, Leskov, Pisemski and others, was either not published at all under Stalin, or in small editions for specialists; other classics were carefully edited. Hitler banned the works of Heine and other Jews; no other German classics, with the exception of Lessing's *Nathan der Weise*, were banned. Nazism, being less ideological in character, took less interest in cultural affairs; it had not time in half a dozen years to ripen into full totalitarianism. In order to survive (with some notable exceptions) it sufficed not to be anti-Nazi; in the Soviet Union a far greater measure of active participation and affirmation was needed. This is, I think, an important point that has not been given sufficient attention. The glaring exceptions in Nazi Germany were in architecture, painting, and sculpture. Here there is a curious parallelism with Stalin's Russia; for all dictators apparently have a weakness for monumental buildings, statues, and portraits. Psychoanalysis was banned in Nazi Germany (as in Russia) and it became difficult to do serious work in biology in either country.

In comparing the state of literature in Nazi Germany and in Stalin's Russia one finds some striking differences. Many German writers compromised themselves by signing political manifestos and, by and large, nothing of great importance was written in the era of the Third Reich. Yet there was no pressure on German writers to describe in their poems Hitler's boyhood in Braunau, or in their novels his military exploits as an N.C.O. in World War I. Their works were mainly an ineffectual kind of escapism. With the exception of an exceedingly small group who had a special commission to do so, they did not deal with the history of the Nazi party in their works. In the Soviet Union the "cult of personality" was incomparably more pervasive; the Leonidzes and Pogodins, the Pavlenkos and Virtas, the Alexei Tolstois and Surkovs devoted poems, plays, and novels to the leader. Yet not only the hacks created such literature; the greatest contemporary writers made their contributions too—Leonid Leonov (*Slovo o pervom deputate*) for instance, or Konstantin Fedin (*Uncommon Summer*) or Sholokhov (*Virgin Soil Upturned*). So did many who are now in the forefront of the battle for a more liberal course in Soviet literature—Alexander Tvardovsky (in *Strana Muravia*), Margarita Aliger, Konstantin Simonov. Even the authors of children's literature made their contribution. I have been rereading what Soviet writers wrote on the occasion of Stalin's seventieth birthday in December 1949—and it is a painful experience. It has since been argued that the "cult of the individual" was indeed very harmful but that, nevertheless, some great works were produced even in that dark period. The underlying idea is that one could delete the scenes or anecdotes where Stalin is introduced just as an entry from an encyclopedia could be omitted. This may be so in a very few cases where the Stalin episodes were quite obviously added more or less artificially to a poem or novel (perhaps after some outside prodding). Yet by and large such surgery is quite impracticable. The books and poems and plays did not merely express fulsome praise for the leader; they were permeated with the spirit of the epoch. According to one of the proverbs which Chairman Khrushchev likes to quote, a little gall suffices to spoil a barrel of honey. . . . The situation in other fields—whether we take the cinema in the early 'fifties or philosophy or political economy—was not very different. The intellectual impact of Stalinism was no less lasting than its social results; the Soviet Union will have to bear the consequences for a long time to come.

If Hitler was evil, the element of calculated cruelty was much smaller in Stalin. To equate the Nazi extermination camps and Stalin's labor camps, as some writers do, betrays, it seems to me, a lack of knowledge, or imagination, or both. Stalin was evil "from necessity" (the ideological argument ran); he used terrible means to reach a humanist ideal; he killed in the name of liberty and for a better future. All this may not have made a noticeable difference to his victims, but it did in fact put certain limitations in his way—limitations which Hitler, for obvious reasons, never faced. It is debatable whether, and to what degree, Stalin still believed in the future ideal society towards the close of his life; or whether, as far as he was concerned, the means had become the ends themselves. (I have heard it said in Russia that "only the methods were deficient but the basic idea was—and is—good. . . ." Others have insisted that "the way Stalin set about introducing Communism was bad, but the basic idea wasn't much good either. . . .") It certainly appears now to have been naïve, and naïveté in politics (as Stalin observed in one of his articles in 1917) "borders on the criminal." There is one important mitigating circumstance: Hitler's tyranny was entirely of his own making; Stalin's dictatorship was very much in line with his own character and style, yet the ground was largely prepared by historical circumstances: Tsarist *samoderzhavie* and the kind of régime established by Lenin in 1917 with its built-in tendency towards autocracy. The following year Rosa Luxemburg predicted accurately how it would all end—and at that time there was no Stalin in sight.

Seventeen thousand historians in the Soviet Union (according to the figures of October 1961)—and add to that a handful outside Russia—face then a touching dilemma: how to explain the phenomenon of Stalinism in terms of Marxian historical materialism? Engels wrote that whether in a particular country at any particular time a particular individual emerged was "pure accident," but if that man were removed the demand for a substitute would immediately arise and the substitute would be found *out Lion qua mal* Plekhanov, the "father of Russian Marxism" who wrote the classic work about the role of the individual in history, was even more emphatic:

> It has long been observed that the great talents appear everywhere, whenever the social conditions favorable to their development exist. This means that every man of talent who becomes a social force is the product of social relations. . . . A great man is great not because his personal qualities give individual features to great historical events, but because he possesses qualities which make him most capable of serving the great social needs of the time. . . .

What social and political conditions existed in Russia in the 'twenties that favored the appearance of Stalin and Stalinism? What social relations produced Stalin—and what qualities did he possess that made him "most capable of serving the great social needs of the time?" These are admittedly diffcult, not to say awkward, questions, and it is not surprising that we have not yet had a Marxist explanation from Russia. Since it is rather unlikely that Soviet historians will find Marxism completely satisfactory on the role of the hero in history, they will inevitably have to play down the role of Stalin. Perhaps he was not so important after all? In the most recent Russian historical works Stalin is not mentioned (or quoted) at all, even where for obvious reasons he should figure quite prominently. Instead, such circumlocutions as the "leadership of the party" (*Rukovodstvo* KPSS) are used; this is somewhat threadbare for it is not exactly a secret that one man constituted the leadership of the party for many years. Such sleight of hand will not serve very well on the stage of history. The Russians, with very few exceptions, suffered a great deal under Stalin. One can, perhaps, make Trotsky an "unperson" but not Stalin; it would be inhuman and, incidentally, ineffective to belittle Stalinism. Since the Russians are very human and desperately eager to "rehabilitate" their past, the present leadership has been steering a middle course: from the release of the Kremlin doctors in April 1953 to the publication of *Ivan Denisovich* in November 1962. But as George Orwell once wrote (in September 1946!), with that uncanny insight of his:

> In five years it may be as dangerous to praise Stalin as it was to attack him two years ago. But I should not regard this as an advance. Nothing is gained by teaching the parrot a new word.

Broadly speaking, four periods can be discerned in the process of de-Stalinization. The first began almost immediately after the death of the dictator in March, 1953; the purges were discontinued, the leadership re-organized, some secret police chiefs were removed. In this period Ilya Ehrenburg wrote his novel *The Thaw*. There was as yet no open criticism of Stalin, but his name was mentioned less often in public speeches, the press, on the radio and in scholarly publications. Some of the Old Bolsheviks were now rehabilitated, albeit posthumously. Publicity was given to these rehabilitations only after the famous Twentieth Party Congress in February, 1956, which constitutes the beginning of the second phase of de-Stalinization. This congress proclaimed the consolidation of "socialist legality" and the return to "Leninist norms of inner-party democracy." The official party history (the famous *Short Course*) was criticizel for the first time. The highlights of this congress, Khruschev's famous speech on February 25th (the text of which became known several weeks later) was a most effective debunking of Stalin all along the line. Yet it was a *secret* speech and has not been made public in the Soviet bloc to this very day. The Soviet leaders preferred to move with great caution. ("We had to tell the people the truth," Khrushchev said later). Word got round, nevertheless, and the second wave of de-Stalinization reached its peak in the summer of 1956 with a great debate among the Communist Parties. The moment it appeared that the reaction might get out of hand, instructions were given to apply the brakes—as the Central Committee's resolution of June 30, 1956 (on the "cult of personality") and *Pravda* editorials (to the effect that Stalin's terrorism was necessary) bear witness.

In these circumstances there was a strictly limited scope for an intellectual ferment that found expression in a number of anthologies, novels, and poems. Even the most famous novel of the period, Vladimir Dudintsev's *Not by Bread Alone* was not really directed against Stalin and Stalinism but merely against certain negative features in the society and a certain type of leader (*"Drozdov"*). Yet once the immovable controls had been removed, the borderline between what was permissible and what was taboo was no longer quite clear. A kind of no-man's land came into being and some courageous men dared occasional forays—and beat their retreat when they sensed that the cross-fire was too dangerous. The old leadership (the Molotovs and the Kaganovichs) warned against sweeping de-Stalinization; they were willing at most to criticize specific aspects of the Stalin epoch, but they refused to damn Stalin himself—both because they did not believe in the new-fangled methods of leadership and because they had been so deeply involved personally. Once de-Stalinization really got under way, where would it all end? Would it not cause (as did "de-Nazification") an unending chain of mutual recriminations and purges? Khrushchev, and Mikoyan too, had been members of the Politburo under Stalin, yet they intended to carry de-Stalinization further than the diehards; for them, and for the younger generation of leaders, this was a necessity in order to win the freedom essential for carrying out a policy that differed in some essential respects from Stalinism. Such revisions could only be made once they had dissociated themselves clearly from the legacy of the past.

After the diehards had been excluded from the party leadership, the stage was set for yet another step forward, which came at the Twenty-second Congress of the CPSU in October, 1961. This time there were public speeches about the horrors of the Stalin era, ranging from a somewhat perfunctory statement by Mikhail Suslov to the touching spiritualist account of Madame Lazurkina about Lenin's visitations and what he had told her about Stalin. This congress, like the one five years earlier, provoked heated discussions in the Communist camp. Again it appeared at one stage that the reaction would be too violent. Again, as in summer 1956, the limits of "the thaw" had to be stressed. Yet in contrast to 1956, fresh impetus was given to the anti-Stalin campaign by the publication of a number of literary works such as Evtushenko's *Stalin's Heirs* in October, 1962, and the first books in a new genre hitherto only known in the West—the labor camp literature. This brings us to the fourth stage—or has de-Stalinization now become a continuing and paramount part of the revolution from above?

It is too soon to say. We are more certain about the limits of this movement for the time being. Everything Stalin did after 1935 can (in fact *must*) now be criticized in Russia; it is freely admitted that he committed "political mistakes"

in 1917 and 1923/4, that collectivization was unduly "harsh."
Yet he is almost exclusively denounced only for what he did
to his own supporters, the men and women who were willing to follow him almost blindly. He has not been taken to
task for what he did to the opposition in the party (let alone
to those outside it). Evidently Trotsky, Zinoviev, Kamenev,
as well as Bukharin and Tomski, still remain political adver-
saries of the CPSU of 1963. True, they were no longer "criminals," "enemies of the people," "German or Japanese spies,"
admissions that were made rather grudgingly, and so far
implicitly. It seems fairly likely that within a few years the
right-wing deviationists will be partly rehabilitated (rumors
to that effect seem to have been premature). If they committed political mistakes, didn't Stalin? The left-wing opposition of the 'twenties presents greater difficulties to
Khrushchevian historiography, and no solution seems to be
in sight. Yet all these are tactical problems, so to speak; the
basic issues have not yet been faced.

According to the currently valid version, Stalinism was
not inherent in Leninism, was *not* its natural and logical successor, but merely an aberration, a form of degeneration.
The structure of Soviet society remained sound, economic
reconstruction continued, and foreign policy was "progressive," even during the darkest years. Some have compared
—wrongly I believe—Stalin to Napoleon spreading the
achievements of the French revolution. (It is an ungainly
comparison anyway. Do Soviet historians regard Napoleon's
invasion of Russia as a progressive event? Didn't Napoleon's
aggression produce an anti-liberal, chauvinist reaction all
over Europe? Didn't Stalin do serious, perhaps lasting, harm
to the Communist cause?) Real problems are not so easily
solved. Those who maintain that "it can't happen again" are
apparently willing to rely on the subjective factor of human
goodwill (surely a very un-Marxist view) unless one insists
that Russia has already made the jump "from necessity to

freedom" and that the laws of historical materialism have therefore ceased to function. It would be most in line with Marxism if they argued that Stalin was a regrettable necessity but that the phenomenon cannot possibly recur since Soviet society has now reached a "higher stage" of social development and that therefore there is no longer a conceivable "objective need" for a Stalin. It is doubtful, though, whether such an answer will satisfy even the determinists. A high degree of economic development is not a guarantee against tyranny, and dictators often have an unfortunate tendency to appear without reference to "objective need."

The general trend in Russia, as far as the internal party and government is concerned, is now "back to the 1920s" Admittedly, the 'twenties are greatly preferable to the 'thirties and 'forties; yet this was the decade that proved so conducive to the growth of Stalinism. If Stalinism was some form of aberration on the part of the ruler, was it not made possible by a parallel process among his subjects?

Ludwig Quiddle, in his study on Caligula, notes that specific Caesarean madness is "the product of conditions which develop from the moral degeneracy of monarchic peoples, or at any rate, their upper classes." Omit "monarchic," and is this not a fairly accurate description of modern forms of dictatorship? Has Soviet society basically changed? Have new checks and balances come into being to bar the way of a new dictator? Despite notable changes in the Soviet Union during the last decade, the answer is still negative. Political power is still in the hands of a very few people; the rest have no way of influencing political decisions. Robert Rozhdestvenski says in a recent poem:

> *We say no longer*
> *That somebody thinks for us*
> *Because we know now how this ends. . . .*

Independent thought may at some future date produce independent action; for the time being the independent thinker has to trust the good intentions of his rulers. The most that can be said is that, as in the 'twenties, various developments are possible—both towards the perpetration of tyranny and towards a greater measure of liberty and even democracy.

Relative optimists (I among them) may add that with the Stalinist experience behind us all, historical prospects could only be for the better. Some optimism is based on the agreeable assumption, hitherto unproven—that a totalitarian state may in time "wither away" or may in time somehow normalize itself. Maybe. But it has not happened yet. (Is Kemalist Turkey really a suitable parallel?) Something approaching a public opinion may again develop in Russia in the course of years. An opposition outside the state party is extremely unlikely, but factions inside the party may gradually emerge and be recognized as a normal development, not as a deviation. Instead of a multi-party, there would at least be a multi-faction system. If there is polycentrism within the Communist camp, why shouldn't there be a similar development within the parties? But this, too, could happen only on the basis of mutual tolerance which at present is certainly not the norm.

These were the political problems of the Soviet Union of the 'sixties and, with luck, of the 'seventies and 'eighties. Whatever their outcome, they are hardly likely to influence our appraisal of Stalin very much.

What did Stalin accomplish? Above all, a rate of growth somewhere between 12–14% during the 'thirties. In terms of economic efficiency Stalin was a success—he did deliver the goods, or at least some of them. Against this, on the debit side, there has been untold suffering and millions of victims (during and after the collectivization campaign, the purges, and the early stages of the war). Politically and culturally it was a monumental wasteland.

I have read some verses (mostly by Central Asian poets) which compared Stalin to a "mountain eagle"; some future historians may come to regard him as an ass in lion's skin. Does this sound preposterous today? Can it be that the gigantic image of the man, the legend of the all-powerful father of the people has loomed too large for a whole generation? I feel it is too easily forgotten how almost any image of almost any person can be fabricated in a totalitarian state. How much will remain of Stalin's iron will, his steely nerves, his tenacity, once the archives are opened and real demythologization begins? There still is a widespread belief that extraordinary (if not superhuman) qualities are needed to reach the top in a dictatorship. Yet the essential qualities —the will for power, self-confidence, and single-mindedness —are not that uncommon. Historic luck seems to be much more important. Stalin was very lucky indeed.

Communism in contrast to Nazism is, I think, in the main tradition of Western civilization, a heresy perhaps, or a utopia, but corresponding to some deep-seated traditional aspirations. Even the most inhuman Stalinist actions had to be justified by humanist arguments. Since Stalin's death, words and meanings have not yet come out of the jungle, but standards of public behavior have certainly changed. Russia has again become conscious of its Western heritage; Russians are at great pains now to stress that, regardless of political and social differences, their country is part of the mainstream of Europe's cultural life. Is there any greater insult now than the argument that Russia has really "belonged to Asia" all along? This is an encouraging development, I think (and one should not be unduly worried by the critics of Europocentrism). Stalin will mainly be remembered as the ruler who tried to divorce his country from the Western tradition. In this he had a great, but one hopes, not a lasting success. Even God cannot change the past, but men can shape the future.

(1963)

RUSSIAN ROULETTE

AS ON PAST OCCASIONS, a visit I have just made to the Soviet Union produced in me conflicting impressions: striking advances and equally striking backwardness in many fields. There was readiness to talk to strangers, greater curiosity about events in the West. The late President Kennedy is still a hero in the eyes of most Russians. Some of them wanted to know whether Mrs. Kennedy and the children had been provided for. There was a willingness to discuss almost any topic under the sun, including the merits and demerits of Mr. Khrushchev, but little comment about his successors. And it was my clear impression that this reluctance to talk about them stemmed not so much from fear and suspicion, as from the belief (which I have shared for some time) that it was not at present of tremendous importance whether Russia was ruled by Brezhnev or Kosygin, by Polyanski or Titov, Podgorny or Kirilenko. The question of promotion and demotion mattered greatly under Stalin, since not much else was or could then be known; and it became a matter of growing fascination in the years after the death of the dictator. In retrospect, however, it seems doubtful whether the "kto-kovo" (who-whom) was of decisive importance for the country as a whole. Would Malenkov have followed a policy radically different from Khrushchev's? In present circumstances an analysis of the main political, social, and economic issues facing the Soviet

Union in 1965 is a more fruitful approach than an appraisal of its rulers, particularly since much more is now known about Soviet problems than about Soviet personalities. I want to make a number of unkind remarks about Kremlinology. But I ought to stress at the outset that while I do not share Mr. Robert Conquest's conviction that Kremlinology is the Namierism of Soviet political history, I reject the popular image of the Kremlinologist even more emphatically. It is both unfair and stupid to regard the Kremlinologists as crackpots or charlatans. Those who professionally follow the struggle for power in the Kremlin are neither less intelligent nor less honest intellectually than their colleagues in other fields. Kremlinology has attracted some very good minds for the same reason as Chemistry (or Alchemy) did in the Middle Ages: because there were so many unkown factors involved in the riddle, and because of the intrinsic importance of the subject.[1]

Kremlinology, of which Mr. Rush's book[2] is a fairly typical example, is a legitimate subdivision of the general field of Soviet studies. Its main weakness is that it has too often to make bricks out of straw; its main temptations to claim too much on a slender factual basis. Namier had many—too many—historical sources at his disposal; the Kremlinologist, alas, has only *Pravda* and the Soviet provincial press, which provide few clues about what is happening in the Soviet corridors of power. The Kremlinologist is thus reduced to intelligent guessing. If the late Lavrenty Beria did not appear at the Opera in 1952 or 1953 this could have been a fact of the greatest significance. The absence of his successor on a similar occasion may simply mean that he

[1] Interested readers should consult a recently published book in which the case both for and against Kremlinology has been stated, ably I believe, by a number of practitioners of this art and their critics. Having edited the volume I cannot say more (*The State of Soviet Studies, MIT Press, 1965*).

[2] Myron Rush, *Political Succession in the USSR* (1965).

had a bad cold. If Mikhail Suslov failed to mention Khrushchev in two speeches in 1958—Mr. Rush makes heavy
weather of this—this may have been pure coincidence. (For
all we know, a Soviet leader may sometimes do this simply
to annoy the western Kremlinologist.) Mr. Rush assumes,
rightly I think, that there are factions in the Kremlin; but we
know very little about who belongs to which factions, and
what they stand for.

At this point, for want of factual knowledge, all kinds of
doubtful hypotheses are applied. Conquest and Rush attribute great importance to the origin of Soviet leaders and
their date of birth, their employment in various government
and party agencies, for instance the fact that many are
either ethnic Ukranians or have worked in the Ukraine, etc.
If, to put a fictitious case, Comrade Petrov is elevated to a
leading position in the Kremlin, it stands to reason that he
will take along with him a few of his cronies; these things
happen everywhere. But I would be most reluctant to draw
far-reaching conclusions from the fact that Petrov and Ser-
geyev were born in Odessa in 1915 and that they worked
together in Kharkov in 1939. It may mean, of course, that
they have come to love each other dearly; it might just as
well mean the opposite. Stalin and Trotsky were born within
a few months of each other in 1879; Lenin and Kerensky
first saw the light within a few blocks from each other in
Simbirsk. It did not make them friends. Early in his book[3]
Mr. Conquest compares the political biographies of Polyanski, Shelepin, and Semichastny, born in 1917, 1918, and
1924 respectively; they are the three up and coming leaders
in Moscow, at this moment at any rate. On the basis of
biographical data he notes that they are typical products of
the Stalin era, and that nothing good can be expected from
such people. His skepticism may be justified. In a similar

[3] Robert Conquest, *Russia After Khrushchev* (1965).

way, an observer of the French political scene in 1794 would no doubt have written off Barras as a staunch supporter of the Jacobins. After all, Barras had voted for the execution of King Louis and excelled in the suppression of the counter-revolutionary rising at Toulon. Clearly a most unlikely man to liquidate the French revolution!

Mr. Rush, and particularly Mr. Conquest, deal at great length with the respective chances of the main contenders for power. They comment on Brezhnev's age handicap, on Voronov's experience in agriculture, on Polyanski's relative inexperience in top positions. There is much penetration and inventiveness in this kind of game, but the equation has too many unknown factors.

Whenever facts are lacking, historical parallels come in handy, and Mr. Rush deals at length with 1923–26. I doubt whether this will greatly enlighten us. The situation in Moscow during Lenin's last illness and after his death differed in many essential respects from the present state of affairs. According to the Kremlinologists' rules of the game, Stalin, the unpopular and relatively inexperienced Georgian, should never have emerged as the supreme leader in the 1920's. Khrushchev was ruled out in view of his "age handicap" and for a great many other reasons. The Kremlinologist knows some basic biographical data; all the rest, including such unilluminating adjectives as "conservative," "brilliant," "independent," etc., is at best intelligent guesswork.

There are so many factors that are not known and cannot be foreseen. It cannot even be taken for granted that a member of the presidium or the secretariat is thirsting for more power; at this moment there seems to be a notable reluctance to act as number one. Khrushchev's fall is of recent date and may act as a temporary deterrent. There is little else that can be taken for granted. If Petrov made certain pronouncements five or seven years ago about the state of Soviet literature or agriculture, it does not necessarily follow that Petrov still holds these views. Very often it is not the strongest pretender (on paper) who is successful in the end; frequently there is a stalemate, and as a result some apparently colorless compromise candidate emerges. Having acceded to power, this non-entity may suddenly reveal totally unexpected energy, character, and even highly individualistic opinions.

Mr. Conquest believes that the present political leaders fail to carry conviction:

> Kosygin and Brezhnev, Shelepin and Podgorny, Suslov and Polyansky are not the men to rule a great country beset by a general crisis.

How can we know? Stalin in 1923 carried even less conviction, and how many people put their money on Khrushchev in 1953? There is no room for the public display of individual talents and independent views near the seats of power in Moscow; it is only the man on top who can show the qualities that carry conviction. And don't we know that in our day and age an image of strength and leadership can be created, even if these qualities are largely absent? All in all, it is much more difficult to forecast the outcome of the struggle for power in the Kremlin than the outcome of a horse race, or some athletic competition. Few gamblers anyway would put their money on a horse on the basis of such scanty information as there is at the disposal of the Kremlinologist.

It is no doubt very important to follow closely the changes in the Soviet leadership, the texts of official pronouncements, the order in which the names of the pretenders are mentioned. Such information, in the form of interim reports, situation and position papers, will be needed for practical purposes. But is it really enough for a full-length book? In writing a book there is sometimes a strong temptation to engage in model-building, in generalizing and theorizing, even if the factual basis is very slim indeed. Mr. Rush's "cyclical theory of Soviet politics" is an example. Such theories usually state the obvious in a roundabout and laborious way. Mr. Rush, for instance, tells us that the period of succession is usually a time of crisis in dictatorships, and especially so in the Soviet Union; that the contenders have to fight for power after the death (or disappearance) of the former boss; that in this inertia period there is instability, and that dissident groups within the leadership have a greater opportunity to influence politics. All this could be said in simple language in three to four pages. Mr. Rush, with much erudition and with the benefit of modern political theory, says it in 214 pages. He also says in the end that no particular strategy for the West can be deduced from this cynical theory of Soviet politics.

Mr. Conquest deals with a great many non-theoretical subjects in addition to Kremlinology, and his book is therefore more interesting. He discusses, albeit sometimes in a stream-of-consciousness manner, the important problems of contemporary Russia; much of this is very intelligent. He overrates, in my opinion, the extent of the economic crisis in the Soviet Union and, above all, the degree of dissatisfaction among the population. He thinks (with Orwell) that the regime will either democratize itself or perish. This is an undue dramatization. The chances are that in the near future the regime will neither become democratic nor will it perish. Mr. Conquest also discusses the possible disintegration of the Soviet Union into succession states. The prospect of an independent Tadjikistan or Byelorussia does not necessarily fill one's heart with joy. There are of course centrifugal trends in the national republics, but there are also strong forces of cohesion which Mr. Conquest clearly underrates. On the other hand he overestimates the importance of ideology ("any real change in communism must involve an evolution in ideology"). In my view, doctrine will probably be the last thing to change in the Soviet Union; to a surprising degree, it can be adjusted to new realities as has been shown in history time and again. The "specific weight" of ideology is never constant; a régime may be mainly or largely motivated by ideology at a certain stage of its development; later on the impact of ideology usually diminishes sharply.

The weakness of Kremlinology is its alienation from its subject. However critical of the Soviet régime the Kremlinologist may be, *Pravda* remains his daily bread. What an unsatisfactory mirror of Soviet reality! Once upon a time *Pravda* was almost the only sourse of information about things Soviet. Need it be said that there have been changes during the last decade, and that Soviet life (and even Soviet politics) is much more complicated and more interesting than its reflection in the Soviet press?

A prolonged visit to the Soviet Union, if it was feasible, would have a beneficial effect on most Kremlinologists and would help them to view their field of study in a broader context and in fuller perspective. True, they would not get the answer to such questions as whether Shelest was given full membership in the party presidium in November 1964 to counterbalance Shelepin's influence, or whether a Ukranian group relying on Titov and Semichastny at the levers could become the dominating power in the Kremlin (I am quoting Mr. Conquest). These important problems can admittedly be studied at greater leisure in New York and London. But what about the dynamics of Soviet policy and society—social and economic trends, the general mood, the character of the new generation? I don't think they are fully reflected in *Pravda*—to put it mildly. My own reading of the situation and the outlook differs considerably from that of Mr. Conquest, and, I suspect, of some other Kremlinologists.

I don't think it is of great importance whether the Soviet Union will be ruled by Brezhnev and Kosygin or Podgorny and Shelepin.

While the question of succession may not be settled, the régime as a whole is in a relatively stable phase. The general course in domestic and foreign affairs has been set; the style may differ, the substance hardly so. It does of course matter whose finger will be on the trigger, but all that the Kremlinologists will be able to tell us, I fear, is whether the man at the end of the hot line is a member of the "Ukranian faction" or a "Leningrader," and this may not be too helpful. The number of choices facing the rulers seems to be limited for quite a few years to come. Grave problems confront them, as the rest of the world. I do not see any good reason to expect a (non-nuclear) explosion; all the signs seem to point to a period of relative stability. Mr. Conquest says somewhere that everything is possible in Soviet politics. I agree. I may be mistaken and Mr. Conquest's predictions may be borne out by subsequent developments—but if so, hardly for the reasons he adduces.

The bulk of the Soviet population "never had it so good"; they are enjoying now some of the good things in life promised them for many decades but not delivered before. Living standards are rising, housing conditions improving. There is a great demand for more of the same. There is discontent about bottlenecks and insufficient supplies of consumer goods. There is, perhaps, the beginning of "a revolution of rising expectations." But whoever thinks there is an overwhelming demand for political freedom is fooling himself; effective government is wanted, not political freedom. Part of the official doctrine is no longer taken seriously by anyone, part is universally and unquestionably accepted. Many young Russians no more think of doubting Lenin's wisdom and goodness than Luther doubted the wisdom of God. There will be new developments, but there is no good reason to expect basic change; that will come only when the leaders of the generation that entered kindergarten after Stalin died succeed the men whose names figure so prominently in Mr. Rush's and Mr. Conquest's Kremlinological studies.

(1965)

IV
GERMANS
AND NAZIS

NAZISM AND
THE NAZIS

On the Difficulties of Discovering the Whole Truth

WHO, OR WHAT, is a Nazi?

Legally speaking, a Nazi was a member of the Nationalist Socialist German Workers' Party, founded in Munich on September 20th, 1920, or one of its auxiliary groups. Since it was a very small group, and wanted to appear larger than it really was, it began numbering its members at 500— Hitler's party card was No. 555. By January, 1933, the party had about 1-2 million members; then the great rush started. Two years later the number had doubled, although in April, 1933, restrictions had been imposed to keep out "time-servers" and "opportunists." So the legal definition does not take us very far. In fact, it can be rather misleading, as Allied de-Nazification courts found out after the war. Many thousands in the S.S., the régime's élite guard, had not belonged to the Nazi party. Among the *Waffen S.S.* still fewer had been party members. Heinrich Mueller, appointed head of the *Gestapo* in 1935, became a member of the party only six or seven years later. On the other hand, some perfectly innocent engineer, who had never been politically active at all, might find himself in serious trouble after 1945, because he had belonged (or been compelled to belong if he didn't want to lose his job) to the association *Deutsche Technik,* a subsidiary of the Nazi party.

To define a Nazi one must define "National Socialism"— a subject about which, several decades after the end of the Third Reich, surprisingly little is known. One knows, of course, that it must never happen again. But this ought by now to have been fortified by a closer understanding of the character of Nazism, its motives, components, and structure; one cannot effectively oppose something that remains inexplicable.

A young American historian, who specializes in contemporary German history, remarked to me the other day that William Shirer's book on the Third Reich, which has had such a phenomenal success, was "really very bad indeed"; not a "scholarly work"; mistaken in countless details, wrong in its basic theses. I tried hard (but I fear unsuccessfully) to convince him that this was largely the fault of the professional historians. True, there have been some very good monographs, some excellent biographical studies, countless footnotes to the history of Hitler's life and times. But where is the definitive history of the Third Reich, or of the Nazi party? Where is the comprehensive account of how justice came to be perverted in Germany, of how the intellectuals reacted, of how the apparatus of terror worked, of how the German economy was managed? On Italian fascism there is a much smaller literature; yet the subject seems to be more fully covered, since Italian writers have apparently been less inhibited in dealing with it. The difficulties, to be sure, are staggering; only those who have tackled the subject can be fully aware of them. Thousands of people who were in leading positions in the Nazi era are still alive— diplomats, higher civil servants, party leaders, police officials. Their evidence would be invaluable; yet they are most reluctant to talk. The only exception is the generals, and some of them have been too garrulous.

A few years ago, I went to Munich in the vague hope of locating and interviewing one or two of the leading members of the Nazi party of the very early period. Much to my surprise there were a great many still around; I had forgotten that most of them had been quite young in 1923, so that some of them had not turned seventy. All showed apprehension: "Who told you about me? . . . How did you get my address?" My assurance that the local telephone directory had been my only guide set them somewhat at ease. But some remained reluctant to talk; and other presented a version that had undoubtedly been carefully rehearsed over the years, and that was both untruthful and useless.

There is thus a strange and striking contrast between ex-Nazis and ex-Communists. The latter, as a rule, are only too willing to tell one their experiences. I can think of only a handful of former Nazis who have given such personal accounts; most of them were very young at the time and held no influential positions. Their attachment to the party was often less close than that of the Communists; their disillusionment, if it came at all, came only after 1945; there was no radical break while the Party and the *Reich* still existed. These ex-Nazis have done with politics, and are only anxious not to attract attention now. A very few keep the flag flying, hectically justifying the Nazi era in little pamphlets published by obscure neo-Nazi publishing houses; about their own past they remain curiously silent. Perhaps they think the time is not yet ripe; perhaps they have manuscripts hidden away to be published at some future date. But I doubt it. One of the most important sources for the study of Nazism, therefore, remains closed.

The Documents
What about the Nazi documents? There is certainly no shortage here; the amount of paper produced and preserved by a modern bureaucracy is staggering. Much was de-

stroyed, of course, during the last months of the war, and immediately after; 1945–46 was a hard winter and there was a shortage of fuel. Some of the top secret files were seized, I suspect, in 1945, by people professionally interested in top secret files. Even so, hundreds of tons of paper remain. Some material is not accessible, either because it is in Russian hands or because the Allies or the West Germans have put an embargo on it for the time being. This applies, for instance, to the personal files in the Berlin Document Center of all former members of the Nazi Party. (I had, for example, great difficulty in getting to see the personal file of Alfred Rosenberg, though Rosenberg has been dead many years.) The reasons are, of course, "political" and not very creditable; but there may be legal complications as well. The embargo is not always effective, however, as copies of material classified in the United States can be found in other files in England and Germany—and *vice versa*.

Despite the losses and restrictions there is still so much that all but the boldest are likely to be awed. The American Historical Society has been micro-filming for years now the documents held in Washington, publishing every two or three months a detailed catalogue. Before me is No. 39, *Records of the Reich Leader S.S. and the Chief of the German Police (Part III)*—and it contains 563 files with, I estimate, between a quarter and half a million pages. In these files there is much that is not, and never will be, of interest to anyone: administrative memos, excerpts from newspapers, an application (in quadruplicate) by Richard Strauss' son-in-law for a hunting licence. Then, suddenly, among a mass of local gossip, pay checks, requests for compassionate leave by office cleaners, there is a document of absorbing interest and great importance. One such catalogue, for instance, lists a full run of the internal *Gestapo* newspaper, published two or three times a week between 1939 and 1944, and an indispensable source for the internal situation in Germany during the war. There are documents of equal relevance for other European countries.

True, very little can be taken at face value without further checking—which may prove impossible. Three examples, chosen at random, should suffice.

1. A detailed report on the visit to Germany in 1938–39 of a young Englishman—bearer of a well-known name—who is described as "a British fascist." (But the same report also calls him "a member of the British Secret Service"!)

2. This concerns a man now prominent in German political life, an ex-minister who maintains that he was an anti-Nazi: according to this document he supplied information to Ribbentrop's private information service. (But, from the document, it is not *absolutely* certain whether he did this knowingly, or whether he was used by others. It is just conceivable that he was playing a "double game.")

3. A Russian officer who fell into German hands in 1942 had some sensational stories to tell about events in the Kremlin in the late 1930s. But much in the report is obvious fantasy—he really believes Bukharin was "a German spy." How is one to know whether he is telling the truth in this case?

These three examples are not of great political importance. But there are hundreds of similar cases, and they underline the necessity of great caution.

What has deterred many historians from using these documents is not so much the fear of legal complications, as lack of time. Writers on foreign policy mostly take as their source the published volumes of *Documents on German Policy* edited by teams of British, American, and French historians. Historians concerned with other aspects of Nazi Germany base their researches on the Nuremberg Trial material, which for the most part has not seen the light of day. Much scholarship and industry has gone into editing the "*Documents.*" But the editors, for obvious reasons of space, could select only the most important documents on German diplomatic relations with other major countries. This goes for the far more voluminous Nuremberg material too—their editors had to fulfil a specific task, and considering the very short time at their disposal, and their conditions of work, they did an admirable job. But their collection contains only a small fraction of all the relevant material, and it covers only certain aspects of Nazi rule in Germany and Europe.

Fortunately, there have been, and are, some scholars with the urge and the opportunity to study the original documents. Frequently these are men and women on the staff of archives or research institutes—who else has the time to cope with so much material? I am not saying that this surfeit of source material is the most serious obstacle for the study of the Nazi era, but it is certainly a formidable one. Some have doubted the value of this research—are the great effort and industry that go into sifting and analyzing this evidence really warranted? Will it produce conclusions likely to affect the general picture that already exists? May it not be a source of confusion rather than clarification? These doubts are not altogether baseless; the number of historians specializing in modern history is limited. Can they afford to lose themselves for years in the minutiae of some aspect of Nazism? We know, after all, without having refrence to the archives, that Hitler was an anti-Semite. And yet, in the end, the only way to shed more light on the whole period is to find what really happened and, perhaps, why it happened. I want to give a few examples.

Revisionists

Some years ago an American historian published a book about Germany's economic war preparations in which he found that, far from gearing her industry to a totalitarian war economy, Germany had done surprisingly little in this direction before 1939. The facts cannot be disputed—the German industrial war effort reached its maximum output only after Stalingrad. American isolationist historians, and their German adaptors, pounced on this book; was it not decisive proof that Hitler had not really wanted the war? Did it not clear up the question of responsibility for World War II once and for all—Halifax and Beck being the main culprits, not Hitler? The argument is childish. One could argue as well that since Hitler lost the war he cannot have wanted it in the first place. Even an elementary knowledge of Nazism should have shown Messrs. Tansill, Barnes, and Hoggan[1] that Germany's comparative lack of readiness in 1939 was a sign not of Hitler's will to peace, but of his general lack of interest in economic affairs and his belief that German armaments were sufficient for a lightning war—a belief which was painfully close to the truth.

I have recently been exposing myself, as it happens, to a massive dose of "revisionist historiography" on the Third Reich—the writings of German neo-Nazis and ultra-conservatives, American Roosevelt-haters, and also certain British contributions. Much of this literature has been published in Germany, and in Germany only; there is an Institute for German Post-war History and a *Deutsche Hochschullehrerzeitung* in Tübingen which specialize in these publications. It is only fair to add that no reputable German historian would be seen dead in such company, and that the most detailed refutations of the pro-Nazi writings have come from Germany. I admire the enterprise of the German and Swiss historians who have shown in convincing detail on what massive ignorance and wilful suppression of the truth this new literature is based. But I doubt whether a rational

[1] David L. Hoggan, *Der erzwungene Krieg* (Tübingen, 1961).

discussion will have much effect; one could as well discuss philosophy with Alfred Rosenberg. Those who want to whitewash Hitler will never be at a loss for arguments. Ordinary mortals are apparently impressed by footnotes; they find it difficult to believe that a book may have a scientific apparatus of fifty pages and yet be a bad joke. Rosenberg's books and those of other Nazi pseudo-historians and philosophers were full of historical references; no serious historians would deign to refute them. There is no danger that the present-day revisionist literature will be taken seriously by members of the profession; the danger is that it will serve effectively as propaganda. In the circumstances it is remarkable how little effect it has had in Germany so far: most of the spadework has been done by foreigners, not by Germans. In a way this is perhaps not surprising. For most Germans know what really happened; for them Hitler was a living reality. (They may dislike the Poles, but they know that Hitler attacked Poland, and that he was bound to do so—not the other way round.) For American and British revisionist historians, on the other hand, Hitler and his whole system appear to be as strange and remote as some Assyrian king, despite footnotes, quotations, and historical references.[2]

[2] German attitudes towards past and present have been documented by polls, conducted by the "Institut für Demoskopie" (Allensbach).

Six years after the end of the war—in the year 1951—"the time in which things went best for Germany" was identified by 42 per cent as the years between 1933 and 1939, i.e., the Nazi "peace years." Altogether, 94 per cent looked backward, to Weimar, to the Kaiser, in "remembrance of things past."

Eight years later, in 1959, the replies to the question, "When in this century do you feel things went best for Germany?" indicated that 42 per cent now felt that "Heute" (today, now) was best. Even the myth of the "Kaiserzeit" began to fade.

This trend has continued. The poll conducted at the end of 1963 reveals that the positive feeling for the present had grown to 62 per cent.

For some Americans of the older generation it is merely a continuation of the quarrel about the responsibility for World War I; for others, it is simply an extension of their vendetta against Roosevelt. There are a few Germans who believe that Hitler's main crime was to be "unlucky." An occasional Englishman probably wants only to shock his audience with paradoxical statements. Of more interest, perhaps, is the Frenchman who was sent by the Hoover Foundation to cover the Auschwitz trial in Frankfurt and who was thrown out by the Germans as a neo-Nazi! He had been a socialist, a *Maquisard* from the beginning. Arrested by the Gestapo in 1943, he spent two years in a camp. Yet after the war he published a series of books according to which the Nazi crimes had been "grossly exaggerated" if not altogether invented; his writings became the standard fare of the neo-Nazi movement all over Europe. A fascinating case, no doubt, for the student of political psycho-pathology.

(The backward-looking figure was now 32 per cent.) The Institut notes that the partition of Germany into two states is a factor in the relatively hesitant German reconciliation with the present. This was suggested by a comparison with the Austrian results of a similar poll. In 1961, in reply to a question about "when in this century things went best for Austria," 82 per cent replied "die Gegenwart" (the present).

QUESTION: *"When in this century do you feel things went best for Germany?"*

	October 1951 %	June 1959 %	End 1963 %
IN THE PRESENT, TODAY	2	42	62
WORLD WAR II	—	—	1
BETWEEN 1933–1939	42	18	10
BETWEEN 1920–1932 (WEIMER REPUBLIC)	7	4	5
BEFORE 1914 (THE KAISER-REICH)	45	28	16
DON'T KNOW	4	8	6
	100	100	100

Monopoly Capitalism?

Some time ago there was a lengthy polemic between the German trade unionists and the Institute of German Industry about the role leading German industrialists and bankers had played in the Third Reich. It generated more heat than light; the trade unions, I believe, had the better of the argument. It was a far cry from the discussion in the '30s about Nazism and finance capital; the real force behind fascism, the Communist argument ran then, was "monopoly capitalism." My own favorite was Ernest Henri, whose books attracted a great deal of attention in the 1930s. He was introduced by the *New Statesman* as a German refugee with exceptional sources of information. Actually, he was a Russian. According to Henri's articles and books Fritz Thyssen, the great magnate of the Ruhr, not Adolf Hitler ("Fabius Cunctator") was the prime mover of German fascism. Thyssen was "the inspiration," the "brain of the whole system," the "driving force behind it." Thyssen had given Hitler orders to launch a grandiose offensive. Hitler was but a puppet in the hands of this German tycoon—just as the Italian industrialist, Toeplitz, was Mussolini's master. In fact, Thyssen was rather dim; Hitler would no more have heeded his advice than that of his valet. He was also relatively courageous; in 1939 he broke with Hitler and went into exile; his property was seized, and after the fall of France he was sent to a concentration camp. So much for the "prime mover behind Hitler," and a book that was called by Bertrand Russell at the time "extraordinarily interesting and valuable."

The monopoly-capitalism theory which is still propagated in some quarters to this day—though with decreasing conviction—was not confined to the Communists; many Social Democrats and Liberals subscribed to it. In a more sophisticated form it was advocated in Professor Franz Neumann's famous book entitled *Behemoth.* Its success was not altogether surprising; great catastrophes often appear inexplicable to their contemporaries; they provide fertile ground for advocates of the conspiratorial theory of history. How could a little lawyer from Arras overthrow the monarchy in France without the assistance of the freemasons and the *illuminati?* How could Lenin have been successful without the assistance of the Kaiser's agents on one hand, and the Elders of Zion on the other? How could a half-mad Austrian corporal conquer Germany, and almost the whole of Europe, without some sinister and darkly powerful backing? It sounded quite plausible at the time. But since 1945 we know what really happened, and a very different picture emerges. The captains of German industry to whom such far-sightedness, diabolical cunning, and, above all, unity of purpose had been attributed, appear in a very different light. They were limited and short-sighted men; not daring, but spineless toadies. Their self-confidence had disappeared in the great slump; they only wanted to be left alone. To attribute such Machiavellian strategies to them was a pathetic misreading of the situation. They did not make Hitler; they jumped on his bandwagon. (True, some of them had paid Hitler for some years. But far, far more money had gone to the small center and right-of-center parties.)

The record of the German captains of industry in the Third Reich is not a pretty one, and it is not improved by the fact that Nazism had support among all classes of German society. The East Germans unearthed and published some time ago a very damaging document about the "Circle of Friends of Heinrich Himmler." This was a group of about thirty leading German bankers and industrialists (and about fifteen leading state and party officials), who met about once a month, were told about the activities of the S.S., and were taken to visit concentration camps on one or two occasions. Himmler's "friends" paid for this privilege—in 1943, for instance, they contributed more than a million marks, which was handed over to Himmler to be used at his own discretion.

What were these privileges for which his "friends" were permitted to pay all that money? They did receive occasional orders from the S.S. (including the supply of cyclone B gas for the death camps). They got slave labor for their factories. But above all they got reinsurance. One of the highest S.S. leaders said about this circle in Nuremberg. "They wanted to have a direct line to Himmler for emergencies, such as when the *Gestapo* made trouble in their factories." The omnipotent German monopolists were paying Danegeld, protection money for the privilige of not being molested by the political police. . . .

The issue at stake is not the record of German industry, which was very bad! after 1933 they did all they could to ingratiate themselves with the new masters. There was some resistance to Hitler among the working class, and less frequently among the middle class and the aristocracy. There was no such opposition from the industrialists; the only one who openly disagreed with Hitler was, ironically enough, Fritz Thyssen. German industry collaborated with Hitler—about this there can be no two opinions. The régime did great favors to some of them and they reciprocated by loyally serving it. But was their help decisive in bringing Hitler to power? Did they at any stage in the Third Reich influence Hitler's policy? On this too there can be no two opinions; they were never asked whether they wanted the war or how it would affect their profits. The myth of an all-powerful monopoly capitalism disappears into thin air. It was based on the false assumption that, to put it in its most primitive form, economics determines politics in the totalitarian state. We now know, beyond a shadow of doubt, that the relationship between political and economic power was exactly opposite: the state made the economy subservient to its own non-economic purposes—such as war and armed aggression.

The Resistance

"Hitler was a very ordinary German. The Nazis were Germans. They won more votes at a free election than any other German party ever received. . . . The German resistance was a myth." Thus Mr. A. J. P. Taylor in a recent pronouncement. Of course, nobody has ever argued that the Nazis were not Germans. But Hitler was definitely not "a very ordinary German." Nor did the Nazis obtain the highest *percentage* of votes before 1933—the Social Democrats in 1919 did better.

What, then, of the German resistance? How many troop transports or deportation trains were derailed? How many S.S. men were killed inside Germany? These questions (put by Mr. Taylor) have to be faced by the Germans. Again: how many Germans were arrested under Hitler? According to *Gestapo* files, the number of persons arrested and held in prisons and concentration camps for political reasons in April 1939, was 301,000. Thousands were executed—well before 1944. Among them were dissident Nazis and unpolitical persons who had been seized following mere suspicion or a denunciation. A few were Jews, considered enemies of the régime anyway. But three hundred thousand is a large figure; it is not "a myth."

The history of German opposition to Hitler, like so much else in the Third Reich, remains to be written. There are a great many books on individual people and groups, but no objective study putting the whole phenomenon in wider perspective. West German accounts frequently ignore the Communists' share; in Professor Hans Rothfels' scholarly study of *The German Opposition to Hitler*,[3] one looks in vain for a just appraisal. Yet the Communists were very active, and credit should be given where it is due—even if it took them a long time to realize that Hitler, and not the Social Demo-

[3] Hans Rothfels, *The German Opposition to Hitler* (London, 1961).

crats, was their "main enemy," and even if they virtually closed down shop between the 1939–41 time of the Hitler-Stalin pact. The Gestapo reports show that among these anonymous people, the rank-and-file militants, there were indeed real heroes, whose memory should not be forgotten. It was, relatively, easier to be a resister in France and Yugoslavia; we should remember what it meant in Germany.

Sodom and Gomorrah, we are told, would have been saved by the presence of ten just men. There were many more than that in Germany, but historical dimensions have changed; on the day of judgment their number was found insufficient. Yet respect should be paid to all who did resist, even if the Communists do not make it easy for the rest.

Among the many gaps in the annals of German resistance, that left by the intellectuals is probably the largest. Or is it merely the most conspicuous because they were unlucky enough to put their views and feelings on paper, while no records exist of the opinions of others? An otherwise not very distinguished German littérateur wrote in February, 1933:

> The dictatorship does not need to give them orders, they stand to attention of their own volition. They began marching even before they got the order. They write what is expected of them.

Re-reading the enthusiastic declarations, the exultant manifestos of German intellectuals in 1933, one can find few mitigating circumstances, apart perhaps from the fact that the stand of writers such as Thomas Mann, Jakob Wasserman, René Schickele, who for a variety of reasons had already been rejected by the régime, was not exactly heroic at that time. But what about 1939, what about 1944? The literary supplement of Dr. Goebbels' weekly *Das Reich* during the war years reads like a roll-call of the "Other Germany." True enough, these non-committed writers were deliberately cultivated by the propaganda ministry; there was temptation—

but they were too easy victims. There were a few German bishops, some generals, there were even German judges who showed courage. But how many writers decided to cultivate their garden rather than serve the régime? Not long ago the Anglo-American public was treated to a book on problems of contemporary history by a German writer who had not been a Nazi and who explained that treason and resistance were really very relative things, with no moral absolutes involved. I am not certain whether the message was fully understood; the book received very good reviews over here. This same author had been a distinguished contributor on Goebbels' own paper—not in January, 1933, but in December, 1944, many months after the July revolt which should have settled the remaining doubts of any thinking German. What made her do this? Would she have been shot had she refused to contribute? Was she asked to contribute, or did she volunteer? But singling her out is grossly unfair; it is like fastening the blame for the defeat of an army on a confused private— who probably did not even know how he came to be on the field of battle.

My point of departure was how to define Nazism. What made people join this movement? The term Nazism (or fascism) has been used rather indiscriminately over the past decades, and particularly since the war. A great many people have been called "fascists" by their political opponents: Greek kings and Austrian chancellors, Polish marshals, French generals, and Latin American adventurers, the Pope, Sigmund Freud, Trotsky, and Stalin. Recently a group of Nuclear Disarmers who spent a night at a police station complained about "Gestapo methods" and "concentration camps" because the mattresses were not soft enough. The letter of a lady who wrote nonsense about birth-control is likened to a "Hitlerian manifesto." A literary critic who offended a poet is denounced as "a fascist."

It makes one wince, but perhaps it is only natural; Nazism has receded into the distant past, it remains as a figure of speech. Historians and political scientists, let alone propagandists, have been somewhat too liberal with the Nazi label. There has been a tendency to dub any régime that persecutes the opposition "fascist"; and if such a government also uses a certain amount of social demagoguery, there is no doubt about its "fascist character." In consequence, the decisive difference between fascist régimes on one hand, and military dictatorships and authoritarian governments on the other, is more and more overlooked. Hardly anybody bothers any more to ask whether it is really very helpful to use one and the same term to define both Hitler's Germany and Italy under Mussolini. Yet there were essential differences between the two régimes: the one ripened into full totalitarianism, whereas the other had to coexist with the monarachy and the church. Some have suggested that we ought to differentiate between "left-wing, centrist, and right-wing" fascism. There is something to be said for such an exercise; but is not certain whether it takes us very far. So-called left-wing fascism may be closer in inspiration (and in policies) to left-wing parties than to right-wing fascism which is nothing but the extreme fringe of traditional conservatism. There is no "ideal type" fascism that can serve as a yardstick for all fascist movements.

If Nazism had been nothing but a conspiracy among millions of criminals our task would be much easier. Its leaders were a singularly unattractive lot, devoid of moral scruples. There was a fair percentage of gangsters (but then the gangsters proved, as a rule, "more human" than the bureaucrats like Heinrich Himmler). Some anti-Nazis have never quite understood this—Bertolt Brecht, for instance.

Arturo Ui, in Brecht's play, is the leader of a little gang in Chicago which runs a protection racket among the local greengrocers. After a short while, he and his cronies establish mastery over the cauliflower trade, having terrorized all their opponents into submission. Their only aim is "cutting their slice of meat out of any cow that the good God has made." Amusing, perhaps, but nothing could be more misleading than this image of Nazism. For Nazism was not only terror. A movement for which millions of people were willing to fight and to die cannot be explained in terms of Al Capone and Jack "Legs" Diamond. There have been many gangsters, but there was only one Hitler; Brecht's formula does not explain the success of the Nazi movement, the enthusiasm it generated, the lack of resistance to it. Among the young people who joined the Nazi movement during the early years there were not a few idealists. Much later, a young man who had resisted the temptation described the dilemma facing his contemporaries:

> If only a few took up a clear position and maintained it, this was not because resistance was so impossible; the fact was that National Socialism offered all that a young man in his most secret and proudest imagination would desire—activity, responsibility for his fellows, and work with equally enthusiastic comrades for a greater and stronger fatherland. It held out official recognition, and careers that had been unthinkable before; while on the other side there were only difficulties and dangers, an empty future and heartrending doubts.

Everybody agreed that Germany was a "cruelly oppressed" country, that it had been "most unjustly treated" in Versailles in 1919, that it ought to get back some of "the lost territories," that reparations were mere "exploitation." We tend to dismiss these grievances as manifestations of aggressive German militarism. But at the time all Liberals and Socialists and Communists, including most left-wingers in England and America, supported these demands. And so millions of young Germans gave their support to the leaders of what they thought was a National Revolution. Some had misgivings about the terroristic character of the Nazi movement, or its hostility to the Church. Some regretted its extreme anti-Semitism. But few were greatly worried, and who was going to fight for democracy or the Jews anyway? These were seen as minor blemishes in the great movement towards Germany's rebirth. Nazism was dangerous precisely because it appealed not only to the meanest instincts. It was temptation on the grand scale. The Germans' ancestors would have been more sceptical; in the medieval theater Antichrist used to appear in the guise of Christ the better to deceive the folk.

Dozens of attempts to "explain" Nazism have been made in our time by Liberals and Conservatives, Socialists and Communists, Jews and Catholics, psychoanalysts and sociologists. Almost all of them contain a grain of truth, however small. My own feeling is that the earliest correct assessments of Nazism came not from political parties but from individuals who had no preconceived thesis to defend or to prove—this, at any rate, is what emerges from a study of the contemporary literature. Only very recently has an attempt been made to integrate all that is of value in the varius interpretations of Nazism. One day, perhaps, we shall all be of one mind. Meanwhile there should be unanimity on the fact that Nazism was not just a "right-wing dictatorship," but had a very distinct character of its own. It was reactionary, but not really conservative; in its own perverse and inhuman way it did want to change the world. It was profoundly anti-Marxist and yet used methods similar to (and sometimes identical with) those of its enemies, sharing their enmity to liberal democracy. A huge variety of motives made people join the Nazi party. In the last analysis, the main source of the evil was moral relativism and indifference: the plain fact that too many people in Germany were unable, or unwilling, to differentiate between right and wrong. It was the classical state of sin as the Greeks would have seen it: sin being the result of *hubris, hubris* producing *ate,* that state of moral blindness in which "the evil appears good."

Nazism came into being in particular conditions and at a specific time; these have passed, and with them the chance of a comeback. To say this is not to advocate complacency or a lessening of that eternal vigilance which is said to be the price of liberty. But misplaced vigilance is not a virtue. Brutal and inhuman dictatorships will recur, but they are unlikely to owe their inspiration to Nazism. Neither by accident nor "by popular demand" will there be a repeat performance.

RUSSIANS AND GERMANS

A RECENT RUSSIAN VISITOR to West Germany found that, all things considered, Russians and Germans had "more in common" than he had originally assumed. For one thing, both the Russians and Germans were "capable of weeping" (unlike those inhuman Englishmen, unable to give free flow to their feelings, if indeed they had any). The former editor of *Izvestia* had gone to Bonn to pave the way for his father-in-law, the former Soviet prime minister; whether he was an experienced and knowledgeable judge of national character is a moot point. (He seemed to be unaware that the Anglo-Saxon taboo on weeping is of comparatively recent date, and has been disregarded from Pitt and Fox to Curzon, Churchill, and Gaitskell.) But he was not alone in stressing the common traits of character, the bonds of interest and sentiment, and the general affinity between Teuton and Slav. Any discussion of Russian-German relations during the last two hundred years which ignores the tremendous German impact on Russia and the strange fascination Russia exerted on so many Germans is incomplete and misleading. There has been a great deal of goodwill, friendship, and even admiration in both countries towards each other which goes back far into history and has outlasted Adolf Hitler. It is equally unrealistic to ignore the profound distrust and the enmity towards each other, deeply embedded in the national consciousness of both Russians and Germans. Relations between groups are even more complex than those between individuals, capable at the same time of loving, hating, admiring, and despising each other. To say that a "love-hate relationship" has prevailed between Moscow and Berlin for a very long time is to state no more than the obvious; but it is nontheless a basic fact of modern history, which has contributed to the outbreak of two world wars, and one that even now periodically aggravates the world situation. Much of the tension between the two countries in the past was caused by genuine conflicts of political and economic interest. But relations between the two nations have been affected at least as much by prejudice, fear, and misunderstanding.

In 1902, the *United Services Magazine* published an article with the somewhat mystifying title, "The Russian Battle of Dorking." It described the surprise and the growing anger of a Russian Rip van Winkle who had fallen asleep in December 1897 to wake up at the end of thirty years, only to find that his country had in the meantime been taken over by the Germans. There had been a six-weeks war. Because of their decisive superiority, especially in the field of science, the Germans had simply crushed the Russians. The Tsars had disappeared, Finland and Bessarabia were no longer part of Russia, the capital had been moved to Nizhni Novgorod. What remained of Russia was a German dependency, while almost everywhere the Jews were in charge of local government (the *zemstvos*). Throughout all the Russian lands the natives were reduced to the status of hewers of wood and drawers of water.

Such fantasies were not uncommon at the time and reflected the very real fear that had prevailed among many Russians for a long time—that their country would somehow, some day, be taken over by the Germans. It would be idle to deny that these fears had no basis in fact; Peter the Great's 18th-century reforms had brought many foreigners to Russia, and with them they imported the German language and German customs. Some decades later the Birons, Muennichs, and Ostermanns, and other German courtiers really did gain control of Russia albeit for a very short time. Even so, *Bironovshchina* is remembered to this day not only as a particularly brutal and corrupt episode in Russian history but as the very symbol of foreign domination and exploitation. Whether government in Russia was any less arbitrary or corrupt before of after (as some maintain) is quite immaterial; for it was obviously less annoying to be oppressed by local than by foreign tyrants. This resentment against German invaders and usurpers, fanned by the old nobility and the new gentry alike, was the first assertion of Russian nationalism. Russian national consciousness thus came into being in opposition to German encroachments.

If the Germans were disliked, they were nonetheless needed in Russia as technical specialists, merchants, private tutors and, above all, in the army and the civil service. The higher posts usually went to the Baltic Germans; the tutors, technicians and artisans were more often newcomers from Germany proper. The Russian aristocracy and the emerging intelligentsia showed no particular eagerness to join the civil service—it was neither highly remunerative nor highly esteemed. Some Tsars (*e.g.* Nikolai I) actually preferred Germans because they were bound to be more pliable tools than his own subjects in carrying out unpopular and repressive policies. Even in the 1880's, at the height of the Pan-Slavist propaganda, about 40% of the senior commissions in the Russian army were held by officers of German origin. In the ministry of foreign affairs and some other government offices they actually constituted a majority!

Anti-German feeling took various forms. Among the aristocrats there was contempt for "the obsequious, submissive German." Turgenev never forgot how his father had bodily thrown from a first-floor window a German tutor who had provoked his displeasure. This awkward, clumsy German tutor (or artisan, or minor government official) has been a stock figure of ridicule in Russian literature from Fonvizin to Gogol and beyond. Fonvizin (himself the scion of a completely assimilated German family) had written in 1784 after a visit to Central and Western Europe "that everything with us is better, and we are bigger people than the Germans. . . ." This was probably one of the first manifestations of the contempt of the Russian *shirokaia natura* largesse vis-à-vis German *philistinism* (or *meshchanstvo*).

In the eyes of the Russian observer the German lacked warmth, humanity, feeling, heart. One entire dimension was missing in his character and temperament. He did not really *live*. There was admiration for the French in Russia even while Moscow was burning in 1812—and derision for the German lack of *savoir vivre* even while Russia and Prussia were close allies. In their admiration of Goethe, Heine, and particularly Schiller, the Russians were second to none, but these great writers were thought to belong to "all mankind," *i.e.*, there was nothing "specifically German" about them. When Johannes Kohl, the author of a *Baedeker*-like guide book, visited Moscow in 1840 he reported a conversation with the writer Polevoi. Of Schiller and Goethe, Polevoi spoke with the warmest enthusiasm, as well as of Herder's *Ideas* (which was apparently in the hands of all educated Russians). But of the Germany of that day he exclaimed, raising his hands above his head, "My God, where has the genius of Germany hidden itself!" What annoyed Bakunin (and many other visiting Russians) was the philistinism of so many Germans: "Of their rich cultural tradition, not even the tenth part had been absorbed into their life!" He noted the inscription a Berlin tailor had affixed under the Prussian eagle which ornamented the front of his workshop: *Unter deinen Flügeln kann ich ruhig bügeln.* Ivan Kireyevski, an early Slavophile writing from Germany in the 1850s, compared it to a prison, a coffin in which people were buried alive.

> "There is no nation on the entire globe so dull, so soulless, so vexing as the Germans—in comparison with them the Bulgarians are geniuses."

Years later one could hear similar remarks from Russian Jews about their German co-religionists. Chaim Weizmann's memoirs are illuminating in this respect. About the Ballins and Warburgs, Weizmann wrote:

> "the usual type of *Kaiser Juden,* more German than the Germans, obsequious, super-patriotic, eagerly anticipating the wishes and plans of the masters of Germany. . . ."

The German Jews in their turn did not think highly of the *Ostjuden:* unkempt, loud, disorderly, talked through the night and got nothing done by day.

I have quoted the opinion of an early Slavophile about Germany; many Russian Westerners shared these feelings though sometimes for different reasons. Radical Russian writers were never permitted to forget for long that the head of the "Third Department" (the chief political policeman and censor) was named Benckendorff, and his successor Dubbelt. For Alexander Herzen the high German official was a symbol of restriction, of everything oppressive and reactionary in Russia—"*l'empire knouto-germanique,*" as Bakunin called it. Since so many Germans had chosen to serve Tsarist autocracy, Herzen and many of his contemporaries formed the mistaken opinion that autocracy was really "un-Russian," and only a German importation.

Up to the 1860s the presence of so many Germans in high places had been resented, but it was not really thought to be a mortal danger. For no one was behind these men-without-a-country. Germany at the time was "a geographical term," not a major power. The situation changed in 1870, when the second *Reich* emerged almost overnight as a dominant force in Europe and a potential foe of Russia. The whole equilibrium of the Continent was upset; there were fears in Petersburg that Germany would claim the Baltic provinces and restore an independent Poland.

"Everyone up to the very highest society is against us," von Schweinitz reported from the Russian capital towards the end of the Franco-Prussian war. Russian industrialists now felt threatened by their more efficient and longer established German competitors; Russian landowners complained about the heavy duty Berlin had put on the import of Russian grain. The Pan-Slavists were solemnly announcing that only the sword would deliver them from the baneful influence of the intriguing intruder, that a struggle between Teuton and Slav was inevitable, a struggle that would be long, sanguinary, terrible. Statements of this kind filled the columns of large sections of the Russian press for many years.

Reading the Russian and German diplomatic reports of that time, one might think that but for the existence of the press the First World War would never have happened. Those who have studied the pre-history of the War have published many of the exchanges between ambassadors, foreign ministers, and emperors. Far too little attention has been paid to public opinion, and, above all, to the impact of the press.

What happened was, very briefly, this. A Moscow journal would feature a sensational article on the "organization of German espionage in Europe," in which Prince Bismarck was accused of striving for German world rule. Soon other Russian papers, not to be left behind by their competitor, would follow suit. Meanwhile, a Russian General would give an interview to one of the Paris revanchist papers or publish a pamphlet about the desirability of a Russo-French alliance to defeat Germany. After a short while the German press would launch a counterattack, drawing attention to the Russian military build-up in Poland or elsewhere. Russian diplomats in Berlin and their German colleagues in the Russian capital would spend a good deal of their time commenting on some newspaper article, denying it, explaining it, in any case continually preoccupied one way or another with the press.

Apart from this permanent tension, there was a major war scare every two or three years. Many people, including some in high positions, persuaded themselves that war between the two countries was "just around the corner." After a while, tempers would simmer down. There would be a temporary *détente*. Then some new sensational publication would start it all over again. This newspaper war went on, almost without interruption, for forty years. Von Schweinitz, Germany's ambassador in Russia in the '70s and '80s, noted in his diary that never and nowhere had the press exerted a more negative influence on foreign policy than in Russia. In other countries it was merely *one* of the factors shaping public opinion; in Russia it was the only one, and the government hardly ever counteracted. One ought to add that the German press was little better; the papers of the *Alldeutsche* were slightly worse. But why blame the press? The attacks did not come out of the blue. The newspapers printed only what they thought the public would like to read or, in some instances, what they were paid to publish.

From about 1880 war against Germany would have been more popular in Russia than against any other nation (except, of course, Austria). Not everybody was blind to the danger. Giers, the Foreign Minister, said in 1888 that all those who wanted to overthrow the existing order wanted

war. He exaggerated. Neither Social Revolutionaries, nor
Mensheviks, and certainly not the Bolsheviks, can be held
responsible for the outbreak of the First World War. But
it certainly is true that the argument of the arch-conservative circles, especially after 1905, that Russia could not
afford a war because it would mean the overthrow of the
Romanovs and the victory of revolution, made little impression on public opinion.

How could anyone actually have *wanted* war? We tend
to forget that those Russians and Germans who had convinced themselves by 1910 that "war was inevitable" thought
in terms of 1853, or perhaps 1870. They had not the faintest
idea what war would involve, or that it would mean the
end of the world as they had known it, triggering off a chain
reaction of which the so-called "Great War" was but the
first link.

Typical of the unconcern, even the frivolity with which
the "inevitability" of a war between Russia and Germany
was envisaged is the unpublished report of a little episode
which happened in Potsdam in November 1910, at the time
of the Tsar's visit to Germany. It involved an anonymous
German, probably a fairly high-ranking officer, and a few
members of the Tsar's entourage, undoubtedly also military men, who were in conversation (probably at a well-
known Berlin restaurant) in the early hours of the morning.
The Russians argued that there were economic conflicts
that could not be peacefully solved: Germany was basically
an industrial country which the Junkers had artifically made
into an agrarian country producing wheat and potatoes.

"We Russians have to buy your industrial products but
you close your border to our grain imports. Your press, being in the hands of the Jews, is almost uniformly anti-Russian. . . ." It was a distorted picture but apparently a widely
accepted one.

"Too bad," the German said in his reply. "If so, war is now

a possibility. Both sides will do their duty. But this should not prevent us having a very nice get-together in the Ritz in Paris after the war, when we shall tell each other how it was on the other side *(und wir koennen uns damn erzaehlen wie es hueben und drueben war)."*

The records do not show whether that meeting in the Ritz ever took place. I rather doubt it. If it did, those present were undoubtedly much wiser and much sadder men.

It has been the fashion in Russia for some years to charge the German ruling classes with "hatred and contempt for all things Russian ever since the middle ages. . . ." Such generalizations are of doubtful value, especially if they go back to a time when there was practically no contact between the two peoples. In the 19th century, at any rate, Prussian official policy was all in favor of friendship with Russia. When Nikolai I died, the arch-conservative *Kreuzzeitung* announced "Our Emperor has died. . . ." Anti-Russianism in that period was found mainly among the Liberals on the Left, where there was much sympathy for the Poles —and considerable enmity towards the country that had emerged as the great bulwark of despotism in Europe, the main pillar of the Holy Alliance. German Left-wing nationalists regarded Russia (not without good reason) as the major obstacle to the unification of their country and proclaimed the necessity of a holy war against Russia. It was then that Freiligrath wrote his famous poem about the two camps into which the world was divided:

> *Zwei Lager zerklüften heute die Welt*
> *Und ein hüben, ein drüben nur gilt.*

Everybody had to stand up and be counted; the free peoples of the West would in a last decisive battle defeat the slaves of the East. But this was the voice of the German Opposition, not of the Establishment.

In this confrontation between the "revolutionary West" and the "reactionary East," German democrats tended to equate Tsarist rule and the Russian people. For a Russian public opinion which dissociated itself from Tsarist policy was scarcely audible in the West. Many of the early enemies of Tsarist autocracy regarded the "Polish question" as a family quarrel between brother Slavs; Western democrats suspected that both were really thinly disguised Pan-Slavists who wanted to conquer all Europe. Even if radicals (such as Herzen and Bakunin) took an unequivocal stand on the Polish question, this did not allay the fears of men like Karl Marx and Friedrich Engels. The events of 1848 had taught them that Russia was a counter-revolutionary nation, and, in their eyes these "aggressive Western Chinese" (as Moses Hess put it) had all the faults but none of the virtues of primitive people; they were "barbarians," their victory would bring "perpetual night on Europe," a Slavic invasion would spell the "destruction of all civilization and culture." Hatred of Russia (as Engels wrote Bakunin) was the "first revolutionary passion of the Germans." Russian history was interpreted by Marx in very unfavorable terms. What indeed could be expected of a people "whose very character had been formed by centuries of Mongol, Tartar, and Tsarist despotism," a nation which "had made territorial conquests far beyond her natural frontiers"? These pronouncements, needless to say, have been a source of embarrassment to latter-day orthodox Marxists of the Russian persuasion.

True, the attitude of the German Left was affected by the emergence of a strong Russian revolutionary movement towards the end of the century. But Tsarism remained the most dangerous enemy of socialism. Engels, as well as August Bebel and Karl Liebknecht, continued to justify a revolutionary war against Russia in the 1890's. Only with the revolution of 1905 did the downfall of Tsarist absolutism become a distinct possibility. Its failure, however, caused little surprise. Most German socialists had no high opinion of their Russian comrades. With their perpetual internal strife they had been a source of anxiety and embarrassment for the whole international movement. When the first World War broke out, the German Social Democracy, almost without a dissenting voice, stood for what their spokesman called "the defense of German civilization" against corruption by primitive Russia. In the name of progress and a higher culture they joined the struggle against Tsarist despotism, for this, in their eyes, coincided with the interests of the international proletariat.

Not all Russophobes in Germany before 1914 were on the Left. There was a small but highly influential group which made a decisive contribution to the shaping of the German image of Russia in the 20th century. These were German Balts. Contrary to common belief not all of them were "Barons"; in many respects they were an attractive people with high cultural and moral standards, certainly more civilized than their equals in the *Reich*. But they had been a privileged minority for a long time, and it had made many of them haughty and overbearing. Their privileges came under attack around the middle of the 19th century; their cultural, religious, and educational anatomy was slowly whittled away by the Tsarist government. If the Balts had previously taken a poor view of how things were managed in Russia, their bitterness now became more pronounced. In answer to one of the leaders of Pan-Slavism their spokesman indignantly rejected the Russian claim to a "world mission." The Russians were, he admitted, a very gifted people —but seriousness, moderation, perseverance were not among their virtues. They were too subject to moods and emotions and lacked discipline. Was there any other people so blind to the tremendous discrepancy between its aspirations and its real abilities? . . .

Among those Balts who subsequently migrated to the *Reich* (to constitute the nucleus of German experts on Russia!) there was one, Victor Hehn, who, more than any other, developed an almost systematic "theory of Russophobia" and thus exerted a tremendous and baneful influence on the course of recent German history. It is unlikely that Hitler even knew of its existence; the *Führer* took his views on things Russian from Alfred Rosenberg, but what Rosenberg had to say on the subject was pure Hehn—often in literal quotation. Victor Hehn, naturalist and historian, is now remembered, if at all, as the author of a very learned history of "domestic animals in the Roman Empire" and some other monographs. What interests us here is a posthumous work entitled *De Moribus Ruthenorum* (a contribution towards a characterization of the Russian *Volksseele:* Leaves from a Diary, 1857–1873).

Hehn had spent many years in various parts of Russia as a young man, and he had found nothing to admire. The Marquis de Custine's famous critical work reads in comparison like the prospectus of a travel agency trying to sell sunny, fascinating Russia to the rest of Europe. Other contemporary writers found fault with the Russian government and the ruling classes, but Hehn reached the conclusion that there was nothing in the myth of the allegedly unspoilt common man either. The Russian, he insisted, lacked idealism and depth of feeling and emotion. Even Pushkin's talent was imitative; it lacked moral profundity and was enfeebled by a streak of frivolity. The age-old despotism had enervated and corrupted these "Western Chinese" who had no conscience, no honor. They were ungrateful, and loved only those whom they feared. They had no perseverance and were the world's greatest liars. They had no talent, and had never produced a single statesman of stature. They lacked the elementary gift of putting two and two together and lost their heads in any emergency; no Russian was able,

for instance, to become an engine driver. Hehn did not like
their looks any more than their character and he discussed
at length their brutal faces, their lifeless skins and other
physical attributes. The absence of cleanliness, the preva-
lence of fleas, ignorance of hygiene, made him despair. The
Russians, he once wrote, are civilized only in the presence
of others. They had invented nothing. They could be de-
leted from the list of civilized nations without any loss to
mankind. (This is only one of his *obiter dicta* which recurs
time and again in Rosenberg and Hitler.) They had no creative genius, no soul, no fantasy. They displayed "the terrible inability of a people which could not advance mentally
beyond the stage of a German secondary school pupil. . . ."

The educated Russian, too, was a miserable creature, and
at the same time a great danger for Europe; after all, there
were so many of these Slavs. Perhaps one day there
would be a new Battle of Chalons: the Mongols had once
reached Silesia, and the Russians might well some day advance to the Atlantic. Hehn had only sarcasm for the Russian predilection for intellectual fashions; of course, they
jumped at every new idea, *e.g.*, socialism; they had no tradition, no roots, no culture of their own to fall back on; all
they possessed had been imported from abroad.

In an interesting passage he discussed "the future of socialism in Russia." Socialism and communism, Hehn wrote,
presupposed a very high degree of social and cultural development; for that reason Russia was the least likely place
in which such an experiment could succeed. Harsh orders
and the whip alone could induce the Russian to commit acts
of heroism. It was a wonderfully amorphous mass ready
to be shaped by a strict master—whether Varagians or German corporals. How could freedom and humanity grow in
this moral climate?

And so it goes on and on, the ravings, one would say in

retrospect, of a madman, a German racialist and chauvinist. But Hehn was nothing of the sort, not at any rate when he wrote this diary. Much of his criticism stemmed from his opposition to Tsarist autocracy. He, too, had been among the suspect revolutionary elements to be arrested at some time or another by the "Third Department." Nor had he any illusions about the role his fellow-Germans played in Russia. In the eyes of the Russian people, he wrote, they were on the side of the bloodthirsty rulers, the corrupt court, and the obscurantist church: they had no heart for the sufferings of the Russian people. Hehn lived in an age in which "culture and civilization" counted for more than "race"; at times he was bewildered by the enormous cultural discrepancy between the Germans and the Slavs, despite their racial affinity. It is true that he made much of "Russian degeneracy," but he was not the only one to do so. These were dark years in Russian history, when Chernyshevski was writing about "that miserable nation, a nation of slaves from top to bottom, nothing but slaves. . . ." There was not all that difference between Hehn and Russian radicals in their *analysis* of Russian society. The difference was in the prognosis, for Hehn saw no redeeming features at all, no prospect of change and improvement.

Hehn's views were a classical if extreme expression of German Russophobia. It would be tedious to discuss in detail the contributions made by his successors. Some, like the Pan-Germans, thought primarily in terms of German expansion eastward up to the Saratov region; others, like Paul Rohrbach, were liberals of sorts and advocated the "dissection of the Russian colossus" into its natural historical and ethnic components. Russia, he argued, could be split like an orange without cut or wound, and would yet survive, unlike Germany or France. An early sexologist named Stern published two huge volumes on what went on behind the stoves in the *izbas* of Russian villages during the long winter, providing more ammunition for those who thought that Europe ended at Ostrowo or Augustowo. During the First World War there was a fresh outbreak of this kind of writing both on the political and literary level in Germany, matched in the Russian magazines by the slogan "from Kant to Krupp." The literateurs tried to write like politicians, and the politicians like Dostoievsky scholars. There was much talk about the imponderabilia of "the Russian soul," the deep instinctive "rejection of Romano-German culture," the nebulous *folie de grandeur* that was said to pervade the blood of every Russian. Nobody explained what all this meant, except that it was something aggressive, destructive, dangerous.

Many of these half-baked ideas were subsequently absorbed and amplified by Nazi writers. Their only new contribution, borrowed from H. S. Chamberlain, was the concept of "racial chaos": Russia had somehow got into this mess because of its inferior blood-mixture. The Russophobia remained, only the ideological justification was somewhat modified. The German "cultural" mission in the East of 1914 became a "racial" mission in 1941.

There were, and are, in most European countries, philosophers, historians, and poets who have held violent or idiosyncratic views about their neighbors. The decisive question was (and is)—how important were they? In Wilhelmian Germany they did matter. Schiemann, who was Hehn's pupil and editor, was also the Kaiser's closest adviser on Russian affairs. When Wilhelm II ascended the throne he said that he did not want war with Russia "merely to satisfy a hundred crazy Junkers." But in his later years he became more and more convinced that war between Slavs and Germans was inevitable, was only a question of time. Towards this feeling of inevitability the German Russophobes undoubtedly made a major contribution. They had another field day under Adolf Hitler, when the clash between Bolshevism and Nazism added an additional dimension, as it seemed, to the age old conflict between German and Slav.

In between there was a more promising interlude. During the Weimar Republic, relations between the two countries were friendlier than ever before or after. True, Germany was still capitalist, but it had the best and strongest Communist party in the world. Versailles, as some Right-wingers put it, had reduced Germany to the status of "a proletarian nation . . . very much like Soviet Russia." What was more natural than close collaboration between the two? The result was Rapallo, a name to conjure with to this day (although its real political importance was small, something like a marriage contract that is only partly consummated).

Germany did not stay a proletarian or a pariah nation for long. A few years later the "Eastern orientation" became a liability in the eyes of most German foreign-policy makers. Stalin, certainly, could not help Stresemann to get what he wanted from Paris and London. There was resistance in Germany to a *rapprochement* with Moscow. The Social Democrats were resentful, remembering what happened to their comrades in the Soviet Union, and the constant attacks on them by the Communists did not make them more friendly disposed. The churches had been antagonized by Soviet atheism. German industrialists were concerned about profits and the future of capitalist society in general. But there was indeed close co-operation between Germany's *Reichswehr* and Russia's Red Army, and cultural and economic relations between the two countries prospered. There was a new wave of pro-Russian enthusiasm among German intellectuals—*Battleship Potemkin,* the Five-Year-Plan, the "Love of the Five Oranges," everything was eagerly accepted and discussed. Karl Radek wrote for arch-bourgeois newspapers like the *Berliner Tageblatt.* Many Soviet novels were translated into German immediately after they appeared in Moscow and found, like Soviet films and plays, enthusiastic audiences. Soviet trade with Germany was much more extensive than its economic exchanges with any other country.

But how much goodwill did it generate? Eager exporters still tell us that foreign trade enhances the prospects for world peace. I have a suspicion that it accomplishes about as much in that direction as international soccer matches. Trade between Russia and Germany has been highest on the eve of a war or a grave international crisis—in 1913/14, in 1932, and in 1940/41, *Absit omen*.

The Russian Communists had, as Lenin once said, a special relationship with Germany. Marx and Engels, after all, were Germans. Before 1914 the Russians had looked up to the German party as the most advanced in the International. True, the Soviet leaders disliked the latter-day German Social Democrats and tried whenever possible to deal with pro-Russian conservatives instead. This made sense from their point of view, for a Count Brockdorff-Rantzau would not lecture them on the virtues of democracy and the necessity of freedom in a socialist society. As for Hitler and Nazism, the Russians do not appear to have understood what it was really all about until it was quite too late. In 1930 they firmly believed that "Hitler was finished" (the German bourgeoisie did not need him any more and had dispensed with his services, or so the *Soviet Encyclopedia* said). Previously they had called Nazism "a radical petty-bourgeois movement"; later on they defined it as "the praetorian guard of monopoly finance-capitalism." Even an experienced observer like Radek did not think that Hitler could really succeed; there were "no facts and figures" in his speeches, only "unbridled emotion." Surely this was not good enough for sophisticated people like the Germans?

The Soviet leaders never sensed the enormous appeal of

nationalism *à l'outrance,* nor could they comprehend that Hitler was nobody's guard or servant or tool. Even when Moscow realized that the Nazis were up to no good, the Soviet leaders failed utterly to give a realistic appraisal of what they called "German fascism"; they assumed it was a new, somewhat streamlined edition of Wilhelmian imperialism. Many detailed Marxist-Leninist studies were published in the U.S.S.R. on far away countries in which there was scarcely a working class, much less a Communist party; one would be hard pressed to point to any Soviet book which attempted to analyze Nazism. Stalin certainly gave no lead to his ideologists; he never attacked Hitler personally, and about Nazism, too, he was singularly reticent. After the Pact of August 1939, anti-Nazi movies and books had to be withdrawn, only compounding the confusion.

Of the new *Reich* the Russians knew next to nothing. They had known the Germans for a long time—sober and industrious, if somewhat pedestrian, people. Parts of Russia had been occupied by the Germans during the first World War, and it had not been a particularly horrible experience as occupations go. Psychologically and politically, the Russians were quite unprepared for what was to come.

If Stalin misjudged Hitler, Hitler in his turn entertained the most fantastic notions about "Judeao-Bolshevism." He did not, of course, believe for a moment all the *Unsinn* about socialism, planned economy, historical materialism, class war, collectivization. These were mere phrases, a smoke-screen to hide the real motive and driving force behind it—which was a gigantic conspiracy by "the racial scum of the earth" against the "Aryan" race. The Nazi press provided chapter and verse. The body of the bishop of Voronezh had been cooked to make soup which the monks of the local monastery had been forced to eat by the *Cheka.*

A monument had been erected in honor of Judas Iscariot. Fifty to seventy per cent of the Communist leaders were syphilitics. Trotsky had been an informer for the Tsarist police, and later was director of a firm of furniture movers in Petrograd. Stalin was a former stevedore in the harbor of Tiflis. . . .*

Occasionally, Hitler took Bolshevism more seriously. In a speech in 1932 he predicted that the Communist *Weltanschauung* would slowly shatter the entire world; if unchecked, it would change the world as completely as Christianity had done. It was not merely a question of a different 'mode of production"—

> "if the movement continues to develop, 300 years from now Lenin will be regarded not only as one of the revolutionaries of 1917, but as the founder of a new world doctrine, and he will be worshipped as much perhaps as Buddha. . . ."

But these apocalyptic visions never lasted long, and soon gave way to Hitler's more usual cocksure aberrations. In a way he did not regret the victory of Bolshevism in Russia (he said), for it made it much easier to carry out the great task which was the destiny of the German people—to expand eastwards. For Bolshevism, once challenged by a superior political and military power, would collapse like a house of cards. He regarded the Soviet Union as an extension of the German Communist Party, and he would defeat the one as easily as he had destroyed the other.

Some Nazi leaders (including the early Goebbels and the Strasser brothers) did not share this view of Russia and at

---

* The rise to power of Joseph Stalin presented difficulties for the racialists—for had not Stalin removed the Jews from the supreme leadership? At this point the Nazis realized that if they persevered in their racial comments, they would soon have to change their whole approach to Communism. This for a variety of reasons they could not do; hence the decision to pursue their anti-Communist campaign regardless of what Stalin had done to his Jewish rivals.

one time advocated a German-Russian alliance against the West. In 1925, in a little book called *The Second Revolution,* Joseph Goebbels had written,

> "Russia is an ally which nature has given us against the devilish temptation and corruption of the West. . . ."

He said he had not the slightest intention of joining the chorus of bourgeois liars and ignoramuses defaming Soviet Russia. But in the end it was, as usual, Hitler's wishes and visions that prevailed. The Nazi press carried daily stories about the impending downfall of the Soviet régime through sheer inefficiency, corruption, and self-destruction. Nazi Sovietology had one single assignment—to prove the Jewish descent of all Bolshevik leaders. There was no particular difficulty as far as Karl Marx was concerned, but the case of Vladimir Ilyich Lenin was more difficult,* and with Djugashvili Stalin and most of his underlings it became very difficult indeed. But they were inventive chaps in Berlin. Kerensky was a Jew (Kirbis) and Lunacharsky was "re-translated" into German *(Mondschein).* Moonshine, indeed.

All in all, therefore, Russia was a country ruled by "racial scum," therefore doomed. The Nazis were in for a great surprise in 1941.

There has thus been a curse on Russian-German relations. Some say that Nikita Khrushchev's attempts to lift it were premature. The time, needless to say, is more propitious now than ever before. The war years had been a profound shock for the Russians, but it is now twenty years after and the Russians are bad haters. They have begun to re-

---

* Mr. Louis Fischer, in his recent biography of Lenin, has critically sifted all the evidence about Lenin's maternal grandfather, a physician named Blank, who was presumably the basis of the tale of Lenin's "Jewishness."

alize that their predictions about post-war Germany have *not* come true. There has *not* been a "neo-Nazi revival"; the "revanchist attack against the East" has *not* taken place. As for the small-nation military power of the *Bundesrepublik*, Russian reflexes are conditioned, understandably perhaps, by the near defeats of 1941. They have absurdly exaggerated the military importance of the new Germany in a nuclear super-power age. Only recently has it dawned upon them that since 1945 Russia and Germany have been playing "in different leagues," and that for Bonn there is no possibility of promotion; militarily and politically the *Bundesrepublik* is no longer a major factor.

There has been, I think, a certain softening of West German attitude towards Russia during recent years.† Dr. Adenauer understood that Russia was "no friend of the West"; in other respects he preferred to ignore a subject which basically did not interest him. For his compatriots Russia was more than ever a sinister riddle wrapped in dark mystery. Millions of them had been to Russia during the war, and the poverty and misery they saw there, greatly aggravated no doubt by the occupation régime, made it appear as if the Nazi slogans about the Slavic *Unter-Menschen* had ample foundation. And yet the Russians fought back with undeniable heroism, and showed great capacity to improvise and even to develop weapons that were sometimes better than any the *Wehrmacht* had at its disposal. Post-war events did not make the Russians popular in Germany; there was the question of the remaining prisoners of war, and above all the problem of a divided Germany.

Let us not be unfair to Konrad Adenauer; vis-à-vis Stalin's Russia it would not have made much difference had his understanding of "the Russian question" been more sophisticated. In the middle '50s, however, certain changes began

† Since this was written and published (1965), there has been Chancellor Willy Brandt's diplomatic mission to Moscow (1970).

to take place in the Soviet Union which German public opinion almost completely ignored until fairly recently. For in West Germany "Bolshevism" or the "Communist régime" always mean the East German DDR, or, as they prefer to say, the "Soviet Occupation Zone." What happens there overshadows, in German eyes, everything else in the Communist orbit. It is perhaps a natural reaction, but it is not one conducive to a balanced view of European and world affairs.

East Germany, everyone agrees, is the most disagreeable of the East European satellites. Economically the situation has improved, but there have been no concessions to popular needs and views as there have in all other East European countries. Instead there came the Wall, the very symbol of failure. Consequently, Ulbricht and his comrades are now regarded as "Stalinist die-hards." But is this really accurate? Given more suitable conditions he could certainly have tried to play the role of a Novotny or a Gheorgiu Dej, if not of a Janós Kádár. But these conditions do not exist; three-quarters of Germany lies outside his rule and has a tremendous attraction for the great majority of his citizenry. In these circumstances, Communist rule in East Germany is either repressive or it disintegrates. Ulbricht and his circle have bitterly complained about the criticism directed against his policy by his East European comrades, in whose "revisionist" eyes he has become more and more of a liability. *They* can well afford liberal gestures, but how could he, in an exposed position, bear "the brunt of capitalist penetration"? That is the official psychology of East Berlin.

East Germany, then, remains the great stumbling-block on the road to any kind of "Russo-German *rapprochement.*" Some Western observers (and, of course, the Chinese) have argued that Khrushchev was willing to give up East Germany as "part of a bigger deal." The same was said at the time of Stalin, and, in 1953, of Beria. I think they are demonstrably wrong. Faced with the Chinese threat, Khrushchev wanted to "normalize" the situation in Central Europe. But could he do so at this price? The German problem involves all of Germany's European neighbors. A united Germany, even if neutral—even if Communist!—would be a major threat in Polish and Czechoslovak eyes. The dilemma facing his successors is very much the same.

What, then, is the outcome likely to be? Certainly no new "Tauroggen," no new "Rapallo," for there is no common enemy against which Russia and Germany could now unite. West Germans are still convinced that though the idea of a divided fatherland may be intolerable, to have no homeland at all would be worse. The most then that one can hope for in this new phase of Russian-German relations is some understanding to "leave well enough alone in Berlin" or to find a new *modus vivendi* acceptable to both sides. Ulbricht surely deserves a rest and will be replaced one of these days by an Erich Honecker or a Willi Stoph. How much will change? There is scope for an extension of trade between the two parts of the country, and one or two minor issues could fruitfully be discussed. But there is not much room for maneuvre on the *major* problems. Like Jupiter, Brezhnev may well say of himself *"Me quoque fata regunt"* (his predecessor would have preferred an earthy Ukrainian proverb to Ovid).

Is there no escape from destiny? Are the Russians and Germans fated to be enemies in the future as in the past, with the difference in social systems adding virulence to an old conflict? The long-range outlook is less bleak than appears at first sight, for the passage of time sometimes helps to solve the most intractable problems or at least reduces them to more manageable proportions. If Germany and France have buried the ancient and much bloodied hatchet, new global tensions and conflicts may make the strife in the central and eastern parts of the European sub-continent appear equally small and senseless. Will one day the walls come down and new generations of Russians and Germans, untroubled by bitter memories of the past, work together in the "quest for a better world"? It is, I think, a noble vision and not altogether fanciful. But today, alas, these new horizons are not even visible. At best, it will be a very long drawn-out process. At most, there will be the first few and hesitant steps in that direction.

(1965)

"BONN IS NOT WEIMAR"

Reflections on the Radical Right

CHRISTMAS EVE in a West German City. The rain has been falling steadily for days; soon it will turn into snow. Last-minute shoppers hurry home with their gift parcels. Enormous Christmas trees are displayed in the shop windows, also shepherds and cribs, tinsel angels with clouds of silvery hair. The main roads are illuminated, the trolleybuses overflow, and it is difficult to find a taxi. People gather in front of the church, where a choir is singing the song of the fir tree, "O Tannenbaum" At the nearby university, students are demonstrating against the war in Vietnam.

A meeting of the National Democrats has been announced for that evening; it is to be addressed by the deputy leader. There is a great deal of curiosity in the air. In the big hall there are perhaps two thousand people; a few hundred who could not find seats have to remain outside. The deputy leader arrives, there is some applause, but not very much; about half the audience seems to be hostile, or at any rate passive. He clears his throat and begins to speak. The deputy leader is quite good-looking, immaculately dressed; he bears a vague resemblance to one of Germany's leading film stars. But he has aged in recent years and there is little of that

*boyish charm which fifteen years ago made his fellow mem-
bers of the Bundestag call him, somewhat derisively, "Bubi."*

*The tenor of the speech is serious; he does not tell jokes,
and barely indulges in sarcasm. He finds it difficult to make
an impact on the audience, remains cold and quite remote.
Only toward the end does the deputy leader warm up a bit:
"We are not Nazis," he claims, "that is a base calumny." The
National Socialist party was the creation of one man, Adolf
Hitler; his movement disappeared together with him. Nor are
we obscurantists, backwoods men, as our enemies so often
claim. We are open to all new influences, "weltoffen." We are
not anti-democratic, we simply want to make democracy
work, we want to do away with the excesses and shortcomings of what amounts to a party dictatorship in Bonn. We
want a united Europe. But we also want to be treated as
what we are—a great people in the heart of Europe, not a
nation of criminals. An independent German policy is overdue, we ought to put our own interests first. . . .*

*He goes on for a few more minutes about the need for a
sensible economic policy. He does not mention Jews in his
speech, and says very little about Russia and Communism.
He ends with a forecast: the party will go from strength to
strength; we had never expected to do as well as we did in
Hesse and Bavaria. Deep among the people there is a growing wish for change—and we now constitute the only alternative.*

*Then, rather abruptly, it is all over. No singing of patriotic
songs or hymns, no shouts of "Heil!" Quietly, the audience
disperses, while some of the party stalwarts peddle their
newssheet, "Deutsche Nachrichten." It is all very orderly
and unexcited. There had been some heckling during the
speech, but the ushers had been given strict instructions not
to intervene.*

This, then, is the great national upsurge. What a contrast with another upsurge I had witnessed in this same country as a boy. My earliest political memory is of listening on the wireless to the results of the 1930 elections in which the Nazis emerged as the second strongest party. This was at a time when thousands of unemployed people were demonstrating, when street brawls and political murder occurred every weekend. It was the age of Hitler and Goebbels, of monster rallies, of electrifying speeches and wild mobs. It was a period of frenzied clamor, of "Deutschland Erwache! and "Juda Verrecke" of shots in dark alleys and the sirens of police cars, a time when political enemies were trampled to death, and uniformed gangs terrorized passersby. It was, in other words, an era quite different from the present; whoever lived through those years cannot help but regard this latter-day revival—if it is a revival—as an anti-climax. The demagogy is subdued; the crowds are passive; there may be resentment but there is no enthusiasm. A large part of the crowd had come to listen to the speaker out of plain curiosity —next time they will watch on television. But on television the National Democrats, like Joe McCarthy, do not look good. True, Hitler, Goebbels, and Goering were greatly underrated in 1930. And yet, for all that, the overwhelming impression, as one observer has put it, is that these people will not set the Rhine on fire, let alone the Reichstag.

Outside their meetings, the National Democrats are not easy to locate. A Cologne sociologist told me the following story: Together with a small group of people, he had gone to a remote little village in Hesse, in which 53 per cent of the population had recently voted for the National Democrats. For two days they had interviewed practically every inhabitant, but no one admitted having voted for the NPD. The peasants had given expression to their resentment in the elections, but they also felt embarrassed about it.

But then one does occasionally meet a member of the NPD in the most unlikely of places. Walking in the street one day,

I saw a man who looked vaguely familiar. He introduced himself. I had known Hirsch (as I shall call him) when we went to the same school; I had not heard from him since. He was a "half Jew" according to the Nuremberg laws. Soon he began to tell me his life story: how he had served in the German army for a while, but—as a "Non-Aryan"—was transferred to a labor battalion in 1940; how he barely survived the war and the persecutions, but lost his parents. Yet, despite his personal misfortunes and all he had suffered under Hitler, he had preserved his belief in the national regeneration of the German people. For was not the destiny of the nation far more important than the fate of the individual? Hitler had been a disaster, but were the Russians and the Americans any better? Was it not their fault that Germany was now divided and that the Eastern territories had been lost? Was it not a fact that the country needed strong leadership and that the National Democrats were the most likely to provide it? A few days later a letter arrived, forty pages single-spaced, in which he developed this theme at greater length. The deputy leader of the NPD once said that his party had two Jewish members; he could not remember their names and addresses. For all I know, he may have been telling the truth—or, to be more precise, the half truth.

On Monday, November 21, 1966, the day after the Bavarian state elections, the London *Daily Express* carried the banner headline: NEW NAZIS WIN AGAIN. The *Sun* proclaimed: NAZIS MARCH TO VICTORY; the *Daily Mirror*, NEW NAZIS STORM TO TRIUMPH; and the *Daily Mail*. ANOTHER TRIUMPH FOR NEO-NAZIS. In the body of the reports it was stated that the National Democratic Party (NPD), a right-wing extremist group, had polled 7.4 per cent of the total vote in the Bavarian elections, having obtained 7.7 per cent in the state of Hesse a few weeks before. A poll of 7 per cent is not usually interpreted in London in terms of a "march to victory," let alone a "storm to triumph;" a candidate polling that much in Britain would, in fact, automatically lose his deposit. But this was clearly an extraordinary event. If the headlines of the British press were somewhat alarmist, most other European newspapers also took a serious view of the outcome of these elections. So did most responsible German observers, though only a few went as far as the advertiser in a Munich newspaper who announced that he had decided to emigrate when he heard of the results—would anyone be interested in a comfortable, spacious, three-room flat in a good residential area?

After the headlines came the editorials, resolutions by various organizations in New York and Milan, Tel Aviv and London, protest meetings, open letters, and a demand for action. Never mind the figures, said some of the experts in the Western capitals; Hitler's party had polled much less in 1928, a mere 2 per cent, and yet five years later it was in power.

How was it that a new party, modeling itself in some essential respects on the old Nazi party (the *NSDAP* without the *SA*, as the saying goes), had done so well in its first attempt? How to explain its achievements in the light of the fact that the party organization was relatively weak and amateurish, that its leaders were, as rabble rousers, not remotely in the class of Hitler and Goebbels, that the party had no major financial backers? How to explain it against the background of an economic situation which, despite a slackening of the boom, could not possibly be compared with the crisis of 1929–33? Some of the election successes of the NPD had been won in areas which had been traditional Nazi strongholds but, inexplicably, there were breakthroughs in other areas as well. How to account for all this?

Many Germans have tried to provide an answer to these questions. Their first reaction had been one of indignation at the sensationalist headlines in the foreign press. Was this not another instance of the double standard used by the West *vis-à-vis* Germany? Did not every country have its extreme right wing? Had not Poujade in France and the Italian neo-Fascists in their time polled even more votes than the NPD without causing a similar commotion? Had not some Western commentators been predicting an imminent return of the Nazis almost since the end of the war and had not their prophecies, time and time again, been belied by the course of events? The more thoughtful German observers realized, of course,, that, in the perspective of recent German history, even a comparatively small success by right-wing extremists was bound to have repercussions far beyond its intrinsic importance. They understood that what really bothered their neighbors was not the figure of 7 per cent, but the question: what next?

The basic reasons behind the emergence of the NPD have been known for a long time, and they can be summarized in a few sentences. In every democratic country a certain section of the population gravitates toward the extreme Right. There has always been an extreme Right in Germany; during the first years after the defeat it was submerged; during the 1950's and early 1960's it was split into many little groups and therefore did not constitute an effective political force. This led some observers to believe that the extreme Right had all but ceased to exist. But all along, some 10 to 20 per cent of the population has been firmly convinced that Hitler did more good than harm—apart from such excesses as killing the Jews rather than deporting them, and apart from such miscalculations as starting a war which he was bound to lose. In past elections, some of these men and women abstained from voting altogether; others voted for a variety of right-wing splinter groups; still others, for lack of a suitable alternative, supported the right wing of the Christian Democrats, or in some instances the Free Democrats. In 1966 there was, for the first time since the war, a movement of the extreme Right which had a real chance of gaining representation in Parliament. Hence its startling successes. The extreme Right, hitherto submerged, had now surfaced. In the process it has gathered strength, rallying to its banner many who, while in sympathy with the aims of the NPD all along, had not in the past had an opportunity to express their feelings. One of the main election slogans of the NPD was *"Man kann wieder wählen"*—you can choose again,[1] there is a real alternative. But this explanation raises many new questions: why did it happen now? How explain the impact of the NPD on some sections of the youth? Who are its leaders and what do they really want? What, above all, are its chances of making further headway?

At this point, a brief historical detour is necessary. Most leaders of the NPD began their political careers in one of the right-wing splinter groups of which there were at least eighty in Germany in the postwar period. There was the German *Reichs* party, the Socialist *Reichs* party, the European Social Movement, the German *Rechts* party, and many more. Despite economic and social conditions that favored the growth of such groups (such as, for example, the presence of millions of refugees from the East), none of these groups attained much influence. The only exception was the Socialist *Reichspartei* which, before it was banned in 1952, polled 10 per cent and more in parts of Lower Saxony and elsewhere in North Germany. But its influence, too, was regionally limited. The party was about to disintegrate anyway; its leaders —like those of other right-wing splinter groups—quarreled on both ideological and personal grounds; some were staunchly anti-Communist in inspiration, while others favored a neutralist line in the Cold War, and a few were even compromised by having accepted subsidies from East Germany.

[1] *Wählen* having a double meaning in German—both to vote and to choose.

Even so, some of them did not despair. They realized that although their organizations attracted only a few hundred members, or at best a few thousand, there was a considerably larger reservoir of good will around them. The sentiments expressed by the Bundestag and by the intelligentsia on such subjects as, for instance, recent German responsibility for the crimes committed by the Nazi régime, were not necessarily shared by the small-town *Stammtische*. There was a great deal of resentment about the lack of a "firm national policy," about the denigration of all national values by "left-wing intellectuals," about foreign workers, indulgence toward sex criminals and murderers of taxi drivers, about restitution to the Jews and aid to Africa, about German miniskirts and German *Gammler* (beatniks). Whichever resolution was passed by the Bundestag in Bonn, a majority of Germans had persuaded themselves by 1966 that the time had come to put an end to the war-crimes trials. Another hopeful indication was the success of right-wing extremist literature, above all the *Soldaten Zeitung*, which subsequently became the *Nationalzeitung*. Dr. G. Frey, its editor, is a man in his thirties and could not therefore be charged with support of Hitler. But the inspiration of both Hitler and Goebbels was unmistakable in every issue of what became within a few years one of the more influential as well as one of the more widely read of West German weeklies.

Among the groups that contended for the leadership of the extreme Right during the '50's, the *Deutsche Reichspartei* was the most prominent. But in the elections of 1957 it polled a mere one per cent of the total (about 300,000 votes); five years later, it did even worse. It was further weakened by a number of petty scandals. Its Cologne branch had to be closed after it was discovered that several of its members had daubed swastikas on the local synagogue at Christmas 1959. There was a constant tug-of-war between a minority which favored a neutralist foreign policy and the majority, which was militantly anti-Communist. The party was too radical, and, above all, too sectarian to be a popular success. Adolf von Thadden, who had been its leading figure, realized that in this form the party had no political future. In order to gain real influence in German political life, a transformation was needed to establish a new movement that could both serve as a haven for all the shipwrecked right-wing splinter groups *and* attract the dissatisfied of all classes in West Germany to whom a strongly nationalist and authoritarian policy would appeal. Von Thadden persuaded most of his colleagues to dissolve the old party and, in November 1964, to establish a new movement, the NPD. At its first convention, von Thadden said that the party hoped to attract ten thousand members during its first year, and to double the membership during the following year. These goals were fullfilled earlier than had been assumed possible: the NPD now has twenty-five thousand members, perhaps a bit more. These are modest figures, but such statistics do not provide much guidance in Germany as to the real strength of a political party. Almost immediately after its establishment, the NPD began to contest local elections with greater enthusiasm than its predecessors. To be sure, it attracted only 644,000 voters (two per cent of the total) in the West German general elections of September 1965, not yet an impressive achievement. But subsequent regional elections have shown that there may be greater things to come. The party did well in Hesse, which is ruled by the Social Democrats, and generally considered to be an exemplary state *(Musterländle);* it scored above its own expectations in Bavaria, the traditional citadel of political Catholicism. If it could do that well under unfavorable conditions there was every reason to assume that it would do even better in some of the Protestant areas of Northern Germany which have a strong nationalist tradition.

The leadership of the new party puts the accent on respectability; strong-arm methods are strictly discouraged. This is partly a device of self-preservation, because the party is still too small to engage in methods similar to those practiced by the Hitler movement between 1930 and 1933. But this is not the only consideration. Bonn—to quote the title of F. R. Allemann's famous book—is not Weimar; the general climate of the Federal Republic is not conducive to street battles. In the 20's and 30's, tens of thousands of toughs could be mobilized without much difficulty. It is much harder to find such people at a time of full employment. Moreover, large-scale rowdyism would antagonize more people than it is likely to attract. The present leaders of the NPD want to enter parliament, not to engage in direct action. The president of the new party, Fritz Thielen, is the very symbol of respectability, solidity, and similar bourgeois virtues. The owner of a Bremen cement factory, he has been successful in local politics, but until recently was hardly known outside his native city. An indifferent speaker, heavy and slow in manner, he is not exactly a charismatic political figure. Thielen never belonged to the Nazi party; his family tradition is *Deutsch-National,* the conservative, right-wing nationalism of Wilhelminian and Weimar Germany. His deputy, Adolf von Thadden, is far more in demand as a public speaker; he also has greater political flair and experience, being a former member of the Bundestag. Thadden (who is forty-five), comes from the East-German landed gentry; his grandfather was one of Bismarck's closest friends, his half-sister, Elizabeth, was executed as a traitor by the Nazi regime. An officer in the German army during the war, von Thadden, like Thielen, was not a member of the Nazi party. Not too much importance should, however, be attributed to this. When the war broke out von Thadden was barely eighteen—too young to qualify for party membership.

Among the eighteen members of the party executive, the

ex-Nazi element is admittedly much more strongly represented; about two-thirds of this group belonged to the party
or to one of its auxiliary organizations. None of them was
very prominent at that time—they were the lieutenants, captains, or, at most, the majors of the party units. There are a
few journalists of the Goebbels-Rosenberg school, and a national bard of Third-Reich vintage. The names of most of
these men are known to the student of German post-war
right-wing radicalism; they belonged successively to a series
of parties, wrote for the party press, and spoke on behalf of
the party at election meetings.

In conversation with the press and foreigners, some of the
propagandists of the NPD sound eminently reasonable. Otto
Hess, one of the deputy leaders, said that his party did not
want to gloss over anything that had happened, least of all
the horrible treatment of the Jews. "But you cannot ask mere
mortals for a permanent 'Mea culpa.' " Thielen, the leader,
made comments to the same effect; Von Thadden, when
asked about anti-Semitism said: "Oh well, there are only
twenty-five thousand Jews in Germany." As an afterthought
he added: "Well, I think anti-Semitism is a bad thing *per se.*"
And on another occasion: "The foreign workers are for us
what the Jews were for the Nazis." Other NPD propagandists sound on occasion less statesmanlike, especially in their
internal assemblies; speakers have strict orders not to be too
extreme, but quite often their demagogy carries them away.

During the 1965 election campaign, the NPD held fifteen
hundred meetings and distributed several million leaflets.
Even so, the party apparatus is comparatively weak; there
are few full-time organizers. During the one Bavarian election, a *Bundeswehr* captain supervised the preparations in
the strategically important Nuremberg region. There are no
paramilitary units like the storm troopers, no elite groups
like the SS, no uniforms and no badges. According to the
present constitution of the NPD, the party is divided into

regional units (*Länder* and *Kreise*). Members meet about once a month in closed session, usually in a local public house belonging to a sympathizer, and pay their dues (about 75 cents per month). Some meetings are open to the public. In addition, there are special gatherings for younger members, Christmas parties, dances. Studying the party calendar for one specific month (December 1966), one finds a heavy concentration on small and medium-sized towns in Northwest Germany and also, incidentally, in the neighborhood of army camps. Among the speakers, apart from the members of the party executive (located in Hanover), one finds local dignitaries—lawyers, physicians, shopowners, a few clergymen and army officers. The party finances are obviously based on more than membership fees alone, but there is no reason to disbelieve the claim of the party leadership that it receives many small contributions rather than a few big subsidies.

The NPD has no program. Its leaders frequently say that a detailed program would only create confusion and unnecessary disputes; there is, however, a twelve-point manifesto, with Gaullist undertones, calling for a united independent Germany. This manifesto calls for a determined effort on the part of the Germans to take responsibility for their own destiny. Without a reunited Germany, there will be no united Europe.

Germany first, then Europe: Germany to the Germans, Europe to the Europeans. We proclaim a German policy independent of foreign interests.

The first of the twelve general principles enumerated by the manifesto calls for the elimination of waste and corruption; the second, for a reasonable economic policy. Points three and four promise support to workers and peasants respectively. Point five advocates the limitation of foreign aid and restitution payments, if not their total cessation. Points six to eight concern health and education, and include a protest against the heavy emphasis on sex in literature, the arts, the press, television, and cinema. Nine calls for an end to the "one-sided trials" of Nazi criminals. Ten:

> We reject the eulogies of high treason and the statement that Germany alone is to blame for all the unhappiness in the world.
> . . . We demand an end to the lie about the sole German responsibility whereby thousands of millions have been extorted from our nation.

Eleven:

> Germany claims the territories where Germans have lived for centuries. We contest with no nation the land where it has settled, but insist with equal determination on the right to our own land.

The last point asks for an end to the "evil spirit of submission," and states that only those conscious of their own national dignity can hope to gain the respects of the world and the friendship of other nations.

Party programs are notoriously vague, but this manifesto is even more meaningless than most. Some of these demands are common to all right-wing parties, others are vague or contradictory. They express sentiments rather than a political platform. For an understanding of the character of the NPD, the data about the social composition of the party and its electors are more helpful.[2]

The typical NPD supporter is Protestant, in the forty-five

---

[2] Sociologists, political scientists, the various German opinion polls, and sundry other institutions have tackled the NPD phenomenon with all the techniques of modern social investigation. Much factual information has already been amassd, above all by Professor E. K. Scheuch, a Cologne sociologist. Several published books also deal with the NPD: F. Richert's *Die nationale Welle*, and *National oder Radikal* by Bessel-Lorck.

to fifty-nine age group, lower middle class, and lives in a small town somewhere in Northwest Germany. The proportion of refugees and expellees is only slightly higher in the NPD than the West German average. The younger generation is underrepresented (23 per cent in comparison with 28 per cent of the total population), but the NPD has gained support among this group during the last year. Only 24 percent of the party's supporters is Catholic (Catholics account for 43 per cent of the total population). In the recent Bavarian elections, the party polled between 11 and 16 per cent in predominantly Protestant towns like Ansbach, but only 3 to 6 per cent in Catholic areas.

Is the working-class immune to NPD propaganda? The sociologists do not think so. In their view, the NPD finds it more difficult to gain a foothold in working-class areas, but once the party takes root there, the pattern conforms with that of the country as a whole. These facts and figures shed some light on the social composition of the NPD, on the kind of people the party is likely to attract. They do not explain the reasons for its appeal. These can be understood only against the general background of current German politics.

During the last few years or so, the political climate in West Germany has changed palpably, and certainly not for the better. For the first time in their post-war history, the Germans have faced a number of emergencies and crises, and they have not exactly passed these tests with flying colors. Under the long paternal reign of Chancellor Adenauer, many Germans became accustomed to a degree of stability and security that is unusual in the modern world. Dr. Erhard, his successor, was a weaker man, an advocate of laissez-faire in both economics and politics. A creeping dissatisfaction began to be felt, which culminated in a real crisis when a deficit of $750 million was discovered in the national budget that had been prepared for 1967. This was due to an increase in public expenditure of about nine per cent over the previous year, whereas industrial production had increased by only 3.5 per cent. But underlying this was a general crisis of confidence; the conviction that "Erhard must go" became widespread in the ruling Christian Democratic party, and various heirs-apparent began to stake their claim to the succession. The subsequent acute parliamentary crisis lasted several weeks, because the search for a new government ran into difficulties. It was resolved only after protracted negotiations by the formation of a CDU-SPD coalition under Kiesinger and Brandt.

This kind of crisis is not unknown to other European democracies. While not exactly welcomed as an ideal state of affairs, it is accepted as part of the normal democratic process. Not so in Western Germany. The idea of being without a strong central government, even for a little while, seemed too great a psychological burden for many citizens. There was a great deal of criticism of the Bonn *Schwatzbude*[3], of the good-for nothing parties, of soft politicians without stature or backbone, interested mainly in feathering their own nests; the notion that these might be the normal growing-pains of a democratic régime seems not to have occurred to many people. It was not so much the German sense for order which rebelled (though this, too, may have played a certain part); what was revealed, above all, was the immaturity of the democratic tradition, the fear of standing on one's own two feet, the longing for the kind of security which only a strong leadership can provide.

That particular parliamentary emergency is now long since over, but crises in economics and foreign policy persist. Although these crises originated in some real difficulties facing the country, they are nevertheless "normal," in the sense

---

3 Literally, a place for mere idle chatter.

that neither of them constitutes a serious danger to the existence of the *Bundesrepublik*. But instead of facing them realistically, many Germans reacted by magnifying them out of all proportion, by persuading themselves that the situation was very grave, if not actually hopeless. By long tradition, Germans hold the manly virtues in high esteem, but there is perhaps no other nation which passes so quickly from exaggerated self-confidence to despondency.

A German economic crisis nowadays tends to be largely psychological in origin. No doubt, the rate of growth in productivity and production can slacken. But no one in the know really expected that it would continue to expand at the same startling rate as that of the 50's and early 60's. Western Europe in general enjoyed a great economic boom during this period (with Britain and Belgium lagging somewhat behind), and also experienced a similar process of slackening. The rate of industrial growth in Germany in 1964 and again in 1965 was among the highest in Western Europe (8.8 per cent and 5.5 per cent respectively), compared with 7.6 per cent and 2.5 per cent in Britain, 7 per cent and 2 per cent in France, 0 per cent and 4.4 per cent in Italy. Admittedly, industrial development is not uniform; the chemical industry, for instance, has advanced much more quickly, whereas there have been difficulties in building, steel, and coal-mining—the last mainly as the result of the transition to other sources of energy. By and large, however, the country continues to prosper. Christmas spending reached all time highs. (In a Düsseldorf jeweler's shop I saw a Christmas tree made of solid silver and decorated with diamonds, sapphires, and pearls.) If unemployment has been rising a little, there are still more job openings than there are unemployed, and private incomes, too, are still going up.

Economic barometers often point to temporary recession, but there would be no cause for alarm even if the situation were to deteriorate further; such recessions occurred in 1950–51, and again in 1957–58, and Europe and Germany survived them. But such is the insecurity of many Germans that talk about a major economic crisis has spread like wildfire. According to a leading opinion poll, a crisis of 1929 dimensions was either definitely certain or rather probable in the eyes of not less than 62 per cent of the population! Such a reaction strikes the outside observer as more than somewhat fanciful. Unfortunately, hypochondria in economics is not a joke, and such dire prophecies could have a self-fulfilling effect. Psychological motives play a major, sometimes perhaps a decisive, part in triggering off severe economic crises. Healthy as the German economy is, it may not be strong enough to weather, without grave consequences, such serious and wholly unnecessary crises of confidence. For despite the great strides of the post-war period, many German industrial concerns are still under-capitalized, and bank credit is relatively difficult to obtain. Public reluctance to invest and to buy could have a snowballing effect within a short time. Even Volkswagen, that most flourishing of concerns, could be forced to stop production (for seventeen days in the first quarter of 1967).

In the attitude of many Germans to world affairs, the symptoms are often worse—a touch of paranoia, a belief that Germany has no allies and is about to be sold down the river by the United States, a fear of complete isolation. All German politicians have for a long time tacitly accepted the Oder-Neisse line, and they know that there is no chance of German reunification in our time. But few have dared to say this in public; those who did have usually come to grief. In this respect there has been a perceptible change in mood during recent years, but for large sections of the public it has taken the form of a rude awakening. There has been a growing resentment of America and an increasing sympathy for "Gaullism" or, to be precise, for certain desirable aspects of Gaullism such as a greater degree of independence from the United States. (This stems mainly from the fear that America will have to neglect Europe, and perhaps, eventually, leave it altogether as the result of American involvement in Southeast Asia.) But one cannot merely accept one half of Gaullism, and ignore the fact that the policy also entails a rapprochement with Russia and Eastern Europe, the recognition of the Oder-Neisse line, and eventually, no doubt, the recognition of East Germany.

The demand for a more independent German policy has two major sources. Up to a few years ago there was great and genuine enthusiasm, especially among the younger generation, for a "united Europe," and not merely as an economic convenience. This dream was killed by de Gaulle; in historical perspective, that act may outweigh all the good he has done. As a result there has been a considerable clamor for national *Selbstbesinnung*—one of those impossible German catchwords that cannot be translated adequately— meaning a return to oneself, a stronger emphasis on the national interest.

The other reason was hinted at by Chancellor Erhard (in a speech in November 1965) when he said that as far as Germany was concerned, the postwar era had ended (meaning the two decades that had been completely overshadowed by the consequences of World War II). The new period, however, had engendered new problems. A new generation had grown up which could not be made to feel responsible for Hitler and the Third Reich. Germany had been on probation for twenty years, but it could not remain so forever. It ought to be permitted to have its own policy, even if that implies, occasionally, making its own mistakes. These sentiments, stated vaguely at first, were shared by the majority of Germans. They represent in many ways a natural demand, and one that was certainly not unexpected. But this demand was accompanied by political manifestations that were far from reassuring. On the Left, a comparatively small but vocal group of intellectuals, entrenched in literature, the arts, and, more importantly, the mass media, withdrew into an almost entirely negative attitude, displaying the well-known Weimarian syndrome: wholesale semi-anarchist attacks on the state and on all political parties. Their critique of a philistine society—justified, if occasionally overdone—led them to write off the state altogether. With a few laudable exceptions, such as Günter Grass, they have made little attempt to influence politics; it is as if Germany were not their state or their country. The frightening polarization of political forces, the legacy of the 1920's, seemed to be starting all over again; Tucholsky and his friends were once again jeering at the Social Democrats.

Politically more significant has been the growth of a new nationalism. The chief spokesmen of this trend are Franz Josef Strauss, the head of the Christian Democrats in Bavaria, and, to a certain extent, Eugen Gerstenmaier, the president of the Bundestag, as well as some of Strauss's advisers like Winfred Martini and Armin Mohler. Their argument, taken up in many editorials and speeches, runs as follows: After two decades of hard work, sacrifices, and sincere attempts to face the past, Germans have earned the right to be recognized by others as equals. But there is still far too much ill will toward Germany in the world, despite the best efforts of the German people since the end of the War. While many countries have indirectly benefited from the German economic miracle, none has been willing to accord Germany a political status commensurate with its economic importance. But (the argument continues) in the long run, it is quite impossible to treat an economic giant like a political dwarf; Germany cannot become a normal nation unless it is treated like one. A return to the national traditions is part of this process of normalization. Germans, as Mohler wrote, should cease to be afraid of history, of politics and power. Not everything in Germany's past was criminal; the younger generation should again be educated in a spirit of healthy nationalism. A nation cannot survive if it has no faith in itself and its values. The excessive self-recrimination, "fouling one's own nest," the nihilistic attitude toward Germany's past and its national values, the denigration of faith and honor and patriotism—all this must cease. Germany must be a democratic country, but this does not give anyone license to attack its national values and traditions indiscriminately. Germans, to be sure, should not be arrogant, but they ought to be far more independent and self-confident. They should regain their self-esteem and the esteem of others. And all this can be achieved only through a national regeneration. . . .

It would be unjust (except in regard to the NPD) to equate this new nationalism with the spirit of the pre-1933 right wing. And yet it is a dangerous trend, for moderation has never been a German virtue. Traditionally, the rarest thing in Germany has been a patriotism that was not self-consciously aggressive. Patriotism has never come naturally to this late-comer among Western nations. Attitudes considered self-evident elsewhere had to be discussed at great length in Germany, often in metaphysical terms, and then pursued relentlessly to the excessive final consequence—nationalism above everything else, and German nationalism above all others. German nationalism has been more exclusive of other aspirations and values than other nationalisms, and for the most part it has been anti-democratic in character. In the German scale of values, the Nation has been traditionally placed above Freedom and Justice.

After 1945, of course, there has been, not unnaturally, a revulsion, especially among the young generation, against the entire national phraseology. True enough, the fact that

Hitler operated with notions such as *Vaterland,* faith, honor, devotion, and sacrifice, does not necessarily invalidate them. But it does make one suspicious of the present use of such slogans in a country in which they can so easily be perverted, and among a people which, broadly speaking, has in its recent history suffered precisely from a surfeit of nationalism. Moreover, in present-day Europe these slogans are at least to some extent anachronistic—whatever de Gaulle might have claimed. In the specific German context they are also dangerous, even when they happen to be voiced by idealistic and well-meaning persons.

The new mood of nationalism is reflected in German public life in countless newspaper articles, speeches, and private conversations. It has come into being against a background of some genuine grievances. More than twenty years after the end of the war, Germany was still divided, and there is no hope for reunification in the foreseeable future. There have, of course, been a great many official expressions of moral support, but, to put it quite bluntly, most Americans, Englishmen, and Frenchmen (not to mention Russians or Poles) could not care less about the division of Germany. Many believe, in fact, that this division is the best safeguard against a resurgence of German aggression and militarism. The debate about German unification is to a large extent academic because it is not in the power of the West to bring unification about. But there is perhaps insufficient awareness in the West that the permanent division of a country is not a normal state of affairs, and that no people would easily put up with it. It is bound to breed irridentism, for it is unrealistic to expect a native of Frankfurt to regard his cousin in Leipzig as a stranger in a foreign country. Instead of reiterating time and again platonic support for reunification and thus nursing unfulfillable hopes, would it not be more honest and, in the long run, more helpful, to admit that nothing can be done about it at present? (And, indeed, some Germans may have to be reminded from time to time that the division of their country is the direct result of Nazi aggression.) No one, to be sure, can ask them to give up the hope of reunification altogether, but all they can do now is engage in a policy of what Willy Brandt has called *kleine Schritte,* "little steps," even though it is not clear whether these will have any long-range effect.

The NPD benefits from the general nationalist trend. By itself, right-wing extremism does not constitute a grave danger in Germany. But there is a great reserve army of the eternally dissatisfied, of the non-committed German believers in know-nothingism. The NPD is a movement of protest by the discontented of all classes, particularly in the more backward areas, and it expresses the mood of a sizable section of the population—frustrated village schoolmasters and impoverished vintners, ambitious lieutenants and small businessmen under pressure from the large concerns, victims of denazification, expellees from the East, and other stepchildren of the economic boom. The lower middle class, as usual most prone to be affected by its propaganda, now includes, thanks to the Economic Miracle, the upper reaches of the former working class which have been absorbed by it and have adopted all the lower-middle-class attitudes and most of its prejudices. Like Poujadism, however, this movement of protest lacks purpose and a clear policy. Although there are many Nazis among its leaders, by and large the party is probably nearer to the Nationalist party of the Weimar Republic. This is not to embellish its character or to play down the danger: the *Deutschnationale* were a pretty vicious lot, profoundly anti-democratic, and their responsibility for Hitlerism was grave.

The leaders of the NPD are aware that Germany is no longer a great power and that there is no hope of regaining great-power status. They are anti-American and anti-Russian and do not think much of NATO.[4] They have a weakness for France and, strangely enough, for China. Some of the "beer-table politicians" in the little towns of Bavaria and Lower Saxony dream of an alliance with Mao's Cultural Revolutionaries against Russia, Poland, and the decadent West. They stress their attachment to the lost territories beyond the Elbe and the Oder (whether this also includes Austria and the Sudetenland is a question which they prefer to leave open). They have the haziest notions about foreign policy; if pressed for practical proposals to achieve their aims, they will grudgingly admit that Germany has very little freedom of maneuver. They want the British and the American forces out of Germany, but so far they have not pressed for a bigger German army (a demand, after all, which would be the logical outcome of their position). They protest against the influx of foreign capital and its takeover bids in various branches of industry—but they know that the German economy needs foreign money to assure continuing prosperity. They attack the presence of 1.3 million foreign workers in Germany—but they realize that many of them play a vital part in the economy; few Germans would be willing to accept the menial jobs done by Turks, Greeks, and Sicilians.

Their policy on the Jewish question is equally contradictory. Party speakers have strict orders not to make anti-Semitic attacks, not to be drawn into a discussion of the Jewish problem or of Nazism in general. Partly, again, this

---

[4] Their attitude to Russia and Communism is ambivalent. On the one hand there is the traditional anti-Communism of the German lower middle class. On the other hand, there is the powerful attraction of a régime such as the one in East Germany, which is so much more authoritarian and "orderly," which encourages family life and makes the beatniks work, which does not tolerate avant-garde culture—a country in which life is so much quieter than in West Germany, because it has not yet been "Americanized. . . ."

is an act of self-preservation, for according to the German Basic Law *(Grundgesetz)*, open anti-Semitic propaganda could lead to their suppression. Partly there is genuine confusion. Yes, they are willing to accept Jews as members, provided these Jews are as loyal to Germany as the Israelis are loyal to their country. At the same time there are vicious attacks on the restitution of looted Jewish property. One leader quoted Martin Buber with approval; another said that he was willing to make a pilgrimage to Auschwitz if the allies would make a similar pilgrimage to the cemeteries of Dresden. So far, the NPD leaders have not been to Auschwitz; they did, however, go to the cemetery of Landsberg prison to lay wreaths on the graves of some of those sentenced to death in the war crime trials. Thielen, the leader of the party, stated that he would lose no time in expelling from the party anyone trying to justify the murder of defenseless people. There is no longer a Jewish problem, von Thadden said in conversation with a British journalist. He stated that most of the thirty thousand Jews now living in Germany were old; the younger ones leave when they can. But instead of the Jewish problem, he added, there is now Israel, which engages in diplomatic blackmail: "They never stop moaning about the past and continually demand more. The Bonn government accedes each time—how long is this supposed to go on?" Speakers at NPD meetings have declared that no crimes were committed on the soil of the Reich, that the war broke out because international Jewry wanted to destroy Germany, and that the Germans killed by the Allies perished no less inhumanly than did the Jews in Poland. Anti-Semitism, open or implicit, is a plank in NPD propaganda, though the term "Jew" does not appear in the party manifesto. But anti-Semitism is not a decisive political issue, and it is most unlikely to become one.

What are the long-term prospects of the NPD? The party

is likely to do well in Schleswig and Lower Saxony. The Catholic Rhineland will be difficult territory for it, though the extreme Right did have traditional strongholds in the Pfalz. The Berlin climate, on the other hand, does not suit it; the party will be reluctant to contest elections in the former German capital.

The present recession will probably be overcome within a year even if a return to the impressive rates of growth of the 50's and early 60's seems unlikely. The coalition will no doubt try to be more assertive of German interests in foreign affairs.

What, then, should be done about the NPD? The suggestion made by some Christian Democrats to "overtake them from the Right" is impractical. Such a course would be dangerous and it would fail to carry conviction, for a small opposition group can always afford to be more extreme and demagogical than a large responsible party. Some outside observers have suggested that more should be done to enlighten German youth on Nazi crimes. This sounds like a sensible suggestion but it is not at all certain whether it would have the desired effect. The German schools have, it is true, been somewhat deficient in this respect, but by and large the young generation has taken in massive doses of information about the Nazis via radio, television, books, and films. Beyond a certain limit, the showing of films about Auschwitz and Maidanek yields diminishing returns, and provokes psychological resistance. A spirit of tolerance cannot be inculcated by textbooks, however excellent, and an increase in the number of lessons devoted to political education in the democratic spirit will not necessarily strengthen their impact. Travel abroad is probably more important. The young generation of Germans, the majority of which abhors dictatorial rule, has learned, and will continue to learn, far more about the democratic way of life by living example— by studying it in action during visits to other countries, by private contacts, and by personal observation—than it will by officially sponsored lectures.[5]

Finally, there is the possibility of outlawing the NPD. Under Article 21 of the German Basic Law any group can be declared unconstitutional if by its goals or behavior, it aims at impairing or abolishing the free democratic order; this ban has been used against the Communist party. The general feeling is that this paragraph should be applied only in an emergency, for it is in conflict with the freedom of association guaranteed in the constitution. Most German politicians believe that anti-democratic parties should be banned only if they actually constitute a danger to democracy, and they are willing to accept the risks involved. If the NPD should grow, if its anti-democratic character should become even more manifest in its propaganda and political action, the demand that paragraph 21 be applied will no doubt increase. But at present most Germans would regard such a ban as an unnecessary admission of weakness.

All things considered, the appeal of the NPD is fairly narrow and its prospects are not brilliant.[6] The belief that history in Germany is always bound to repeat itself is a fallacy: nothing is easier than drawing parallels, and nothing is more misleading, for it blinds one to the changing historical con-

[5] German student politics has changed radically. In the Weimar period, the Nazis were the leading party in the university, long before the party scored its successes in national elections. Of those politically active in the universities today, the majority is oriented toward the Left, and some of the most vociferous belong to the extreme Left. They read Mao and Marcuse, and some factions have gone as far (if not further) than the American *S.D.S.*

[6] I would qualify this statement in one respect only: the influence of the NPD in some circles of the *Bundeswehr*, the new German army, is a matter of concern and may make action necessary. Contrary to belief outside Germany, NPD sympathizers are more often found among sergeants and lieutenants than among colonels, many of whom support the Social Democrats.

text. Bonn with all its weaknesses (let it be said once again) is not Weimar. While democracy is not yet firmly rooted in Germany, some of the traditional bases of authoritarianism have been uprooted. To justify this cautiously optimistic assessment would require a long excursus into such topics as school and family life, the general post-war mood, the trade unions, the character of the young generation, and the acceptance of a democratic order by a majority of the German people.

The victory of the Nazi party was possible only in the context of specific historical factors. These included the antidemocratic opposition of the big landowners, the army, and quite a few of the industrialists, who did so much to weaken the Weimar Republic. The church, the family, and the schools were to a considerable extent authoritarian in character; the judiciary and the civil service were, as far as the majority of the population was concerned, above criticism. The democratic character of the republic of 1919 was simply not accepted by a large part of the population. The West Germany of today has many defects and will, no doubt, have to face various crises in the future, but its weaknesses are not those of the Weimar Republic. The *Junkers* have gone, the army officers—whatever their views—do not meddle in politics, and the industrialists identify themselves with the present state; they have done very well in it. The patriarchal character of the family and the authoritarian style in public life in general has lessened, and is no more pronounced in Germany today than in most European countries. The people, by and large, are reconciled to a democratic order, preferably one with a trusted father-figure at the head. The experience of Nazism and of World War II, when all is said and done, have had a deep impact on the German national consciousness.

These observations are unlikely to convince those who know instinctively that Germans will be Germans, that national character is unchangeable. They are presented here as the assessment of one who has had the opportunity to watch the German political scene from a fairly close angle. To summarize: it is unlikely that the NPD will become a decisive factor in German politics. The prediction, however, that the new ("respectable") nationalism will become the prevailing mood in West Germany cannot, unfortunately, be dismissed with equal certainty. But whatever happens, we should never forget that the dimensions of the German scene have changed. As the result of the War, the political and military importance of the country has been greatly reduced. A further growth of right-wing extremist influence could cause serious harm to Germany's prestige. It is difficult to imagine how it could adversely affect anyone else. Everyone now knows that the Nazi movement in the early 1930's was underrated by many observers inside Germany and abroad. Consequently, there is now a tendency to sound the tocsin too early, and perhaps too often. There are lessons to be learned from past history, but they are not as obvious and straightforward as some of us believe.

(1967)

THOUGHTS AT
THE WALL

Bernauer Strasse

WEDDING, a small village in the 13th century, a spa in the eighteenth, and Berlin's most typical working-class area ever since, is now a Western enclave in East Berlin. Germany's leading electrical plants, such as Borsig and the AEG, first set up their factories here some 140 years ago, and re-emerged after the Second World War. This was *Rote Wedding*—the reddest district of Red Berlin. The Communists were the strongest political party in the German capital in 1932; in Wedding they held on to their plurality even in March, 1933, after Hitler had come to power. Wedding held a unique position in German communist folklore—in novels, pictures, and songs *("Der Rote Wedding Marschiert");* it always offered the true proletarian setting. Thirty years later it is a prosperous lower middle class district, commonly called the "green Wedding."

Bernauer Strasse was little known outside the area, though it gave its name to an underground subway station. But then it became part of the Frontier between East and West Berlin, and the border between the Soviet and the French sector ran down the middle of the street. When the wall went up in August 1961, this was for a short time the main escape route. East Berliners used to jump to freedom from the third, fourth, or fifth floor, some into the nets held out by Western fire brigades, others to their death. There are several wooden crosses on the pavement; from a passing bus, tourists photograph them. The windows of these houses were then walled up and the houses evacuated. But East German border police peep out from their loopholes. On the Western side of the street it is business-as-usual, with the exception of one *Bierstube* which has closed down; there is a table in the shop window with a verse to the effect that so near to the *Mauer*, both the wine and the general mood has become *sauer*. The pub-keeper has retreated to Schoeneberg (have the guests followed?). A small group of Indian students passes: "Not very nice here." They are neutrals; they try hard not to commit themselves.

This is not the only divided city in our time. There was Trieste, and the division of Jerusalem was even more complete. But even the neighborhood of the Mandelbaum Gate in the North of the Holy City, desolate as it was, was never quite so depressing. The line between Israel and Jordan was fixed following an armistice between two warring nations. Bernauer Strasse divides one nation.

Berlin & the British
Englishmen have rarely had a feeling for the former German capital. To them, Berlin stood for Prussianism, stiffness, hard work, ugly streets, a funny and somewhat repulsive German accent, and the late Dr. Goebbels. But it also stood (for a few) for the roaring 'twenties: the Kurfuerstendamm, the youth movement, "*Wer hat denn den Kaese zum Bahnhof gerollt?*", German expressionism, Sally Bowles and Family Landauer. Was it really "a city without culture," "without *savoir vivre* or elegance"?

Of the real Berlin, few Anglo-Saxons have ever been properly aware. It had its own peculiar popular culture, from Nante, the character standing at the street corner watching the girls go by, to Paul Lincke and his marches, from Heinrich Zille and his drawings to the monstrous *Resi* ballroom of our days (where the customers send flirtatious special delivery messages via table-side phones and pneumatic tubes). There was the Berlin of the liberal and Jewish intelligentsia, and also the Berlin of Theodore Fontane. Few outside Germany have heard of Fontane apart perhaps from students of German literature; curious that the works of the greatest German novelist between Goethe and Thomas Mann have not been translated. In the 'forties and 'fifties of the last century Fontane spent years in London as a correspondent and wrote half a dozen books about life in England, Scottish Ballads, and the London theater. True enough, it took the Germans themselves some fifty years to discover Fontane. In one of his poems he describes the unexpected guests who showed up on his seventy-fifth birthday. Fontane was the bard of Frederic II and his generals, and had described in great and loving detail the city and its countryside; his work had been one long paean of praise for the great Prussian families who were the heroes of his historical novels. But the Arnims, Treskovs, and Zitzewitzes did not show up to honor him, only the old aristocracy of a very different race. The poem ends: "Come on, Cohn." . . .

Can the deep ignorance in the West of the real Berlin be without political consequences? As things are, many British and Americans care no more about Berlin than about Bogota, and does anybody lose sleep over Bogota?

Berlin & Bonn

Many Germans, too, have disliked Berlin intensely. Beethoven wrote that he found the Berlin public "very well educated" and Schiller praised its great "personal freedom" and its lack of "restraint." But for many others it was the hydrocephalus of Germany; it did not seem to have grown organically, it was a parvenu of a city. There is a whole literature of opposition to Berlin's attempt to dominate German art and letters. "*Los von Berlin*" was the slogan of right-wing extremists and south German particularists alike; Berlin was the image of "international fashion," and not of "our German national character." It took the post-war years and the capital's transfer to provincial Bonn to make them realize what had been lost. Bonn (as a Swiss journalist put it) is located between Brühl and Bad Godesberg—Berlin between Washington and Moscow.

On Walls
Chinese love walls, Americans don't. A Chinese city is not complete without walls. "Walls, walls, and yet again walls form the framework of every Chinese city," says a writer on Chinese architecture. They even use the same word, *chen'g,* for city and city wall. Americans prefer the wide open spaces: "something there is that doesn't love a wall" (Robert Frost). The wall as a symbol: oughtn't one to look it up in Stekel?

The wall is a reality: the Berliners had several walls before; the most famous was erected by the Great Elector. He faced a difficult task after the Thirty Years war: of the 1200 houses of Berlin, one third had remained empty and the rest were utterly neglected. It was probably the dirtiest city in Germany; the inhabitants kept pigs, usually in the open streets. A special ordnance was needed in 1641 to remove them. The old wall came down with the expansion of Berlin in the last century. The Great Wall of China has not yet come down; it was built by the emperor Shih Huang Ti, who carried out a vast program of reforms. Historians report that the system of decentralization and militarization broke down immediately after his death "not through any inadequacy but because there were not enough efficient men available. . . ."

Ulbricht and After
Efficient men there will be after Ulbricht, but how many true believers are there among the younger generation?

Many Western observers have gone on record with dire predictions about East German youth, which, they say, will be "lost" if Germany remains divided for long. They uttered the same prophecies ten, and fifteen years ago, but experience so far has not borne them out. In contrast to the Hitler Youth, the "Free German Youth" of East Germany does not appeal to emotions and instinct alone, but also provides a "scientific philosophy." This produces citizens far more "conscious" and ideologically sophisticated than National-Socialism ever did. But it works both ways. The "young pioneers" enthusiastically identify themselves with the ideals of communism and the hatred of its enemies. At seventeen or eighteen, on the other hand, young men and women become a bit more reserved in their attitudes. Having left school and come in contact with realities, they discover to their consternation that there is a vast gulf between the ideals of "socialism, democracy, and humanism," and the society around them in which these ideals are supposed to be realized. At this stage a Marxist-Leninist education often turns out to be a mixed blessing; young men and women apply the rational and dialectical thinking they have been taught to their own surroundings, and usually the results are heretical, if not subversive.

And yet, in some respects, the effect of this education is incomparably more lasting than that of the Hitler Youth. They will almost certainly lose faith in the Ulbricht régime, but they will probably retain their belief in "a socialist order." They have little sympathy for the West German *Wirtschaftswunder* and its social climate. They think that their own "social services" are vastly superior, that everyone should have "equal opportunity in schools and universities." The West Germans, on the other hand, are not disposed to see any positive achievements at all in the East. The Ulbricht régime has made "socialism" a dirty word in West Germany. "When they hear the word socialism," a leading

Social-democrat said to me the other day, they think of the
H.O. [the state trading organizations which are a synonym
for inefficient service, poor quality, high prices, limited
choice]. Ulbricht has, in a way, made it almost impossible
for the Social-Democrats to win a national election in West
Germany (until 1968, that is), despite their transformation
from a class party into a popular movement.

East German Culture
The differences between East Germany and the Soviet
Union are probably most striking in the cultural field. In
comparison with the shrill Goebbelesque vituperations of
Neues Deutschland, Izvestia reads like a paper edited by a
group of tolerant and liberal elder statesmen. *Sonntag,*
which used to be the only readable East German weekly,
recently published the results of an inquiry: "What is holding up the creative work of our artists and writers?" It mentions all kinds of reasons except the decisive one: that there
simply is not that essential minimum of freedom in East
Germany. It is highly dissatisfied with the misplaced liberalism of some neighboring countries—Polish writers have
scarcely been translated during the last five years; and even
Czech writers come in for strong criticism. One of the more
daring Soviet films was cut by forty minutes for its performance in East Germany. I found very revealing the attack by Alfred Kurella (the East German Zhdanov) on Ilya
Fradkin, a Soviet critic who, in an essay published in East
Berlin, had outlined the new tasks of the Soviet writers: not
to embellish life, not to gloss over the bad effects of the
"cult of personality," but to be truthful. All this was thought
to be very dangerous in East Berlin and Kurella stepped in.
If Kurella were an ignorant and insensitive hack, it would
be easier to explain the affair. But he is an educated man,
well versed in Russian, German, and French literature. For
many years he was under a cloud and escaped arrest in the

Soviet Union only by retiring as a language teacher to a little town far from Moscow. His brother, Heinrich, was arrested and never came back from the camp; Kurella himself
was permitted to return to Germany only ten years after the
end of the war. And yet, after that, he seems to be content
to carry out Ulbricht's cultural policies, adding some petty
and irritating restrictions of his own.

Russia in West German Eyes

Coming from London, one dislikes the strident tone, the
intransigent approach prevailing in West Germany; the cold
war is always a few degrees cooler there. Gradually one re-
alizes that it is essentially a reaction to enormous pressures.
Talking to some German Sovietologists, I get the impression
that nothing has changed or is likely to change in the Soviet
bloc. A professor at Berlin's Free University observes, at the
end of a long treatise on Soviet foreign policy, that bourgeois governments which project their own pragmatic attitudes onto Soviet policy are most likely to misinterpret Soviet Union, and Communist China is a perfect illustration. . . ." This may be so, but is Germany the ideal observation point for Soviet bloc developments? Whatever happens
beyond the Curtain is obscured for the Germans by events
in "the Zone." They say Khrushchev or Kosygin and mean
Ulbricht. Ten years ago this did not greatly matter, for conditions throughout the Soviet bloc were more or less alike.
Since then "polycentric trends" have emerged, and there are
now considerable differences between the various communist states. Some have carried de-Stalinization fairly far; Ulbricht has marked time. He had his good reasons: the more
popular dissatisfaction there is, the more dangerous it is to
relax controls. Ulbricht conceivably told Khrushchev that
de-Stalinization may be all very well in Russia and even
Bulgaria, but that in the "front line of imperialist aggression" one could not possibly engage in experiments which

might lead to explosions (as in June, 1953, or October, 1956). The West Germans have been looking fixedly at East Germany where nothing much has happened since the last Soviet party congress (apart from an Ulbricht speech of some 35,000 words).

Germany & Marxism

Of all the European nations the Germans have the longest record of speculation about Russia. It began in the 16th century, when travellers, philosophers, and theologians debated whether Moscow was with or without "the true knowledge of God," whether it was the last piece of Europe looking Eastward, or the beginning of that barbarous East which constantly threatened the West. Romantic pro-Polish enthusiasm in the late eighteenth century caused much anti-Russian feeling, but the aristocracy expected that the old order would be saved by intervention from the East. In the nineteenth century speculation about the "European destiny of Russia" became something of a national sport. After 1917, too, Germany remained the leading country for Soviet studies, but 1933 put an end to all that: according to Hitler and Rosenberg, there was no Soviet ideology, only a "Judaeo-Masonic conspiracy" to dominate the world. As a German historian subsequently wrote:

> The intellectual discussion of Marxism was rejected as superfluous and even dangerous. . . . When the war ended in 1945 many Germans knew scarcely anything of Marx except the name and that he was a Jew.

In the post-War period Marxism became *Soviet* Marxism, Ulbricht's ideology, and it did not thereby become a promising subject for dispassionate enquiry. True, some Protestant and Catholic clergymen have made a brave effort to discuss Marxism *sine ira et studio*, but it has been very abstract indeed—*entfremdung* (alienation) and all that. We owe to them some good textbooks and stimulating debates (Professor Wetter's *Dialectical Materialism;* the Protestant *Marxismus-Studien*). But this hardly ever filtered down to those trying to analyze current Soviet policies. As far as the impact of ideology on Soviet policy is concerned, most German students of Soviet affairs are as much at sea as the rest of the world, only more so.

Berlin's Future

Like every major crisis, the Berlin problem is embedded in broad layers of misconception and illusion. The most common in Britain is the assumption that Berlin is somehow the cause—not the result—of West-East tension. From which it follows that a "reasonable compromise"—which could easily be reached if only the Germans were not so stubborn—would bring about a lasting détente. It is very disheartening at this late hour to come across such elementary misunderstandings about cause and effect in the present world situation.

To be sure, in West Germany both government and opposition have their own private myths. According to the governmental version, it will be possible to pursue the present policy of the non-recognition of the DDR and the Oder-Neisse line indefinitely, and all else that is involved—e.g., the so-called Hallstein doctrine, according to which Bonn is obliged to break off relations with any country extending diplomatic recognition to the DDR. The Opposition, on the other hand, often claims that "the German question (including Berlin) could have been solved in March 1952" (they refer to some ambiguous statements by Stalin and Grotewohl at the time). If only Germany had followed "a national policy" instead of "blindly obeying the West"! I would not want to deny that Stalin in his last years was no longer responsible for his actions and there is no telling what he might have done. Yet, everything considered, a careful analysis of the situation in 1952 makes it clear that there is little basis for the political myth.

Some Western observers (Joseph Alsop and Walter Lippmann, among others) argued that the erection of the Wall was actually "a positive step," conducive to lessening of tension; they ascribed to the Communists a defensive mentality which, unfortunately, has yet to be exhibited. The Wall was urgently needed to stop the mass exodus from East Germany. But it was at the same time an important *offensive* step; as the recurrent incidents have shown, it has by no means reduced tension. On the contrary, a dangerous new source of conflict has come into being.

Others argue that the Communist demand that West Berlin cease to be "a center of Western agents and cold war propaganda" is not unreasonable. But since the Wall went up "Western agents" which, in Communist parlance, does not just mean Mr. Allan Dulles and his successors, but everybody who is not a Communist, have been unable to reach the DDR except by broadcasts; it would not make the slightest difference if the radio stations were moved 150 miles to the west.

The Communists could not, of course, care less whether Rias and *Radio Freies Berlin* broadcast in future from West Berlin or from Hannover; their designs are most ambitious. They have pursued their offensive cautiously so far; since it began (on November 27, 1958, to be precise), and they have since pressed home their program patiently though relentlessly. The men in the Kremlin are not unreasonable—they are willing to give the West time to surrender—they fully understand that some psychological readjustment is involved. But they may not be able to wait indefinitely; they are always under some fire from other comrades within their own camp. There have been certain setbacks (the agricultural front and elsewhere), and they may feel obliged to bring stronger pressure to bear on the West. There is little the West could or should do (as Richard Lowenthal has often argued) to help Moscow to find a way out of a crisis that is of its own making. The Soviet leaders *seem* to realize (quite correctly) that while they may bring about a Western surrender over Berlin following an ultimatum, such a chain of events would lead at the next world crisis with near-certainty to nuclear war. The most disturbing and complicating factors in these circumstances is, on the one hand, Ulbricht (who may try to convince the Soviet leaders that his régime is doomed unless the East gets Berlin), and on the other some well-meaning but short-sighted Western "partisans of peace" who indirectly encourage the Russians to take an aggressive line on Berlin. So far the Soviet leaders have wisely resisted these temptations and one ought to be grateful for their good sense in realizing that the stakes are too high. As good chess players, they try to think several moves ahead. Unfortunately, there is no telling what inner tensions may be generated in the Soviet bloc and what their consequences may be.

If that were all, the outlook would be bleak. But the Soviet leaders make *world* politics these days; they see not only Ulbricht but also the men in Asia, Africa, and the Middle East who hold power. They know that the frontier between East and West in Europe has been frozen for a long time; even if they were to get a "neutral Berlin" it would take them a long time to incorporate the city into the DDR. The gain in substance would be small, the gain in prestige not much larger, and all this at very considerable risk. By contrast, the situation in some of the underdeveloped countries seems much more promising. There everything is, as yet, in flux; anything can happen. There are, in fact, definite signs of a more militant Soviet line in the *tiers monde*.

Which takes one far afield from the grey brick walls of Bernauer Strasse. This is still a good vantage point from which to watch the clash of East and West in Central Europe; it is less well suited for tracing Eurasian developments. And are the Russians themselves truly "experts on the East" as they fancy themselves? Stalin used to say: "You Westerners don't understand the Asians." Ivan Maisky, former Ambassador to the court of St. James and now a member of the Soviet Academy of Sciences states in a contribution to a recent *Voprosy Istorii:* "The only conclusion that can be drawn from our analysis is that Jengiz Khan's entire activity did much harm to the cause of human progress. Such is the final conclusion from the point of view of Marxist-Leninist science." Some Westerners, we are reliably told, held this point of view for a long time—possibly even before Marx was born. And what are the Leninist historians in Peking writing about traditional Asian expansiveness over Neutrals?

Red Square, next stop[2], may be a better place for meditation on these topics.

(1962)

---

2 See Ch. 12.

WEIMAR CULTURE

THERE WAS no place like Berlin in the 1920's. The capital of the modern movement in literature and the arts, pioneering in the cinema and theater, in social studies and psychoanalysis, it was the city of "The Threepenny Opera" and "The Cabinet of Dr. Caligari," the cradle of the youth movement and the haven of unheard-of sexual freedom. The Mecca of a whole generation of Isherwoods, it has entered history as the center of a new Periclean age.

Only a few were aware of its true importance at the time; most Germans emphatically rejected what Peter Gay calls Weimar culture and what, to all intents and purposes, was the culture of Berlin. "Shallow," "rootless," "destructive," "cultural Bolshevism," "*asphaltliteratur*," these were the most common epithets used by its critics.

The advocates and the enthusiastic followers of this avant-garde movement came from a small unrepresentative layer of German society; left-wing or liberal, largely Jewish, it was concentrated in Berlin and a few other big cities. It had no popular success at the time; in the list of contemporary best-sellers one looks in vain for the famous names of the 1920s. Yet internationally these men were the only ones who counted, and in Germany, too, there has been in recent years a spectacular revival of the golden twenties.

After 1933 many of these intellectuals and artists were

forced to emigrate; their impact in foreign lands has been considerable. For Weimar-Berlin culture was the heir to a great tradition; intellectually most of the world has been subsisting until recently on what was created by two or three generations in the German cultural sphere, which then included Prague and Vienna as well, and even Budapest. These emigré scholars were usually men of great erudition, and the artists had a degree of sophistication uncommon at the time; they helped create new disciplines and provided fresh intellectual impulses in various fields. Some of the goods perished in transit; German expressionism, for instance, was not an article for export. Other ideas, movements and personalities succeeded in their new surroundings beyond all expectations, as the Brecht revival and the great interest in the Bauhaus have shown. The present-day youth movements, too, owe more to Berlin than Herbert Marcuse.

Professor Peter Gay's absorbing essay,* its other merits apart, is of considerable topical interest, for "Weimar culture" anticipated many intellectual trends and fashions now current in the West. The author has tried to portray this fascinating phenomenon without sentimentalizing or sensationalizing—not an easy task, for the temptation to be sentimental about it is great and the sensationalism is inherent in the topic. His book has clearly been a labor of love, and despite the difficulties of doing justice to so many disparate trends in various fields, he has succeeded exceedingly well.

One could dispute details endlessly. For instance, Professor Gay hardly deals with the popular culture of the day which, I believe, was of considerable interest. Paul Abraham the composer (who is not mentioned) has already outlasted Karl Abraham the psychoanalyst (who is), and I suspect that the music of Paul Lincke (who does not appear either) will still be performed when many of the worthy academics have

* *Weimar Culture: The Outsider as Insider* (1968).

been forgotten. But what matters is the broad outline, and on this count it is difficult to fault Professor Gay's judgment; he has recaptured the spirit of this exciting decade and he provides a reliable guide to it.

Weimar Culture was such a splendid failure that there is a strong temptation to ignore its weaknesses. It was magnificent while it lasted, but it also carried within itself the seeds of its own destruction; it was sick, and Hitler's advent to power only hastened its demise. Four decades later the causes of its downfall seem all too obvious, especially against the background of New York in the late 'sixties; there are fascinating similarities between the intellectual milieu of the two cities, though perhaps not in achievement.

Moral relativism among all too many intellectuals, on both right and left, was characteristic of postwar Germany, as were political naiveté (Thomas Mann and Brecht were two famous cases), the dominant position of all sorts of fake gurus, enthusiasm for revolutionaries in far-away countries and a lack of tact and common sense. Behind the feverish activity and the quest for new, revolutionary forms and contents there was a great deal of sterility, and there were strong self-destructive tendencies.

Shortly before Hitler seized power, Ernst Eckstein, one of the leaders of the socialist Left, declared at a party congress that there was little to choose between the Nazis and the (relatively democratic) government of the day. Some people told him that it might be the difference between life and death, but he and his friends shrugged off such warnings. Less than a year later Eckstein had been trampled to death by the Storm Troopers; he too was a symbol of Weimar.

One should not make too much of the responsibility of the intellectuals for the disaster. It was after all Hitler and not the satirist Kurt Tucholsky who buried the Weimar Republic. But many intellectuals too had been merrily gravedigging; for them the democratic Left, not the extreme Right, was the main enemy. This has a familiar ring. "Things fall apart, the center cannot hold"—and who cares? One of the most popular songs of the period ended with the words *"denn das dicke Ende kommt ja sowieso,"* which freely translated meant *"Après nous le déluge."* The intellectuals were quite *weltfremd,* divorced from reality, and operating in a vacuum. This lack of roots in their social milieu frequently limited their intellectual impact as well.

The Weimar period has entered history as the age in which all the major questions of our time were posed and none was solved. By the time Hitler took over, many (admittedly not all) of the intellectual currents had exhausted their original impulse and lost their momentum. The fruitful time of the Frankfurt Institute of Social Research was over, the German school of cinema had petered out, the youth movement faded away. Not much of consequence was added to psychoanalytic thought in the early 1930's and the limitations of Karl Mannheim became only too obvious. There was a truce in the conflict between the generations (of which Professor Gay makes rather too much). All the sons had killed all the fathers, at least on the stage; the fathers had gotten their revenge, at least in the cinema, and both sides had become a little bored in the process. The great recession was on, with millions of unemployed in the streets; the intellectuals faced real issues and the quasi-problems of the 'twenties seemed suddenly rather unimportant.

In short, the first German Republic was a most exciting period for intellectuals; its cultural heritage should be studied and admired—from a safe distance. It is not there to be copied; absorbed in massive doses it is bound to produce unfortunate effects.

THE ROOTS OF NAZISM

FOR MOST PEOPLE who have not lived in Germany, the essence of Nazism remains a riddle. Americans, Russians, Frenchmen, and the British usually try to interpret it in terms of Militarism, anti-Semitism, extreme Nationalism, and Imperialism. All these were elements in Nazism, yet they existed in other countries as well. I suspect that some of the obstacles to understanding are linguistic in character; for whenever one tries to describe and analyze what was unique in Nazism—the *voelkisch* ideology, the blood and soil doctrine, the whole Nordic hero myth—one runs into a language barrier and communication breaks down. The very word *voelkisch*, for instance, is untranslatable, and not only in English. (In Russian it was rendered for a long time as *narodnicheski, i.e.,* populist. One can easily imagine the resulting political confusion.) A courageous effort has been made from time to time to explain in English what Nazi doctrine was all about, but the result was either utterly confusing or downright comic, and the topic was, after all, not in the least funny.

Now for the first time a successful attempt has been made to explain in English in an intelligent way this intangible (and untranslatable) part of Nazi doctrine. Masterly in presenting the ideology of Nazism, Professor Mosse's book*

* George L. Mosse. *The Crisis of German Ideology: Intellectual Origins of the Third Reich* (1964).

shows convincingly that the doctrine of Hitler's movement was neither a mere propaganda trick nor the outpouring of a small group of unbalanced minds. On the contrary, Nazism is based on a body of intellectual doctrine that goes back for at least a century. Whereas Marxism is considered to be a movement with deep historical and intellectual roots, Nazism is usually thought of as a temporary aberration in the history of a nation. It is to Mosse's great credit that he shows this is simply not so.

Attempts to examine the roots of Nazism have been undertaken before; during the Second World War Rohan Butler tried to trace Nazism back to certain authoritarian and chauvinistic trends in German history. (So, of course, did Peter Viereck, and a few others.) Valuable as these books were, they did not really touch the core of the problem, because manifestations of extreme nationalism could without difficulty be discovered in the history of other nations as well. What made Germany different was not its chauvinism but its *voelkisch* tradition, and this is the subject of Professor Mosse's book.

This tradition of thought goes back to the romantic era with its heavy emphasis on sentiment (rather than intellect), on nature and landscape, on history and on rootedness. Like Novalis it contrasted the heroic (and happy) middle ages with the degeneracy wrought by modern times. The golden age, in this view, had existed in the distant past, and it was never quite to be recaptured in the future, for the industrial revolution had uprooted the folk, and rural rootedness with all its virtues had given way to urban dislocation— with all its vices. Heritage ("blood") was of the greatest importance, and the stress was on the basic differences between races and peoples. This was coupled with the idea of the superiority of the German (Nordic) race over all others —first developed, incidentally, by two non-Germans, Gobineau, who laid the scientific (or pseudo-scientific) foundations, and Houston Stewart Chamberlain, the renegade Englishman who popularized them in the philosophical jargon of the day. There were a great many other minor thinkers who established a whole "system" on this basis—but the Schemanns, Woltmans, Ammons, *et al.* are now forgotten even in their native country and there is not much point in resurrecting them for the benefit of the Anglo-American reader. All that need be said is that in their view *voelkisch* stood for the union of the people with a transcendental essence, which might also be called "nature" or "mythos." It was fused with man's innnermost nature, the source of his creativity and the depth of his feeling. The *voelkisch* thinkers were all anti-modern, anti-industrial, anti-big city, and of course anti-Jewish, for the Jew stood for modernity with all its destructiveness: were the Jews not among the pioneers of finance capitalism in Germany, especially after 1870? And had they not gained access to many positions in German cultural life?*

This *voelkische Weltanschauung* was a closed system with a firm grip on successive generations of Germans, especially students and teachers. Various crackpot schools had their heyday—astrologers, occultists, preachers of Nordic body culture, and apostles of extreme nature mysticism. Even the top Nazi leaders were not immune—Himmler believed he was a reincarnation of Henry the Fowler. But the main body of this doctrine was formulated in philosophical and quasi-scientific terms among respectable academic circles, and gained wide currency in right-wing circles and political parties. This was the chief source of inspiration for most leaders of Nazism too, and it undoubtedly helped greatly to pave the way for the victory of Hitler's party.

---

* Their influence, needless to say, was often greatly exaggerated. They were said to have, among other things, a stranglehold on German literature; but in the German best-seller lists of the first part of the twentieth century, among the eighty books which sold 800,000 copies or more, there is not one by a Jewish author.

The growth of *voelkisch* thought into a political movement, the mainsprings of its impact, and its gradual transformation into a real way of life for at least one section of the German people, is described, for the first time in any language, in this excellent book. The author has scanned not only all the political manifestos but also the *belles lettres* produced by and for the movement, and has used much unpublished material in German archives which adds substantially to our understanding of the origins of the *voelkisch* movement.

The Crisis of German Ideology is a milestone in the study of National Socialism. It is at the same time a somewhat controversial book. There are some unwarranted generaliza tions, occasionally a faulty perspective, and criticisms that are sometimes too sweeping and indiscriminate. Professor Mosse argues, for instance, that *voelkisch* thought in 1932–33 was so widespread and dynamic that even if Nazism had not taken the lead, another such group stood ready to do so. But this is not so: the Nazis were the only *voelkisch* group who had any grasp of the mechanics of political power; the others were Ultra-Conservatives divorced from the masses, or simply faddists. It was only the genius of Adolf Hitler—as Mosse notes elsewhere in his book—which wedded the *voelkisch* flight from reality to political discipline and efficient organization. He should have added that Hitler, who drew much of his inspiration from the *Voelkische*, had the lowest possible opinion of them as a political force, and in *Mein Kampf* wrote about them with great contempt.

Most authors are inclined at times to exaggerate the importance of their chosen subject, and Professor Mosse has not always resisted this temptation. According to the picture that emerges from his book, German Jews were already socially isolated before the first World War as a result of the spread of *voelkisch* thought among the German middle class. He quotes one report which asserts that it was then highly unusual for German and Jewish pupils to share the same table at school. I do not know about school tables, but there are statistics about inter-marriage, which was about seven or eight times higher in Berlin than in New York. Influential as the *voelkisch* doctrine was, it did not by itself become a political force, nor did it extend beyond a vocal minority. The many millions who chose Hitler in 1933 did so for a great variety of reasons, of which the Nordic mythology was certainly not the most important.

Sometimes Professor Mosse casts his net too wide in tracing *voelkisch* influences. Certain grievances of the *Voelkische* and some aspects of their critique of modern industrial civilization were neither specifically German nor altogether unjustified. They were shared by a variety of thinkers from Rousseau to Tolstoy, and from Thoreau to D. H. Lawrence. One has the feeling that, but for their Jewish origin, Martin Buber and Simone Weil and some others would have been claimed by the *Voelkische* as fellow-travelers. Perhaps Mosse also slightly overshoots the mark in his criticism of German historians who claim that the ideological evolution which led to National Socialism was not "typically German," and that other countries also had such movements. That many German historians try to play down the role of the predecessors of Nazism goes without saying, but Mosse's counter-argument that in France "the young people rallied to the cause of the Left," whereas their German contemporaries became *voelkisch*, is, stated this way, quite untenable. Gobineau, after all, had a far greater impact in 19th-century France than in Germany; towards the turn of the century anti-Semitism was certainly as prevalent in Paris as in Germany. It is too easily forgotten now that sixty years ago "race thought" was widespread even in England and America. A recent writer has recalled that the majority of late-Victorian English and American historians accepted the view that the "Anglo-Saxon race" had not only a manifest destiny but also a unique capacity to rule; Seeley and Sir

Henry Maine should be consulted by those who doubt this. After the First World War, the impact of the famous *"Protocols of the Elders of Zion"* was, for a while, greater in Britain than in Germany; the idea of a Jewish world conspiracy influenced even Winston Churchill at one point. All this is now happily forgotten by all but our elder contemporaries and a few historians, but it should be remembered from time to time.

Racialist thought admittedly never grew such deep roots in France and England because in the last resort it did not fit into the pattern of French rationalism or British pragmatism. (The Romantic school, in a similar way, was more deeply rooted in Germany than in any other country.) But it did exist and was not entirely confined to the right wing either. The fact that racialist thought eventually prevailed in Germany cannot be explained solely in ideological terms. It had to do with the economic crisis, and a number of other political, social, and economic trends which contributed to the rise of right-wing racialist movements common to many European countries. These movements, as Dr. Peter Pulzer's book* describes them, were composed of ex-servicemen—particularly ex-officers unable to adjust themselves to civilian routine—of axed officials of Empires no longer on the map, debt-ridden peasants, students and teachers. In general, they were those whose social and economic position had been destroyed, or was being threatened. Germany was much the most prone to succumb to this infection, but both the virus and the conditions for its spread existed elsewhere.

Dr. Pulzer, who is known to a wider public as one of Britain's leading psephologists, in a somewhat more specialized monograph traces the theoretical background of modern anti-Semitism back to its beginnings in the second half of the nineteenth century. His book to some degree overlaps

* Peter G. J. Pulzer. *The Rise of Political Anti-Semitism in Germany and Austria* (1964).

with Mosse's, but it breaks fresh ground, especially in the section on Austria. There have been many studies of German anti-Semitism, but hardly any of anti-Semitism in Austria, though before the First World War it was far more widespread and virulent there. The Germans in Austria, in contrast to those in Germany, faced a most serious nationality problem; they were, in fact, a minority. Once an undisputed master race, they were now involved in a losing struggle against the other contenders for power. In this situation, racial hate and national resentment reached a high pitch—and much of it came to be directed against the Jews, despite the fact that the Jews were among the most faithful German *Kulturtraeger*. While Mosse is mainly interested in the history of ideas, Pulzer approaches the problem as a political scientist. Above all he is interested in the impact of anti-Semitic ideas on the everyday politics of the two Empires. His book, too, is a valuable contribution to the historiography of modern Germany; it is full of fascinating facts and figures and information about, for instance, the social composition of the pan-German associations.* Pulzer explains the victory of Nazism, rightly I believe, as the triumph of the South-German-Austrian *voelkisch* ideology over the classical nationalism and chauvinism of Prussia and the North; and he argues that anti-Semitism flourished in Austria because of the failure of Liberalism to provide adequate answers to both the Empire's economic needs and the clash of nationalities. Private enterprise, constitutionalism, religious tolerance were a source of weakness, not of strength.

Neither of these two books discusses what may broadly be called the "Jewish problem" in Central Europe between

---

* One Josef Schneider, of Vienna, is described as a *Personaleinkommensteuerschaetzungscommissionsmitgliedersatzmann*, which is to say: a deputy member of the commission assessing the amount of income tax to be paid by individuals.

1870 and 1933. This problem assumed different forms in various countries: in Berlin and Vienna it consisted mainly in the emergence of a strong Jewish middle class, very heavily represented in such fields as trade and commerce, journalism, the law, medicine. It is idle to ignore the fact that Jewish emancipation during the first half of the 19th century created serious social problems. Even though these tensions in themselves do not explain modern German and Austrian anti-Semitism, their existence was well known not only to anti-Semitic authors but also to the early Zionist writers. Of late it has become somewhat unfashionable to mention it, but there was anti-Semitism long before Hitler, and individual psychopathology cannot entirely explain it. Is a satisfactory analysis of racialist thought and policy possible without a consideration of the situation of the Jews in these places at the time?

Much of this comment has been taken up by critical reflections, but it is only sterile and insignificant writing that never excites dissent. These excellent books, indispensable for any serious student of 19th- and 20th-century Europe, will provoke not only assent and criticism but, above all, discussion, which is much needed and long overdue.

PLOTTING AGAINST
HITLER

IN THE RESEARCH LIBRARY in which I usually work there is almost an entire roomful of books and pamphlets on German resistance against Hitler. When visitors are shown round our building they often express surprise that so many people have devoted so much time to writing so many books upon a non-existent subject. Similar opinions have been expressed by widely read authors (such as Hannah Arendt and A. J. P. Taylor): they are commonly held in England and in the United States. But what of the thousands of German enemies of Hitler who perished in prisons and concentration camps? True, these dissidents were singularly ineffective, but is it just to ignore them altogether? The question of the German resistance against Nazism, its inspiration, aims, and effects, is one of the most complicated and vexing of modern history. Hence the flood of books about it in many countries. That the issue happens to be also of wider significance need hardly be stressed: the problem of resistance in a totalitarian régime has not, unfortunately, become a purely academic one since 1945.

No other modern dictatorship has had such a wide popular appeal as Nazism had in Germany. Up to the outbreak of the War, to give but one example, Germans could travel abroad freely; no other totalitarian régime has felt secure enough to give its subjects similar license. But we also know, on the basis of much evidence that has come to light since

1945, that the Third Reich had far more enemies inside Germany than was commonly assumed at the time. How does one explain this apparent paradox? Most of us have come to measure the importance of political groups in terms that make sense only in a democratic régime. Since Hitler's opponents were not much in evidence after 1933 it has been assumed that a German resistance did not exist. But a totalitarian régime and a strong opposition exclude each other like fire and water; wherever there is an organized opposition, the régime is not yet, or is no longer, totalitarian in character.

German opposition to Hitler was ineffectual but so far as sheer figures are concerned it was not negligible. This was partly due to the fact that the Nazis never tried to win over political opponents; they were very confident of their hold and refused even to consider admitting to their ranks leading Communists or Social Democrats who might have been willing. Neither were "bourgeois" leaders permitted to play a role of political importance in their Reich beyond that of specialist assignments.

"Resistance," admittedly, covered a very wide range of activities; not all of which now strike us as very dangerous. One of the heroes of the German resistance was a Professor of Romance languages who had decided to sabotage the war effort by mistranslating Spanish documents. Much of the opposition of the Communist militants consisted in listening to Radio Moscow. Twenty years later, these do not seem to qualify as great acts of heroism; but at the time they involved the risk of years in a concentration camp, and possibly a death sentence. Those who have not had personal experience of living under a totalitarian régime ought to be careful in their judgment.

Not that all members of the resistance were angels: Goerdeler, the political leader of the July 1944 plot, gave all his fellow conspirators away without even being exposed to undue pressure. Arthur Nebe, another member of the conspiracy, would have been condemned to death by the Allies had he not been shot earlier by the Gestapo. (He had been the commander of one of the leading *Einsatzgruppen* in Russia; some 70,000 Jews were killed in White Russia under his personal command.) But there were also tens of thousands of Germans who resisted Hitler to the best of their ability, aristocrats and Communists, colonels and trade unionists, some Catholics and a few Protestants and ordinary, decent people who thought that Nazism was an outrage to their own people and humanity. Of these thousands paid with their lives, and it is a matter of elementary historical justice that their sacrifice should at least be recorded, even if it was inconsiderable in terms of political efficacy. In a country like France or Yugoslavia, many sympathized with the resistance; it was the patriotic thing to do since the Germans were the foreign invader. In Germany, German opponents to Hitler found themselves not only in almost complete isolation, swimming against the apparently irresistible wave of the future, but in the eyes of most other Germans they were simply traitors, breaking the oath to their supreme commander, stabbing their own people in the back. Those who braved not only the danger of arrest and execution, but moral and political isolation, deserve full credit.

This, at any rate, is Mr. Terence Prittie's opinion. He knew Germany during the 1930's, was there as a prisoner of war, and for many years now has covered the German scene for the (Manchester) *Guardian*. Mr. Prittie has obviously been worried by the anti-German frame of mind of many of his compatriots both on the Left and on the Right. There is, admittedly, much in this wave of British anti-Germanism (which has been fashionable ever since the middle 1950s) which has more to do with resentment of German economic achievement than with genuine anti-fascism. Organs of the press which were in the forefront of appeasement in the '30s are now leaders in the sport of Germany-baiting; they seem to dislike Adenauer and Erhard more than Adolf Hitler. Be that as it may, Mr. Prittie has done well to present in broad outline the development of the various German resistance groups.[1] Or perhaps one should talk about individuals rather than groups. The churches, the former political parties, and trade unions did not resist, but quite a few individuals from these milieus did. Mr. Prittie mentions them all: the Kreisau Circle (which included most of the men of the 20th of July); the *"Rote Kapelle"* (a fellow-traveling group which combined anti-Nazi propaganda with military espionage on behalf of the Russians); Jehovah's Witnesses who steadfastly refused to join the army and had to pay the penalty, Probst Lichtenberg, who protested from his pulpit against the deportation of Jews—and perished himself in a concentration camp. Even so, Mr. Prittie's book is not an exhaustive history; it certainly was not written for other historians but for a much wider public. It could have been a very good book had the author taken a little more time, but Mr. Prittie was chief diplomatic correspondent of his newspaper and the incessant international crises presumably left him little time for other activities. It is, however, a useful book which will help to dispel some of the sillier ideas about the Third Reich—like the assumption that there was no resistance at all.

West and East German historiography have, quite predictably, not been able to agree with the importance of the attempt on Hitler's life in July 1944. West German books (Professor Hans Rothfels' history of the German opposition, for example) often ignore the Communist opposition to Hitler, whereas for the East Germans the July plot was merely

[1] Terrence Prittie, *Germans Against Hitler* (1964).

a desperate attempt by a handful of professional soldiers, Junkers, and other Anglo-American agents acting in accordance with their class interest when defeat was already certain. The Russians, it is only fair to mention, have of late taken a somewhat more objective view—Major General Milstein in his book *Zagovor protiv Gitlera* describes von Stauffenberg (the man who deposed the bomb in Hitler's headquarters) as a great hero, a man of "boundless courage."

There have been several descriptions of the July plot since the end of the war, how it was hatched and why it failed; Manvell and Fraenkel,[2] who have shown familiarity with the German scene in their previous work, went over the whole evidence again, uncovered some that is new, and frankly admit that they do not have all the answers. Some unsolved questions still persist. There is, for example, the all-important telephone call from Hitler's headquarters to Berlin on July 20 which was to inform the conspirators whether the attempt on his life had succeeded—and for which, during many decisive hours, they waited in vain. The part of some of the *dramatis personae* either during the plot or after their arrest also remains in question; not all the documents are available and some of the survivors have apparently not been helpful in providing historical evidence. Manvell and Fraenkel's book is well-written and accurate. My main criticism is that it has no real beginning nor end. It does not set the plot into historical perspective, and there is very little about the Nazi political reaction to the plot. Something like the original plebeian character of Nazism again emerged after these "degenerate aristocrats" had tried to kill the *Füehrer*. (In Italy, too, fascism again became much more radical in its last phase—the Republic of Salo.) These shortcomings are unlikely to affect the success of the book which in Germany is already high on the best-seller list.

[2] Roger Manvell and Heinrich Fraenkel, *The Men Who Tried to Kill Hitler* (1964).

Hitler escaped almost unhurt from an explosion that, according to all established rules, was bound to kill him. As Prittie puts it, this was "an act of God"—though it is not easy to think of any reason why the Almighty should have preserved Hitler's life. But even after the plot to kill the *Füehrer* had failed, the revolt might still have succeeded, had the conspirators acted boldly and decisively. They held so many key positions in the army command in Berlin, Paris, and elsewhere; there was still a good chance that the troops would have followed them. But, as Fraenkel and Manvell delicately put it, there were certain flaws common to human nature. There was, literally, a breakdown in communications. There was also weakness and irresolution and lack of civic courage. The colonels and generals wavered, and went on looking for someone who would relieve them of taking initiative and responsibility, until the Gestapo came and arrested them all. The Germans have been the least effective rebels against authority in modern history. When the Social Democrat Scheidemann proclaimed the German Republic in November, 1918, his comrade Ebert told him "You had no right to do that . . ." Of all Germans, the senior officers were the least likely candidates to lead.

PROPAGANDA
AND TERROR

IT IS SURELY here to stay, Harold Lasswell wrote in 1934 in his entry on "Propaganda" for the *Encyclopedia of the Social Sciences*. How right he was. We have all been taught about the origins of the word in its modern sense—Urban VIII, the Jesuits, and all that. But if the term is of relatively modern date, propaganda itself surely is not, for what were the Crusades if not a masterfully envisaged (if poorly executed) exercise in propaganda and political warfare? Napoleon, too, was no mean practitioner of the art. On a wide scale propaganda was first used in World War I; in 1917–18 the *Entente* dropped some 100 million leaflets over the German lines. Their content, their make-up, the means of distribution, were extremely primitive by modern standards, but they had some effect on the morale of the German troops.

Above all, they had a profound impact on those Germans who after the end of the War pondered the causes of the defeat. Lord Northcliffe became a magic name in right-wing extremist circles in Munich and Berlin; and Hitler wrote in *Mein Kampf:* "I have learned a tremendous lot (*unendlich viel*) from enemy propaganda in the World War." (He also learned from socialist propaganda and ridiculed the bourgeois parties to whom the "art of propaganda is almost entirely unknown.") He did not need Gustave Le Bon to make him realize that the masses were stirred not by logical argument but by appeals to passions. He also seems to have understood fairly early that a lie that goes undetected for a long time, acts as a truth. Above all, Hitler was firmly convinced that propaganda was a terrible weapon in the hands of the experts. He was thinking primarily of the spoken word; there was always the danger that newspaper articles would be clever and sophisticated, *i.e.*, the very opposite of what effective propaganda should be, the crude and persistent hammering home of a single theme (Kill the Jews, Destroy Marxism, Defeat the Enemy).

Hitler was fortunate in finding a very able lieutenant in Joseph Goebbels, an agile and fertile mind, a competent writer and excellent speaker, who combined organizational know-how with a total lack of inhibitions. He was a cripple who looked even less than Hitler himself the part of the ideal Nordic hero which played such a great part in Nazi doctrine; his only heroic exploits were in the beds of movie stars. His enemies inside the party called him a "shrunken Teuton gone dark (*nachgedunkelter Schrumpfgermane*)." For all that his was the best mind among the Nazi leaders. He was critical of his colleagues, but boundlessly devoted to the *Füehrer* to the very end. Goebbels was the creator and chief operator of the Nazi propaganda machine from the very beginning, supervising each phase and every field of activity. Unlike Mussolini, he realized the tremendous importance of the radio as a means of carrying propaganda to the last hamlet and cottage in the country and thus reaching a far wider public than ever before in history.

Dr. Bramsted, a native of Germany who worked in London in the 'thirties with Karl Mannheim and now teaches at the University of Sydney, has produced in a massive tome the most thorough study of the house that Goebbels built and which, together with Himmler's terror machine and the

Wehrmacht, was one of the three pillars of Nazi power.[*] His book is based on much hitherto untapped documentary material; if some of the observations that follow are critical in character, it ought to be stressed at once that *Goebbels and National Socialist Propaganda* is an important book which will be consulted as a standard reference work by all students of modern German history for many years to come. (To my own surprise I find myself recommending many recent books on Germany; we have been having uncommonly good years as far as Central Europe is concerned, and Dr. Bramsted's book takes its place in this series.) The author, rightly I believe, takes Northcliffe as his starting point and then passes on, wrongly I think, to a discussion of the influence of one almost totally forgotten right-wing Munich publicist, Paul Cossman. Cossman, whose origins were partly Jewish (which probably caused his arrest in the third Reich), was an old-fashioned extreme nationalist. There was literally a world of difference between a spokesman of the old order like Cossman and a semi-nihilist like Goebbels, who had on various occasions expressed great admiration for Lenin and Bolshevism and ridiculed the "stupid anti-Semitism" and anti-Bolshevism of the traditional German right.

The core of Bramsted's book is devoted to an analysis of the organization of Nazi propaganda, the coordination of the press, the radio, the cinema, the theater, and all other means of mass communication. He examines the treatment of foreign correspondents, the tactics of soft-pedaling for foreign consumption while Germany was as yet unprepared, and subsequently, the all-out preparation for Hitler's conquests (Austria, Czechoslovakia, Poland). In wartime the main task of German propaganda was, as before, the projection of the Hitler image. In addition the belief in German invincibility had to be strengthened and, after Stalingrad and El Ala-

[*] *Goebbels and National Socialist Propaganda 1925–1945*, by Ernest K. Bramsted (Michigan State University, 1965).

mein, morale had to be kept up on the home front by, among other things, appeals to fear. Separate chapters in the book are devoted to Nazi attitudes towards Britain, the anti-Jewish propaganda, and (somewhat incongruously) to a very detailed discussion of the counter-propaganda of the British Broadcasting Corporation in wartime.

The general conclusion, not quite surprisingly, is that Goebbels's propaganda was more effective while German armies were advancing than when they retreated. Even so, with its promises of miracle weapons, a sudden break in the Allied coalition, and references to sudden changes of fortune that had happened before in German history, it helped to prevent a breakdown in German morale up to a very late stage in the war. The strong effect of this propaganda, its aggressive character, its utter mendacity, and the impact produced on the masses by constant repetition are unlikely to emerge from a scholarly book. It is fortunate that some of Goebbels's main performances are now available on records. The spoken word, the frenetic applause, the whole atmosphere transmitted in sound conveys to those who did not live through that period a far more tangible impression than any literary description.

That Goebbels was a cynic appears, for instance, from his campaign in the late 1920's against Dr. Weiss, the Jewish deputy commander of the Berlin police at the time. Goebbels relentlessly attacked Dr. Weiss, bestowing on him the Jewish nickname "Isidor"; he became in the Nazi press the very symbol of the sinister Jewish forces which were brutally abusing the German people. Years later Goebbels admitted that the propagandistic transformation of this "harmless fool" into some super-Frankenstein had been one of his greatest achievements. But Goebbels was not only a cynic. There was in him a great deal of blind belief, and it is the difficult task of the historian to establish where the one ended and the other began.

It is an exaggeration to argue, as some have done, that

in National Socialism propaganda filled the place of a doctrine. But it is certainly true that in Nazism and in Nazi propaganda *Weltanschauung* played a much smaller role than, for instance, in Communism. Precisely for that reason an *"apparatchik,"* a top executive, would not have been able to conduct Nazi propaganda; a brilliant and malignant mastermind like Goebbels was needed. He was also, incidentally, a very hardworking man. I do not know of anyone in a similar position in our time who produced each week both a newspaper article and a broadcast script as Goebbels did over and above his other duties during the last years of the War.

There is no lack of documentary evidence on the Nazi era; on the contrary, there is an *embarras de richesse* of millions of files and frames of microfilm. It is almost impossible not to lose one's way from time to time in this maze of documents, and Dr. Bramsted, too, seems occasionally to have been overwhelmed. This shows in the organization of the material, a certain sketchiness, a concentration on some admittedly very interesting and revealing aspects, to the detriment of a full coverage of the subject.*

Messrs. Manvell and Fraenkel have produced over the last few years biographies of Goebbels, Goering, Himmler, and the men who tried to kill Hitler in 1944. These biographies are workmanlike and well written; to the best of my knowledge there are no better biographies in existence. They have come in for some attacks of late because they are, as some purists argue, not up to the highest historical standards. I do not attribute too much weight to such criticism;

---

* He wrongly attributes to Goebbels the authorship of the phrase, "Iron Curtain *(der eiserne Vorhang)."* Winston Churchill is often said to have adapted the phrase from him. But in fact the term is much older. To give but one example—Ethel Snowden, who went to Russia with the first Labor delegation, wrote in 1920: "We were behind the 'iron curtain' at last . . ." (*Through Bolshevik Russia,* London, 1920, p. 32).

it is doubtful whether the basic picture to emerge would have been essentially different even if Manvell and Fraenkel had worked for ten more years on each volume. For my own uneasiness about these books, and particularly about the Himmler and Goering biographies, there are different reasons. It is exceedingly difficult to write a biography of anyone but the supreme leader in a totalitarian dictatorship; I am not convinced that it is worthwhile to try to write about the others. The life of the great dictator himself can usually be well documented; about his lieutenants we mostly do not know enough for a study in depth. All the important decisions, moreover, are taken by the great dictator himself, not his lieutenants, who were, so to speak, merely dancing the Gopak. Himmler as a person is not that interesting, and I think the authors could have shown in a long essay rather than a book* how this unprepossessing youth grew into an obsessively scrupulous and very superstitious man with a schoolmasterish attitude to life. Biographers of the men "next to Hitler" (or Stalin or Mussolini) are almost certainly bound to inflate the importance of their villain-hero; there will be much general politics and little biography. A book on Goering, in other words, will deal mainly with the German air force, a book on Molotov with Soviet foreign policy. This Himmler biography deals largely with the S.S., its main figures and activities. This is a legitimate subject, for the definitive work on the Nazi terror machine remains to be written. Manvell and Fraenkel's new book has all the good qualities of their previous biographies, but it adds few new facts or fresh insight—and it is certainly not the long-needed definitive study of the S.S.

Professor McRandle's book, *The Track of the Wolf*** is more ambitious and more exasperating. In his five long es-

---

* *Himmler,* by Roger Manvell and Heinrich Fraenkel. (Putnam's, 1965).
** *The Track of the Wolf: Essays on National Socialism and its Leader, Adolf Hitler,* by James H. McRandle. (Northwestern, 1965).

says on Nazism and its leaders he is above all concerned
with Hitler's destructiveness as opposed to his creative powers, with his suicidal tendencies, and with the origins of his
ideas. In "Warrior and Worker" he deals with two stereo-
typed figures of German 20th-century literature which later
became part and parcel of Nazi ideology. Professor Mc-
Randle, in other words, wants to find out what made Hitler
tick. This kind of book, needless to say, is a far more courageous enterprise than the attempt to write a historical monograph on some little known aspect of the history of the
Third Reich. The writer of the specialized monograph is
bound to come up with something that is new, provided his
subject is sufficiently obscure. With the authors of studies
that want to go straight to the core of a great problem and
to explain it, it is very often all or nothing; they are either
great successes or miserable failures. I admire Professor
McRandle's daring spirit, but I do not think his effort is a
success.

He writes well and knows the literature about Nazism.
I agree with some of his arguments—he stresses, for instance, the central importance of the personality of the
Füehrer in the history of Nazism; elsewhere he emphasizes
that the Nazis were not just an extreme right-wing group
as some historians still believe. I sympathize with his attempt to apply the psychoanalytical method to shed light
on Hitler's real motives. But these valuable approaches and
ideas are more than offset by an uncanny tendency to ask
the wrong questions and to complicate simple issues. One of
the main essays, which gives its title to the whole book, is
"the track of the wolf." Professor McRandle describes how
Hitler, when hiding in Bavaria in 1922, once used the
pseudonym "Herr Wolf" while visiting a friend in a neighboring village. The choice of this nickname—McRandle
thinks—is most significant, nor was it pure coincidence that
his headquarters during World War II were called *Wolfs-*

schanze and *Wolfsschlucht.* On this Professor McRandle builds his theory about Hitler's dual character—the dawdling dreamer with aspirations towards the artistic life, and the ravening wolf hungering for and attaining political power. Thus a small grain of truth becomes the basis of an elaborate theory. I felt prejudiced from the very beginning. For reasons which are of no public interest I once chose "Wolf" as a first name and I can assure Professor McRandle from my own experience that unconscious motives are not the only ones that matter in the choice of a name or a pseudonym. There is in history as in psychoanalysis the danger of missing a clue, but the pitfall of reading deep significance into meaningless action has also to be avoided. Lenin, I believe, once chose the pseudonym "Herr Richter." I wonder what Professor McRandle would have made of this. Was Lenin really a judge *manqué?* Was he basically a right-winger?

The longest essay, "The Suicide," is even more startling. It asks why Hitler committed suicide. The obvious answer to this question, namely, that he had no alternative, is far too simple for the author, and so we are told—100 pages and 213 footnotes later—that we shall never know exactly why Hitler killed himself. In between there are statistics about suicide in Japan and Egypt, in urban areas, in Catholic countries, in West and East Berlin since the last War. We learn that artists have a higher suicide rate than non-artists, and soldiers commit suicide more often than civilians. We are given to understand that according to Ringel's fundamental study about married persons committing suicide, those having marital difficulties are in greater danger—an unstartling conclusion, if there ever was one. We know that Hitler committed suicide on a Monday at 3:30 in the afternoon. According to Ellis and Allen's investigation, more people commit suicide on a Monday than on any other day of the week, and in Europe most people commit the fatal deed either in the morning or the early afternoon. We are told what Stengel, Zilboorg, and Menninger think about suicide. Hitler's performance at his secondary school, which was quite wretched (he failed in German, mathematics, and shorthand) is also discussed in detail. Professor McRandle has even studied the literature on suicide in Dutch—and yet one remains firmly unconvinced. There may have been a suicidal streak in Hitler, and over the years he may have made some vague threats or announcements pointing in this direction. If so, what a roundabout way for a man to achieve his aim! I have the greatest admiration for the authorities on suicide quoted by Professor McRandle, but I suspect he invoked them unnecessarily. Hitler really had no alternative on that Monday afternoon. His situation therefore radically differed from that of all other people who took their lives on the afternoon of that day. If someone is still looking for a pattern to understand Hitler's behavior during the last few weeks of his life, I recommend a study of the "Song of the Nibelungs," which, I submit, is likely to shed more light than—with due respect—an article on "automobile accidents, suicide and unconscious motivation."

MIDDLETOWN, GERMANY

MR. WILLIAM SHERIDAN ALLEN, a student of history from Evanston, Illinois, went in the early 1950s to a small town in the former kingdom of Hanover to write about its history during the fateful years 1930–1935. I happen to know from experience that authors are not always responsible for what is printed on the dust jackets of their books; this one claims that the German townspeople revealed their innermost thoughts to Mr. William Sheridan Allen. Few people are willing to share with strangers their innermost thoughts on any subject. It is hard to imagine small-town Germans being frank and open when asked by an American student in search of material to reminisce about their own and their neighbor's doings under the Nazis.*

In these circumstances, interviews in depth or other such techniques will be of little help. The citizens of Thalburg (as Mr. Allen calls his Middletown) may be narrow-minded, but they are no fools. In his preface, Mr. Allen also says that he attempted in his study to contribute to the understanding of one of the central political and moral problems of the twentieth century. This is a formidable claim. Can one really study the central political and moral issues of our time on the basis of the gossip of the good citizens of Thal-

*William Sheridan Allen, *The Nazi Seizure of Power: The Experience of a Single German Town, 1930–1935* (1965).

burg? I was about to dismiss Mr. Allen's book as yet another dissertation which by mistake had found its way into print. This would have been a great mistake, for Mr. Allen, as I soon came to realize, has written a first-rate study of absorbing interest. It shows how accurately and how vividly a knowledgeable and intelligent observer can retrace the events of those years in a predominantly Protestant little middle-class town. Above all, I had clearly underrated the enterprise and diligence of Mr. Allen, who has not only read every single issue of the *Thalburger Beobachter,* the *Grae-fische Hofscurier,* and similar local newspapers (there were surprisingly many of them); he has studied with equal attention the annual reports published by the local secondary school and the museum, the town budgets and the mimeographed sheets reporting the work of the municipal departments; he has also looked into local crime statistics and court cases. Nothing that was published in or about Thalburg between 1930 and 1935 seems to have escaped the attention of this formidable researcher. Out of this mass of revealing material (which seems more reliable than the uncertain memory of the *dramatis personae*) Mr. Allen has woven an account that is both convincing and surprisingly well written.

He describes the whole climate of those days—the effect of mass unemployment in 1931/32, the demonstrations and clashes, the general feeling of helplessness and of impending disaster which so decisively helped the Nazis in their quest for power. He relates how the center parties simply melted away and how the Social Democrats, led by decent but uninspired and ineffectual people, gave up one position after another.

January 30, 1933, came and passed almost imperceptibly in Thalburg. The leader of the local Nazis, Kurt Aergeyz, the owner of a hardware shop, an indifferent businessman and alcoholic, became the head of the city administration and provided surprisingly effective government. In July 1933 there were no longer any unemployed in the city, by 1935 all external signs of the Depression had vanished, construction was booming, the city looked much better, the streets were cleaner, a "green belt" had been developed, the houses had been repainted. There was even a new open-air theater set in a natural declivity in the Thalburg forest.

At what price was all this achieved? Mr. Allen provides the answer in sections headed "The Terror System" and "The Atomization of Society." I think he tries to prove too much on the basis of the experiences of a little town—typical perhaps for other small towns but not for Germany as a whole. There was intimidation in Thalburg, but not that much terror. In fact no one came to serious grief. Three Social Democrats were sent to a concentration camp—but this was in the middle of the war, many years later. No one was beaten to pulp in the street, no one sentenced to a long term of imprisonment. There was hardly any resistance and there was no need in Thalburg for terror on a grand scale. "The resistance clique showed its defiance by singing in the church choir"—this about sums it up.

There also were limits to the "atomization of society" in a small town, where, unlike a big city, everyone knew everyone else. True enough, the club for mixed choral singing, the Retail Merchants' Association, the Common Good Construction Club, not to mention the rifle societies, were *gleichgeschaltet, i.e.,* they received a Nazi leadership. Some organizations were dissolved but the beer and card evening circles and other such groups continued to exist. I strongly doubt whether it is true that "people often simply stopped coming together," whether society in fact "had been destroyed." True, one had to be careful about what one said but this did not mean "that to a great extent the individual was atomized." I suspect there was not that much difference between the quality of life in Thalburg in 1932 and 1935, and

I think Mr. Allen is wrong in his assumption that, by 1935, in the eyes of most Thalburgers the bad of the new system outweighed the good and that consequently free elections might have resulted in a defeat of Nazism. Two-thirds of the voters, considerably more than the German average, had supported the Nazi party before January 30, 1933. There was no earthly reason for them to change their views three years later, since the Nazis on the whole kept their promises. Mr. Allen makes the important point that

> Thalburg Nazis created their own image by their own initiative, vigor, and propaganda. They knew exactly what needed to be done to effect the transfer of power to themselves in the spring of 1933 and they did it apparently without more than generalized directives from above.

Hitler did not seize power single-handed.

What were the mainsprings of this massive support for Nazism in Thalburg? Mr. Allen refers to the middle class's paranoid fears of the local Social Democrats: "they were determined to put the clock back to a period when the organized working class was forcibly kept from exerting influence." This is very true, but there were other equally valid motives: the impoverishment of the middle class through inflation and the world economic crisis, the general feeling that strong leadership was needed to overcome the Depression and the deep attachment to extreme nationalism. But whosoever views Nazism exclusively in terms of a middle-class movement misses a vital clue. Nazism was such a great success precisely because its influence, unlike that of the traditional right-wing parties, extended much *beyond* the middle class.

Then came the war; eventually the Allied armies arrived after Herr Aergeyz had departed in a Mercedes with (Mr. Allen reports) two blondes and several cases of *schnapps*. Later the refugees from the East arrived; by 1950 the population had doubled, today it is probably even larger than that. Thalburg is, I imagine, a hardworking town, enjoying the fruits of the Wirtschaftswunder. It is also still, I suspect, quite reactionary. All the big towns in Germany now have a Social Democratic majority, while most small towns, especially in North Germany, are right wing. It would be interesting to know more about the recent past of this German Middletown. To find out, a student of history will be needed as informed and as indefatigable as Mr. Allen, who has shown us how much of interest can be extricated from the most unlikely places.

V
JEWISH
QUESTIONS

THE TUCHOLSKY COMPLAINT

THE STUDY OF GERMANY during the Weimar period has become a fashionable subject of late, and it is not difficult to see why. My American students certainly find it more interesting than the history of Britain and France—not to mention Italy or Russia—during that period; it all seems, to use the inevitable adjective, so relevant. The study of this Periclean age of *avant-garde* culture, youth revolt, sexual experimentation and radical politics seems to provide not only interesting raw material for dissertations but also inspiration for the present day. There are undoubtedly certain parallels, some of them rather disturbing in view of what followed the Weimar period. In a review in the New York *Times* (24 Nov. 1968) of Peter Gay's fascinating little book* I singled out some of the achievements of this exciting decade, as well as the moral relativism and political naiveté so characteristic of that epoch, the dominant position in it of so many fake gurus, the enthusiasm for revolutionaries in far-away countries, the lack of tact and commonsense among the intellectuals. Reading Mr. Deak† and re-reading Mr. Gay I now realize that there is one aspect which is usually neglected

---

* PETER GAY, *Weimar Culture*. Harper & Row (New York), and Secker & Warburg (London). See my comments above, in Ch. 21.

† ISTVAN DEAK, *Weimar Germany's Left Wing Intellectuals*. (University of California Press).

or glossed over, perhaps because it is so delicate and yet it is one of the key issues.

I mean, of course, the Jewish question.

Mr. Deak's book, I ought to add in explanation, is a political history of the *Weltbühne* and its circle; the *Weltbühne* was an independent left-wing weekly, immensely stimulating and highly readable, often very witty, the implacable enemy of both the nationalist Right and the Social Democratic establishment. The majority of its contributors and, no doubt, most of its readers were Jews. Mr. Deak is a little too generous towards his heroes:

> They were never destructive [he writes] on the contrary, they aimed at redemption, they dreamed of a socialist society with democratic instrumental forms. . . .

The evidence does not bear out such charitable assumptions. Kurt Tucholsky, the leading spirit of the circle, said that since 1913 he had belonged to those people "who think that the German spirit is poisoned almost beyond recovery, who do not believe in an improvement, who regard German democracy as a façade and a lie." How could he be anything but destructive if he did not believe in a possible recovery? True, the members of the circle had their dreams of a socialist society, of pacifism and humanism, but the writers of the *Weltbühne* lacked the political and economic experience (and often also the necessary common sense) to provide any valid answers to the most pressing problems facing Germany at the time. The singular lack of impact of this circle, its political sterility, is surely connected with the fact that these were Jewish writers who, with all their talent, were quite oblivious to one basic existential fact: that they were living in an intellectual ghetto, that the great majority of Germans did not just dislike them, but disputed their very right to have a voice as far as the future of Germany was concerned. The fact that these *Weltbühne* contributors believed that they were *das andere Deutschland,* the other Germany, the conscience of the German nation, was not of the slightest significance to anyone but themselves. Nor did it matter that most of them had no longer any tie with the Jewish community, or like Tucholsky were actually converts to Protestantism.

To explain their singular lack of resonance and to illustrate the whole background against which they worked, it may be useful to refer to a controversy that had taken place a decade earlier.

In March 1913 a young Jewish writer named Moritz Goldstein published an article entitled "German-Jewish Parnassus" in the fortnightly *Kunstwart* which created something of a minor scandal, provoked some 90 letters to the editor, and was discussed for years throughout the German press. Goldstein argued, to put it briefly, that the Jews were managing the culture of a people which denied them both the right and the capacity to do so. The newspapers in the capital were about to become a Jewish monopoly; almost all directors of the Berlin theaters were Jews; so were many actors. German musical life without the Jews was almost unthinkable; and the study of German literature was also to a large extent in Jewish hands. Everyone knew it, only the Jews pretended it was not worthy of notice; for what mattered, they claimed, were their achievements, their cultural and humanistic activities. This, said Goldstein, was a dangerous fallacy for "the others do not feel that we are Germans." We could show the others that we were not inferior (his argument continued), but wasn't it naïve to assume that this would in any way diminish their dislike and antipathy? There was a basic anomaly in the Jewish situation. The liberal Jewish intellectuals were good Europeans, but they were also split personalities, divorced from the people amidst whom they were living. They could make a great contribution to science, for science knew no national borders. But in literature and the arts (and he should have added: in the political sphere) any major initiative had to be rooted in a popular and national framework. From Homer to Tolstoy all the really great works had their origins in the native soil, the homeland, the people. And this "rootedness" the Jews were lacking, despite all their intellectual and emotional efforts.

Among those who answered Goldstein there was the poet Ernst Lissauer, who during the first World War received notoriety in connection with his "Hate England" song. He bitterly opposed any attempt to restore a ghetto on German soil or a "Palestinian enclave"; on the contrary, the process of assimilation was to be carried to its successful conclusion. If so many Jewish intellectuals were radicals and had as yet no feeling for the German national spirit, this was, no doubt, because they were as yet discriminated against in so many ways. But once these barriers would fall they, too, would be fully integrated into the mainstream of German life.

Ten years later a republic had been installed, and Jewish intellectuals were no longer impeded in their professional careers: they became professors, government officials, even cabinet ministers. Many still belonged to the radical fringe, more, in effect, than in Wilhelminian Germany. This affinity between Jewish intellectuals and radicalism had deep historical roots. Lissauer's explanation was at best only half true; the people he was writnig about had not been radical in politics because they were out merely for personal betterment. At least in passing it ought to be mentioned that the political commitment of these intellectuals did not by any means reflect the orientation of the German Jewish Community as a whole which, as Professor Touri has recently shown in a massive and highly informative study, was always surprisingly "*Staatstreu*," giving consistent electoral support to the center parties. But who was interested in the voting patterns of half a million Jews? What mattered were the men and women in the limelight, from Marx to Rosa Luxemburg, from Kurt Eisner to Kurt Tucholsky: that was the "Jewish element" in German politics as far as public opinion was concerned.

In 1928 Tucholsky published a copiously illustrated volume of little notes and essays: *Deutschland, Deutschland über alles*. This was a broadside against the *Reichswehr*, the Church, the judiciary (formerly the people of *Dichter und Denker*, the Germans had become a nation of *Richter und Henker*, Judges and executioners), the beer-drinking students, Hindenburg, the Social Democratic commanders of the Prussian police, Stresemann, trade union secretaries, and almost everyone else in a position of authority. It was an all-out attack not just against the German *Philister*, his customs, the way he arranged his bourgeois home and educated his children but against the German way of life in general, a denunciation not merely of militarism but of national defense as such. ("There is no secret of the German army I would not hand over readily to a foreign power," Tucholsky wrote.) He ridiculed not just the veteran associations with their chauvinistic slogans and parades, but derided systematically and with great skill all and any manifestation of patriotism. The impression that emerged was that everything specifically German was *a priori* bad, and had to be eradicated. In an article on "The Face of a German" Tucholsky depicted the average German *à la* George Grosz:

> A rather thick-set head, a none-too-high forehead; cold, small eyes, a nose that likes to lower itself into a drinking glass, a disagreeable toothbrush moustache. . . .

It was a caricature of Weimar Germany, some of it quite true, much of it distorted—all in questionable taste.

"For 225 pages we have said *no*"—Tucholsky concluded his book, "now we wanted to say *yes*. Yes to the landscape and to the countryside of Germany." But there are beautiful landscapes all over the globe. Tucholsky in any case preferred Paris to Germany. ("Here no one steps on my toes, here people are kind and polite, here the cars travel smoothly and fast, here clouds are still clouds and stones are still stones, here it still makes sense to be alive.") Some of the pictures in the book are very funny indeed; others are embarrassing or, in a perspective of 40 years simply inexplicable. The one which scandalized most people at the time was a *photo montage*, "Animals Look at You," showing eight somewhat decrepit and rather ugly gentlemen, aged 65 or above, most of them in military uniform. It is a pathetic sight, but there is nothing particularly animal or evil about them given the unfortunate fact of life that men usually look more handsome and virile at thirty than at seventy and that babies are more likely to smile than retired generals and admirals. Did Tucholsky mean to imply that the German army and police needed better-looking officers? If so, they certainly got them a few years later; Heydrich, for instance, was a man of striking appearance.

In an essay not long ago Gordon Craig noted that Tucholsky's great weakness, shared by most of the engaged writers of his period, was a lack of selectivity about his targets; he was indiscriminate in this respect and immoderate in his expenditure of ammunition. Tucholsky and his friends thought that the German Judge of their day was the most evil person imaginable and that the German prisons were the most inhumane; later they got Freisler and Auschwitz. They imagined that Stresemann and the Social Democrats were the most reactionary politicians in the world; soon after they had to face Hitler, Goebbels, and Goering. They sincerely believed that fascism was already ruling Germany, until the horrors of the Third Reich overtook them. Their period was

one of unprecedented political freedom in Germany, when
the leaders of the Weimar Republic—to quote another recent historian—exhausted their energies in hard combat with
Hugenberg and Hitler:

> Tucholsky stood aside and jeered at them. They could have used
> help. All they got was scorn and laughter.

It is easy to understand the reasons for the present Tucholsky renaissance among the New Left in West Germany today.

What concerns me in this context is not so much the view
of the *Weltbühne* circle and their judgment of the political
situation. I happen to believe that it was, to say the least,
grossly oversimplified. But even if their appraisal had been
correct, if German democracy was a sham in 1929, if fascism
to all intents and purposes had already prevailed, the publication of books like *Deutschland, Deutschland über alles*
would still not have served any useful purpose. This is not
to say that a man or a group of men should not stand up
for their convictions however radical, and however dangerous the consequences. But Tucholsky and his friends
should have at least understood what dilemma they were
facing. They could have argued that as Europeans and hu-
manists, as socialists and pacifists, they had a sacred duty to
resist the rising wave of chauvinism. Since they lived in
Germany and wrote in German they considered they had a
right to have their say on Germany's future and to be listened to with respect. Unfortunately, this is not how most
other Germans saw it. Since they were Jews their position
in German politics and society was shaky anyway—and a
man like Tucholsky remained a Jew even if baptized seven
times over. By making no effort whatsoever to differentiate
between patriotism and maniacal chauvinism, between legitimate or normal national interests and aggressive revanchist

politics they finally disqualified themselves even in the eyes of their friends on the Left, socialists and Communists alike. If Tucholsky was convinced that there was no longer any hope, that the corruption had proceeded too far, what indeed was the point of carrying on the struggle? These were not insensitive men but they had no real roots themselves and, therefore, they lacked the sensorium for the patriotic feeling of their fellow-citizens. They were incapable of understanding anyone who reacted differently from the way they did.

Moritz Goldstein, who wrote that controversial and prophetic article before the first World War, emigrated to the United States when Hitler came to power. On one occasion, in his old age, he again wrote about the affair and commented on its implications. Comparing the German and the American situation, he dwelt upon the heavy concentration of American Jews in all branches of literature, the theater, films, music, etc. But he also noted the profound differences. The European concept of culture was not fully valid on the other side of the Atlantic; there was no talk about that semi-mystical entity called *Volksseele*, the inner mind of the nation. There was no fear that the mind of the nation would be polluted by any foreign admixture. On the contrary, America was the classical country of immigrants; everyone was equal, and belonged to the nation; every divisive trend was disparaged, and considered unpatriotic. "Antisemitic utterances in private or public seem to be unknown," Goldstein wrote. No opposition had been voiced against the participation of Jews in cultural activities. But, he added almost as an afterthought, the day may come when the Americans, too, will be concerned about the true mind of their nation, and then the question will be raised whether American Jews are Americans or strangers.

Mr. Goldstein's second article was written in 1956; when

he said "the day may come" he meant "in a hundred or even two hundred years hence." Events during the last decade have moved faster than he anticipated. There has been something of a problem all along, and it has become more acute in recent years. In some American circles the Tucholsky Syndrome has been rapidly spreading. (Perhaps I am doing an injustice to the late star of the *Weltbühne;* in comparison with the author of *Macbird* he was, of course, a giant.) A radical force has come into being even more emphatic in its rejection of America, its way of life and the aspirations of most of its citizens than the opposition of the writers of the *Weltbühne* to the Weimar Republic. Its more extreme members are firmly convinced that fascism has already prevailed, that American prisons are worse than Nazi concentration camps, that American policemen are more vicious than the *Gestapo.* There are countless publications which take up with a vengeance the theme of *Deutschland, Deutschland über alles* opposing not just American policy at home and abroad but deriding patriotism, the national symbols, traditional values, venerable traditions. Many leaders of the movement and a high percentage of their followers are of Jewish origin. Everyone knows it, though it is still not often mentioned in public. The majority of American Jews has not much sympathy with the movement. But this is of no great consequence. As in Germany in the Weimar period what matters are those who are in the limelight; it is Mark Rudd and not the Hassidic rabbis of Brooklyn who determines the public image.

Jewish intellectuals are drawn towards the camp of progress and social justice in politics following an old and honorable tradition. They feel (to quote an early forerunner, the German radical democrat Johann Jacoby) every folly and every misery of mankind as if they were personally affected. Those with a particular Western European background have realized more acutely than others the great dangers of Nationalism. It is, perhaps, not without relevance in this context that in Israel too the movement for an Arab-Jewish *rapprochement* from the very beginning has been largely constituted by Jews from Germany and the United States. But by this very same tradition they have had (with the exception of the Zionists), no feelings for the importance of the national element. Having been for so long in their history a people without a state and a homeland, total rejection has always come much easier to some of them than to most of their fellow citizens.

I hope I shall not be reminded that present-day America is in a hundred ways different from Weimar Germany and that history never exactly repeats itself. This, of course, goes without saying. But it is equally true that there are certain recurring patterns in Jewish as in general history. The issues are complex, and a discussion of their many aspects leads one beyond the confines of a brief essay. I do not want to carry my argument beyond this point and to speculate about the future place of American Jews in the cultural life or the radical movement of their country.

But there is reason for concern: problems of this character are not usually resolved by turning a blind eye.

THE DILEMMA OF THE
ZIONIST LEFT

DID HERZL KNOW that Palestine was not an empty country? Martin Buber relates that Max Nordau, his close colleague, was deeply concerned when for the first time he became aware of the presence of Arabs in Palestine. Greatly agitated, he went to see Herzl and told the founder of political Zionism: "I did not know this—we are committing an injustice! . . ." To this day it is widely thought that the early Zionists did not know that Palestine was inhabited by Arabs, that their successors continued to ignore the problem, and that this was the primary cause of the tragic Arab-Jewish conflict, which in our day has taken on such dangerous dimensions. It sounds plausible, but it does not correspond with the known facts. Buber's anecdote is probably apocryphal. Herzl knew that Palestine was not empty, and before him the Russian "Lovers of Zion" had frequently referred in their writings to the existence of an autochthonous population. Their reasoning was, very briefly, that the inhabitants of Palestine would greatly benefit from the immigration. When Rashid Bey, a character in Herzl's utopian novel *Altneuland,* is asked whether Jewish immigration had not ruined the Arabs and forced them to leave, he replies: "What a question! It was a blessing for all of us."

The early Zionists argued that the Jews needed a country of their own, that there were no longer any empty spaces on earth, that the inhabitants of Palestine numbered no more than half a million, and that modern methods of cultivation would make Jewish mass settlement possible without any need for the Arabs to leave. Palestine at that time was part of the Ottoman empire and a Palestinian national movement did not exist. It was only after the revolution of the Young Turks (1908) that such a movement came into being, and it was also at about this time that the Zionists first became aware that they were facing a major political problem. They still thought that, with tact, patience, and a little good-will on both sides, it could be solved. These early hopes, needless to say, were thwarted, and the question has been asked ever since whether the conflict was inevitable or whether it could have been prevented.

Aharon Cohen,[1] a member of a left-wing *kibbutz*, believes that it could; a protagonist of the idea of the bi-national state, he has devoted many years to the cause of Arab-Jewish rapprochement, maintaining that, left to themselves, Jews and Arabs would have been able to reach mutual understanding and that the Jewish national renaissance in Palestine might have integrated peaceably with the Arab national movement in the Middle East. Unfortunately, the imperial interests of Turkey and Britain, the villains in this story, were incompatible with such an understanding. Moreover, although some of the Arabs were misguided and obstinate, the Zionist leaders let slip many opportunities to reach agreement with their neighbors.

Mr. Cohen's massive book lists these missed opportunities; yet it leaves the reader unconvinced. The facts as given are not wrong, though they are regrettably incomplete, and the selection is often highly arbitrary. He rightly argues that the Zionist leaders should have given much greater attention to the Arab question, should have tried even harder to

---

[1] Aharon Cohen, *Israel and the Arab World* (London, 1970).

win friends among their neighbors. The catalog of sins of commission and omission is substantial: the new immigrants should have been more tactful, they should have studied the language and customs of the Arabs, more could have been done to see that the Arabs shared in the economic benefits of Jewish immigration. There were possibilities of influencing Arab public opinion, of explaining that the Jews did not intend to dominate the Arabs. Whether this would have dispelled Arab fears is more than doubtful. The trouble with Mr. Cohen is that, after all these years of studying Arab-Jewish relations, he seems not to have understood the basic character of the conflict; that, as in a Greek tragedy, each step follows the preceding one as its necessary consequence, with few surprises and no *peripeteia*. He is reluctant to acknowledge that politics is about power—a curious aberration in a Marxist.

The Arabs resented the Jews for the same reason that mass immigration has always and everywhere been resented. These tensions could perhaps have been overcome, but what disturbed the Arabs above all was the future plans of the Zionists, and they were no doubt correct in the essential point, namely, that the Jews wanted to establish in Palestine something more than a cultural center. However exemplary their behavior, the decisive question would have remained open: to whom was the country eventually to belong?

The Arabs sensed the logic of events more correctly than did the Zionists, who at the time were not thinking in terms of political power. Present-day Arab historians are mistaken in their conviction that Zionism was *ab initio* out to expel them, relentlessly striving to establish a Jewish state by force of arms. The early Zionists were liberals and pacifists, confused about their ultimate aim and lacking in political instinct. The first to perceive the contradiction was the sociologist Gumplowicz, who wrote in a letter to Herzl:

You want to found a state without bloodshed? Where did you
ever see that? Without violence and without guile, simply by
selling and buying shares?

Zionist leaders did not see it that way at all. Instead they
talked about the common ties between Jews and Arabs,
about the great Semitic brotherhood, about the cultural revival that would ensue if the two peoples joined forces. One
of the few dissidents at the time was Richard Lichtheim,
a young German Jew, who represented the Zionist executive
in Constantinople before the first World War. In a report
to his superiors he agreed that it was vital to make every
effort to win the good-will of the Arabs, but he had few
illusions about the outcome of such a policy:

> The Arabs are and will remain our natural opponents. They do
> not care a straw for the joint Semitic spirit. . . . I can only
> warn urgently against a historical or cultural chimera. . . . They
> want orderly government, just taxes, and political independence.
> The East of today aspires to marvels, none other than American
> machinery and Paris plumbing. Of course the Arabs want to
> preserve their nation and develop their culture. What they need
> for this, however, must come from Europe: money, organization,
> machinery. The Jew for them is a rival threatening their pre-
> dominance in Palestine.[2]

Lichtheim, of course, is one of the villains in Cohen's book
(a man "imbued with contempt for the alien peoples of the
Orient"); but he seems in retrospect to have understood certain aspects of Arab-Jewish relations more clearly than his
contemporaries.

Lichtheim's views were heretical; his friend Ruppin, the
chief representative of the Zionist executive in Palestine at
the time, certainly did not agree with this pessimistic appraisal and he continued to work for Arab-Jewish under-

[2] Quoted in: Yaakov Ro'i: "The Zionist attitude to the Arabs 1908–
1914," *Middle Eastern Studies,* April 1968.

standing. Twenty years later he sadly realized that his work had been in vain. "What we can get today from the Arabs we do not need," he noted in his diary. "What we need—we can't get. What the Arabs are willing to give us is at most minority rights as in Eastern Europe."

Mr. Cohen argues that there was a real chance of Arab-Jewish understanding in 1913–14, of which nothing came, largely because the Zionists were procrastinating and took a "frivolous view" of the Arab national movement. The contacts between the two peoples have in recent years been the subject of scholarly studies based on archival material, and the picture that emerges from them is very different from the one painted by Mr. Cohen. It is a little surprising that he has not incorporated these findings in the English edition of his book and revised it accordingly. (The original Hebrew version of *Israel and the Arab World* appeared in 1964.) Let us assume the unlikely, that an agreement of sorts had been reached in 1914: such an alliance would have made sense only if it had been directed against the Turks. This would not have remained a secret for long, and it is not difficult to imagine how the Turkish authorities would have reacted. Arab Palestine would have survived; whether the Jewish communities would, is much less certain. Above all, such a pact would not have outlasted the storms of war. Once Turkish rule was overthrown, the struggle for Palestine was bound to become a free-for-all and the Arab-Zionist conflict would have reappeared with a vengeance.

Many attempts were made by the Zionists during the 1920's and 30's to reopen the dialogue. The official Zionist line was parity; as the 17th Zionist Congress resolved, neither people should dominate or be dominated by the other. The principal idea guiding the *Brith Shalom* (Peace League), a group of Jewish intellectuals, was that Palestine should be a bi-national state in which Jews and Arabs should enjoy equal civil, political, and social rights, without distinction of majority and minority. The lack of response from the Arab side was total. "What is the point of reaching agreement among ourselves if there is no one on the other side?" Ruppin wrote after years of effort to Magnes, President of the Hebrew University and one of the chief advocates of Arab-Jewish understanding.

The members of *Brith Shalom* feared that without agreement between Jews and Arabs there would be perpetual strife, creating a situation in which it would be impossible to build a society such as Zionism had originally envisaged. Magnes remained an opponent of the idea of a Jewish state up to the very end. Even in 1946 he did not rule out the possibility that in a military conflict the Jews would defeat the Arabs, but this would not bring peace: However the frontier was drawn, irredenta would be created on either side of the border, and this would almost certainly lead to further war. Prophetic words, but what was the alternative?

The predictions of the peace-makers were correct, but they could not point to any practical solution. Only now, after more than forty years, some Palestinians have come to accept the idea of a bi-national state. This may be all to the good, but by now a Jewish state exists, and the Zionists regard the recent converts to bi-nationalism with some suspicion. Whereas in their English-language publications they propose the establishment of a multi-national, democratic, secular Palestinian state, the Arabic original usually refers to an Arab state in which only those Jews (and presumably their offspring) would be considered citizens who were residents before the beginning of the "Zionist invasion" in 1917. To come out unambiguously one way or another does, of course, present the Arabs with a delicate problem; a little double-talk in politics may on occasion do no harm. But on a decisive issue like this there must be clarity. The Palestini-

ans, after all, will have to live not with Mr. Christopher May-
hew and Mr. Anthony Nutting, but with the Israelis, and it
is the Israelis that they should persuade.

In the 1930's the Arab demand was for the total cessation of immigration. Palestine was an Arab country, the
argument ran, and the Jews had no historical connection or
claim. Nor were the Arabs willing to accept the 400,000
Jews already there. "If 70 million cultured and civilized
Germans could not tolerate 600,000 Jews, how could the
Arabs be expected to do so?" Auni Abdul Hadi, the leader
of the *Istiqlal*, asked the Palestine Royal Commission in
1937. When the Mufti of Jerusalem was asked by Lord
Peel on the same occasion: "Does his Eminence think that
this country can assimilate and digest the 400,000 Jews
now in the country?" the answer was a brief and categorical
"no."

These were the years of growing anti-Jewish persecution
in Central and Eastern Europe; there were six million Jews
doomed (in Weizmann's phrase) to be pent up where they
were not wanted, and for whom the world was divided into
places where they could not live and places which they
could not enter. England (which had given shelter without
any ill effects to 120,000 French Protestants after the revo-
cation of the edict of Nantes) had absorbed 19,000 by March
1939; the United States ("give me your tired, your poor, your
huddled masses") took 6,000 in 1935. As *The Times* put it in
its "Review for the year 1938": "The great surplus Jewish
population remained an acute problem."

Palestine thus became the only hope for millions of Jews,
and as the Arabs continued to insist on an end to immigration, the Zionist leaders despaired of ever reaching agreement with them. Even before Jabotinsky's party, the Revisionists had reached the conclusion that Zionism did not
make sense without a Jewish majority. Jabotinsky is Mr. Cohen's *bête noire*, but it is difficult to deny that from the

Jewish point of view his ideas had a certain logic and consistency. The Arabs love their country as much as we do, Jabotinsky wrote in the early twenties, "their decision to resist us is only natural." Every people would fight immigration and settlement by foreigners, however high-minded their motives. There was no "misunderstanding" between Jews and Arabs, as most other Zionists were asserting at the time, but a real conflict.

Jabotinsky did not argue that justice was all on one side: "Of course the Arabs have a strong case, of course they would prefer Palestine to be the fourth, fifth, or sixth independent Arab state," he told the Peel Commission. "But when the Arab claim is confronted with our Jewish demand to be saved, it is like the claims of appetite versus the claims of starvation." Justice, he said, had to be done according to the overmastering and terrible balance of need: the Jews were facing destruction, the Palestinian Arabs—minority status. Jabotinsky was considered an extremist by the standards of those days, and his enemies in the Zionist camp called him a "fascist." But the Arabs regarded him as an honest enemy, whereas those Zionists who advocated a bi-national state, or, like Weizmann, refused to discuss the ultimate aim of their movement, were mere tricksters.

Ben Gurion and other members of the Zionist executive continued to meet Arab leaders throughout the 1930's in an attempt to discover common ground and to open a dialogue. The Arabs listened politely but eventually told them that there was no use in discussing basic problems, for there were no misunderstandings between Arab and Jew; they understood the Jewish national movement only too well. There was a fundamental clash of interests which could not be resolved through talk. The Arab argument was irrefutable, and it is disingenuous to claim that the conflict could have been resolved by some diplomatic legerdemain.

Unlike some of the valuable academic studies which have

recently come out of Israel (such as Eliezer Be'eri's *Army Officers in Arab Politics and Society* and Uriel Dann's *Iraq under Qassem*), *Israel and the Arab World* is basically an ideological *apologia pro vita sua*—and a very sad one at that. As a historical work its value is strictly limited, but it does compel the reader to rethink the whole complex of Arab-Zionist relations. Zionist leaders were indeed short-sighted and narrow-minded, and they underrated the intensity of Arab national feeling; some of them refused to recognize that there was a Palestinian Arab people. But unfortunately there is every reason to believe that even if they had done all the things Mr. Cohen accuses them of failing to do, even if they had all behaved like Kalvarisky, there still would have been no peace with the Arabs.[3]

Left-wing Zionism has not been very lucky with its prognosis regarding the Arab question. Ber Borokhov, the founder of the Zionist-Marxist school, sincerely believed that the Palestinian Arabs would in due course be culturally assimilated, that, in other words, they would one day become Jews. Borokhov laid down the law from far-away Poltava; his Palestinian disciples were a little more knowledgeable. They envisaged a common Arab-Jewish struggle for the victory of revolutionary socialism in Palestine. Once an Arab proletariat emerged, then Left would be able to speak to Left. The Zionist Left was bitterly opposed to British imperialism, but did not explain how its mem-

[3] C. M. Kalvarisky, who died in 1942, is the main hero of Mr. Cohen's book. An agronomist who settled in Palestine in 1895 and a public figure with many Arab friends, he devoted his life to Arab-Jewish rapprochement. He was a man of great charm, boundless energy and goodwill, indefatigable in his quest for Arab-Jewish understanding, never discouraged by setbacks. That he was also known as a man who liberally distributed *baksheesh* among Arab politicians only enhanced his reputation. The author prefers not to mention this fact, an act of piety no doubt, but not the way to write history.

bers would ever have settled in Palestine and established their kibbutzim without the help of the British. When Arabs attacked their settlements, as in 1929 and again in 1936–39, they claimed that these attacks were not progressive but reactionary, because the Arab leadership was feudal and clerical in character; the British and the *effendis* were to blame. This was not even a half-truth, for the Arab national movement of 1936 certainly had broad popular support. The "feudal" leaders would never have succeeded in inciting a major revolt but for the deep resentment among the Arab masses. The Zionist Left thought that by organizing joint Arab-Jewish strikes they were laying the groundwork for an understanding between the two nations. Yet, ironically enough, willingness to cooperate with their Jewish colleagues (on a strictly limited professional basis, to be sure) was far more pronounced among Arab merchants and orange-grove owners than among the workers. The Zionist Left realized, as the *Brith Shalom* had done earlier, that without Arab-Zionist understanding there would be permanent warfare. But if it found from time to time a few interlocutors on the other side, these were usually not men of the Left; they were unfortunately quite unrepresentative of Arab public opinion, and if they had the courage to speak up, they virtually signed their own death warrant.

The Zionist Left was equally unsuccessful in enlisting the support of the world revolutionary movement dominated by the Communists and the National Liberation forces in Asia. The argument that the Jewish masses had to leave Europe under threat of physical extinction did not cut much ice with the Comintern. If Gandhi told Buber in 1938 that the German Jews should on no account leave Germany, but practice *satyagraha* (passive resistance), the Communists were telling the Jewish workers—if they had any message for them at all—to join the revolutionary struggle wherever they lived and wait for the world revolution which would eradicate anti-Semitism and solve the Jewish problem once and for all. The Soviet attitude has been a source of great agony to Mr. Cohen; how could a progressive régime with an otherwise almost unblemished record have such a blind spot, such a prejudice against the Jews, inducing Moscow "to behave in a way that has no parallel or precedent"?

The story of the Zionist Left is one of bitter ideological disappointment which reached its climax in the last decade. It is not difficult to see why, and there is nothing dishonorable about it. Men and women who grew up in the tradition of the old Left—of Marx and Lenin, of Rosa Luxemburg and Otto Bauer, of Syrkin and Borokhov—sincerely believed in internationalism, humanism, and democracy. They find it difficult to adjust to a new world in which they are dismissed as bankrupt reactionaries, in which individual terror and extreme nationalism, even racialism, is glorified as the wave of the future, in which fascist cut-throats can get away as progressive heroes provided they use the currently fashionable revolutionary verbiage.

There is, as we have said, something very sad about the story of Mr. Aharon Cohen and his friends, if only because they invested so much idealism and good-will in trying to bridge the abyss between the two peoples. Arab-Israeli relations have reached an impasse and it is more necessary than ever to find a way out. "It is essential to cut short the road of pain which is so totally devoid of fruitful purpose or historical justification," the author says towards the end of his book. Old misconceptions die hard. That the conflict serves no fruitful purpose goes without saying, but an ostrich-like denial of its historical roots does not contribute to a solution either. Jews and Arabs will have to find a way to co-exist in Palestine, for the only alternative is mutual extermination. It is not at all clear what forms such co-existence will take. For bi-nationalism it is probably too late, and historical experience in other parts of the world has not exactly been encouraging. If Flamands and Walloons, Greeks and Turks, Hindus and Muslims, French and English Canadians find it difficult to live together in one country, the prospects for Jewish-Arab cooperation after decades of bloodshed cannot be rated high.

Events in Jordan may offer a key to a solution, or at least to a new beginning. The Palestinians have realized that they cannot rely on the Arab governments, all pursuing their own political aims, which are by no means identical with those of the Palestinian cause. If they will at last accept that the state of Israel has come to stay, and if at the same time the Israelis make an offer which could be the basis for a new departure, some good may come of the Jordan civil war. Imagination will be needed as well as statesmanship. Mrs. Golda Meir will have to realize that the Palestinians have as much right as the Jews to a country of their own, and the Palestinians will have to accept at long last the fact that hijacking some more planes will lead them exactly nowhere, even if it is gravely called "Revolution Airstrip." The trouble with some Israelis is that they still hope to wake up one morning to find that the other side has disappeared. But this is unlikely to happen. Nor should the Arabs be misled by the Crusader parallel, if only because the Crusaders did not have the capacity to produce nuclear arms.

There are many "ifs" involved, and it is unfortunately quite probable that the present chance will pass unused. The alternative is more death and destruction, and ultimately the acceptance of a compromise, either because both sides will be too exhausted to fight on, or because a solution equally disliked by both sides will be imposed by a big power which will come to rule the Middle East. The fate of East Central Europe could be a useful object lesson. History, Schopenhauer once wrote, should have as its motto: *the same always different.*

BETWEEN NEW YORK
AND JERUSALEM

A RECENT INTERVIEW given by Saul Bellow in Israel
provoked sadness and disbelief on the part of the literary
editor of *Ma'ariv*. Our appraisal of the American-Jewish
scene must have been seriously mistaken, he wrote, or perhaps things have changed very quickly and this has escaped
our attention. Saul Bellow's account had been neither startling nor controversial. He mentioned the lack of interest in
things Jewish among many U.S. intellectuals; the wish not
to be identified as Jewish, but as American writers; the attraction of the establishment and the "New Left" counter-
establishment; and also the fact that among some of the
younger generation there was a tendency to attack Israel as
"a tool of American Imperialism." The reaction of the literary editor was one of genuine shock: We had always regarded Bernard Malamud and Leonard Bernstein, Professor
Sabine and Isaac Stern, and the tens of thousands of good
Jews coming enthusiastically to Israel as typical good-will
representatives of American Jewry. Had we been wrong?
Was it true that the American Jewish intelligentsia had been
afflicted by the same fatal disease that had taken such a
high toll of Central and West European Jewry—were they,
too, eaten by Jewish self-hatred, driven by the typical *galut*
complexes? Many European Jewish intellectuals had become
unhappy creatures incapable of living at peace with them-

selves, or with the world around them. It would be all the more tragic, the literary editor concluded, if this disease were to affect the American Jewish intelligentsia at the very time that Israel needed the help of the whole Jewish people more than ever before.

Reactions of this kind will strike American readers as more than a little naive. A whole decade of American Jewish life seems to have by-passed the Israelis, absorbed as they were in their own problems. One need not look far for the underlying reasons. Only few of those critical of Israel ever visited the country. The journals expressing the new moods and ideologies among sections of the Jewish intelligentsia are not widely read in Tel Aviv and Jerusalem. The new American culture heroes are virtually unknown there; the Hebrew translation of *Portnoy's Complaint* was the great non-event in Israeli book publishing in 1969. It is therefore not surprising that Israelis, confronted for the first time with ideological trends and moods currently fashionable in America, are more inclined to regard it as a disease of the mind or the soul than as a movement of great promise and consequence.

The lack of understanding is mutual. The Israeli reaction is bound to offend not a few American Jewish intellectuals and will be regarded as backward if not downright reactionary and chauvinistic. Did not Mr. James Reston of the *New York Times* report some time ago that Spiro T. Agnew would feel happy in Israel? Moreover, sympathies for Israel have diminished as the result of recent events in the Middle East. To some, the Israelis now appear as conquerors and annexationists; others find fault with Israeli society because it is no longer dominated by the Kibbutz and has moved towards becoming a second-hand America. The editor of a leading radical journal is said to have expressed surprise during a recent visit to Israel that students there have not yet protested against defense research undertaken by some of their professors;

still others have been antagonized by Israel's dependence on the United States, and feel embarrassed by the hostility towards Israel displayed by "progressive" and "third-world" forces. The uncertain future of the country has made it less attractive even for those intellectuals who have no *a priori* ideological reason for antagonism.

Israel and an influential section of the American-Jewish intelligentsia have been moving apart. Israelis have certainly not moved with the *Zeitgeist*. Provincial as they are, they will not readily understand why American Jews should be in the forefront in defending organizations which, whatever their other merits, are anti-semitic in character. The virtues of "Women's Liberation" and of Mao's little Red Book are not obvious to them; and they find the fashionable pseudo-radical language and underground style incomprehensible even if the individuals and groups concerned profess their commitment to Judaism and Israel. In so far as they are Marxists, the ideological training of the Israelis stopped with Lenin, Rosa Luxemburg, and Otto Bauer; they are reluctant to take the writings of Herbert Marcuse, let alone those of lesser figures, as guide-posts to a better future. The scenes that could be witnessed in 1969/70 around Harvard Square, or in front of the buildings of some other leading universities, remind an Israeli visitor not so much of Smolny in the Petrograd of 1917, but of Bedlam as Hogarth depicted it. If an Israeli Usbek (the hero of Montesquieu's *Lettres persanes*) were to report back today to his friend Ibben about the scenes he witnessed in New York or Cambridge, Mass., the speeches listened to, the books and newspapers he read, he would no doubt express his utter bewilderment at the new American-Jewish guilt-culture trying hard and not wholly unsuccessfully to overcome its strong life-instinct. Usbek might point in his letters to psychic epidemics not unknown in past ages, or he might refer to a disharmonious ego structure of a whole group of people splitting up under relatively low conditions of stress. An optimistic Usbek would be likely to predict that Reason was bound to prevail again in the not-too-distant future; but in his darker moments he might well conclude that the disease was widespread, the prospects for full recovery uncertain, and that even if all should go well, the curative process is bound to take a long time.

The first and most obvious fact which strikes one is the conspicuous part taken by Jews in what is loosely called the radical movement. There may be more in the opposite camp, but they are less vocal, less in the limelight, and so the public at large is much less aware of them. The Jewish part in the revolutionary sects of the 1930's was no doubt even larger, but the "movement" of the 30's was a marginal phenomenon; outside of a few cities, public opinion was hardly aware of it. The first difficulty which confronts the observer today is one of definition: "Radical" as well as "liberal" does not mean in America what it does elsewhere, and it does not apparently mean the same now as it did in the past. A radical may be a dedicated revolutionary, but the term may equally well refer to a wealthy book publisher or a prosperous dentist who, on the way from his bank to his yacht, mutters that the situation is "hopeless," that America is fast becoming "a fascist country," and decides to make a contribution to the Black Panthers. Today's Jewish radical resembles his predecessor of a bygone age in some respects but not in others. The Jewish revolutionary was by tradition a believer in reason and progress, and there was often a substantial dose of scepticism in his mental make-up. He had no use for beliefs or traditions which did not fit into a rigid rationalist framework, and his opponents usually criticized him for his "arid intellectualism." This is a charge which can hardly be made against the present-day radical; whatever his virtues, a surfeit of rationalism is not among them. He is

not a sceptic, but a true believer, though there is little optimism in his *Weltanschauung*. A sense of humor and of
irony, so typical of the earlier radical, is notably absent. He
belongs, in other words, to an altogether different species,
with far fewer of the qualities considered at one time "typically Jewish." The new radical shares with his predecessor
the belief that existing society is doomed because of its inequities, and that he is called upon to precipitate the radical
change which has become necessary.

The recent upsurge of radicalism has come as a surprise
to most observers. In an article published some twelve years
ago Professor J. L. Talmon noted that most Jews, disen-
chanted with the communist message, were turning away
from the extreme left; the majority of them were living in
countries unaffected by messianic ideologies, and so the
leftist trauma was dispelled by the cold, hard impact of
events. This was the age of "the end of ideology," but those
who trumpeted this message clearly undervalued both the
magnitude of the problems as yet unsolved, and the human
(and specifically Jewish) capacity for discontent. To tolerate
the *status quo*—to accept piece-meal change and reform—
would have gone against the intellectual grain, would have
meant that the intellectuals had given up their role as the
critics of society *par excellence*. There was, in retrospect, no
good reason to assume that such basic changes would occur
in our time. The intensity of the critique of society does not
necessarily depend on the objective situation. On the contrary, despair and *Kulturpessimismus* usually spread in ages
of affluence and boredom rather than at times of real crisis.
If the Kremlin god has failed for the radical intelligentsia
there still were Mao, Che Guevara, Ben Bella, Sukarno,
Nkrumah, Frantz Fanon, and other *dei minorium gentium*.
And even if there would have been no new gods at all to
worship, this would not have made the existing order any
more acceptable. In effect, the upsurge of Jewish radicalism

in present conditions must be more of a surprise to the believer in historical materialism than to the student of human nature and behaviour. It is clearly not in the material interest of the middle-class Jewish radical to rebel against the liberal order which has emancipated him socially, politically, and economically, and whose overthrow may put these achievements into dire question. If he is, nevertheless, drawn to negation and rebellion, he is obeying urges of a different kind, and of which he may be largely unaware. At this stage it is necessary to pause for a brief historical detour; while the past may have no ready-made lessons for the present, it does occasionally throw some light on it.

In the participation of Jews, or lapsed Jews, in left-wing politics during the last century, two basic facts stand out: the prominent part they took at one time or another, and their subsequent disappearance from positions of influence and command. Jews provided the ideological leadership in 19th-century Germany; according to some current definitions, not only was Moses Hess a Zionist, but Marx and Lasalle as well. Later on, Jews were among the leaders of the revolutionary wing (Trotsky, Rosa Luxemburg), the "centrists" (Russian Menshevism), and the "revisionists" (Bernstein, Leon Blum *et al*). The leadership of Austrian socialism ("Austro Marxism") and Hungarian communism was almost entirely Jewish, and there was not a single non-Jew in some East European delgations at the congresses of the Second International before the first World War. If they gradually faded out from the leadership of these movements that was not just the result of Stalinism and the impact of Nazi rule. To provide but one example: most of the founder members of the German Communist Party in 1918, including the most prominent among them, were of Jewish origin. Only thirteen years later there was not a single Jew among the hundreds of Communists chosen by the party to run for election to the *Reichstag*.

The attraction exerted by the Left on the Jews, especially of the first two or three generations after the European emancipation, is too obvious to need further elaboration. The French Revolution had bestowed freedom on them; the conservative parties of the Right, on the other hand, opposed the granting of full civic rights. The case of Ludwig Börne is typical of a whole generation of young Jews. This *Juif de Francfort*, as his passport described him, was the greatest publicist of his age. He left a graphic description of the position of the Jews in his home town:

> They enjoyed the loving care of the authorities. They were forbidden to leave their street on Sundays so that the drunks should not beat them up. They were not permitted to marry before the age of twenty-five, so that their children would be strong and healthy. On holidays they could leave their homes only at six in the evening, so that the great heat should not cause them any harm. The public gardens and promenades outside the city were closed to them and they had to walk in the fields—presumably to awaken their enthusiasm for agriculture. If a Jew crossed the street and a Christian citizen shouted, "Pay your respects, *Jud!*", the Jew had to remove his hat; of such measures the intention no doubt was to strengthen the feelings of love and respect between Christians and Jews.

Some young Jewish intellectuals dissociated themselves from the pariah people, once the walls of the ghetto had come down. It was only natural that others should join the democratic republican forces which promised to lead the Jews out of their degradation. Börne, who migrated to Paris, was attacked by his critics for his "anti-Germanism." He replied that he loved Germany more than France, because it was the unhappier country, but who could not admire France, the citadel of liberty?

The economic position of the Jews in Central and Western Europe improved rapidly during the first half of the nineteenth century, but their social and political standing rose much more slowly. It was therefore only natural that many Jewish intellectuals should be in the forefront of republicanism and the radical Left. For although their economic interests might have made them hostile to socialism, the radical Left stood for a world in which all men would be free and equal. Even if there was occasional anti-semitism on the Left, Jews could be politically active there, whereas by and large the parties favoring the established order, excluded them from their ranks and leadership. Neither the ardent idealism nor the burning ambitions of these generations of young Jewish intellectuals should be ignored.

It was at this time that the image of the "typical Jewish intellectual" emerged. When Ferdinand Lassalle discarded the old religious beliefs (as Hermann Oncken, his biographer has written), he turned to the other extreme, to atheism and materialism. He did away with his own past and had therefore no particular respect for tradition in the history of the Christian peoples. He felt deeply aggrieved and resentful: for centuries the Jews had been held in contempt, yet they had continued to regard themselves as the chosen people. The emancipation—for the time being only partial in character—provided for the first time a channel for the release of tension.

Georg Brandes (born Georg Morris Cohen), an earlier biographer of Lassalle, was the first to point to one of the most pronounced features of his hero and others of his contemporaries in radical politics—"*huzpah*"—which he defined as "presence of mind, impertinence, audacity, intrepidity, insolence." The Jews had been timid, forced into subservience; once they were emancipated and felt the impact of *Kultur*, some of the intellectuals among them were bound to gravitate towards extremism in politics.

It is usually forgotten that this affected only a minority. The majority of European Jewry west of Russia gravitated to radical and revolutionary parties only at certain, relatively short periods; in the wake of a widespread revolutionary wave, such as before and during the revolution of 1848, and on certain occasions later on. They gave their vote to the Social Democrats when there was no strong liberal party, or in the face of a right-wing anti-semitic danger. A great part of European Jewry was middle-class in character, and it supported middle-of-the-road liberal and democratic parties (left of center, but not too much so). They were patriotic and, to a large extent, conformist. They joined the revolutionary movement only if facing (as in Eastern Europe) a government which opposed assimilation and integration. The history of the Jews in the radical movement is, therefore, largely the history of sections of the Jewish intelligentsia; and it continued well after emancipation had been completed.

Various interpretations have been offered for the particular fascination exerted by the party of radical change on the Jewish intelligentsia. The anti-Semitic thesis of the "ferment of decomposition" is well-known. It has frequently been repeated in different variations in many countries: unable to establish a state of their own, reduced to a marginal, parasitic existence among the peoples, Jews developed over the centuries an overwhelming destructive urge. If they had no fatherland, why should anyone else have one? The more extravagant anti-Semites regarded this as part of a worldwide conspiracy to subvert the Aryan peoples and establish Jewish world rule. The more moderate regarded the trend towards radicalism as the unfortunate heritage of an unhappy people, understandable in the light of their past, but dangerous for law and order and the preservation of the traditions and values of the non-Jewish peoples.

Among Jews and within the radical parties, the subject

was not often discussed. Marx, Lassalle, and many other Jewish socialists completely dissociated themselves from Judaism and Jewry, for which they had nothing but contempt. Their choice of revolutionary socialism implied for them an absolute break with tradition. But was their decision in favor of the radical Left entirely unconnected with their Jewish origin and heritage? The anti-Semites (such as Bakunin) were not the only ones to think so. A Jewish contemporary of Marx wrote that radical politics were a new and different manifestation of religion.

> One goes to the democratic club, as the religious believer to his house of worship.

Deprived of its transcendental character, religion became politics, and the new secular messianism preached freedom and happiness on earth.[1]

Gustav Mayer, the distinguished historian of German socialism, saw the models of Marx's strict faith in the prophets of Israel. He compared Marx's analysis of early industrial capitalism, with its ravages and inequities, with Isaiah's dire predictions concerning King Ahas' rule. Leon Blum, writing at the turn of the century, pursued the theme of the Jewish disposition towards socialism further. They would play a great role, he predicted, in the destruction of the old order and the building of the new. Insofar as their race had a collective will, it was towards revolution. Their critical faculties were strongly developed; they would turn against any idea, any tradition which could not be justified by reason and did not conform with the facts. Their Messiah was the symbol of eternal justice. If Christ preached love, Jehovah stood for justice. The transformation of the social order according to reason and justice was, of course, scoialism.

[1] See Jacov Touri, *Die politischen Orientierungen der Juden in Deutschland* (Tuebingen 1966), p. 73 *et seq.*

Even the Jewish millionaires would not oppose socialism; they had learned by long experience not to resist great historical trends.[2]

Not many Marxists held these views. Most of them preferred to believe with Karl Kautsky that to the extent that Jews were affected by messianic aspirations, these were leading them towards reactionary Zionism. If socialism had a particular attraction for the Jews it was simply because they were city-dwellers, and as such had the specific qualities required for the progress of humanity. Though small in numbers, the Jew of Western Europe had produced Spinoza and Heine, Lassalle, Marx and other geniuses. But these spiritual giants became effective forces only after they had broken out of the fetters of Judaism. Their struggles were carried on outside its sphere, within the realm of modern culture, usually in complete and conscious opposition to Judaism. As Kautsky concluded: "The Jews have become an eminently revolutionary force, while Judaism has become a reactionary factor." Similar views have frequently been expressed since, most recently by the late Isaac Deutscher in an essay, "The Non-Jewish Jew," which, while it does not mention Kautsky by name, is essentially a paraphrase of Kautsky's pre-1914 thesis.

Jewish revolutionaries striving for the liberation of mankind obviously had no use for Jewish nationalism which most of them regarded as an atavistic throwback, a reassertion of the tribe over humanity, a retreat from internationalist ideals. It is only fair to add that such an approach was by no means specifically left-wing-revolutionary, but of the "bourgeois-assimilationist" heritage of the nineteenth century. The liberal argument against Zionism voiced among others by the "protest rabbis" and the Pittsburgh Platform was that divine providence had scattered the Jews in the

[2] "Nouvelles Conversations de Goethe avec Eckermann," in *L'oeuvre de Leon Blum* (Paris, 1945), Vol. I, pp. 264–66.

dispersion so that they might appear as witnesses all over the globe to the omnipotence of the idea of God and to promote the realization of the prophetic ideal. Jewish revolutionaries accepted this argument as Marx adapted Hegel: they stood it on the head. However, of all the arguments against Zionism (of which there are doubtless a great many) this has been traditionally the weakest. Some of the advocates of universalism believed sincerely in what it involved; but for many others it was simply a convenient pretext: "messianic mission" really stood for the fleshpots of Europe and America. A few revolutionaries may have genuinely thought that in view of their vulnerability and rootlessness the Jews were (as Deutscher put it) the natural protagonists of cosmopolitanism; the advocates not of nation-states but of internationalism. But most simply preferred the wider stage of European politics to the narrow confines of the Jewish community.

One explanation of the Jewish inclination towards left-wing radicalism several generations after Börne and Marx, is that it is an outgrowth of messianism. But this has been assailed on the grounds that those who embraced communism were not, after all, orthodox Jews; on the contrary, they did so, *inter alia,* in order to dissociate themselves from Judaism. This argument is not altogether convincing, for the immanent urge towards social justice, which for thousands of years found expression in the Jewish religion, could well manifest itself in a secular movement in the post-religious age.

But the basic assumption, namely that the Jewish religion is somehow more "leftist" in character than others, and that Jews are therefore predestined to join revolutionary parties, does not stand up to closer investigation. The Jewish religion is essentially conservative. The messianic impulse towards eternal peace and social justice has been as clearly

evident in other religions, and the strict emphasis put on
allegiance to the religious-national entity in Judaism does
not by any means predestine a practicing Jew to cosmopolitanism. Having been an oppressed minority and the victims
of persecution for so long, it may be only natural for them
to show sympathy for and give support to other unfortunate
groups even after their own emancipation had been nearly
completed. This would account for a political position left
of center, but to explain an attitude which negates the
values of the society which liberated them such an interpretation is clearly insufficient. The utopian, abstract element in revolutionary politics may have been a powerful
attraction. It is an undisputable fact that whereas Jews have
excelled in many fields of human endeavor, their contribution to politics has not on the whole been outstanding. Traditionally they have shown great ability on the level of abstract thought, but politics also involves instinct, common
sense, wisdom and foresight, and in this respect their record
has not been impressive. The inability to understand the
imponderables in the life of peoples has been a great handicap. It has led them time and again into belittling national
traditions, one of the main reasons for the failure of the
radical Left everywhere. Not one of the ideologists of revolutionary socialism foresaw that in all countries internationalism would give way in our time to national socialism,
a trend which has had unfortunate consequences for Jewish
socialists, for the Jewish communities, and for the world in
general.

Historically these Jewish weaknesses are not difficult to
explain. Not having had a state of their own for two thousand years, it would have been a near miracle had they
shown political instinct, the responsibility and maturity peculiar to a sovereign people with century-old traditions of
statecraft. (Which is not to imply that, with the establishment of the state of Israel, wisdom again reigns in Jeru-

salem.) Individual Jews have devised clever ideological constructions which had every quality but the essential ones. They were hopelessly wrong. Those who are appalled by some of the inanities of present-day radical thinkers on Judaism or Israel would do well to re-read the works of some writers of the 1930's. I refer to Otto Heller's *Downfall of Judaism* (*Untergang des Judentums*, 1931) in which the author demonstrated in great detail that in Eastern Europe, under communism, the Jewish question had been solved once and for all and that anti-semitism had lost its social foundation. "What is Jerusalem to the Jewish proletariat?" Heller asked. "Next year in Jerusalem! Next year in the Crimea! Next year in Birobidzhan! . . ."

William Zukerman's *The Jew in Revolt*, published in 1937, was an ambitious analysis of the Jewish situation and it makes now even stranger reading. He attacked in the sharpest terms the various schemes for promoting Jewish emigration from Nazi Germany, for the German Jews were deeply rooted in German soil and bound to their country by a thousand spiritual ties.

> It is a gross slander on the German Jews, whose love for their fatherland is proverbial [Zukerman wrote] to represent them as being ready to rush in panicky haste from it in a mass exodus at the first approach of misfortune . . . After all, the Jews are not the only victims of persecution in Germany today. Why not a wholesale exodus of German communists, socialists, pacifists, liberals and Catholics?

If the Jews were to adopt the exodus plan, this would mean the voluntary acceptance of the entire Nazi point of view, a complete capitulation to the racial theory of Hitlerism, playing the Nazi game "in a manner which Hitler himself probably never dared to hope that the Jews would do." Zukerman believed that the responsibility for the despicable plan for Jewish emigration from Germany fell squarely on the fanatical Zionist bourgeoisie:

The fact is that as much as the exodus plan has now become a popular solution for the Jewish problem, it is due more to a number of Zionist zealots and to a few big Jewish financiers than to the fascists. Of all the paradoxes of our times, this one will probably go down into history as the most curious of all.

But he had no doubt that the Zionist project for the mass emigration of Jews from Germany would fail:

In spite of the brutal Nazi persecution, the bulk of German Jewry will remain in Germany and they will be there long after Hitler is gone . . . They bear the cross of their suffering witᵗ dignity and fortitude as behoves an ancient people who has seen martyrdom and knows that tyranny, no matter how powerful temporarily, cannot forever turn back the wheels of history.

It sounds altogether incredible, but it was not just a case of one outrageously mistaken appraisal of the Jewish and German situation. Zukerman's thesis was based on a careful ideological analysis. The Soviet Union had solved the Jewish question; "economically, politically and psychologically," Zukerman wrote, an end had been put to the scourge of Jew hatred. "The very meaning of the word anti-Semitism is rapidly forgotten. It has certainly evolved a perfect solution of the Jewish problem." The shining example of the Soviet Union provided a lesson to be learned. The golden age of liberalism was at an end; there was only one road open to the Jew, whether he approved of everything going on in the Soviet Union or not: "As a Jew he can do nothing but follow the road shown by the Soviet Union for the solution of the Jewish problem." The Jew is the "faithful, old, brass-buttoned lackey kicked by fascism down the steps of the palace of capitalism which he has done so much to erect and over which he has watched devotedly for so many years." But adherence to the revolutionary socialist movement would atone for everything, Zukerman concluded with something approaching Fanonian pathos. Spiritually it would

save the Jews for the world. By revolting against the existing order they were revolting also against themselves—"and
there is no greater, and morally more cleansing, revolt than
this one. . . ."

The author was not, I believe, a member of the Communist party. His views were shared at the time, if in somewhat more moderate form, by many well-meaning and apparently sane people; they did not reflect the temporary
aberration of an individual or a small group. And this raises
the disturbing question: does the instinct for survival which
preserved the Jewish people during the long ages of persecution still exist?

The question of survival is not an issue likely to perturb
the Jewish radical concerned with world revolution to the
higher interest of which the concerns of individual nations
have to be subordinated. Seen from this vantage point, the
Jewish problem is certainly not the most important: Jews are
expendable; other nations have come and gone in history.
Trotsky relates in his autobiography that, from his earliest
childhood, nationalist passions and prejudices were incomprehensible to him, producing in him a feeling of loathing
and moral nausea. Rose Luxemburg wrote Mathilde Wurm
in 1917:

> Why do you come with your special Jewish sorrows? I feel just
> as sorry for the wretched Indian victim in Putamayo, the Negroes
> in Africa . . . I cannot find a special corner in my heart for the
> ghetto.

It was, in a way, an understatement, for, to judge from her
writings and speeches, she actually cared less for the Jewish
victims of persecution than for the victims of colonial oppression. It is difficult to imagine that Lenin, an internationalist second to none, would have referred with such dismay to "special Russian sorrows."

At this point Zionists usually underscore the phenomenon of Jewish self-hatred, well known even before Theodor Lessing published his study of the subject in the 1920s. But self-hatred is a more complex phenomenon than the critics of assimilationism maintain. *"Le moi est haïssable,"* Pascal wrote. Self-hatred is found not only among Jews, but among underprivileged groups in general, and among Jews it has been (and is) by no means limited to radicals. On the contrary, it is easier to understand an Otto Weininger cursing the disgrace and shame, the metaphysical guilt of being a Jew, for he and self-hating Jews like him wanted to be completely assimilated to the host nation. For an internationalist revolutionary the issue of being totally accepted is not a very important one. The key to the specific Jewish propensity towards guilt feelings ("it is our fault that we are hated") has been seen by some to lie in "religious tradition." Since the Jewish religion does not put more emphasis on individual and collective guilt than Christianity, this explanation remains unconvincing. Feelings of inferiority would seem to be of greater relevance in this context than feelings of guilt; but the importance of the issue as it concerns Jewish radicals today should not be exaggerated. It plays a lesser role now than two generations ago in Europe, and historical parallels are likely to be misleading.

The young Jewish radical who supports, at least in theory, Fatah against Israel *("a steady patriot of the world alone, the friend of every country but his own")* is not as a rule motivated by self-hatred. To be Jewish is for him largely meaningless; he does not feel himself part of the community into which he was accidentally born. He is not a traitor: one cannot betray what one does not believe in and what one feels no allegiance to. His rejection of Jewish solidarity is in the tradition of Rosa Luxemburg, but also of that Anglo-Jewish Cabinet minister who wrote in 1917 that the suffering of Russian Jewry was not a cause of special concern to him. The young radical does not violently reject his Jewishness; he is simply not particularly interested. The process of the disintegration of the diaspora Jewry was retarded by Hitler and the holocaust but, as we now realize, not for very long. There is admittedly a special cutting edge to the rejection of Judaism and Zionism by the young Jewish radical of our time. The old Left did not feel any special solidarity with the Jewish people either, but having lived through the greatest catastrophe in Jewish history, they felt it would be unbecoming to dissociate themselves publicly from this community. For the young Jewish radical, on the other hand, Jewish history begins in 1960 or thereabouts, and he has therefore no such inhibitions. In some cases there may be the desire to shock the older generation by outrageous statements ("the death camps were set up and run by the Zionists in cooperation with the Gestapo," or "the destruction of Israel would benefit mankind"). But it is doubtful whether this applies in many cases; recent social studies have shown that most young radicals grew up in left-wing homes, without any strong ties to the Jewish community. They did not have to rebel against tradition.

The political and social position of American Jewry has for a variety of historical reasons been less vulnerable than that of European Jewry, but the general crisis affecting America at the present time has dangerous implications for its Jewish citizens. This would be the case even if Messrs. Jerry Rubin, Abby Hoffman, and Mark Rudd, the Jewish Weathermen and their supporters had never appeared on the scene. The fact that Jews have been prominently associated with declarations and actions abhorred by the majority of Americans (such as desecrating national symbols, disparaging and deriding deeply cherished traditions and values), the danger implicit in the argument that the Vietnam war was lost in New York, not in Southeast Asia—these and other aspects of the present crisis provide fuel for a reaction which will be not just anti-Left or anti-intellectual, but anti-Semitic. No great demagogic skill will be needed to single out the Jews as the main culprits for the evils which have befallen America in recent times. If this happens, the New Left will enter history, ironically enough, as a movement which, albeit in an indirect way, delayed the full integration of American Jewry, kindled the dimly shining candle of Jewish consciousness, and (for all one knows) promoted a substantial increase in *aliya* to Israel. This would be what Hegel called the cunning of reason. It is a different question whether these incidental benefits would be worth the price that may have to be paid.

Until fairly recently, most Israelis, as we noted, have been unaware of internal developments in the United States and among American Jewry. Only during the last year or so have terms like *SDS, Yippies, Weathermen*, become known outside a small circle of *cognoscenti*. Previously, members of the Israeli establishment mainly met official figures in New York and Washington, and there was nothing particularly disquieting in what they heard from them. They would probably have disbelieved the truth anyway, for to the generation of Israelis who grew up on Berl Katznelson and shared his contempt for Jews willing to fight the social and national struggle of every people but their own, the "movement" must have appeared totally incomprehensible.

Some of the younger ones have been more receptive. Like most small countries, Israel faces the danger of cultural provincialism. There is the fear of being cut off from the main centers of world culture, the desire not to miss a single intellectual fad and fashion. Within the limits set by climate and good sense, the young generation, not surprisingly, are prepared to follow the sartorial fashions of America and

Western Europe. They have adopted the Beatles, the Rolling Stones, and other exponents and features of the youth sub-culture. Drugs have made certain inroads, as have the movies expressing the new spiritual climate; students have been restless, demanding (quite rightly) a greater say in running the universities. But for the more extreme cultural and political antics of American-Jewish radicalism, Israel does not provide promising soil. There is a small New Left *(Smol Israeli Hadash = Siah)*, and, a more extreme, a tiny but vociferous quasi-Trotskyite movement *(Mazpen-Compass)*. Many of the members of *Mazpen* have migrated to Europe and the United States—not because of police chicanery and persecution, but for sound ideological reasons. The position of a member of *Mazpen* is not unlike that of a Jewish communist in Mandatory Palestine in the 1920's or 30's: once he reached the conclusion that Jewish Palestine was *ab initio* imperialist and counter-revolutionary, a "colonialist society," that it could not be transformed but must be destroyed, the only logical, sensible, and honest conclusion was to emigrate. For the chances of integrating himself within the Arab national movement, however close he felt to it politically, were minimal.

But, on the whole, these political and cultural influences do not go very deep, and the impact of the marginal groups is very limited. There is a world of difference between the mood of the American Jewish radical intelligentsia and the state of mind of Israel. It is one thing to engage in the systematic disparagement of America, to predict its further decline and eventual downfall, or at the very least to insist on a radical reorientation in the scale of national priorities. To say this, to be politically active on these lines, does not involve any mortal danger, nor does it usually affect one's pay-check. Israel, on the other hand, is a beleaguered fortress; its priorities are dictated by its enemies. Any action likely to weaken defense is not merely unpatriotic

in the abstract sense, but endangers the very existence
of the state and the safety of its citizens. The danger to
its existence is immediate and total—whereas for America
the question is whether or not to withdraw an army from
a far-away country. Even if those who contend that America should drastically cut its defense effort and cease
playing a leading role in world affairs should succeed in
pressing home their demands, this would not constitute an
immediate physical danger to them and their families. For
if you live in Newton or Scarsdale, Russia is far away, and
neither Canada nor Mexico, nor Cuba is likely to invade
Lexington and Great Neck. From Maoz Haim and Metulla
the world looks different. Even if Israel had more options
and were not fighting for physical survival, its whole attitude would probably still be different. Like all new countries, it is intensely patriotic, immensely proud of its achievements. The children in the school opposite my Jerusalem
apartment last winter seemed to be singing patriotic songs
(Anu ohavim otech moledet) almost all day long. Where else
could this have happened?

These and other manifestations of Israeli patriotism, and
the conspicuous lack of guilt feelings, are no doubt strange
and more than somewhat offensive in American radical eyes.
The Israeli set of values, still strongly imbued with the pioneering spirit of several generations of halutzim, must seem
as outdated and square as the tradition of the frontier in
American history. The American radical derides the values
of bourgeois society, appropriate to an age of scarcity but
irrelevant in the contemporary world. Leaving aside the
question how much these values owe to bourgeois society
or to scarcity, there is the simple fact that Israel, like most
of the world, has by no means moved beyond scarcity. The
American radical critique is based on its denunciation of
capitalist culture—but Israeli culture was never capitalist.

For the Israeli, the American Jewish radical is the Galut

Jew *par excellence,* immature, irresponsible, tormenting himself and others with sundry imaginary problems, full of
verbal revolutionism, but no great believer in the unity of
theory and practice. If he comes to Israel, he will join a
kibbutz full of enthusiasm; but the adjustment to a labor
discipline will not be easy for him. He will have to face
the fact that even in a revolutionary society cows have to be
milked in the early hours of the morning and that all kinds
of unpleasant jobs have to be done conscientiously and on
time. It will be no great surprise to the old settlers if our
revolutionary should leave after a few months on the ground
that a kibbutz is "not radical enough," and return to America, either to join the less demanding and more glamorous
struggle for liberation as practiced there or (more likely) to
be absorbed by the soft bourgeois society he scorned. For
the young Israeli his American contemporary, restless, neu-
rotic, always seeking something new, is basically unserious,
and he will be little inclined to take his ideological critique
earnestly.

This refers above all to the criticism regarding Israeli's
inability to come to terms with its Arab neighbors. Everyone wants peace, but the advice the Israelis receive from
their American well-wishers is not usually very helpful. A
bi-national state may be a wonderful concept, but where
has it ever worked? The Israelis are told that their country
should stop being "a nationalist-racialist state," become socialist and truly democratic and that on this basis a rapprochement with the Arabs will be possible. But even if
the basic assumption is accepted, namely that states will get
along better if they become more alike (which seems to me
highly doubtful), the opposite course of action would seem
to be indicated. To become more like the revolutionary Arab
countries Israel would have to introduce a military dictatorship with a one-party system, in which civil liberties are no
longer respected, which ideologically is an admixture of

Islamic, Communist, and Fascist elements. Such a régime would be similar to that in Egypt, Syria, and Iraq, and perhaps on this basis a common language with the Arabs could be found. I doubt it. In any case, who would want to live in such a state? What good is it to argue, as Noam Chomsky does, that it will be possible to find a solution to the conflict once nationalism is overcome, if even the extreme left-wing of the "Arab liberation movement" is intensely and exclusively nationalist in character, if internationalist slogans are advanced by only a few individuals of whom, moreover, it cannot even be taken for granted that they really mean what they say? "Arab-Jewish working-class solidarity" usually figures prominently in these peace plans, but the lesson of the past is not encouraging. Property-owners on the two sides of the fence (such as owners of orange groves) have, on the whole, found it easier to collaborate than have Arab and Jewish workers.

The Israelis note the genuine concern behind such advice, but they will as a rule reject it out of hand, not just because they consider it totally removed from realities, but mainly because these well-wishers usually have no wish to link their own fate with that of the state of Israel. Some Israelis have by now reached the conclusion that they may be better off without a certain type of immigrant who, affected by the "American disease," has only negative criticism to offer and who is moreover temperamentally ill-suited to life in a country which in most respects is still much harsher than in the United States.

The estrangement between Israel and sections of American Jewry is not a problem to be dismissed lightly. Once Russian Jewry were the main bulwark of Zionism, and the big prosperous Jewish communities of Europe; but since the end of the second World War, Zionism and the state of Israel are more dependent than ever on American Jewry.

While American Jewry has given invaluable political and financial help to Zionism and Israel, only a few American Jews have in fact settled in Israel, much to the disappointment of the Israeli leaders, who were well aware that this was what ultimately counted.[3] But how realistic was the assumption that sizable numbers of American Jews would immigrate? Zionists have always believed in the rejection of the diaspora; Israeli school-children are taught to this day that life in the diaspora is both physically unsafe and intolerable for proud, self-respecting Jews, and that sooner or later the "ingathering of the exiles" is going to take place. On a higher level of sophistication, it is argued that the American crisis (black anti-semitism, the breakdown of liberal pluralism, and other social processes) will make assimilation more difficult, if not impossible, that there will be a new national revival among American Jewry affecting hundreds of thousands, if not millions, and leading them towards mass emigration. At the same time, the hope has been expressed that even the New Left Jew will sooner or later have to confront the question of his identity and that, as a result, he will realize that Israel is the only place where he can live as a human being, free of the pressures and distortions of the diaspora.

It is not easy for me to understand on what these assumptions are based. There is a Jewish problem in America, and it will probably be aggravated in the years to come, partly as the result of the general American crisis, partly because of the New Left and other social and political trends. But it may be useful to recall that there was a far more acute Jewish problem in Central Europe well before Hitler, and

[3] I once had a long interview with David Ben Gurion, in the course of which I asked him who in his opinion was the greatest American-Jewish leader.

"Magnes," he said without hesitation, much to my surprise.

"But you quarrelled with him constantly."

"Yes—but he was the only one who settled in Palestine."

that it did not result in mass immigration. Zionism has never quite accepted the fact that a few idealists apart, people leave their native lands only as a result of extreme economic or political pressure, such as is unlikely to arise in America. Even if Jews should be squeezed out of certain professions, there will be openings elsewhere; even if their political influence should decrease, they will not be defenseless—unless a catastrophe were to occur which would jeopardize the prosperity and security of America, and not only its Jewish inhabitants.

Zionist ideologists, even the most far-sighted and perspicacious among them, have usually been reluctant to accept the differences between the position of American and European Jewry. When in 1928 M. Reisen wrote (in *Yisrael be Amerika,*) "Don't shout '*Galut, Galut*' in a country in which there is no *Galut*—only that persisting in the mentality of individual Jews," Zionists countered with dire predictions about the end of American prosperity and its political repercussions on American Jewry. Typical of this approach was a fascinating long essay by Chaim Arlosoroff published in *Hatekufah* in 1929 (entitled, incidentally, "New York ve Yerushalayim"). It contained many brilliant observations, but his basic theory was mistaken; it was that American Jewry, not being rooted in primary production, but overrepresented in various marginal professions, was bound to be hit severely by a crisis and by the trend toward concentration and bureaucratization in the American economy (such as the squeezing out of small shopkeepers by the department stores). Having been told in Cleveland that among a hundred thousand Polish-Americans there were only 30 lawyers, and among the same number of Jews 1900 lawyers, Arlosoroff wrote: "When I heard this, I said that if a young Jewish lawyer in Vienna named Herzl had not already published the *Judenstaat,* it would have been written thirty years later by one of his colleagues in Cleveland. . . ." Arlosoroff noted that at the time very few Jews held a prominent place in American cultural life, in the press and in literature, but he also pointed to the growing number of young Jews streaming into these professions. Sooner or later, he predicted, there would be voices complaining about the "complete Judaization of the press and literature of the country. . . ."

Arlosoroff erred in attributing paramount importance to the lop-sided Jewish social structure; he failed to see that in the country as a whole the numbers employed in agriculture and mining were in fact declining, whereas science and technology, no less productive branches of the national economy, which were to provide work for many Jews, were expanding rapidly. Arlosoroff was no Marxist, but in his analysis of the prospects of American Jewry he attributed great significance to economic factors, which, he thought, would make the Zionist solution inevitable. Events in Germany a few years later showed that anti-semitism in its most rampant form came to the fore not as the consequence of economic and social competition but as the result of political developments which had their own momentum.

There has been in Israel much talk of late about the necessity of a "dialogue" with the New Left. Nothing should be done to dampen the enthusiasm of those eager to try their luck, but no one familiar with the problem will feel very sanguine about the outcome. Whoever believes that Mao or Fanon or Guevara are the great political thinkers of the century, that LeRoi Jones is a paragon of socialist humanism, and that the American political system is worse than Nazism, is bound to denounce Israel as a puppet of American imperialism. The thought of "the movement" has a certain logic and consistency; whoever accepts all the other basic premises cannot stop short where Israel is concerned.

Israelis have heard of various Jewish radical groups in the United States and most of them should not be bracketed with the anti-Jewish, anti-Israeli sections of the "movement." While opposed to the Jewish establishment, these groups have a deep commitment to their own Jewishness; some of them claim that they "identify strongly with Israel although not necessarily with her policies." Their doctrines betray strange and contradictory ideological influences. Some of its spokesmen like Mr. Waskow of Washington advocate a return to the ideas of the *Bund* as he understands them (minus Yiddish and the other essential planks of that organization), while others claim to have rediscovered Ber Borokhov.[4] The *Bund* played an important role in educating the Jewish masses of Eastern Europe and Borokhov was a man of considerable intellect and erudition, even though he was not among the greatest political prophets. He predicted, for example, that the Palestinian Arabs would be absorbed by the Jews as the result of a process of cultural assimilation. But whatever the past merits of the *Bund* and Borokhov—and many of their views were mistaken even sixty years ago—their present relevance for American Jewry is roughly comparable to that of the dispute about the use of amulets between Rabbis Emden and Eibeschütz in the 18th century. In other words, it is difficult to take them at all seriously.

Israelis will be as distrustful of the professed commitment of some Jewish radicals to Israel as these radicals are of the generation of their parents, and for very similar reasons: the discrepancy between their words and their actions. The radicals accuse the Jewish establishment of hypocrisy. But what does a "strong identification with Israel" mean unless it in-

---

[4] Some sixty years ago Borokhov attempted to find a Marxist-Zionist synthesis. He believed that Palestine would be built as the result of "stychic" forces, *i.e.* objective economic trends which would drive both Jewish capital and the Jewish proletariat towards a Zionist solution.

volves settling in Israel? To get 15 credits for living six months on a kibbutz is not quite what was understood by the *halutzim* as "*hagshama azmit*" in the olden days. If the committed radicals disapprove of Israeli policies, the place to do so, after all, is not at MIT or Berkeley. Admirers of Lenin, some radicals obviously do not subscribe to his ideas about the unity of theory and practice, certainly not in respect to Israel. They find it as difficult to defend their position against the anti-Israeli New Left as Borokhov's followers did against the Russian Marxists, and not just because the Bolsheviks were the stronger party. Their commitment to a "critical radical political ideology" involves opposition to American foreign policy, not only in Vietnam, but opposition *tout court*. Some want to see America defeated in the global contest; others simply advocate a drastic reduction in defense spending, a retreat from world politics for a decade or two, until the main domestic problems are solved.

At this point commitment to the basic tenets of the New Left clashes with the interests of the survival of Israel; and no ideological legerdemain can dispose of the dilemma. Even Jean-Paul Sartre conceded that it was absurd to regard Israel as a "spearhead of American imperialism." But given the constant geo-political factors and Soviet ambitions in the Middle East, the survival of Israel depends on the global balance between the two super-powers. If this balance is radically upset, if America is seriously weakened, the Soviet Union will emerge as the predominant power in the Middle East. Such a development would have, to put it cautiously, grave consequences for the independence and the very survival of the state of Israel. This is the basic political fact in Middle East politics; and for the Jewish radical there is no way out of this dilemma. Any action which weakens the United States is bound to upset the balance of power, strengthen the Soviet Union and jeopardize the existence of Israel. The anti-Israeli New Left is, of course, quite correct in its criticism of its inconsistent pro-Israeli comrades. Once one accepts the basic assumption that the American establishment is totally evil, that its foreign policy is simply a function of its imperialist, anti-revolutionary character, that the defeat of America is in the interest of world revolution, one cannot logically make an exception of American policy in the Middle East.

Some Israeli students of American Jewish radicalism have argued that every ideological belief has its Achilles heel and that

> one well-placed blow may prove fatal to the whole structure, leaving the believer bereft of his former beliefs with their built-in screening mechanisms . . . The Achilles heel of the Jew on the Left is the problem of his identity . . . Only Zionism has created the reality which the left-wing aspires to. Only Zionism has made it possible for a Jew to exist without the fact of his Jewishness.[5]

Hence the need to persuade the Jew on the New Left that Israel is the only place in the world where Jews can lead a fully human existence.

The argument is quite familiar. Seventy years ago Max Nordau wrote about the young Jewish intellectuals who had become "cripples within and counterfeit persons without, ridiculous and hateful like everything unreal, to all men of high standards, new Marannos who had no longer a faith to sustain them." But America is not Europe, and the New Leftist has a faith to sustain him; his sensitivity about his Jewish origin should not be over-rated. But perhaps he will eventually realize by bitter experience that he is not wanted in the struggle for the liberation of other peoples and that by pushing himself into positions of command and authority, he does more harm than good. Again, such warnings are not novel either.

[5] Zvi Lamm, "The New Left and Jewish Identity," *Dispersion and Unity, no. 10* (1970), pp. 64–5.

Max Nordau, well before the first World War, in a remarkably prophetic speech apostrophizing some of the left-
wing critics of Zionism, predicted that Socialism would
bring them the same disappointment as did the Reforma-
tion, the Enlightenment, and the movement for political
Emancipation:

> If we should live to see that socialist theory becomes practice,
> you'll be surprised to meet again in the new order that old
> acquaintance, anti-semitism. And it won't help at all that Marx
> and Lassalle were Jews. . . . The founder of Christianity was a
> Jew too, but to the best of my knowledge Christendom does not
> think it owes a debt of gratitude to the Jews. I do not doubt that
> the ideologists of socialism will always remain faithful to their
> doctrine, that they will never become racialists. But they will
> have to take realities into account. The anti-semitism of the
> masses will dictate their policy.

Appeals like Nordau's have only rarely impressed Jewish
revolutionaries, who always pooh-poohed the idea that anti-
Semitism was "eternal" (which, to be sure, Herzl and Nordau
never claimed), and that it constituted a serious handicap
in the struggle for social liberation.

The Zionist conception of the deep-seated vulnerability
of the Jewish radical devoting his life to the liberation struggle of other nations, but eventually returning to his own
fold (the notion of "the return of the prodigal"), was exaggerated even in Nordau's day. It is, I fear, now very much
out of date. Sixty years ago, a young East European Jewish
intellectual could drift from Bolshevism or Menshevism to
Bundism or *Sejmism* or Zionism (or vice-versa) without great
difficulty; he was only half a generation removed—if that—
from Jewish tradition. The Jewish radical of the 1970's is no
longer part of that tradition, and I doubt whether the situation would change if Jewish education were to look in the future (as has been suggested) to Leon Trotsky, Isaac Deutscher, and Karl Marx "to provide a meaningful study of the

culture of Judaism, of the political genius of that tradition."[6]

The hope that anti-Jewish radicals of this generation will again become "good Jews" is a slender one, comparable perhaps to the hope of a psychoanalyst for the recovery of a patient with a weak ego structure or a deficient intellect. Individuals may rediscover their Jewish identity and consciousness, but a catastrophe of the magnitude of Nazism would be needed to effect a mass reconversion of people so far removed from Judaism. Such a disaster is not very likely. Jewish radicalism in America is, of course, a form of assimilation, part of a much wider historical process. The assumption shared by most (not all) Zionist thinkers that assimilation is not possible has been proved correct in some countries, but not in others. Assimilation in the Western world was retarded by the holocaust, which strengthened Jewish consciousness, created a favorable atmosphere for Zionism among Jews and non-Jews, and made the creation of the state of Israel possible. But the shock has passed. A new generation of Jews and non-Jews has grown up which no longer feels a special obligation and commitment. Even many radicals who express concern for Israel are increasingly preoccupied with American domestic policies. This is a natural development, and similar processes have taken place in the past. In Russia, before the first World War, left-wing Zionist groups became more and more involved in Russian revolutionary politics, and this despite the fact that there was far less freedom of action for a Jew in the Czarist empire. Eventually what was then called *"Gegenwartsarbeit"* became their paramount concern, and most of them ceased to be Zionists.

It can be predicted with reasonable certainty that specifically Jewish preoccupations will gradually be relegated to a less and less important place in the scale of priorities of many wavering radicals. They already figure lower than

[6] J. Brandow in *Jewish Spectator* (New York), June 1970.

Cambodia, Pollution, Women's Liberation, and the Race Question, and will no doubt decline even further. This may be all to the good, for the present stance of the Jewish radical is a halfway house, morally and intellectually inconsistent, and thus untenable in the long run. They will have to take a decision: "Committed Jews" who devote almost all their time and energies to act as catalysts for what they regard as "progress" in a Gentile society will find that their Jewish commitment becomes more and more meaningless and even irrelevant (to use the currently fashionable term). Israel will be an embarrassment to them, and they will want to wash their hands of it. The interests of world revolution, after all, override those of a small country in the Middle East which, if the rhetoric of its leaders is taken as the criterion (*i.e.* the frequency of the use of terms such as "revolution," "progressive," "anti-imperialist," "exploitation") must be less close to their hearts and minds than Egypt, or Syria, or Iraq.

Yet, with all this, the outlook for relations between Israel and American Jewry is probably brighter than would appear from this analysis. I have been concerned here with the activities of a relatively small, if highly vocal section of American Jewry. While Jewish Maoists support *Al Fatah* and the DFLP, the number of American immigrants to Israel is increasing from year to year. The great majority of American Jews, those in between the champions of "liberation" and the others who have opted for settlement in Israel, are full of apprehension; and so are the Israelis, who know to what extent their fate depends on the future of American Jewry. The four decades which have passed since Arlosoroff wrote "New York and Jerusalem" have witnessed an immense advance of American Jewry in almost every field; yet at the end of the period the problems besetting them, though different in character, are at least as formidable as those described in 1929.

THE JEWISH
QUESTION TODAY

IN AN ESSAY written in 1966 and recently republished, Professor J. L. Talmon noted in passing that the term "Jewish Question" is never mentioned these days.* But if the term has gone out of fashion the thing itself has not; the fate of Jews, as individuals and in their communities, continues to feature prominently in the world news. The fateful terminology, to be sure, is subject to change. According to a resolution of the Central Committee of the Czechoslovak Communist Party (10 December 1970), "Czech Zionists" made the Soviet intervention necessary in 1968. But Krigel, Loebl, Goldstueker, Pelikan and the other villains are no more Zionists than are Brezhnev and Kosygin. The Black Panthers have attacked Abby Hoffman and Jerry Rubin as "Zionists," though their attitude to the state of Israel does not essentially differ from that of Eldridge Cleaver. In so far as the Jews are concerned, some of their enemies clearly

---

* Talmon's collection of essays on recent Jewish history, *Israel among the Nations* (Weidenfeld & Nicolson, London 1970) is warmly recommended. The other two books to which passing reference is made in this article deserve equally high praise: Michael R. Marrus, *The Politics of Assimilation: A Study of the French Jewish Community at the time of the Dreyfus Affair* (Oxford University Press, 1971) and Henry L. Feingold, *The Politics of Rescue: The Roosevelt Administration and the Holocaust, 1938–1945* (Rutgers University Press, New Brunswick, 1970). They are scholarly in the best sense, judicious, well written, and very welcome additions to the sadly neglected field of modern Jewish historiography.

prefer to call a spade not a spade but an agricultural imple-
ment. Anti-Semitism is again becoming darkly fashionable
in some circles, but one still has to observe certain conventions and rules in this game.

It is not only in Prague and among the Black Panthers
that Jews have had a bad press. Fifty years ago the *Manchester Guardian* was second to none as an eloquent de-
fender of the Jews against their detractors and persecutors.
A comparison between the coverage of the recent trials of
Burgos and Leningrad shows that attitudes have changed.
("Death Penalty for Basques Shocks World" on the one
hand, and "Israel Moulds Policy of Fury at Russia" on the
other.) But it would be unfair to single out one particular
newspaper in order to demonstrate a general trend; the
liberal press in West Germany *(Der Spiegel, Die Zeit)* and in
France have not reacted very differently. More than a quarter of a century has passed since the greatest catastrophe in
Jewish history. During that period the Jews enjoyed a great
deal of sympathy. There was uneasiness in the West, occasionally even guilt feelings about the fate of millions of
Jews under Hitler. In the menacing years when Central
European Jews still had the chance to emigrate they found
the gates of other countries locked. The stand taken by the
governments concerned was that even if the Jews were their
brethren (a supposition that could not be taken for granted),
they were not necessarily their brothers' keepers. They had
more urgent commitments and obligations. As the Australian
representative said with brutal but refreshing candor at the
Evian conference called in 1938 to find a shelter for the Jews
of Central Europe: "We have no Jewish problem, and do not
wish to import one." Other speakers put the thought more
elegantly; they expressed concern, apprehension and regret.
But the consensus was complete: only the Dominican Republic was willing to risk possible contamination by Jewish
immigrants.

It is not certain whether much could have been done by the Allies between 1941 and 1943 to stop the mass murder; but there is equally little doubt that there was no willingness to try. The argument used by Allied spokesmen in 1944 that bombing Auschwitz would have been "counter-productive" because it might have provoked more vindictive action on Hitler's part is, to say the least, disingenuous. For, as Mr. Henry Feingold has rightly pointed out in his study *The Politics of Rescue,* what "more vindictive action" than Auschwitz was possible, or even conceivable, remained the secret of the Allied leadership.

Over a quarter of a century has passed. There are no more guilt feelings, and if terms like "genocide" or "Auschwitz" are still part of the political vocabulary they are applied to very different events and situations: "Auschwitz" is now used to describe life in a black ghetto, "genocide" is supposed to refer to the underrepresentation of Negroes in American universities. The "Jewish Question," in other words, has become something of a nuisance and a bore, even though it still persists and is no nearer a solution than a century ago. The Jewish state, whatever its achievements, has not provided what Theodore Herzl thought it would: "a modern solution of the Jewish question," to quote the subtitle of his famous pamphlet. As for liberalism and revolutionary socialism, the two ideologies which claimed to have a grand solution, events of the last three generations have not, to put it mildly, borne out their predictions.

Several generations of Central and West European Jews grew up in the optimistic spirit of the Enlightenment. With Herder, they believed that the time would come when no one in Europe would ask whether someone was Jewish or Christian because the Jews too would live according to European laws and contribute their share to the common good. Eastern Europe with its massive concentration of Jews was different, but outside Russia and Rumania even the rise of racial anti-Semitism towards the end of the 19th century did not greatly affect the general optimism. There were some Cassandras, not necessarily all of them Zionists. Ehrenberg, the Jewish businessman in Arthur Schnitzler's undeservedly forgotten *Weg ins Freie* (1908), tells his young acquaintance, a Jewish socialist, that he will fare no better than the Jewish liberals and Pan-Germans before him:

> Who created the liberal and the German national movement in Austria? The Jews. Who deserted them, who spat on them like dogs? The liberals and the German nationalists. Exactly the same is bound to happen with socialism and communism. Once soup has been served, you'll be chased from the dinner table!

In 1929 the editor of the semi-official *Gazeta Polska* wrote:

> I like the Danes very much. But if there were three million of them I would pray to God to take them away. Maybe we would like the Jews very much if there were only 50,000 of them in Poland.

Four decades (and twenty-five years of socialism) later, there were less than 50,000 Jews left; but the Poles still did not like them.

It was not only in Vienna and Budapest that the shape of things to come was felt so acutely. No German-Jewish writer felt himself more closely tied to his country of birth than Jacob Wassermann, whose books were so popular during the years before and after the First World War. And yet even Wassermann reached deeply pessimistic conclusions about the cultural symbiosis:

> Vain to seek obscurity. They say: Why does he take such liberties with his Jewish obtrusiveness? Vain to keep faith with them as a comrade in arms or a fellow citizen. They say: He is Proteus, he can assume any shape or form. Vain to help them strip off the chains of slaves. They say: No doubt he found it profitable. Vain to counteract the poison. They brew new venom.

These were, admittedly, lonely voices at the time. The great majority of German Jews (and French or British Jews for that matter) were neither writers nor prophets, and followed their personal and professional interests with cautious optimism about the future. They felt that national distinctions were losing their importance all over the world. They had made tremendous progress within less than a century and came to regard anti-Semitism as the rearguard action of reactionary obscurantist groups. They were doubtless annoying, but of no decisive importance. Even a sensitive observer like Thomas Mann thought Wassermann's *cri de coeur* exaggerated. Wassermann, after all, had been very successful —did he not realize that a German writer would never have the moral prestige, the standing as the conscience of the nation comparable to his French colleague ("A German writer? A German martyr . . .")? Did Wassermann not realize that everyone, especially a writer, was bound to run into some trouble sooner or later, that the differences between Jews and non-Jews were not as great as Wasserman imagined? Many years later, when Thomas Mann reread his answer to Wassermann, he freely admitted that he had misjudged the situation.*

Germany and Austria, it could be argued, were special cases, where there was particular reason for concern. France, on the other hand, was the classical country of liberty and tolerance; the Dreyfus case made Zionists of Herzl and Bernard Lazare; but the overwhelming majority of French Jews reacted differently (as Michael Marrus has shown in his fascinating study, *The Politics of Assimilation*). Joseph Reinach, the well-known politician and *homme de lettres*, expressed the view of most of them when he wrote that the French Fatherland was given to the Jews by the Revolution,

---

* Wassermann's credo is quoted from his *My Life as German and Jew* (Berlin 1921); Thomas Mann's reply is printed in Peter de Mendelssohn's monumental history of the S. Fischer Verlag, Frankfurt 1970, pp. 853–57.

and neither the anti-Semites nor the Zionists would induce any Jew to renounce it. Or, to quote another contemporary, Alfred Berl: the only possible defense of the Jews was to strengthen the *idée liberale*, to uphold the ideas of 1789, their right to be Frenchmen like everyone else. Even four decades later, during the German occupation, the great historian Marc Bloch gave moving expression to these feelings:

> Throughout my life I have felt above all and very simply—French. I have been tied to my fatherland by a long family tradition, nourished by its spiritual heritage and its history, unable in truth to conceive of any other country where I could breathe at ease. I have loved it very much and served it with all my strength.

Being "a stranger to both confessional formalism and racial solidarity," Bloch requested, before his execution by the Nazis, that Hebrew prayers should not be said at his grave.

But if Theodore Herzl and Bernard Lazare had been the exception in 1896, the unshaken confidence of a Marc Bloch had become a rarity by 1940. The First World War and its consequences, the rise of Hitlerism and other anti-Semitic movements, had profoundly shaken liberal optimism, and it was never to recover. The only exceptions were on the extreme revolutionary Left. Karl Kautsky was the first orthodox Marxist who gave more than a passing thought to the Jewish question. In his *Race and Judaism,* published on the eve of World War I, he predicted that the Jews would soon disappear: the sooner the better, for society and themselves. Their disappearance would not be a tragedy, like that, say, of the American Indians; it would not be a degrading decline but, on the contrary, an ascent towards an immense field of activity making possible the creation of a new and higher type of man. Not liberalism, but the victorious proletariat would bring complete emancipation. Thereafter the Wandering Jew would at last find a haven of rest.

It is no longer fashionable to quote Kautsky, but a study of his views reveals that he somehow pre-empted all the subsequent arguments of the Communists and the New Left. What Lenin and Isaac Deutscher and Abram Leon had to say about the subject can be found in Kautsky's work, not only in general outline but in considerable detail. Kautsky was certain that the Jews would disappear after the proletarian revolution because only anti-Semitism was holding them together. Most Zionists would have agreed. Herzl and his friends did not argue that anti-Semitism was "eternal," even though such views were often attributed to them by their critics. On the contrary, they thought assimilation a possibility, if only the Jews were left alone for a few generations. They were, however, much less confident than Kautsky, who was convinced that anti-Semitism was a phenomenon specific to capitalism and that with the overthrow of capitalism—the social ground on which anti-Semitism had flourished—it would no longer exist. Jews had engaged in usury in the Middle Ages (so this argument ran); they had acted as the agents of capitalism and they were the ones who had to pay the price instead of the real exploiters, who had used them as lightning conductors. To this day this thesis is still being repeated with a great deal of assurance despite the lack of supporting historical evidence. At the time of the pogroms of the First Crusade, in the eleventh century, Jews did not engage in usury. The practice of usury does not explain the expulsion of the Jews from Spain and Southern Italy any more than it explains their recent misfortunes in post-capitalist Eastern Europe. In fact, it could be argued that in the heyday of liberal capitalism in Europe anti-Semitism was less virulent than ever before or after!

However, despite the unhistorical nature of Kautsky's line of reasoning, it appeared consistent and therefore attractive. It was based on the assumption that the world was moving away from nationalism, away from the nation-state and national sovereignty towards internationalism. According to the thesis developed by Kautsky and pursued by Deutscher, the Jews had a special mission: to be the pioneers and standard-bearers of the world of tomorrow, the apostles of the message of brotherhood and universal human emancipation. It implied that the Jews were called to participate actively in the class struggle in their native countries. The fatal weakness of this vision was that it related, hopefully, to some very distant Utopian future. It was not a practical policy in the Germany of 1933, and it has encountered obstacles to a greater or lesser extent everywhere at all times. The radical Left rejected Zionism as a profoundly "reactionary" movement, not only because of its attempt to revive a nation-state at a time when the course of history was so clearly moving away from it; but also because of its pessimistic prognoses, its disbelief in human progress, its proposal to distract Jews from the struggle for political and social liberation in their own native lands.

Whatever the demerits of Zionist doctrine, these specific accusations are, in my view, largely unjustified. Herzl always stressed that he believed in progress, but that it was agonizingly slow. Max Nordau was the most alarmist of the early Zionist leaders, but he too did not believe in a major catastrophe. In his writings* he expressed his confidence that the horrors of the Middle Ages would never recur; he wrote that he thought it highly unlikely that tens of thousands would be murdered or whole Jewish communities expelled: "I only believe that our Ice Age may still last a long time . . ."

What then was Zionist doctrine? To assess correctly the historical function of this movement one has to dig below the myths and counter-myths which have had intellectual circulation in recent decades. Zionism—to put it very briefly

---

* Max Nordau, *Zionistische Schriften* (Berlin, 1908).

—is the belief in the existence of a common past and a common future for the Jewish people. Such faith can be accepted or rejected; it cannot really be proved or disproved. Its intellectual origins go back to the French Revolution and the romantic wave of national revivalism which followed it. It was part of the liberal-humanist tradition of the Risorgimento, of Louis Kossuth and Thomas Masaryk. Some recent historians of ideas have maintained that Herzl's inspiration was "anti-liberal," but the evidence, to say the least, is quite unconvincing. Professor Carl Schorske* has gone so far as to bracket Herzl with Schoenerer and Lueger, the leading Viennese anti-Semites! Herzl (we are told) sketched out his dream of the Jewish secession from Europe after attending a performance of *Tannhäuser*, "exalted in a fever of enthusiasm akin to possession," with Richard Wagner as the vindicator of the heart against the head. A startling revelation, no doubt, but profoundly mistaken in almost every respect. Herzl's vision of the future state as described in *Altneuland* (Vienna, 1904) was that of a typical liberal, rationalist and optimistic, a model society on a progressive pattern. It was, in fact, so tolerant and cosmopolitan in character that it was bound to provoke resentment among cultural Zionists. Ahad Ha'am rejected it because it was just another modern secular state, one more manifestation of assimilation. If African Negroes (he wrote) managed one day to build a state of their own, it might well be similar in character to Herzl's vision. It was, in other words, a modern, technologically advanced and enlightened state inhabited by Jews, but not specifically Jewish. Nordau, in a somewhat crude but nonetheless effective reply, asked the Eastern European critics: "Do you want to stay forever in your ghetto . . . ?" The rationalist belief in a new and higher form of society was one of the basic articles of belief of the

* Carl E. Schorske, "Politics in a New Key" *Journal of Modern History*, December 1967.

founders of political Zionism. But for this and the assumption that the Jewish state would contribute substantially to the solution of the Jewish question, their interest in Palestine would have been, as one of them once said, mainly archaeological.

It is simply not true that Zionism was the ideology of some Jewish Establishment, supported by the Jewish *haute finance*—as its left-wing critics have so often argued. The Jewish Establishment, such as it was, denounced and ridiculed Zionism. It was the historical tragedy of Zionism that it was abysmally poor and never had sufficient funds at its disposal. When Herzl went to see the Rothschilds, the Hirschs, and the other leading "money Jews" (as he called them in his *Diaries*), he did not get a penny; and the situation did not improve after his death. In the 1920s and '30s the yearly budget of the Zionist movement hardly ever exceeded two million dollars. By 1928 it had run up a deficit of over half a million dollars, and faced bankruptcy, since it was unable to get any fresh loans. These were the material problems facing a movement that sought to build a national home at a critical period of Jewish history.

It was pointed out at the time that the yearly expenditure of one single Jewish community (Berlin, not necessarily the biggest and richest) on social welfare exceeded the total budget of the Jewish Agency by a considerable margin. Left-wing opponents of Zionism have frequently argued that Zionism was implanted in the Middle East to safeguard the interests of Western imperialism. The idea of spreading what used to be called the blessings of Western civilization (a phrase which in our age has come to have doubtful connotations) did figure occasionally in the writings and speeches of the early Zionist leaders. But it may be useful to recall that in this respect there was no basic difference between Zionists and Socialists. Following Marx and Engels, the Zionists regarded the spread of Western ideas and techniques in the East as an *a priori* progressive act needing no ideological justification. Until fairly recently the Jewish immigrants to Palestine were attacked by the Arabs not as "imperialists" and "colonialists" but, on the contrary, as "Communist agents". When the first official Arab delegation went to London in 1922 to demand the abrogation of the Balfour Declaration, it protested specifically against the influx of alien Jews, "many of them of a Bolshevik revolutionary type." M.E.T. Mogannam in her book on *The Palestine Problem* (1936) put it even more bluntly: namely, that the Arabs were deeply offended by the Bolshevik principles which the new arrivals brought with them. This produced an effect not so much by the success of its propaganda but by the genuine uneasiness which it inspired among the Arabs, especially the poorer classes. Jamal Husseini, secretary of the Arab Higher Committee, declared in his testimony before Lord Peel's Royal Commission (1937):

> As to the Communistic principles and ideas of Jewish immigrants most repugnant to the religion, customs and ethical principles of this country, I need not dwell upon them as these ideas are well known to have been imported by the Jewish community . . .

Arab anti-Zionism may or may not be justified, but there is no denying that it has shifted the ground of its attacks in accordance with the changes of *Zeitgeist*.

The real weaknesses of Zionism emerge only beyond the fog of anti-Zionist propaganda. I refer, for instance, to the Zionist attitude towards "assimilation," which they have always regarded as the main danger and enemy. While Zionists have rightly referred to the "objective character" of the Jewish question (meaning the social background of anti-Semitism), they have refused to apply similar criteria to assimilation. With a few notable exceptions (such as Jacob Klatzkin) they have usually regarded assimilation as a kind of weakness of character rather than a historical process with a logic and momentum of its own. Given the general liberal situation and the improved specific position of the Jews in European society in the last century, assimilation was, of course, inevitable. With the disappearance of the common tie of religion, many educated Jews no longer felt any obligation, moral or otherwise, to their community. These lapsed Jews admitted to a common ancestry and tradition but this did not weigh heavily in the scales compared with the overwhelming attractions of European culture, the unprecedented flowering of philosophy and literature, music and the arts. Judaism had nothing to put against the powerful influence of the Encyclopedists, of Kant and Hegel, of Goethe and Beethoven.

The process of assimilation, or symbiosis, was usually one-sided and not an altogether pleasing phenomenon. What had begun as furtive glances, as Gershon Scholem noted, soon turned into passionate involvement. Spokesmen of Eastern European Jewry criticized their co-religionists in the West because the Westerners knew in their innermost hearts that they were unfree since they lacked their own ethnic culture. To justify their uprooted existence they had to become Universalists, to dispute the view that every people had an individual character and assignment. But such criticism ignored the essential difference between Eastern and Western Jewry. Jews in the East were able to retain their ethnic national identity because there were so many of them. Nor was there an overwhelming temptation to accept and assimilate, say, Rumanian or Galician culture. Jewish nationalists in Eastern Europe had a more acute feeling for anti-Semitism and the limits of assimilation, but they totally failed to understand the problems of Western Jews in a milieu so unlike their own. In the West, even Zionists admitted that "if we analyze ourselves we find that 95% of our culture is composed of West European elements."

In their polemics against "the evils of assimilation," Zionists, moreover, forgot that Zionism itself would not have come into being but for the emancipation of European Jewry. The Jewish national revival was not a product of the ghetto but of Europe. To realize this is to be aware of the limits set to the development of a specific Jewish culture and way of life in Israel. Martin Buber, in one of his more extravagant moments, said that "it was up to the Jews whether Palestine would be the center of humanity or a Jewish Albania," the salvation of mankind or a pawn in the game of the great powers. The choice, needless to say, was never up to the Jews, and as normalization in Israel proceeds the more fanciful claims (Zion as a spiritual center, a model for the redemption of the human race) are quietly dropped.

Zionism has been criticized from both Left and Right as being simply a reaction to anti-Semitism, and Zionists, for no good reason, have vehemently disputed this. The charge is of course quite true. In a world without anti-Semitism Zionism would not have flourished. Had it not been for the persecution of the Jews Zionism would have existed as a minor literary coterie affecting individual neo-romantic *Schwaermer*. It became a political force only as the result of outside pressure and not because eccentric Jewish men of letters published stirring appeals. But what does this prove? The fact that a political or social movement developed in response to outside pressure does not invalidate it. Major political movements do not develop in a vacuum. Without the *ancien regime* there would have been no French Revolution—without Tsarism, no 1917.

As far as anti-Semitism is concerned, the Zionist appraisal has been more acute and realistic than the liberal and Marxist assessments. Yet the fact that the analysis is *correct* (as the late Chaim Arlosoroff once said in a moment of spiritual crisis) does not imply that Zionism had *an answer*. It was not just the fact (stressed again by J. L. Talmon) that the planet had been divided by the time Zionism appeared on the scene, and that there were no "empty spaces" left. Zionism was always a movement in a desperate hurry; it never had sufficient internal support when it mattered most. The Balfour Declaration of 1917 and the UN resolution of 1947 both came at the last possible moment. The Arab-Jewish conflict was inevitable, given the fact that Zionism wanted to build more than a cultural center in Palestine (which is not to imply that a cultural center would have been welcomed by the Arabs). Seen from the Arab point of view, Zionism was in the very nature of things an aggressive movement, and Jewish immigration an invasion. The basic weakness of Zionism was not a matter of ethics: there was no people which needed a home, a shelter, more desperately than the Jews. For others, it was a question of dignity, of justified national aspirations—for them, an issue of physical survival. The very act of the creation of a Jewish state on a territory largely inhabited by another people was of course an act of injustice. But throughout history states have developed from invasion, colonization and armed struggle, not peaceful development and legal contract. If Zionism had managed to build a state without the use of violence, it would have been the first such case in the annals of civilization.

The hard nub of the matter is this: Zionism was not strong enough to establish *faits accomplis*. The expulsion of ten million Germans from their Eastern homes (to mention but one recent example) was immediately accepted, and those unwilling to put up with it were denounced as *revanchistes* and "fascist warmongers." For it was obvious that the map of Eastern Europe could not be changed except through a new world war. But there were many Russians and only a few Jews; and unlike the Poles and the Czechs, they had no powerful protector. The rest of the story does not need to be re-told.

The basic aim of Zionism was twofold: to regain Jewish self-respect and dignity in the eyes of non-Jews; and to rebuild a Jewish national home, for Jews to "live as free men on their own soil, to die peacefully in their own home" (Herzl). Zionism has certainly succeeded in carrying out part of its assignment. The establishment of the Israeli state was the greatest turning point in the 2,000 years of Jewish history; it had a profound effect on Jewish life all over the world. But while esteem for Jewish determination and prowess has increased, the position of the Jews has not become more secure. In a world where might counts more than right, Jews are still at the mercy of superior forces. Zionism has not changed this. The fact that Eastern and Central European Jewry was destroyed during the Second World War whereas the Palestinian Jewish community survived does not prove the contrary. But for the defeat of Axis forces by the Allies, Hitler's armies would have reached Palestine, and this would have been the end of Zionism. If there has been a certain lessening of anti-Semitism in many parts of the globe, it is due as much to the revulsion caused by Nazi barbarism as to the Jewish state. Hostility towards the new state on the part of its neighbors has certainly increased. The state created by Zionism thus faces an uphill struggle to be accepted as a fact that can no longer be undone. As long as this struggle continues, the existence and independence of the state of Israel is no more assured than that of other small countries situated in an area where an expansive super-power has staked its claim.

Zionism has achieved the concentration of one-fifth of the Jewish people in Israel. There still is the problem of Russian Jewry. Once the mainstay of the Jewish national revival, it has been cut off from the body of world Jewry for the last five decades. While Soviet Jews did not receive full recognition as a national minority, they were given, after 1917, their own schools, theaters, publishing houses, and here and

there even low-level religious autonomy. Religion was persecuted, Zionism outlawed; but the physical safety of individual Jews was guaranteed. It was tacitly assumed by
Soviet leaders at the time that the Jews would gradually
become completely assimilated, lose their specific character,
and become more or less indistinguishable from the rest
of the population. Up to a point these expectations have
come true. Soviet Jews have adapted themselves to their
surroundings; their place in the social structure has changed;
Russian is their language and culture. And yet there is "a
Jewish problem" more acute than five decades ago. The
reasons are obvious. As the Soviet Union moved from proletarian internationalism to a national brand of socialism,
the problem of ethnic minorities was bound to re-emerge.
The Jews were expected to give up their own specific char-
acteristics, and many of them were only too willing to
oblige. But this did not make them Russians, Ukrainians, or
Uzbeks; they were still something apart—tolerated, but by
no means fully accepted. Whatever the reasons behind the
campaigns against "rootless cosmopolitans" and "national
deviationists," the Jews were made painfully aware that they
did not fully belong. While the Soviet authorities staunchly
maintain that there is no Jewish problem and that "outsiders" would not succeed in stirring up trouble, they have
nevertheless unwittingly managed themselves to create a
major crisis. There is a vicious circle of suspicion and dis-
crimination: the more the Jews become unreliable in the
eyes of the authorities, both in view of their international
connections and as an "internal ferment" (i.e. the high percentage of Jews among the intellectual dissidents), the more
they are discriminated against on many levels. As a result,
assimilation becomes difficult, if not impossible. Ten years
ago, if faced with the choice, only a small part of Soviet
Jewry would have opted for Israel. Today the situation
seems to be quite different, not owing to Zionist propaganda

but as a result of domestic policy. The problem is likely to become even more acute in the years to come. Young Jews, barred from the universities or promotion in their professional careers, are likely to react just as a previous generation did: they will turn against the unjust system.

There may be several ways to solve the problem, or at least to alleviate it, but it does not seem likely that any of them will be adopted by the Soviet leadership. It could try to create ideal conditions for assimilation and absorption. However, the Soviet Union is not a melting pot of nationalities. The "new Soviet man" is a fiction; Russians do not want the Jews to become one of them, nor do the Ukrainians; and the Jews will thus have to retain their special position, whether they like it or not—with all that this implies. To be sure, the Soviet authorities could let the Jews go, but this again is hardly practical politics: it would antagonize the Arabs and at the same time be an admission of the failure of the "Leninist policy on nationalities." The Bulgarians, the Rumanians and the Poles allowed their Jews to emigrate, but the numbers affected were on a much smaller scale, nor did this take place after more than a half-century of Marxist Leninist tutelage. Certain limits are set to the extent of anti-Jewish measures by the official ideology. It is not unthinkable that the traditional Marxist-Leninist ideology will be discarded altogether one day, but as long as it continues to have a certain impact on Soviet life (albeit less so than in the past), open anti-Jewish measures are difficult to justify. This does not make the situation of the Jews any less precarious, for anti-Semitism is not less painful if furtively practiced or given a different name.

Under present conditions no solution is in sight: the problem will persist and probably become more acute. A solution may come about as a result of changes within the Soviet Union itself, for if the trend towards populist nationalism continues, not only the Jewish question but national problems in general will again come to the fore, and some accommodation will have to be made between Russians and non-Russians. Alternatively, it is not inconceivable that a change in the international situation may make it easier for the Soviet government to let a substantial number of Jews go. But this, I suspect, is unlikely to happen in the near future.

What about the Jews in the pluralistic societies of the West? While assimilation was bound to fail in Poland and Rumania, and seems not to work in the Soviet Union, it has indeed made great strides elsewhere. Jewish history does not prove the impossibility of assimilation nor did Herzl rule it out ("if they let us be for just two generations . . ."). Jewish consciousness was strengthened by the anti-Semitic wave of the 1920's and the holocaust, but the loosening of the ties seems to have been retarded only temporarily. As the shock has passed, assimilation has again come into its own. Anti-Semitism in one form or another has persisted almost everywhere, but low-key anti-Semitism has not made assimilation impossible, nor has it acted as an agent on behalf of Zionism. Zionist doctrine, as I have said, has always rejected assimilation. Max Nordau dwelt on many occasions on the rootless cosmopolitans without firm ground under their feet, suffering personal humiliation, forced to suppress and falsify their personalities. But this image of spiritual misery was overdramatized even with regard to the world before 1914; and it bears little resemblance to the present-day world.

Jews as individuals and groups have faced difficulties, but it is certainly not true that "all the better Jews of Western Europe (or America) groan under this misery and seek for salvation." Nordau, who wrote this, never set foot on Palestinian soil, but continued to write from Paris for his European public. Subsequent generations grew up in an environment even more remote from Judaism. Many are no longer religious and ancient Jewish traditions are largely meaningless for them. The new assimilationists are not

"traitors' to their people nor are their personalities necessarily warped, or permeated with self-hate. They have grown
away from Jewish tradition and become indifferent to it. A
historical catastrophe would be needed to stop and reverse
this process.

Assimilation involved a conscious effort in the nineteenth
century when society was imbued with traditions and had
generally shared values and rigid standards. To be fully accepted, the assimilationist Jew had to conform to the standards and values of this society and to give up what set him
apart from it. Present-day Western pluralistic society is different in character. Not only have the Jews much less of
their traditional substance, society itself has lost its old
moorings. Traditional values have been jettisoned; like the
Jew, society has become rootless. This cultural crisis, which
may be protracted, is likely to be conducive to assimilation
while it lasts. But while it helps to break down some of the
barriers between Jews and non-Jews, it also undermines the
fundamental spirit of liberal tolerance on which Jewish
existence in the Western world is based. It is one of the
many ironies of Jewish history that those who work hardest
for the overthrow of Western liberal society are unwittingly
fanning the flames of anti-Semitism, creating new obstacles
helping to perpetuate the Jewish question rather than to
solve it. If Zionism were more Machiavellian-minded it
would give them unconditional support.

The "end of the Jewish people" was one of the main topics
of discussion among Zionists and non-Zionists alike only a
few years ago. Arthur Koestler, who was in Palestine when
the Jewish state was born, was one of the first and most out-
spoken advocates of this thesis. Since the foundation of
Israel the attitude of the Jews who were unwilling to go there
but still insisted on remaining a community in some ways
apart from their fellow citizens, had become an untenable
anachronism. The confused majority of diaspora Jewry (he

argued) perpetuated this anachronism through its inertia "by clinging to a tradition in which it no longer believed, to a mission which is fulfilled, a pride which may become inverted cowardice." To break the vicious circle of being persecuted for being "different," and being "different" by force of persecution, they must arrive at a clear decision, however difficult this might be:

> Now that the mission of the Wandering Jew is completed he must . . . cease to be an accomplice in his own destruction. If not for his own sake then for that of his children and his children's children. The fumes of the death chambers still linger over Europe; there must be an end to every calvary.

Koestler's own decision was clear. Now that the state was firmly established he was at least free to do what could not be done before—to wish it good luck and go his own way with an occasional friendly glance back and a helpful gesture, but nevertheless to find his own path in the Western community whose life and culture he shared, without reservations and split loyalties.* Koestler's views were criticized by the Zionists and ignored by most others. That he put his finger on a very real dilemma was not generally realized at the time. But his theme was taken up by others. Georges Friedman, the distinguished French-Jewish sociologist, wrote in a disturbed (and disturbing) book on *The End of the Jewish People* (1967), almost twenty years after Koestler:

> It seems inconceivable to me that everything possible should not be done to avoid another Auschwitz. Judaism was a historical accident, the spiritual fruits of which for the past twenty-five centuries had been paid for by an infinity of sadness, misery, suffering and bloodshed.

And this price seemed exorbitant and monstrous.

* Arthur Koestler, *Promise and Fulfilment* (1949).

Professor Friedman's argument is unassailable but, like Koestler, he had no recipe for breaking out of the vicious circle. The weakness of the advocates of "the end of the Jewish people," like the weakness of the Zionists, is not on the moral but on the practical level. They underrated (or ignored altogether) a certain biological basis of the Jewish people that seems to exist, intangible, perhaps unprovable, but nevertheless of some importance whatever well-meaning genetic experts may say about the subject. Intermarriage over several generations might be an answer; but so far it has not been proposed as a policy to be systematically pursued. Above all, the advocates of neo-assimilationism have underrated the reaction of the non-Jewish world, as if the disappearance of the Jewish people depended on the Jews alone. For, while religious and national divisions persist in the world, a Jew is bound to remain "different" in various ways; and it is unlikely that either official tolerance or a policy of assimilation, however determined, can decisively affect this state of affairs. There was room for illusions in the last century; there should be none now.

Given time, a minimum of good sense, and a willingness to compromise, it is not unthinkable that the conflict between Israel and its Arab neighbors will be reduced to manageable proportions. Given time, tolerance, and a reasonably stable world situation, it is possible that Soviet Jewry will be spared a revival of the persecutions of the late Stalin era, and Jews in Western society will not have to face yet another major ordeal.

But neither past experience nor current political trends encourage such optimism. It is exactly one hundred years now since Heinrich Graetz wrote the preface to the eleventh and last volume (Leipzig, 1871) of his great *History of the Jewish People*. His lifelong study of the subject was not conducive to optimism, but he ended his work on a note of satisfaction and confidence:

Happier than any of my predecessors, I can conclude my history with the joyous feeling that in the civilized world the Jewish tribe has found at last not only justice and freedom but also a certain recognition. Now at long last it has unlimited freedom to develop its talents, not as an act of mercy but as a right acquired through thousandfold suffering.

A century after Graetz such confidence seems exaggerated, to say the least.

A new age of tolerance and humanism—a second Enlightenment—does not seem a likely prospect for mankind at present. The dark clouds of political unrest, of domestic and international crisis, foreshadow a climate in which existing problems will be exacerbated rather than solved. The Jewish Question has always been a sensitive barometer. All the Jews can hope for is that they will not be exposed yet another time to the full blast of coming storms.

(1971)

PROPERTY OF

AURORA PUBLIC LIBRARY

AURORA. COLORADO

ABOUT THE AUTHOR

WALTER LAQUEUR is the Director of the Institute of Contemporary History (Wiener Library) in London, and founder and co-editor of its scholarly publication, the *Journal of Contemporary History*. He is also Professor of History at the University of Tel Aviv and was until recently Professor of Ideas at Brandeis University. He is one of those transatlantic commuters who feel intellectually at home in both America and Europe.

He was born in Germany in 1921, spent his youth in Palestine (where he lived in a kibbutz), and has lived in England and the U.S.A. since the 1950's. He has been a guest professor of history at various American Universities, including the University of Chicago and Johns Hopkins. He has published four books on problems of Nationalism and Communism in the Middle East, works which scholars have called "indispensable" and which have established him as a recognized world authority on that subject. Among his other books are *Young Germany* (1962), *with an introduction by R.H.S. Crossman*, *The Fate of a Revolution* (1967), and most recently *Europe Since Hitler* (1970).

His work as a journalist has brought him a widespread audience throughout the Western world, and many of his memorable articles have appeared in the *New York Times, Commentary, Dissent,* the *New York Review of Books,* the *Times Literary Supplement, Encounter,* and the *Neue Zurcher Zeitung.*

Professor Laqueur is married and has two daughters.